D1251596

Political, Religious,

and

Love Poems.

Early English Text Society.

Original Series, No. 15.

1866
Re-edited 1903
Reprinted 1965
Price 55*s.*

Political, Religious,

and

Love Poems...

(SOME BY LYDGATE, SIR RICHARD ROS, HENRY BARADOUN,
WM. HUCHEN, ETC.)

FROM

THE ARCHBISHOP OF CANTERBURY'S LAMBETH MS. No. 306,
AND OTHER SOURCES,

WITH A FRAGMENT OF THE ROMANCE OF

Peare of Probence and the fair Maguelone,

AND A SKETCH, WITH THE PROLOG AND EPILOG, OF THE ROMANCE OF

The Knight Amoryus and the Lady Cleopes

BY JOHN METHAM, SCHOLAR OF CAMBRIDGE, A.D. 1448–9.

EDITED BY

FREDERICK J. FURNIVALL

Published for
THE EARLY ENGLISH TEXT SOCIETY
by the
OXFORD UNIVERSITY PRESS
LONDON · NEW YORK · TORONTO

FIRST PUBLISHED 1866
RE-EDITED   1903
REPRINTED   1965

Original Series No. 15

REPRINTED IN GREAT BRITAIN BY RICHARD CLAY
(THE CHAUCER PRESS) LTD., BUNGAY, SUFFOLK

CONTENTS.

POLITICAL POEMS, ETC.

LOVE POEMS, ETC.

RELIGIOUS POEMS.

PAGE

ADDITIONS.

FOREWORDS.

(*Afterwords* are on pages 309–311.)

THIS book is somewhat of a medley, partly for the reason that the Lambeth MS. whence it is mainly drawn—and for the loan of which I am deeply indebted to the Archbishop of Canterbury—is so too. The first three poems, and part of the fourth, should—and, had its editor known of them, of course would—have found a place in the second volume of Mr. Thomas Wright's Political Songs for the Master of the Rolls; some of the rest might have gone into any collection of Love or Religious Poems, and others into any Miscellaneous volume. Of the pieces now issued some have been printed elsewhere, and of most, perhaps better texts exist; but the time that it takes to ascertain whether a poem has been printed or not, which is the best MS. of it, in which points the versions differ, etc., etc., is so great, that after some experience I find the shortest way for a man much engaged in other work, but wishing to give some time to the Society, is to make himself a foolometer and book-possessor-ometer for the majority of his fellow-members, and print whatever he either does not know, or cannot get at easily, leaving others with more leisure to print the best texts. *He* wants *some* text, and that at once.[1] I cannot say that the Lansdowne MS. 699 of Lydgate's *Hors, Shepe, & Gosse*, is the best in being; it is only the best I have met with; and I have collated it with the Roxburghe Club 1822 reprint of the old black-letter version, and the Harleian MS. 2251, from which Halliwell printed its Envoy. In the late Lambeth MS. (printed in my first edition) it has lost its head and tail, and many readings are bad. *La Belle Dame sanz Mercy* may be in the same condition, but it was given for lovers of Keats, who were not owners of black-letter Chaucers. It is now edited from the MS. Ff. 1. 6 in the University Library, Cambridge, collated with MS. in Trin. Coll. Camb., both copied by Mr. A. B. Rogers of the University Library.

---

[1] This excuse is not intended as a justification for an Editor to take no trouble about his work. It only asks that he may be allowed to judge how the trouble he can, and must, take, can be best applied.

I intended at first to print only certain of the pieces in the Lambeth MS. 306, but on looking through the *Piers Plowman* MSS. in the British Museum with Mr. Skeat, to choose the best for the Society's three-text edition, he pointed out to me the Political Poems in Vespasian, B xvi. These I copied, and then cancelled—with the exception of the *Satirical Proclamation* (pp. 12, 13), on finding that they were in Mr. Wright's volume of *Political Songs*.[1] Then a comparison of the Lambeth texts of *Sent Gregorys Trentalle* and *The Stacions of Roome* with those in the rather earlier Museum MS., Cotton Caligula, A ii.,[2] showed that the latter must be preferred to the former, and they were accordingly copied. After this a friend at Cambridge kindly sent me transcripts of some seemingly anonymous poems from the University Library, one of which proved to be a version of a ditty of Lydgate's against Women's Horns, printed in *Reliquiæ Antiquæ* (vol. i. p. 79) and twice by the Percy Society, and the rest inferior copies of others of Lydgate's Poems ; nevertheless, as two of these had been set up they are included here (pp. 46-54, 73-5), for they are sure to meet some eye that has not seen them before. As a substitute for the other cancelled poems, Mr. Skeat with much goodwill copied *Whi art thou Froward* (pp. 141, 142), and (on the late Henry Bradshaw's recommendation) *The Parliament of Love* and *The Seven Deadly Sins*, printed here pp. 76-79, 244-48, and Mr. Rogers has re-collated them. Dr. W. Aldis Wright kindly copied the two poems in the Northern Dialect on pp. 133-40; and Mr. Edmund Brock *The Fifty-First Psalm*, pp. 279-85, besides helping me in other ways. The late O. Cockayne gave me the first verse of *Rats Away* (p. 43), and Mr. George Parker, of the Bodleian Library, the second verse, and a revise of the whole. Mr. G. Parker is also responsible for the text of the Prologue to the Adulterous Falmouth Squire. A reference in *Reliquiæ Antiquæ* sent me to the Harl. MS. 7322, and the early date of the English Poems mixed with its Latin prose more than justifies their reproduction here, pp. 250-70. To Mr. Bradshaw's acquaintance with the Lambeth Catalogue I owe my introduction to the excellent MS. 853,[3] which has furnished complete texts of two poems, 1. *Quia Amore Langueo*, p. 180-8, printed opposite another copy ; and 2. a Complaint of the Virgin, p. 191-92,

---

[1] There is a kind of comfort in narrating one's little troubles. The reader will sympathize if he knows how very small a man feels when he looks at his eagerly-made copy of a good poem, by the side of an after-found print of it.

[2] I hope some day to print the unedited pieces from this MS.

[3] The whole of this MS. has been printed by the Society.

of which a most interesting variation (p. 238–242) occurs in Harleian MS. 3954, between copies of *Mandevill's Voiage* and *Piers Plowman.* From the latter MS. I have also taken a curious A-B-C Poem on the Passion of Christ, though it has, I believe, been printed elsewhere. I have re-collated all the texts from the Lambeth MSS. 306 and 853, and Brit. Mus. MSS. with their originals.

Now as to the contents of the Poems themselves ;—the allusions in the first were not at the outset explained with certainty, even with the help of Mr. James Gairdner, of the Record Office. A man saw Twelve Letters that should save Merry England, in Edward the Fourth's time. These Twelve letters then turn into Eight,—R, W, two E's, F, M, Y, S,—but the R multiplies into three R's (Ares) of three Lords' names, and a fourth and fifth, the Rose that's fresh and will not fade, and the Ragged Staff that no man may escape. The Y, M, S, and W, were explained in the poem to mean the nobles York, March, Salisbury, and Warwick, and the F and E the Feterlock and Eagle. Thus we had four Richards, four nobles, and four badges, of which two, the Rose[1] and Eagle,[2] seemed to mean Edward IV. Did then this triad of fours mean twelve different persons, or ten, or four, or two? An unexpected meeting with an old friend, who proved to be that wonderful being, ROUGE DRAGON, —of whom I had the vaguest possible notion before, not knowing even whether he had not been buried hundreds of years—produced the following happy solution of the problem.

" There can, I think, be little doubt that the Twelve Letters refer to the *Christian names*, the *Titles*, and the *Badges or Cognizances* of the following Four Men—

E. M. F.

EDWARD, EARL OF MARCH, with the badge of the Fetterlock. Afterwards Edward IV.

R. Y. R.

RICHARD, DUKE OF YORK (1415 to 1460), with the badge of the White Rose of the house of York, Father of Edward IV.

R. S. E.

RICHARD (Nevill), EARL OF SALISBURY (1442 to 1460), with the badge of the green Eagle of Monthermer.

---

[1] See *The Wright's Chaste Wife*, p. 20, l. 670.
        (Trevilian)
[2] The Cornysshe Chough offt with his trayne.
        (Rex)
Hath made oure *Egulle* blynde.
    Cotton Rolls, ii. 23, quoted in Wright's *Pol. Songs*, vol. ii. p. 222.

R. W. R.

RICHARD (Nevill), EARL OF WARWICK (1449 to 1471), the King-maker, with the badge of the Ragged Staff belonging to that House.

"The Fetterlock, with a falcon inside it, was a badge of Edmund of Langley (son of Edward III.), who re-built his Castle of Fother-ingay in that shape, and was consequently assumed by his great grandson Edward IV.

"The arms of Monthermer (an eagle displayed) were always quartered, both by the Montacutes and Nevills, Earls of Salisbury. In the 'Rows Roll' (pub. by Pickering, 1845) is a portrait of Richard, Earl of Warwick above-named, who succeeded his father in 1460 as Earl of Salisbury—with the eagle standing at his feet, as a badge.

"The date of the poem is between 1460 and 1471, as Edward is spoken of as King (line 63), and Richard, Duke of York, in the past tense ['He reyny*ed*' (line 44), and that he '*hathe* sofferde grete vexacion'—sc. been slain (line 28)]; so likewise Lord Salisbury, who was beheaded in 1460, is never spoken of in the present tense, while the Earl of Warwick, who lived till 1471, is spoken of as alive.—G. E. ADAMS [later, Cokayne], ROUGE DRAGON [now CLAREN-CEUX], *Heralds College.*"

That this is the true conclusion, and that the Twelve letters repre-sented four persons,—two dead (Richard of York and Richard of Salisbury), and two living (Edward IV. and Richard of Warwick, the King-maker),—I have no doubt. But if the poem is to be taken as referring to living men only (see line 60, etc.), then the four men must be reduced to two; and this can be easily accomplished, because as Edward IV. united in himself his father's title of the Duke of York and his own of Earl of March, so Richard the King-maker united in himself his father's title, Earl of Salisbury, and his own, Earl of Warwick. For the King-maker was Earl of Warwick before he succeeded to the Earldom of Salisbury in 1460, when his father, the then Earl, was beheaded at Pontefract Castle subsequent to his capture after the battle of Wakefield, in which Edward the Fourth's father, Richard Duke of York, was defeated and slain. In this case the poem would describe only Edward the Fourth, and Warwick, who made him king; but no doubt their fathers were included too, as Mr. Adams says.

The second Poem sounds strange to modern ears, dulled by non-intervention talk, accustomed to the threat without the blow, the

bark without the bite, the scold without the scratch. But its tones
fell differently on Edward's ears, we may be sure; and if there had
been no Towton, Hexham, Edgecott, Erpingham, Barnet, and
Tewkesbury, to fight on English soil, and drain the country of its
best blood, we should have heard, I doubt not, of the daring young
king in France in other wise than when he was there in 1475, and
perchance he would have taken the English flag beyond the southern
bounds that the Black Prince so bravely bore it to.

The third piece records how Edward the Fourth was received at
Bristol; and the fourth Poem tells how the Duke of Suffolk, the
unpopular favourite of Henry VI., was caught at sea by the ship
Nicholas, and beheaded; and calls on many of the chief clergy and
laymen to help sing his Dirge and bury him. Of these the following are mentioned in the list in the faded Cotton Roll (Cott.
Charters, ii. 23), printed by Mr. Wright (*Pol. Poems*, v. 2, pp. lvi—
lvii, notes), of unpopular "namys that were enditede at Rowchestre
afore the cardinalle of Yorke, bysshoppe of Canturbury, and the
Duke of Bokyngham, etc., in the feste of the Assumpcioun of oure
lady and (?) festo Laurencii, anno r. r. Henrici xxix°.

Johan Trevyliane, nuper de Londone, armiger, 2.
Johan Say, nuper de Londone,
armiger, 2.
Johannes Polsforde [? Pulford, l.
111]. nuper de Londone, armiger, 2.
Thomas Kent, de London, gen-
tyllmane, alias dictus T.K.,
clericus consilii domini regis, 2.
Johan Penycole, nuper de London., armiger.
Thomas Hoo, de Hastynge in
comitatu Sussex., miles, of, 2.

Reginaldus, abbas Sancti Petri
Gloucestriæ, of, 2.
Jacobus Fynys, dominus de Say, j.
T. Stanley, miles, of, j.
Thomas Thorppe, gentilman, j.
Johan Blakeney, gentilmane, j.
Dominus Iohannes Forstkew, of,
j. miles.
Walter Liarde, episcopus Nor-
wic., j.
Ricardus Wodvile, dominus de
Ryvers, j.
Willelmus Booth, episcopus Ces-
triæ, j."

Our version has sixty lines not in the Cotton copy (Vesp. B. xvi)
printed by Mr. Wright, but omits sixteen lines of the latter. It is,
Mr. Gairdner tells me, in the handwriting of John Stowe, the
chronicler, to whom the Lambeth MS. 306 once belonged, and in
whose handwriting there are many entries scattered through the
volume. Three characteristic ones I copy below.[1]

[leaf 47, back]
[1] Anno d° 1564 . . . The 20 of november, beynge Monday, in y⁵ mornynge
a-bout .vj. of y⁵ clocke, throghe neglygence of a mayden *with* a candell, y⁵ snoff

To explain the fifth piece in this Text, the Satirical Proclamation, nothing better has been proposed by the friends I have consulted than Mr. Cokayne's suggestion on p. 14, that it is a satire by the party of Cardinal Beaufort on the pretensions of René Duke of Anjou, and titular King of Jerusalem, etc., whose daughter Margaret afterwards married Henry VI.

The sixth piece is Lydgate's Horse, Goose, and Sheep, a dispute of these animals before the Lion and Eagle as Judges, as to which is most useful to man and the common weal. The judgment is that they are all useful in their several ways, and are not to quarrel about precedence. Lydgate's moral, in his Envoy, that no man should " for no prerogative, his neighbour not despise " is still much needed

---

ther-of fawlynge in-to an hundryd-wayght of gonne-pothar, thre howssys in bucklers-bury war sore shaken, and yᵉ backar partes of yᵉ same howsys wer all to-blowne & shattard in pecis, & yᵉ aforesayd mayde was so byrnt yᵗ she dyede ther-of *with*-in ij dayes afftar. yf this powthar had bene in a sellar, as it was in a garret, it had donne more harme.

.j. This yere .1564. was a sharpe froste, whiche began on seynt Thomas daye before cristmas, on yᵉ .21. daye of desembar, beynge thursdaye, & contynewyd tyll yᵉ .3. day of Janewarie, beynge wednys-daye, on yᵉ whiche wedynseday it thawyd bothe yᵉ daye & nyght folowynge, & yᵉ morow, beyng thursdaye, allso. this forst, as before is sayde, begynynge on sent Thomas day before cristmas, was so sharpe that on neweyers even men went ovar the Thams as saffe as on yᵉ dry land, not only betwyxt westmystar & lambythe, but in all placis betwyxt lambethe & yᵉ olde swane, they wente bothe ovar yᵉ thames & alonge yᵉ same, from london to westmystar, & from westmystar to london, comynge a lande salffelly (thankis be to god) wher they wolde, between westmystar and yᵉ olde swan whiche is very nere vnto yᵉ brydge ; & yᵉ same newyers even, beynge sondays, people playd at yᵉ footte ball on yᵉ thams by great nombars : on newe yeers day, beynge mondaye, & on twesday & wednyseday, dyvars Ientyllmen & othars set vp pryckes on yᵉ Thams, & shott at yᵉ same, & great nombars of people beholdynge yᵉ same, standynge at yᵉ prykis as boldly and thankis be gyvyn to god a[s] saffly, as it had bene on yᵉ drye lande. And I my selffe who wrate this notte, we*n*tte on yᵉ wedynsday before namyd frome lambythe to westmystar, & ther dynyd *with* M*aster* burre who went thetar *with* me, & then we went agayne to yᵉ comon starys of westmystar, & so vpon yᵉ Thames to yᵉ baynards castell, where we went a land (thankys be to god) as salffe as evar I went in eny place in all my lyffe, where we sawe men shewte at a payre of prykes set vp a-gaynst yᵉ qweens cowrte vpon yᵉ Thams, & costardmongars playnge at yᵉ dysse for aples ; & yᵉ people went on yᵉ thams in greatar nombars then in eny streat in london. The people went ovar yᵉ thams on yᵉ thursdaye at nyght ; & on yᵉ morow, beynge frydaye, was no yce on the thams to be sene, but yᵗ all men myght rowe ovar & a-longe yᵉ same, it was so sodaynly conssumyd.

[leaf 71, back]

Anno .1563. yᵉ .26. of Iune was a mynyster, parson of sent marie abchurche, of sent martyns in Iarmongar lane, & of one othar benifice in yᵉ cuntrie, takyn at dystaffe lane, vssynge an othar mans wyffe as his owne, whiche was dowghtar to ser Myles partryge, & wyffe to wyllyam stokebrege, grosar ; & he beyng so takyn at yᵉ dede doynge, (havynge a wyffe of his owne,) was caryed to brydwell thrughe all the stretes, his breche hangynge aboute his knes, his gowne & his (kyvar knave) hatt borne aftar hym *with* myche honor ; but he lay not longe ther, but was delyveryd *with*-owt punyshment, & styll Inioyed his beneffysis ; they were greatly blamed that prehended hym and comitted hym.

in 'Society' which cuts its poor acquaintances as it rises, and in the Amateur Rowing Association which flunkily refuses to let any Club containing a man who has workt for wages, row in any of its Regattas. The date of Lydgate's Poem has been settled in Germany as 1437–8 : see pp. xix–xx, below.

The seventh piece (p. 43) is the " Rats Away," already alluded to. I cannot construe all the lines, and the MS. is so nearly illegible that Mr. Parker, and Mr. Macray who kindly helped him, had much difficulty in making out so much of the MS. as they have done.

The wise advice given by the next three pieces to purchasers of land, to all mixing with their fellows,[1] and to housekeepers, are in great part applicable now. The six following little bits were put in, either for their oddity, or because I fancied them, not because Directions how to cram Chickens with black Slugs were considered to be a Political Poem. There are plenty more medical recipes in the Lambeth volume.

The Love Poems begin on p. 66, continue to p. 111, and include Lydgate's before-printed appeal against the woman's horns then in vogue—a bonnet trimming seemingly, like a pair of cow's horns, with the junction stuck as a curtain to a woman's bonnet, the horns curling up on each side of the bonnet, and high above it into the air.

The division of Religious Poems starts with a Hymn to the Virgin " to preserve nobyl Kyng Herry." *Saint Gregory's Trental* exalts the power of the Mass, and tells how by singing thirty Masses,—three on each of the ten chief Festivals,—the Saint rescued from hell[2] to heaven, his mother, damned for having two bastard

---

[1] Of this "Like thyn awdiens," Mr. Skeat says : "There are two better copies of it in print—one by Wynkyn de Worde, with several misprints, but with better readings, and one by the *Percy Society*, Early English Poems, vol. ii. p. 173, from Harl. MS. 2235, which is better all round, has the Latin verses at top, and shows what is translated and what original. It is one of Lydgate's."

[2] The *Saturday Review* of Dec. 22, 1866, p. 765, col. 1, says that I clearly misconceive this 'Poem' : *Hell* should be *Purgatory*. A Romanist friend long ago assured me that the Pope's Mother could not possibly have been admitted into Purgatory, because she had murdered her two children and died impenitent as to these crimes. Purgatory being only for the penitent, Hell was the place that Gregory's Mother must have gone to. Compare Hampole, *Pricke of Consience*, p. 72, l. 2631 :

    Bot many soules þat er save
    Ar þai com to blis, payne by-hoves have
    In purgatori, and duelle þar-in
    Until þai be clensyd of al syn
    þat er schryven and noght clensed here,
    And þar be fyned als gold þat shynes clere.

The descriptions in the text, ll. 48-74, p. 116, and the lines

    Among oþur prayeres þey ben good
    To brynge sowles fro helle flodc (l. 201-2, p. 121)

children and strangling them.[1]   The moral teaching of the next
Poem is of a different order, warning adulterers that they shall be

seemed to bear out my friend's assertion ; and the statement in the *Stacyons*
that Masses sung in *Scala Cœli* would bring souls from Hell, through Purgatory,
into Paradise, was consistent with this.   The question turns, I believe, on
whether strangling one's two children and concealing the crime, is a venial sin,
sending the Murderess to Purgatory, or a mortal one, when unrepented of,
sending her to Hell.   To a Saturday Reviewer accustomed to a weekly slaughter
of innocents, and to mistakes, I do not wonder that the offence seems venial.
Having been a father, I hold the crime mortal, and believe the ' misconception '
complained of, not to be mine.—F. J. F.

P.S.—The very Rev. Daniel Rock, D.D., has just favoured me with the
following note on the point, showing that Hell, and not Purgatory, must have
been the place : " A woman guilty of fornication and child-murder, dying
unshriven, unassoiled, and unsorrowing for such deadly sins, is lost for ever.
No prayers, no alms-deeds, no masses will have any effect on her behalf, having,
as you state it, left this world without any sorrow, even at the last moment, for
such tremendous crimes that cry to heaven for vengeance.

" St. Gregory's Trental and the Indulgence of ' *Scala Cœli* ' have been most
egregiously misrepresented, under several points of view.   The reported vision
of St. Gregory's mother in hell is a mere fable.   The mother of that great Pope
was Sylvia, a holy woman in life and in death, which happened to her in a
house of religion which she had founded.   The Trental of St. Gregory came
into use from the saint being inspired with the knowledge that a monk, for a
sin, not a deadly one, but only venial, was suffering the smarts of Purgatory.
He bade one of the monks of the monastery say mass every day for a month, on
the last day of which the suffering dead monk appeared to the living one who
had said the 30 masses for his soul, and told him he was, by the mercy of God
won for him by the holy sacrifice, freed from pain.   Mind, from the pain of
Purgatory—a place of temporary cleansing pain—not from the pains of hell, out
of which when once therein there is no coming. *

" Our Henry VII. got for his chapel in Westminster Abbey, the indulgence
of ' *Scala Cœli*,' all the conditions of which are enumerated in the bull printed
in Dugdale's *Monasticon*, new edition, t. i., p. 320, whereby you will see that
whether applicable to the living or the dead, it must be only to those ' *vere
penitentibus, et confessis :* ' a condition attached to all indulgences."

[1] In this poem are certain terms of the Roman Catholic service which Lord
Denbigh has kindly explained to me.   The *secrete*, p. 91, l. 224, are the *Secreta*,
or Secret Prayers, which when more than half through " The Ordinary of the
Mass," and before he has received 'the Host' and 'Blood,' the Priest recites
(in a voice not audible) with outstretched hands, and which differ on different
days.   The *Post Comen*, p. 91, l. 229, is the Post Communion, or the portion of
the Ordinary after the Host has been given to the laity.   See the *Missal for the
Laity*, pp. xviii, xxx, etc.   Lord Denbigh is anxious that the Roman Catholic
doctrine of Indulgences, much misunderstood and misrepresented by Protestants,
should be stated in the words of a book of authority among his fellow-believers.
I therefore give the following extracts from the *Full Catechism of the Catholic
Religion*, 1863, which he has sent me.

Pages 293-6.

Question 84.   What is an Indulgence ?

An Indulgence is a remission, granted out of the Sacrament of Penance, of
that temporal punishment which, even after the sin is forgiven, we have yet to
undergo either here or in Purgatory.

85.   How does the Church remit the punishment due to our sins ?

By making to the Divine Justice compensation for us from the inexhaustible
Treasure of the merits of Christ and His Saints. . . .

* That the Middle Age belief of some persons was different, see the *Stacyons*, as above,
and this *Trental*.

tortured in hell[1]; and that such teaching was wanted in England in earlier times, when rich men used poor men's wives and daughters even more freely than they do now, no one who knows our history or literature can doubt. (See Robert of Brunne's *Handlyng Synne.*)

The Stacyons of Rome is simply (to me) a puff of the merits of the Papal City as a place for getting pardons and indulgences, in comparison with Santiago and Jerusalem. What is the good of going so far as either of those places—says the writer, in effect,—when you can get more of the article you want, and on easier terms, in Rome? Every time you go to one church you get 7000 years' pardon; every time you give alms at another you get 14,000 years; in every church, more or less of it. Lents are to be had for the asking; relics may be seen without end, from the Virgin's milk to the hay the donkeys ate at Christ's birth. What would you have more? Why should any penitent go elsewhere? Rome is *the* place for him! The date of the Poems is about 1440–5. See p. xxxiii.

For a set of very valuable and interesting notes on this Poem of *The Stacyons*, containing much curious and suggestive illustration of its statements, the Society is indebted to one of its members, Mr. William M. Rossetti, the well-known art-critic and translator of Dante, whose words on this subject will come with an authority that those of few other writers in England could command. To one

---

86. What is generally required to gain an Indulgence?

It is required, 1. That we should be in the state of grace, and have already obtained, by true repentance, forgiveness of those sins, the temporal punishment of which is to be remitted by the Indulgence; and, 2. That we should exactly perform the good works prescribed for the gaining of the Indulgence. . . .

To assert that, by an Indulgence, the Church forgives *sins* past or future, or that she grants Indulgences for *money*, is a gross calumny. . . .

91*. Is it then not true that the Church, by Indulgences, frees us from the obligation of doing Penance?

No; she does not free us from the obligation of doing penance according to our capacity, since, the greater is our penitential zeal and love to God, the more do we participate in the Indulgence; she will only assist us in our inability to expiate all temporal punishment in this life, and thus, by a generous Indulgence, effect what in ancient times she endeavoured to attain by the rigorous Penitential Canons.

92. How many kinds of Indulgences are there?

There are two kinds: A *Plenary* Indulgence, which is the remission of the whole debt of temporal punishment due to sin; and a *Partial* Indulgence, which is the remission of a part of it only.

93*. What is meant by an Indulgence of forty days, or seven years?

A remission of such a debt of temporal punishment as a person would discharge if he did penance for forty days or seven years, according to the ancient Canons of the Church.

[1] To a printed note of Mr. Halliwell's I owe the reference to MS. Ashmole 61, which supplies the Prologue to the story, and identifies the sinner with Sir William Basterfield.

who, like myself, has received for years the untiring aid of this accomplished scholar in the compilation of the Philological Society's Dictionary (now the Oxford English Dictionary, edited by Murray and Bradley), his help in the present volume has been doubly grateful, and I desire to express my warmest thanks for it.

The next Poems are to the Virgin,—the first said to be written in 1508 by a D. T. Mylle—and serve to introduce the series of *Complaints* which contain, in parts, a truer pathos, and touch deeper chords, than anything else in the volume. The pleadings of Christ with the sinner are often beautiful, even to an unbeliever's mind; and who that has heard a mother's passionate cries for her lost one,—those terrible appeals that cut to the heart,—can refuse his sympathy with the stricken mother (though he holds her only a poet's fancy), who swooned at Calvary when her 'dear child' died?

I am sorry that the way in which the text of one of these Poems is here printed, led one learned and much-esteemed friend, Henry Bradshaw,—who (unluckily for us) devoted his spare energy to denouncing the Committee in general and me in particular, instead of editing texts for us all—into calling this volume a pig-stye. Admitting that beings of the species " gruntare, *grunnitor* " can find space for the exercise of their calling within the leaves of the book, I yet believe that, as the matter stood, it was right to leave the first part of the even-page text of *The Complaynt of Criste* (pp. 190, 192, 194, 196, 198), as the scribe copied it. Having secured at a later period a good text and right arrangement of the poems from the earlier Lambeth MS. 853, the question was, What was to be done with the already-in-type poor text, and incorrect arrangement of it, from the later Lambeth MS. 306, the MS. which gave us *The Wright's Chaste Wife*, and of which I had in gratitude resolved to print as much as I could, without seeking for better texts of its contents? Was this poor text, and arrangement of 12-line stanzas in 8, to be cancelled; or to be corrected by the good one opposite it, and retained; or was it to be left as an instructive instance to readers in general, and a caution to careless people like myself, of how one of those scribes to whom we owe almost all our knowledge of our forefathers' minds, had chanced to go astray? Without contending for the position of the greatest scholar I ever knew (the late Prof. Goldstücker) " that the errors of Manuscripts are sacred, and must be preserved," I still think that readers who are kept from mistake as to the original text by the good version of the Lambeth

MS. 853, will be glad to see the most instructive variations and mistakes that time and repeated copyings have brought into the later text of the MS. 306, especially when the writer of it may have argued that as the two poems purporting to be by God and Christ were both in fact by Christ, they had better have one title, and the 12-line stanza of the shorter poem be made symmetrical with the 8-line of the longer one. Should this decision[1] make any reader or reviewer grunt again " Pig-stye," I can assure him that the repeated exclamation will be taken as good-humouredly as the first one was.

Asking again attention to the contrast of the continued wail of *The Virgin's Complaint*, "Filius Regis mortuus est," with the triumphant change of the Harleian version " Filius Regis . . . Resurrexit, non mortuus est," and also recalling readers' notice to the A B C Poem already mentioned, I repeat again thanks to the kind friends who have aided me with this collection, and hope it may help a little towards a better understanding of "the English mind" of former days.

[1] I had intended to leave out the 8-line version in this re-edition, but, on my friend Israel Gollancz's request, have left it in. He is specially interested in all 12-line-stanzad poems and their changes.

Egham, May 31, 1866.
London, October 26, 1899.

NOTE BY PROF. MAX FÖRSTER, Ph.D.,
ON THE DATE OF LYDGATE'S "HORSE, GOOSE, AND SHEEP,"
Pages 15–42 below.

A PUPIL of Prof. Schick has lately published a valuable study of one of Lydgate's most interesting minor poems in a pamphlet, entitled "Lydgate's Horse, Goose and Sheep. Mit Einleitung und Anmerkungen herausgegeben von Dr. M. Degenhart. Erlangen & Leipzig, 1900." Besides a critical text from eight MSS.[2] and four prints, the editor has several introductory chapters, of which the one about the date of the poem is the most interesting. Dr. Degenhart has found out not only the historical allusion, which Dr. Furnivall has noted independently on p. 25 below, in lines 233–6 :—

> Slouhth of my flyht :—for hasty negligence,
> Of presumpcioun, the goose was left behynde
> Whan the famous worthy duke of Clarence
> Rood on Bayard, with his eyen blinde,

---

[2] Viz. Harl. 2251, Rawl. 86, Lansd. 699, Univ. Libr. Cambr. Hh. iv. 12, Leyden Voss. g. G., Ashm. 50 (and 754), Laud 598, Lamb. 306. Dr. Degenhart has not made use of Mr. Huth's MS.

and which proves that the poem was written after 1421, but also the date of the other passage, p. 32 below, lines 409–419, which push the *terminus ad quem* as far on as 1437:[1]—

> The sheepe is cause, and so hath be ful long,
> Of newë stryvës and of mortal werre.   410
> The circumstaunce me list not to deferre:
> Thy wulle was cause and grete occasïoun
> Why that the prowde, forsworn duke of Borgon   413
>
> LX.
>
> Cam before Caleys, with Flemynges nat a fewe,
> Which yave the sakkis and sarpleres of that towne
> To Gaunt and Bruges, his fredom for to shewe,   416
> And of thy wolle hiht hem possessïoun.
> His boysterous Bastile first was beten down;
> Hemself uneth escaped with the lyf: 419
> What but thy wulle was cause of all this strif?

It may easily be seen that this passage refers to the Duke of Burgundy's siege of Calais in 1436 and the Dutch riots of 1437. Philip the Good, Duke of Burgundy, had at first joined the English against the Dauphin in the Treaty of Troyes (1420) and, in 1423, even married his sister to Henry's brother John, Duke of Bedford. But after some quarrels with Gloucester and Bedford, he was inclining more and more towards the French, till, in 1435 after Bedford's death, he openly renounced his alliance with the English and entered into a league with Charles VII. So Lydgate could very well call him "*forsworn,*" and he certainly did so the more indignantly as, during his stay[2] at Paris (ab. 1426–?) in the service of the Earl of Warwick, he must have had ample opportunity of witnessing the good understanding between Burgundy and the English. The first step of open hostility was that, in June 1436, Philip called out 30,000 Flemings (cp. l. 414 of the poem) and laid siege to Calais which, as the most important emporium of the English wool-trade, had for long been a thorn in the side of the Dutch rivals (cp. l. 420). He had high entrenchments thrown up, and a bastille (or movable tower?) erected, which however was soon taken by the relieving force of the English (cp. l. 418), who drove the Burgundian army away from Calais. The disappointed Flemings gave vent to their discontentment in several riots, which, especially in the larger towns, assumed rather severe forms. In one of these, at Bruges, the Duke himself (cp. l. 419) had a narrow escape from being killed (1437). As Lydgate refers to all these events as "*newe stryves*" (l. 410), we may safely conclude that the poem was written not long after 1437, let us say between 1437–1440.

The idea of a debate between a horse, goose, and sheep seems to have been taken from a tale in the *Gesta Romanorum* (ed. Oesterley, no. 261) or a French translation of it by Nicole Bozon (*Contes moralisés*, ed. P. Meyer and L. T. Smith, 1889).

MAX FÖRSTER.

Würzburg, Dec. 3, 1900.

---

[1] In l. 410 and 411 I have taken the liberty of deviating from Dr. Degenhart's text, as, in my opinion, he has not been very happy in his reconstruction of the text. From his variants I have the impression that Ashmole 754 ought to be taken as the basis of the text, which Dr. Degenhart has only used in a late copy (Ashm. 50).

[2] Cp. Schick's *Temple of Glas*, p. xciii.

NOTES ON

THE STACYONS OF ROME

p. 143–173.

BY

W. M. ROSSETTI, ESQ.,

TRANSLATOR OF DANTE, ETC., ETC.

HAVING some—though only a scanty—personal knowledge of the Roman Churches, I have been invited to write a few remarks by way of elucidation of the statements made in "the Stacyons of Rome." In attempting to revise, confirm, or illustrate, those statements, the books to which I have referred are chiefly three: viz.—

1. Roma Ristaurata di Biondo da Forlì. Tradotta in buona lingua volgare per Lucio Fauno ; nuovamente da molti errori corretta, e ristampata. In Vinegia, appresso Domenico Giglio, 1558.

2. Le Cose Maravigliose dell' Alma Città di Roma, anfiteatro del mondo, con le Chiese et Antichità rapresentate in disegno, da Girolamo Francino. Con l'Aggiunta del Dottor Prospero Parisio, Patritio Romano. In Roma, ad instanza di Gio. Antonio Franzini ed Herede di Girolamo Franzini, 1600.

3. A Handbook of Rome and its Environs. 7th edition, carefully revised on the spot, and considerably enlarged. London, John Murray, 1864.—[Murray's Handbook.]

It may first be expedient to say a few words regarding the term "stations." A station may be defined as the appointed visitation of some church, altar, shrine, or other the like ecclesiastic locale, for pious purposes, and with certain spiritual graces annexed. Francino, whose book first received papal approval in 1587, gives a somewhat long—and, I presume, a complete—list of these stations as then existing. I translate the first half-dozen entries, as a specimen. "The Stations which are in the Churches of Rome, both for Lent and all the year, with the accustomed Indulgences. In the month

of January. The 1st day of the year, which is the Circumcision of
our Lord, there is a station at Santa Maria in Trastevere ad fontes
olei. That same day there is a station at Santa Maria Maggiore, and
at Santa Maria in Aracœli. And there is a Papal Chapel at Santa
Maria del Popolo. 6th, the day of the Epiphany of the Lord, there
is a station at St. Peter's, and a Papal Chapel. 7th, to St. Julian,
in his Church. 10th, at the Church of the Trinity, to St. Paul the
first Hermit. 13th, the octave of the Epiphany at St. Peter's.
16th, to Pope St. Marcellus, in his Church." And so on. The
number of stations throughout the year thus specified by Francino
is about 389, or one may say in round numbers 400. The reader
will perceive therefore that, ample as seems the allowance mentioned
in the poem of the Stations, these form in reality but a small
selection of the whole ; and the thousands and hundreds of years of
indulgence or " pardon," and the plenitudes or percentages of remission of sins, which the poem specifies, will in like manner be found,
though often differing from the allowances indicated by Francino,
by way of excess, to differ also, about as often, by way of deficiency,
and not probably to be at all overstated on the whole. Such of our
readers therefore as feel incited to obtain " a Mˡ yere and þou hit
crave," may set off for Rome in tolerable confidence that they will
not, in the long run, find themselves put off with a sorry hundred.
Inscriptions over altars, such as " Indulgentia Plenaria pro Vivis ac
Defunctis," will show them where to go to, if they are not otherwise
aware.

Thus much premised, I proceed to details, following the order of
the poem, and limiting myself almost entirely to such points as bear
directly upon its statements. To diverge into collateral information
concerning the churches would be tempting, but endless, work.

Line 1 to 24, p. 143. The statement that there were 147 churches
in Rome at the date of the poem seems to be rather under the mark
than over. In 1587 there were 108 parishes, each, no doubt, with
its own special church, and others to boot in no small number.
Murray's Handbook speaks to 45 parish churches within the walls
of Rome, and 9 without, and to more than 300 churches altogether,
besides the 13 basilicas, of which 5 are classed as great or " patri-
archal," and 8 minor. The asserted number of chapels, 10,005,
seems startling : it would be more than 61 chapels apiece to the
147 churches—or, to the present number, about 31 apiece (subject
to some deduction for isolated chapels or oratories). The latter may

be a not unlikely number : it is true that the greatest Basilica of
all, St. Peter's, has only 28 chapels above-ground, but few or none
of the other edifices are laid out on so spacious and uncrowded a
plan.   Of the next item, " A-bowte þe walle to & fowrty," I scarcely
understand the bearing : it appears to affirm that the city of Rome is
environed by 42 walls, of which I do not find, nor can surmise, any
confirmation.   The walls, as at present existing, are from 12 to 13
miles in circuit, including the Trastevere and Vatican.   " Grete
towres þre hondredde & syxty" are quite credible : there are said
to have been 633 in the time of the Emperor Claudius, and nearly
300 are yet standing.   The 24 chief gates show less falling-off from
the imperial time : Pliny speaks to 30, of which, however, 7 were
then walled up : 18 only were open in 1587 : at the present day, 20,
with 7 still walled up in addition.

Line 25 to 101, p. 144–6.   *The Basilica of St. Peter, named also
Basilica Vaticana.*   I need hardly remind my readers that, in perus-
ing our old poem, they must not have in their mind's eye the present
world-famous building on which Bramante, Michael Angelo, and
other men of renown, have left their sign-manual.   The old Basilica
was founded by Constantine—it is said, in A.D. 306 : its façade, as
recorded by Raphael in the fresco of the " Incendio del Borgo," would
probably have been nearly the same as that known to our poet.   This
ancient building had become ruinous by 1450, and new works were
then begun.   In 1506 Julius II. laid the foundation of Bramante's
edifice, which may be considered the nucleus of the one now existing.   The 29 steps which our poet speaks to had by 1600 become
35 steps (of marble).   The 7 years' pardon, or indulgence, for each
step ascended or descended, is confirmed by Francino, who adds,
however, the obligation of going up the steps to St. Peter's Chapel.
The Pope Alexander who granted this indulgence is not clearly
identified : it may perhaps have been either Alexander IV., who
reigned from 1254 to 61, or Alexander V., 1409–10.   I find nothing
to elucidate the interesting statement that the solitary chapel of
St. Peter, standing at the head of the steps in question, was the
one wherein that saint sang his first mass.   The 100 altars in the
church are reduced in the note (from the Lambeth MS.) to 80 : as
I have already said, the number of altars, or chapels, in the present
building is far below either of these figures.   The poet next tells us
that 7 of the 100 altars are of more especial honour.   This was still
the case in 1587, the ordinary indulgences being doubled on the

respective feast-days for these altars : and doubtless these privileges
have since continued or increased.   The 1st altar is "þe vernake,"
on the right hand.   As Francino says, " In the tabernacle to right
of the great door is the Veronica, or sacred countenance ;" which
(in Biondo's words) " is the true likeness of our Saviour preserved
upon a veil by St. Veronica."   The reader, no doubt, knows the
legend that, as Christ was going to Calvary, a Jewish lady handed
Him her veil to wipe His face, the image of which was transferred
thereto.   This is the Veronica, which is exhibited on Holy Wednesday, on Good Friday, and on the 18th January, the day set
apart in 1557 for the dedication-feast of St. Peter's Cathedral.   There
is not now any altar to St. Veronica (though there is her statue) in
the upper church of St. Peter's ; but one remains in the crypt.   The
2nd chief altar named is that of the Madonna ; to whom indeed
there are at present two—that of the Virgin, and of the " Madonna
del Soccorso."   The 3rd, to St. Jude—or, as the note from the
Lambeth MS. says, to Sts. Simon and Jude.   The remains of both
these saints were in 1587, and doubtless still are, in the church ; but
it does not appear that an altar dedicated to St. Jude has remained.
The 4th altar was to St. Andrew, to whom there is now a chapel in
the crypt, and another, to this saint along with St. Peter, in the
upper church.   His head is there also, having been brought to Rome
by the Prince of the Morea, in the time of Pope Pius II. (1458–64).
The 5th altar was, and still is, to St. Gregory the Great, there buried.
The 6th, to Pope St. Leo, now accompanied by a very conspicuous
bas-relief of the repulse of Attila by that pope.   The 7th is an altar
of the Holy Cross, or, as now also termed, of the Crucifix : this
chapel contains the principal relics of the church.   Our poet next
gives some details of indulgences.   The statement that, from Holy
Thursday to Lammas-day (1 August), you can obtain 14,000 years
indulgence per day, is modified by Francino to 12,000 years and as
many lents, and remission of one-third of your sins, daily from the
Feast of the Annunciation, 25 February, to Lammas-day.   Similarly
as to the " gret *pardon* " when the Veronica is shown : 4000 [Fran-
cino, 3000] years' indulgence to citizens of Rome, 9000 [6000] to
those who come from without, and 12,000 to such as have crossed
the seas, with one-third of sins remitted in each case : Francino adds
as many lents, and, on the 18th January, plenary remission.   All
these graces are, according to the poem, doubled in lent : according
to Francino, on the festival of St. Peter (29 June), the feasts of the

seven principal altars, and all double feasts. Next we have an account of the relics in this Basilica. Bones of St. Peter and St. Paul. Francino affirms that half of Peter's body, and half of Paul's, were then (1587) under the high altar of St. Peter's—the other halves being under the high altar of S. Paolo fuori le Mura. Murray's Handbook differs somewhat : saying that " the body " of Peter has, since the middle of the 4th century, been in the confessional of the crypt of St. Peter's, whither it was brought from the crypt of St. Sebastian's in the Via Appia ; while the tomb of St. Paul used, before the burning of the Basilica of San Paolo, to be under the high altar of that edifice—the earliest traditions testifying to his remains having been buried there, after removal from the Vatican in A.D. 251. The *present* resting-place of St. Paul does not appear to be further defined in Murray. To the best of my recollection, the local account given to the visitor is that both St. Peter and St. Paul lie in the crypt of St. Peter's. Francino confirms our poet in saying that the bodies of Sts. Simon and Jude (as already stated), and of St. Gregory, are in St. Peter's : as to St. Leo he is silent. " Seynt Parnelle þat holy vyrgyn " is no doubt St. Petronilla, daughter of St. Peter, to whom again Francino testifies as lying here. As for " Seynt Sythe þat þoled pyne," I cannot trace such a saint, nor bring the name into harmony with my authorities, unless (which I strongly suspect) it ought to be " Stephen," of whom, according to Francino, the church contains a shoulder-blade.

Line 102 to 128, p. 146–7. *The Basilica of St. Paul, termed San Paolo fuori le Mura, or the Basilica Ostiensis.* This edifice stands on the Ostian Road, about a mile out of Rome, being founded in A.D. 388 on the spot where the truncated head of St. Paul is said to have been miraculously discovered. It remained as the only specimen of a Basilica resembling the earlier St. Peter's, until its lamentable destruction by fire on the 16th July, 1823. Some portions, however, escaped ; and the building has been reconstructed on the same interior plan. Our poet states that, on the feast of the conversion of St. Paul, 25 January, one may have at this church 1000 years' pardon (which he seems always to use in the sense of "indulgence," as now more generally termed). The note, however, from the Lambeth MS. cuts this down to 100 years ; which is confirmed by Francino, who adds as many lents, and plenary remission of sins. The 2000 years on St. Paul's day, 29 June, figure in Francino simply as plenary remission ; and the 4000 years on Childermas-day (28

December) are not named by that author, but merely that there is then a station in this Basilica. "On Seynt Martyn þe viij day" means, I suppose, during the octave of St. Martin, when, as the text says, this church was consecrated. The 14,000 years and lents, and remission of one-third of your penance, are reduced by Francino to 1000 years and lents, but with plenary remission. In the next item the Lambeth MS. appears again to be correct: it is by going to this church on all the *Sundays*—not necessarily all the *days*—of the year, that you obtain the same pardon as by a pilgrimage to St. James's shrine.

Line 129 to 156, p. 147-8. *The Church of St. Anastasius, or of Sts. Vincent and Anastasius,* stands outside Rome in the Ostian Road, having been consecrated by Honorius I. in 626, and is (as Murray says) "one of the good and unaltered specimens of the early Christian Basilicas." Our author states that 7000 years' pardon [Francino, 6000] is granted in this church daily, with one-third of penance remitted, by grace of Pope Urban—who may be either Urban VI., reigning from 1378–87, or Urban V., from 1362–70. The curious particular as to pardon for such quarrels with parents as do not comprise blows struck at them is not in Francino. The stone before the door of this church whereon St. Paul was decapitated is a short marble pillar: the sword of the executioner is not named by either Francino or Murray. The three wells stated to have sprung up are still to be seen: they mark as many bounds of the apostle's head, and are now enclosed within the adjoining church of San Paolo alle Tre Fontane, built in 1590.

Line 157 to 182, p. 148-9. *The Chapel Scala Cœli* stands near the foregoing Church of St. Anastasius. It was built over the cemetery of St. Zeno, and has undergone restorations from 1582 onwards. It derives its name from a vision of St. Bernard's, who, while celebrating a funereal mass, saw the souls for whom he was praying going up to heaven by a ladder. The text seems to ignore this legend, and to imply that the name "Scala Cœli" is used merely as one of the mystical or figurative names of the Madonna. One feels sceptical as to the 10,000 martyrs slain in the time of Tiberius. Francino confirms the number, without assigning any date, but adding as a relic "the knife which they were killed with:" it must have been a well-tempered one. Murray terms these martyrs the 12,000 Christians said to have been employed in erecting the Baths of Diocletian —a less unlikely era, at any rate. Our poet seems now in the vein, and strides from bold to bolder assertion; saying that he who sings mass in this chapel for a friend releases him "fro *helle*," passing him into purgatory, and thence into paradise. At least the term hell *appears* to be used here in its exact current sense, as against purgatory; though possibly it is intended rather for an equivalent, which might seem to be the case in line 565, "To abate the peyne off helle." Taken in the sense I understand, the assertion is an exceedingly daring one; no pope even, so far as I am aware, having ever professed to release a soul from hell,—the power of the keys is over two keys only, those of purgatory and heaven. As an instance in point may be cited the famous legend of the salvation from hell, at the instance of Gregory the Great, of the long dead and doomed Trajan. It is propounded, not that Trajan passed from hell into either purgatory or heaven; but that God restored him for a while to *mundane* life, wherein becoming a Christian, he died again and went to heaven—or, as an annotator of a MS. of Dante tersely phrases it, "brevi resuscitatus est, et postea salvatus." A still more obvious, though jocular, instance may be cited regarding the papal master of the ceremonies, Messer Biagio di Cesena, whom Michael Angelo, in his Last Judgment, painted among the condemned. "Biagio," says Murray, "complained to the pope in order to have the figure removed: who declared that it was impossible, for, though he had the power to release from purgatory, he had none over hell." Moreover Francino, who could scarcely have omitted so grave an ingredient in this grace at the Scala Cœli, says nothing of hell, but simply, as in any other purgatorial case, "there is the liberation of a soul" upon celebrating mass under the altar on the 29th January. In his next statement, however, our author appears needlessly modest: his "3000 years granted by six popes buried at St. Sebastian's" become in Francino 10,000 years' indulgence daily.

Line 183 to 198, p. 149. *The Church of St. Mary Annunciate*, standing midway between those of St. Anastasius and St. Sebastian, was consecrated in 1220. The legend mentioned in the text "of owr lady yn þe way" (*i. e.* I suppose, Santa Maria in Viâ, the title of another of the Roman churches), and which, as I understand the poem, is inscribed on this Church of St. Mary Annunciate, is not elucidated by Francino. In that writer, the 500 years' pardon of the text swells into 10,000 years' indulgence daily, and plenary remission on Annunciation-day. It will be right to bear in mind, in this and other cases, that the privileges may very well have augmented

between the dates of our poet and of Francino, but are not likely to
have decreased.

Line 199 to 267, p. 149–152. " Fabyane and Bastyane" is *the Basilica of St. Sebastian, called also the Basilica Appiana,* being one of
the eight minor Basilicas : I cannot find any authority for giving it
the name of Fabian. It stands about two miles beyond the gate of St.
Sebastian on the Via Appia. Its foundation has been ascribed both
to Constantine and to St. Lucina ; but the building, as it now exists,
is new from 1611. Our text states that Pope Gelasius endowed
this church with 40 years' pardon and many lents : Francino does
not mention Gelasius, but speaks to many indulgences, including
6046 years and lents daily. The pardons, equal to those at St.
Peter's, on account of the bones here buried, are to be obtained by
entering the catacombs into which the church leads, usually termed
" the Cemetery of St. Callixtus,"—though this would appear, from
modern researches, to be a mistake, and the catacomb under St.
Sebastian's to be unconnected with that of Callixtus. Our poet
appears to be considerably out in saying that the bodies of St. Peter
and St. Paul lay here " fyfe hondred ȝer er þey were founde :" 19
months is the space of time assigned in Murray, and Francino,
though only using a vague term, seems to contemplate some such
moderate period. They lay "in the underground chapel, opening
out of the ambulatory behind the tribune," having been placed there
after being recovered from some Grecian kidnappers or enthusiasts
in the reign of Vespasian : and, in the time of Heliogabalus, who
was constructing a circus at the Vatican, the remains of Peter, which
had been transported thither, were again for a while deposited in
this spot—which hence acquired, specially and individually, the
name of " Catacumbæ," afterwards so widely applied. The statement
which follows in the text as to six popes, mentioned by name, giving
here 1000 years' grace each to all shriven persons, appears to relate
to the indulgences appertaining (according to Francino, as above
cited) to the *church.* The subterranean chapel next referred to
must be the catacombs, or a chapel therein ; the 46 martyr popes
do not appear in Francino, but 18 popes amid the large number of
174,000 martyrs. Both statements may be regarded as considerable
exaggerations ; and the former is certainly a monstrous one—for
there had only been 32 popes altogether up to the time of the conversion of Constantine, A.D. 312. (This date may be used as a
corrective to a previous statement as to the foundation of a Christian

church by Constantine—St. Peter's—in the earlier year 306.)   Francino confirms the plenary remission, but not the salvation consequent
upon dying in this subterranean chapel.   " þe palme," l. 252, next
mentioned ("Palmete" in the Lambeth MS.), should evidently not
be understood to mean a palm-tree, but a footsole; and the term is
here applied to a very famous relic still to be seen in the Church of
St. Sebastian—a slab of white marble with an impression somewhat
rudely resembling that of human feet, or rather with an inartistic
imitation of such an impression, for it seems impossible that any eye
which has looked at the relic should admit its actual authenticity as
a footmark.   The beautiful legend connected with this relic is briefly
related in the text:—the faint-heartedness of that most human,
fallible, and sympathetic of apostles, Peter, in the prospect of death,
which he was fleeing Rome to escape; the apparition of the cross-
bearing Saviour to him on the Via Appia, at a spot now marked by
the small church of Domine Quo Vadis; the question put to Him in
those words by Peter, with the reply that the Saviour was coming to
Rome to be crucified anew, as His apostle shrank from the martyrdom; and the return of Peter, contrite, compunctious, and heroic
unto death.   (Our National Gallery contains a frigid yet observable
small picture of this subject by Annibal Carracci.)   Here, says the
poem, one may obtain remission of sins (confirmed by Francino), and
1000 years' pardon.

Line 268 to 277, p. 152. *The Church of San Giovanni a (or "di-
nanzi") Porta Latina* was founded in A.D. 780; but its present form
dates from the end of the 12th century.   On the festival of the saint,
6 May, a soul may be saved from purgatory—or, as Francino puts it,
there is plenary remission of sin—with 500 years' indulgence daily.
There is also a grace, says the poet, to those who go into the place
where St. John was sodden in oil—more strictly, where he would
have been sodden in boiling oil but for a miraculous interference.
This place is a round chapel outside the Church of the Porta Latina:
it marks the spot where the caldron of oil was set, and dates, in its
present condition, from 1509.   It bears the separate name of *San
Giovanni in Oleo.*

Line 278 to 289, p. 152–3.   *The Church of " Saynte Thomas of
ynde"* is not noticed in Murray; but this is no indication of its not
being still extant.   It must be the same church which Francino terms
St. Thomas the Apostle, or San ·Timmaso in Parione (which is the
name of one of the Rioni, or Districts, of the City of Rome).   The

original church was consecrated in 1139, but had been entirely renewed, somewhat about Francino's time, on the old plan. The pardon of more than 14,000 years, with remission of one-third of one's sins, is not confirmed by Francino : who says, however, that on four feasts (not including the feast of St. Thomas, 21 December), there is plenary indulgence in this church for all sins, and a full jubilee, which had been granted by Pius IV. (about 1560).

Line 290 to 293, p. 153. These four lines affirm that there is great pardon "wher þe stacyones cleped ys," ratified for ever by Pope Boniface. The statement does not appear to have any relation to the immediate context (though it might possibly belong to the sequel, concerning the Lateran Basilica) : it seems more appropriate as a general announcement proper to the opening of the poem.

Line 294 to 477, p. 153–9. *The Basilica of St. John Lateran, or the Lateran Basilica*, occupies in the poem, it will be observed, more than double the space accorded even to St. Peter's. In fact, this is the church of highest traditional rank in all Rome, and even in the whole Latin-Christian world, being the pope's own diocesan church : it stands inscribed "Omnium urbis et orbis Ecclesiarum Mater et Caput." The popes are crowned here, and "the Chapter of the Lateran still takes precedence of that of St. Peter's." This church was built by Constantine ; nearly destroyed in, or shortly before, the time of Clement V., whose reign began in 1305 ; restored and enlarged by him and his successors. It is dedicated to the Saviour, and the two Sts. John, Baptist and Evangelist. Its name, Lateran, comes from the house of the senator Plautius Lateranus, of the time of Nero, on the site of which it is built. The poem intimates that this house was one of the palaces of Constantine at the time of his being healed and converted by Pope Sylvester, and that the Emperor gave the edifice to the Bishop, to be converted into a church : this is, for legendary purposes, nearly enough correct. The " Saluator " in the roof over the pope's see, or the tribune of the high altar, is an image of Christ which is said to have appeared there miraculously at the consecration of the church, 9 November, and to have survived two conflagrations of the building unscathed. The next relic mentioned is the table of the Last Supper, "That Cryste made on h*i*s monde." The phrase might at first be understood to mean that Christ, either in His parental calling as a carpenter, or by the exer cise of miraculous power, actually made this table ; but I do not find any such tradition elsewhere, and should suppose the phrase to

mean rather "On which Christ made His maunday" (mandate, or
eucharistic institution). "The table stands in a recess opening out
of the corridor called the Portico Leonino, surrounding the tribune :
it is of cedar wood, and was once encased in silver." The two
tablets whereon Christ wrote the law for Moses appear in Francino
by the name of the "arca fœderis" (ark of the covenant), which
ark, in the Jewish temple, was said to contain these tablets : perhaps the two writers mean substantially the same thing, especially
as our poet proceeds to name Aaron's rod (the rod of Aaron and
Moses, in Francino), and "Angelles meat," which one may suppose
to be the pot of manna, both preserved in Jerusalem in connection
with the ark. Francino is silent as to the remains of the five loaves
and two fishes wherewith Christ fed the multitude. Our poet is
clearly not quite right about the four brass pillars brought by Vespasian and Titus from Jerusalem : some *other* relics are said to have
been so brought, but not these. They are, on the contrary, four
pillars of gilt bronze, at the altar of the Sacrament, reputed to have
been made by Augustus from the rostra of the galleys taken at
Actium, and set up in the Temple of Jupiter Capitolinus, whence
they were brought to this church : Francino, however, has it that
they are filled with consecrated earth from Jerusalem. The chains
which bound St. John are those used when the evangelist was
brought a prisoner from Ephesus to Rome. The vessel which they
gave him to drink from, but harmlessly, was a poisoned cup presented to him by order of Domitian. The text next specifies a kirtle
of the man who was raised from the dead on that same occasion :
this is modified, by the note from the Lambeth MS., into St. John's
own kirtle which raised three men from the dead, and Francino
concurs in this statement. The "cloþis of Ihesu-criste" are the red
robe which Pilate put on Him, stained with His blood. Francino
confirms "þe askes [ashes] of Iohne þe baptyste," adding a piece of
his haircloth. The next item again appears more correctly, to trust
Francino, in the Lambeth MS.; it should be, not the table-cloth of
the Last Supper, but the towel wherewith Jesus wiped the disciples'
feet. The sark made for Christ by the Virgin, and the blood and
water from His side, are confirmed by Francino. That author is
silent, possibly through a sentiment of decent *retenue*, regarding the
"mylke of Marye þe vyrgyne," and "þe flesh of his cyrcumsyce"
(Christ's) : he specifies, instead, some of the hair and garments of
Mary. The rather earlier author, Biondo da Forlì, upholds our poet

in showing, as regards his latter-named relic, that "men h*i*t holde yn grete pryse." He mentions both this, and the "vase di latte bianchissimo di Maria Vergine gloriosa;" and not only mentions them, but includes them in those few and choicer Roman glories which need to be ushered in with the following peroration, as he winds up his eloquence and his book :—" There are in Rome, however, certain things peculiar to itself, so great, so marvellous, that neither are they found elsewhere, nor can they be transferred elsewhither: and he who has not seen Rome, what *has* he seen? of a surety he has seen nought to marvel at." To return to our text. The foot of the Magdalene is not particularized by Francino, only certain relics of her: " þe clo*pi*s þat cr*i*ste was wonden In" are reduced to the facecloth. The heads of Peter and Paul are said to have been found among the ruins of the older Lateran church in the reign of Urban V. (1362–70): they are over the high altar, in an iron grating. Francino confirms our poet in saying that, when these heads are publicly exhibited, which is done on six several days of the year, there are the same indulgences as at the exhibition (already mentioned) of the Veronica. The author next ushers us into the Pope's Hall, connected with the Lateran. This would appear to have been already more or less destroyed in the time of Francino (1587), who speaks of it as "the old palace," and of its contents as things of the past: the present palace was built by Sixtus V. It seems somewhat singular that the writer of the "Stacyons" should not mention, among the treasures of the old Pope's Hall, its now sole surviving relic (save the chapel Sancta Sanctorum), the famous Scala Santa, said to be the staircase of Pilate's court, which Christ descended after his sentence: no one may go up it save on his knees. Omitting this, he informs us that the Hall has three doors, on passing through any of which you may, if shriven, obtain 40 years' pardon : these vanished doors, says Francino, had been in Pilate's court, and Jesus had passed through them. The next 12 lines, 448 to 459, seem to have dropped somewhat out of their place, and to be more proper to the passage just preceding (430–37) concerning the heads of Peter and Paul. The present passage is of value in tending to fix the date of our poem. It speaks of the indulgences granted by Pope Urban V. when these sacred relics were discovered and first exhibited; and proceeds to say (l. 456–9, p. 159) :—

> "There ys no man now y-bore,
> Nor his fadur hym be-fore,

That of þe heddës haue a syȝth
At þat tyme, but be graᴣe of God almyȝt."

Urban had found the heads in or before 1365. Now the writer
of the "Stacyons" assumes that persons living at the date when he
wrote might in the year of discovery have seen the heads. Suppose
(which seems an ample allowance of time) that he assumes that a
person now aged 90 might have seen the heads when aged 10; this
would leave an interval of 80 years, which, added to 1365, would
bring out 1445 as the latest admissible date of the poem, and probably some few years later than in fact. We are next escorted to
the chapel Sancta Sanctorum—already referred to as being, with the
Scala Santa, the sole remaining portion of the old Lateran Palace of
the popes: it is a handsome Gothic work, consecrated by Nicholas
III. (1277–81) to St. Lawrence. No women, as notified by the poet,
are allowed to enter. The "Saluatowr" in this chapel is a painting
5 feet 8 inches in height, representing the Saviour at the age of
twelve. Our author says that the portrait was sent to the Virgin
Mother by her re-glorified Son after His ascension. This memor-
able detail does not appear in Francino, who attributes the picture
to St. Luke as designer, and to an angel as executant: the less
believing Murray speaks of it as of Greek workmanship.

Line 478 to 513, p. 159–61. *The Basilica of Santa Croce in
Gerusalemme* (one of the 8 minor ones); termed also *The Sessorian
Basilica*, being founded on the site of the Sessorian Palace of Sextus
Varius, the father of Heliogabalus. It was built, in 331, by Constantine, at the request of his mother, St. Helena, famous as the heroine
of the "Invention of the Cross,"—or rather perhaps, as our text says,
by Constantia, daughter of Constantine. Some earth from Jerusalem
was mixed with the foundations, whence the special name of the
church. Its present form dates from 1774. Pope Sylvester consecrated the building on the 10th March. The indulgences, 2005
years every Sunday and Wednesday, are reduced to 300 years and
lents every Sunday, with remission of one-third of sins, by Francino:
the Lambeth MS. gives only 100 years. The *daily* indulgence of
100 years, however, rises in Francino to 6046 years and lents, and
remission as above. That author confirms the statements as to the
sponge of gall and vinegar offered to Christ, the nail from His cross,
and the title written thereon by Pilate; this was covered by St.
Helena with silver, and adorned with gold and gems. The portion
of the true cross here deposited by Helena is still to be seen; also

POLIT. POEMS.   *c* the portion—Francino terms it a half—of the Penitent Thief's cross.

Line 514 to 535, p. 161-2. The Church of St. Lawrence here mentioned is *San Lorenzo fuori le Mura :* there are in Rome at least five other churches dedicated to the same saint. This, which is one of the five larger Basilicas, is on the road to Tivoli, about a mile beyond the Porta di San Lorenzo. It was built by Constantine, and enlarged and altered by Honorius III. in 1260. The catacombs of St. Cyriacus are entered hence. The daily indulgence of 7000 years is reduced in Francino to 748, with lents and remission as in the text. The assertion that the church was consecrated by Pope Pelagius seems to refer, not to the original dedication, but to some re-consecration by Pelagius II., who partly rebuilt the edifice in 578. Sts. Lawrence and Stephen rest here, in a marble urn in the confessional. The statement in the text,

> "And vnþur þe awter ys made a stone,
> There a-bowte þey may gone,"

may perhaps relate to this urn ; or perhaps to one of two relics here preserved—a stone cast at Stephen, and a stone whereon Lawrence was laid after death, marked with his fat and blood. Probably, however, the first explanation is the true one—the passage being followed up by a reference to the "swete smelle of bodyes þat þer be," by which the relics of Stephen and Lawrence would appear to be indicated; I do not find any other bodies recorded. The grace as to release of a soul from purgatory is confirmed in Francino.

Line 536 to 547, p. 162. The Church here named of "seynt sympylle, Fawstyne [Lambeth MS. "Fastym"] and Betrys" ["Beatrice"] may be probably rendered *The Church of Sts. Simplicius, Faustinus, and Beatrice.* I find no account of it in my authorities. Francino does indeed name a church of Sts. Faustinus and Jovita, the patrons of Brescia ; but this was a new foundation of Julius II. (1503–13), and is therefore too late in date, even if otherwise acceptable.

Line 548 to 553, p. 163. *The Church of St. Julian* is at the head of the Via Maggiore, at the spot where the so-called "Trophies of Marius" were found.

Line 554 to 565, p. 163. *The Church of St. Eusebius* is in the same neighbourhood. The inscription on a stone, "I wole the halowe or I goone," seems to suggest something special, but I do not find it elucidated.

Line 566 to 571, p. 163-4. We here return to the aforenamed *Church of St. Julian.*

Line 572 to 581, p. 164. *The Church of San Matteo in Merulana* is on the road between the Lateran and Santa Maria Maggiore.

Line 582 to 590, p. 164. "The Chirche of uyght and modeste" is *the Church of San Vito in Macello,* near the arch of Gallienus. It does not appear that the building is dedicated to Modestus as well as Vitus ; but there is a station there, on the 15th June, to Sts. Vitus, Modestus, and Crescentius—or Crescenti*a,* as quaint old Topsell, the naturalist, says in his account of the king of beasts : "Primus and Fælicianus, Thacus, Vitus, Modestus, and Crescentia, all martyrs, being cast unto lions, received no harm by them at all ; but the beasts lay down at their feet, and became tame, gentle, and meek, not like themselves, but rather like doves." The forgiveness of a quarter of one's sins in this church is not named by Francino, but 6000 years' indulgence on St. Vitus's day. The 7000 martyrs buried here in the time of Antoninus are, no doubt, the same as Francino's "infinite number" of martyrs who were killed on a stone at the same spot. Line 590 runs—

"This is the vij parte of þy synne ondoone,"

and remains without a rhyme to match. It also appears—though not to a certainty—to conflict with the previous line 584, announcing remission of a *fourth* part of sins. Possibly 590 ought to be transferred to follow 723—

"Suche bed of penaunce I not no moo,"

which seems also bereaved of its proper rhyme-sequence, and with which 590 would rhyme, were we to read "ondoo" instead of "ondoone." The first word of the line, "This," would also appear to be a mistake for "There" or "Thus"

Line 591 to 654, p. 164-6. *The Basilica of Santa Maria Maggiore, also called the Liberian Basilica,* ranks third among these great churches. It was founded on the summit of the Esquiline, in 352, by Pope Liberius, and by a Roman patrician named John, and his wife. These three persons had, on the night of the 5th August, a vision enjoining them to build a church on the spot where they should find snow lying next morning : they obeyed, and hence the church was first called Sancta Maria ad Nives. It was enlarged in 432, and the plan then adopted has been preserved in subsequent alterations, so that this church has, more than any other intramural one, retained the characters of the larger Basilicas. The text states that the body of St. Matthew lies at (or below) the high altar. Murray concurs in this statement; but probably Francino is more exact in speaking of the body of St. *Matthias*, and an arm only of St. Matthew. In another part of the church lies St. Jerome. I am not clear as to the statement that the remains of this saint were brought "frome the Cyte of Damase;" which may be presumed to mean Damascus, though the word seems more commonly used for the papal name Damasus. These remains are said to have been transported to Rome in the middle of the 7th century, along with the Præsepe (or Culla) which came from Bethlehem; and Jerome is reported to have been originally buried in Jerusalem, in a tomb which he had ordered at the entry of the cave-sepulchre of Christ. The Præsepe, before which Jerome is deposited in Santa Maria Maggiore, consists of five boards of the manger wherein Christ lay in Bethlehem, now enclosed in an urn of silver and crystal, and placed in a subterranean chapel: a solemn procession to this relic is held on Christmas Eve. The Chapel of "Seynt Agas," next mentioned, I understand to be a chapel of St. Agatha, but do not find any particulars concerning it. The cloth wherein the infant Christ was first wrapped by the Virgin is specified also by Francino: not so the hay which He lay in, nor "of his Flesche the Syrcumsyse," the possession of which, as we have already seen, is assigned to the Lateran Basilica earlier in the poem. The relics of St. Thomas à Becket, specified by our author, are an arm, part of his brain, and his blood-stained rochet; by Francino, his tunicle, stole, and maniple, blood-stained. The image of the Virgin which Luke found ready painted to his hand by angelic agency is now in the rich Borghese Chapel. It represents the infant Christ, as well as the Madonna, and, according to Murray, is pronounced by a papal bull to have been painted by Luke: miraculous powers are ascribed to it, and it was carried in procession to stay the plague in Rome in 590. The papal bull is attached to one of the chapel-walls, and is probably the same document which our poem alludes to. On the festival of this church, termed the day of the "Madonna della neve," the text says there is 1000 years' pardon, with 700 years additional if sued for, and one-third of sins remitted [Francino, plenary remission only]: on every feast of the Madonna, 100 years' pardon [Francino, 1000 years, and plenary remission, on the feasts of the Virgin's Purification, Assumption, Nativity,

Presentation, and Conception]: and from Assumption - day till Christmas-day, 15,000 years of temporal penance remitted—not a very easy statement to comprehend—[Francino, 12,000 years' indulgence; besides ordinary daily indulgence of 6048 years and lents, with remission of one-third of sins].

Line 655 to 684, p. 166–7. *The Church of St. Pudentiana,* near the Novatian Baths, and behind Santa Maria Maggiore, is reputed to be the most ancient of all the Christian edifices in Rome, and to have originally ranked as the Cathedral. It includes, or is erected on the site of, the house of Pudens, a senator with whom St. Peter lodged from A.D. 41 to 50, and whose daughters, Praxed and Prudentiana, that Apostle converted. The name is mentioned in the 2nd Epistle to Timothy, iv. 21 : "Eubulus greeteth thee, and Pudens, and Linus, and Claudia, and all the brethren." The church was consecrated by Pope St. Pius I. in 145 ; restored by Simplicius, who reigned from 467 to 485 ; and brought to its present form in 1597. The late Dr. Wiseman was titular cardinal of this church. The (daily) remission of one-third of sins here, named in the poem, is confirmed by Francino, who adds indulgence for 3000 years and lents. The churchyard of St. Priscilla adjoins it, containing the bodies of 3000 martyrs. The statement that Sts. Peter and Paul "Bothe were harborowed there" may be inferred to apply rather to the Santo Pastore. The further statements that "Seynt Peius founde" [founded?] and hallowed the baptistery, and converted 78 souls on an Easter-day, would appear to refer to St. Pius ; though the peculiar spelling "Peius," and the stroke over the *i* being the mark used for an *er* contraction, might seem to point to Peter as the person really intended.

Line 685 to 702, p. 167. *The Church of St. Praxed,* near Santa Maria Maggiore, was erected by Pope Paschal in 822, on the site of an oratory which had been built in 160 by Pius I. as a place of refuge from persecution. It was modernized by San Carlo Borromeo, its titular cardinal. The poem states that St. Praxed buried in this spot 1300 persons martyred in the reign of Antonine. They lie in a well in the centre of the church, having been put to death on the Esquiline Hill ; or, as Francino says, all over Rome, whence their blood was sponged up by the saint, and drained into this well. We may fairly reject the date of the reign of Antonine ; St. Praxed having been converted by Peter in or before A.D. 50, and the earliest of the Antonines not having succeeded to the throne till 138. A farther number of martyrs, set down as 40, are buried in the chapel named of old the Orto del Paradiso, now the chapel of the Colonna Santa, or of St. Zeno : among them, it is said, are 11 popes. The pardon of 1 year and 40 days, with remission of a quarter of one's sins, doubled in lent, swells in Francino into 12,000 years and lents daily, and one-third remission. The pillar to which Christ was bound is of white and black marble, and was brought from Jerusalem in 1223 by Cardinal Colonna.

Line 703 to 723, p. 167–8. The festival (1 August) and *Basilica of San Pietro in Vincoli*, in commemoration of the fettering of the saint in Jerusalem. Francino confirms the plenary remission on this day in the church : he is silent as to the daily indulgence of 500 years and lents. The church stands on the Esquiline, not far from the Baths of Titus : it is one of the minor Basilicas, and is entitled the *Basilica Eudoxiana*, having been built in 442 by Eudoxia, wife of the Emperor Valentinian III. It was repaired by Pelagius I. in 555, and has undergone other changes, up to 1705. This church has two special claims to remembrance : Hildebrand was here elected pope in 1073, under the name of Gregory VII., and Michael Angelo's Moses is inside it. Our poet, in saying that the church contains a piece of the cross of Christ, is probably less correct than Francino, who speaks only of a part of the cross of St. Andrew. The latter writer does not elucidate the curious legend in the text as to a bed of St. Martin, in this church, insensible to sight and touch. The chains of St. Peter, from which the church receives its name, are enclosed in a bronze tabernacle in the outer sacristy, and are only exhibited from the 1st to the 9th August.

Line 724 to 741, p. 168. The "plase of the postyll*is* twoo" must be *the Basilica of the Holy Apostles or Basilica Constantiniana*, now dedicated, it would appear, to all the twelve Apostles without distinction, but originally to Sts. Philip and James. It stands in the Piazza dei Santi Apostoli, behind the Corso ; and it is stated by Francino to have been founded by Constantine, though the present edifice, in its earliest condition, is only ascribed to Pelagius (555–60), and a re-building took place in 1420. Sts. Philip and James (" Jacobe ") are buried here. " Seint Sabasabyne " appears to represent the names Sts. Saba and Sabina, female saints, of whom each has a church of her own in Rome : according to Francino, however, the saint buried in the Church of the Apostles is of the male sex, St. Sabinus. He confirms the tabard of St. Thomas the Apostle, and the arm of St. Blaise. As to indulgences, all that he names is plenary remission on the 1st May.

Line 742 to 745, p. 168. *The Church of San Bartolommeo in Insula* was built in the Isle of the Tiber, on the site of a temple of Jupiter (or perhaps Æsculapius), by Paschal II. in 1113 : it received its present form in the reign of Gregory XIII. (1572–85). The sub-structions used to give the island the form of a ship, as shown, with quaint attractiveness, in Francino's woodcut. That writer does not confirm the 1000 years' indulgence of our text; but speaks to plenary remission on St. Bartholomew's day, 24 August, and 20 years' indulgence on Palm Sunday. The relics of Bartholomew are preserved in an urn under the high altar, having been brought from Benevento to Rome by the Emperor Otho II.

Line 746 to 809, p. 168–70. *The Church of Santa Maria Rotonda, or Sancta Maria ad Martyres, being the antique Pantheon,* stands in a Piazza between the Corso and the Piazza Navona. The circular edifice, one of the most famous of antiquity preserved for the admiration of modern architects, was dedicated by Agrippa in B.C. 27, and was afterwards worked upon by some of the heathen emperors. Agrippa, our poet informs us, founded the building "for sabillis [I suppose 'the sibyls'' or 'a sibyl's'] and neptuno-is sake," and named it "Pantheon," which appears to have been a very illogical proceeding. There is, however, some considerable conflict of opinion as to the deities to whom the temple was in fact dedicated. Some authorities say Mars and Jupiter; others, Jupiter Ultor; others, Mars and Venus; others, all the gods—which attribution is of course favoured by the name Pantheon. Dion, nevertheless, does not leave even this point clear; for he says that the motive for using the term Pantheon was simply that the temple, being round or round-roofed (θολοειδες), resembled the vaulted heaven, abode of all the gods. Other investigators again, still less easily satisfied, believe the build-ing to have had little or nothing to do with worship at all, but to have been connected with the baths which Agrippa constructed in this neighbourhood—the form (apart from the portico, which seems to be a later addition) being simply that of a "calidarium." Leaving these controversies, our memories may retain one authenticated fact —that Raphael is buried here. Our poet tells a curious legend : That the heathen worshippers made a golden idol of Neptune, and set it up on the roof, peering through an opening thereof; and that the brass covert on this statue's head blew off "with A wynde of

helle" to St. Peter's Basilica, where it might still be seen before the
church door.   I am left to guess at the modicum of foundation
which there may be for this little episode : and I conceive it to be
as follows—amounting simply to two misapprehensions, or gratuitous
assumptions.   1st, the roof of the Pantheon is not entirely closed,
but has an opening, 28 feet in diameter, which supplies the whole
of the light which the edifice receives.   Some legendary imagination,
contemplating this orifice, and not reasoning upon any questions of
antique architecture, jumped to the conclusion that it *must* have
been made for something to be inserted or to project through it; if
something, it *must* have been a statue; and if a statue, why not
Neptune?   2nd, a gilt bronze pine-cone, hollowed, and 11 feet in
height, used once to be at the summit of the Sepulchre or Mole of
Hadrian (now the Castle of Sant' Angelo) ; it was removed by Pope
Symmachus (498 to 514) to the quadriporticus before the Basilica of
St. Peter, probably to the steps of the building.   Dante saw it there,
and speaks of it under the name it still retains, "la pina di San
Pietro :" it is now in the garden of the Vatican Palace.   There was
a story, not probably true, that this pine-cone had been set atop of
the campanile of St. Peter's, and had been hurled thence by lightning
down to the steps.   This, I have little doubt, is the object in which
our author is content to see a head-dress of Neptune's [imaginary]
statue, blown from the roof of the Pantheon, over half the width of
Rome.   He next informs us how the pagan temple, the Pantheon,
was converted, in or about 609, into the Christian Church of Santa
Maria Rotonda, at the prayer of Pope Boniface (the fourth) to " the
emper*o*ure Julius, that was forso*þe* A wele goode man "—in reality,
the Emperor Phocas, whom history indicates to have been a most
fearful ruffian.   The Christian consecration of the building is
assigned in the poem to the 1st November, All Saints' day, and
the church is stated to have been dedicated to St. Mary and all
Saints : Francino names the 12th May instead.

Line 810 to 817, p. 170.   " Seynt Mary Transpedian " can only,
I conceive, be *the Church of Santa Maria Transpontina :* I am un-
able to account for the corruption of the name.   The church used to
stand near the Castle of Sant' Angelo; but the earlier building was
destroyed by Pius IV. (1559–66) with a view to the fortification of
the Castle, and he gave orders for constructing another in the Borgo
Nuovo, near the Via Sestina, preserving the old indulgences, etc.
Francino does not confirm our poet as to the two stone pillars to

which Sts. Peter and Paul were bound; but he mentions as in this church a figure of the Crucified Saviour reputed to have appeared to those saints while under flagellation.

Line 818 to 821, p. 170. *The Hospital of Santo Spirito*, near St. Peter's, in connection with the Church of Santo Spirito in Sassia, is the chief hospital in Rome. It is spoken of as almost a town in itself, and is so richly endowed as to pass by the name of "Il Primo Signore di Roma:" it now receives nearly 13,000 patients in a year. The church was originally built by Innocent III. (1198 to 1216), but a new building was erected towards the end of the 16th century.

Line 822 to 825, p. 170-1. "Seynt Iamys uppon the flome" is probably *the Church of Sant' Jacopo Scossacavallo* (jog-horse), in the Trastevere: there are in Rome at least two other churches dedicated to St. James. The building was erected on the spot where are said to have died the horses which were transporting to St. Peter's, by command of the Empress Helena, the stone whereon Christ was presented for circumcision, and the one upon which Isaac was to have been sacrificed: relics which no efforts availed to move from this spot, and for whose guardianship the church was therefore founded.

Line 826 to 831, p. 171. *The Church of Santa Maria in Trastevere, or ad Fontes Olei* (also called, in some early documents, simply "Fons Olei") is stated to have been the first church erected in Rome to the Virgin Mary. It is said that on the night of Christ's nativity, a great well of oil (two wells in our text) sprang up on this spot, and continued all next day running down to the Tiber: hence the name given to the church, which was founded by Pope St. Callixtus I. in or about 224, and often afterwards altered; the present building belongs almost wholly to the time of Innocent II., 1139, with modifications by Nicholas V. (1447-55). The site is the same as that of the ancient Taberna Meritoria, or hospital for old soldiers. The seven years' indulgence named in the text is not specified by Francino; but 25,000 years' indulgence, with plenary remission, on the feast and octave of the Assumption. Our poet seems to state that the miraculous oil still runs, either permanently or every Christmas night: I do not find this confirmed.

Lines 832-3, p. 171. *The Church of St. Cecilia*, at the end of the Trastevere, near the Quay of Ripa Grande, was built on the site of the saint's own house, in 230; re-built by Pope Paschal I. in 821, and dedicated to God, and Sts. Mary, Peter, Paul, and Cecilia; and

altered to its present form in 1599 and 1725. In the former of
these years, 1599, the body of the saint was found on the spot, with
a contemporary inscription identifying her: the celebrated statue
by Stefano Maderno, now in the church, represents her in the
attitude she was discovered lying in. Francino does not name the
100 years' indulgence of the text, but plenary indulgence on St.
Cecilia's day.

Line 834 to 841, p. 171. "Seynt Petyr and Poullys preson" is
the actual *Oratory of San Pietro in Carcere Tulliano*, at the foot of
the Capitol. It is a portion of the ancient Mamertine Prisons, com-
menced by Ancus Martius, and is consequently one of the very
oldest monuments in Rome. Peter and Paul are said to have been
imprisoned here by Nero, on which account the building was consecrated as above named by St. Sylvester (314–36): over it stands the
Church of San Giuseppe de' Falegnami. The 2000 years' indulgence
daily figures in Francino as 1200 years' indulgence, and remission of
one-third of sins, doubled on feast days. A well is said to have
sprung up on the spot at the prayer of Peter and Paul, to enable
them to baptize their converted gaolers, Processus and Martinianus
("Martuman" in our text), whose bodies are still preserved here.
However, if we may trust Plutarch—not perhaps a much better
authority on such a point than a church legend—this well existed
in the time of Jugurtha.

Lines 842–3, p. 171. *The Church of Santa Maria Nuova*, near
the arch of Titus, was built by Leo IV. (845–55), and restored by
Nicholas V. (1447–55).

Line 844 to 847, p. 171. *The Church of St. Alexius* is on the
site of the house of that saint, on the Aventine: Francino speaks of
certain stairs, then extant, on which the saint, after returning from a
pilgrimage, performed penance during 17 years up to his death,
unrecognized by his father and the other inmates of the house.
The first church on this spot was erected in the 9th century, and
dedicated to St. Boniface. The 2200 years' daily indulgence
diminishes in Francino to 100 years and lents.

Lines 848–9, p. 171. "Seynt Cosme and Demiave" is *the Church
of Sts. Cosmas and Damian*, in the Forum, near the site of, or trans-
muted from, a Temple of Remus (or perhaps Romulus): the church
was dedicated by Felix IV. (526–30), and restored by St. Gregory
(590–604). In this instance Francino exceeds our text as to the
amount of indulgence; naming 1000 years daily, instead of 300.

Line 850 to 863, p. 171–2. *The Church of St. Eustace* was built
by Celestin III. (1191–8). The remains of the patron saint are here,
together with those of his wife, Theopista, and his son and daughter,
Agapetus and Theopista (" ij. *sonnes*," as in the text, does not seem to
be absolutely accurate). "*þesaluator*" next mentioned I understand
to be an image of Christ in this church : Francino, however, does not
specify any such image, but some of the blood and clothes of the
Saviour, some thorns from His crown, and some of the wood of His
cross. One might suppose the separate Church of San Salvatore to
be intended ; but that was only built about 1450, and would consequently appear to be too late for the date of our poem, or, at any
rate, not likely to be therein mentioned without some intimation of
its being a perfectly new building ; moreover, I am not aware that
this church contains any such image. Another conjecture might be
hazarded :—that all this paragraph about the Salvator has dropped
out of its right place, and belongs properly to the Church of Ara
Cœli (lines 882–91), in which is a highly venerated image of the
Infant Christ, named the " Santissimo Bambino," much bejewelled,
and endowed with miraculous curative powers. It is carried about to
the sick in an old brown coach, and has a festival of its own from
Christmas day to Epiphany. This image is said to have been carved
by a pilgrim out of a tree on the Mount of Olives, and to have been
painted by St. Luke after the pilgrim had dozed off.

Line 864 to 867, p. 172. Here we revert to a church already
named, that of *St. Cecilia* (lines 832–3). I do not find any elucidation of the statement that "the Mawdlene" is to be seen in this
church.

Line 868 to 873, p. 172. These lines relate to a chapel near the
Church of San Pietro in Vincoli, either dedicated to *San Salvatore*,
or containing a venerated image of the Saviour. It is not mentioned
in my authorities.

Line 874 to 877, p. 172. Four separate churches : 1st, *St. Jerome* (either the one near the Farnesse Palace, or the one in the Via
di Ripetta, near the Mausoleum of Augustus) ; 2nd, *St. Gregory* ;
3rd, *St. Ambrose* ; 4th, *St. Augustine*. Francino does not confirm
our poet in saying that there is 1000 years' indulgence at each of
these churches ; but he speaks of daily plenary indulgence, and
remission of sins at St. Jerome's near the Farnese Palace,—plenary
remission at St. Gregory's on the day and octave of all souls,—great
indulgences granted by Clement VII. (1523–34) at St. Ambrose's,

—and plenary remission on three several days at St. Augustine's. The Church of St. Gregory stands on the Cœlian Hill. It was the paternal house of that pope, and was dedicated by him, as a church, during his pontificate in 591, to St. Andrew; the edifice was re-built in 1734, and is now connected with the headquarters of the Camaldolese Monks. The Church of St. Ambrose is in the Corso, having been built by the Milanese. The Church of St. Augustine, in the Via della Scrofa, was entirely renewed in 1483 by Cardinal d'Estouteville, and was again restored in 1740.

Line 878 to 881, p. 172. *The Church of San Lorenzo in Damaso* (Murray says, "San Lorenzo *e* Damaso,"—Sts. Lawrence and Damasus), close to the Palace of the Cancelleria, was built by Pope St. Damasus in 370, and termed *the Prasinian Basilica:* the building now extant, however, is the work of Bramante, erected in 1495, at the bidding of Cardinal Riario, nephew of Sixtus IV.

Line 882 to 891, p. 172. "Seynt Mary Rochelle" must be a much corrupted form of the name *Santa Maria di Ara Cœli*, a famous Church on the Capitoline Hill, built on the ruins of the Temple of Jupiter Feretrius, and of a palace of Augustus. The present building is probably as old as the 6th century, when the church was dedicated by Gregory the Great, under the title of Sancta Maria in Capitolio. The origin of the term "Ara Cœli" has been much debated. The popular account is that an altar was erected on this spot by Augustus, to commemorate the prophecy of the Cumæan Sibyl concerning the advent of Christ—which altar was inscribed "Ara Primogeniti Dei." Another, and more matter-of-fact, account is that the church was termed in the middle ages Sancta Maria in Aurocœlio. The "many greses" are 124 (or probably, in our author's time, 121) marble steps leading to the church, made out of the ruins of the Temple of Quirinus on the Quirinal Hill: this staircase was constructed in 1348. Francino does not mention the 2000 years' indulgence; but speaks of plenary remission on the festival of the Circumcision, and infinite other indulgences and privileges, especially on New-Year's day. The image of the Virgin painted by St. Luke represents her as she stood at the foot of the cross. The Friars Minor are still in the adjoining convent, which is the headquarters of the order of Reformed Franciscans, or Grey Friars.

Line 892 to 895, p. 172. "Seynt Mary Merle" would appear to be another verbal corruption, meaning *the Church of Santa Maria de' Miracoli*, so named from the many miracles here wrought: it stands by the wall of the Porta del Popolo, and, in its present form, is a modern building, of the reign of Alexander VII. (1655-67).   The 1000 years' indulgence is modified in Francino into plenary indulgence and remission of sins.

Line 896 to 906, p. 172-3.   *The Church of St. Andrew* here referred to is probably the parish church dedicated to that saint, between the Porta del Popolo and the Capitol, connected with the Company of Clothiers named "di Sant' Uomo-bono:" there are at least four other churches of this saint in Rome.   The graces accorded to persons here buried, and otherwise, are not elucidated by Francino.

Line 907 to 914, p. 173.   Our poet has now vamped his holy wares, as far as his opportunities allow; and can only add that any quantity more of them remain behind,

> "And that I shall with all my myght
> There-off wryte boþe day & nyght."

A formidable promise for any commentator: but, as it remains unfulfilled so far as our text is concerned, I can here conclude my imperfect illustrations of " the Stacyons of Rome."

W. M. ROSSETTI.

St. Pernelle. See her Life in the Vernon MS. (Bodleian Library), leaf 31 vˢ β.
St. Agas; in the same MS., leaf 12 vˢ β. 'Seint Agace, that gode maide, in Cisyle was ibore.'

POLITICAL,
RELIGIOUS, AND LOVE POEMS.

Hodson MS. 39, *on leaf* 3 (A.D. 1483).

𝕶𝖞𝖓𝖌 𝕰𝖉𝖜𝖆𝖗𝖉 𝖙𝖍𝖊 iiij𝖙𝖍.

(10 stanzas of 7 lines each, *ababbcc.*)

[There is a Religious Poem of 6 stanzas next it in the MS., but as this would make a break in the *Political Poems* if put after *Edward IV.* here, it is printed on p. 289, below.]

(1)

Where is
Edw. IV.

who conquerd
France and
Scotland, and
won Berwick?

¶ Wher is this Prynce that conquered his right   1
   Within Ingland / master of all his foon,
And after Fraunce, be very force & myght
   Without stroke / and afterward cam hoom,   4
   Made Scotland to yelde / and Berwyk wan he from,
     Rydyng a hontyng / hym silff to sporte & playe :
     All men of Englond ar bounde for hym to praye.

(2)

His fame was
world-wide.
He was the
doughtiest man
living.

¶ This most dred prince / that was vnder the son,   8
   Through all this wordle renewed was his name,
The dowthiest, the worthiest, withouten comparison,
   Ther was noon siche / but ye reken the same
   Compassed the wordle / so spronge his name ;   12
     And as in batell, the ffresshest I shall say :
     All men of Englond ar bounde for hym to pray.

(3)

¶ Wher is he nowe, that maṅ of noble meṅ, .   15   He kept a royal
  That, in his howsold, kepte the ryaH rowte?   household
Ther is no place in aH the wordle I keṅ,
  but of the Substaunce he hath chosen owte.
  Hit was a wordle to se hyṅ ride aboute   19
    Through-out his landł; And that was day be day :
    AH meṅ of Englondł ar bounde for hyṅ to pray.

(4)

¶ O noble Edward, wher art thowe be-come,   22
  Which fuH worthy I haue seen goyngꞌ in estate?
Edward the iiijᵗʰ I mene, witħ the sonne,   He was our sun,
  The rose, the sonnë-beme / which was fuH fortunate :
  Noon erthly prince durst make *with* hyṅ debate. 26
    Art thowe agoo, and was here yestirday?
    AH meṅ of Englondł ar boundł for the to pray. 28

(5)

The weH of Knyghthode, wit*h*outen any pere   29
  Of aH erthely prynces thowe were the lode-sterre !   the lodestar of
Be-holde & rede ; herkyṅ weH and hyre !   princes,
  In gestis, in romansis, in Cronicles nygħ & ferre,
  WeH knoweṅ it is / þer caṅ no maṅ it deserre, 33
    Pereless he was / and was here yest*i*rday :   peerless.
    AH meṅ of Englondł ar bounde for hyṅ to pray.

(6)

¶ Fy on this wordle ! What may we wrecches say, 36   [leat 3, back]
  That nowe haue lost the lanterne & the light,   We have lost
Oure kyngꞌ oure lorde, (alas and wele-a-wey !)   him, our light,
  In eue*r*y felde fuH redy for oure right,   our lord.
  It was no nede / to pray hyṅ for to fight ;   40
    Redy he was / that was here yestirday :
    AH meṅ of Englondł ar bounde for hyṅ to pray.

(7)

¶ Me thynkith eue*r* this kyngꞌ sholde not be goṅ ; 43
  I see his lordis, I see his knyghtis aH ;   I see his knights,
I see his plasis made of lyme and stoṅ ;   his palaces,
  I see his se*r*uauntes sittyngꞌ in the HaH,
  And, walkyngꞌ amongꞌ theṅ, his MarshaH.   47   his Marshal ;
    What sholde I say? He was here yestirday :
    AH meṅ of Englondł ar bounde for hyṅ to pray.

(8).

but he is gone. ¶ I am be-giled / for He is past and gooɰ ;   50
His men weep   I mette his meɰ wepyng in clothis blake ;
Not ooɰ nor tweyɰ : god wote, many ooɰ,
and wail for him.   Which daily waylith & sorowith for his sake
Hit to endite, hit makith my herte quake,   54
    When I remembre he was here yestirday :
    Aℍ men of Englonð ar bounde for hymɰ to pray.

(9)

Let us pray God to set him among His angels! ¶ Nowe pray we to god, that aℍ this wordle hath wrought,
       Among his Aungelis / this prince may have a place ;
And for his passioɰ that vs so dere hath bought,
    That, of his paynys he may haue his grace.
    Nowe, gracious lorð, remembre weℍ this case !   61
       As wofuℍ synners, we caℍ to the, and say,
       That we of Englond ar bounde for hym to pray.

(10)

¶ Ye wofuℍ meɰ / that shaℍ this writyng rede,   64
       Remembre weℍ here is no dwellyng place.
And let us remember that he is dead, and that we must follow him. Se howe this prince is from vs gooɰ, and dede,
    And we shaℍ, aftir hymɰ, suë the trace :
    Ther is no choise /. ther is nooɰ other grace ;   68
       This knowe ye weℍ / he was here yestirday :
       Aℍ men of Englond ar bounde for hym to pray.

Explicit /

𝕿𝖍𝖊 𝕿𝖜𝖊𝖑𝖛𝖊 𝕷𝖊𝖙𝖙𝖊𝖗𝖘 𝖙𝖍𝖆𝖙 𝖘𝖍𝖆𝖑𝖑 𝖘𝖆𝖛𝖊 𝕸𝖊𝖗𝖗𝖞 𝕰𝖓𝖌𝖑𝖆𝖓𝖉.

(Ab. 1465.)

[*Lambeth MS. No.* 306, *fol.* 134.]

(1)

¹ **E**RLY in a sommeristide
 y sawe in london, as y wente,   A lady in
A gentilwoman⸳ of chepe-side   Cheapside
 workinge on⸳ a vest[i]ment.   4

(2)

She sette xij lett[e]rs on a Rowe,   told me that 12
 And saide, if *that* y myght it vnderstond⸳,   letters
Thorough þe grace of god, ye schule it knowe,   should save
 This lettres xij schaȞ save mery Englond⸳. 8   Merry England.

(3)

A litil while yf ye wille duelle,
 And yeve avdenes vnto me,
what lett*r*es they be y shall you tell*e*,   I'll tell you what
 they were drawe oute of þe .A.b.c.   12   they were,

(4)

They were nether⸳ A. b. nor S.,²
 Of any clarke y take wittnes,
Hit was R. w. And ij ees   R[5]. W. E. E.
 F. M. 3.³ and S.   16   F. M. Y. S.,

(5)

Than stode y stille a litile Sesonc,
 And constred⸳ this lettres or y wente thens,
And Exspoundide theim⸳ after myn⸳ owne wesdone   and they meant,
 After the forme of Exp*er*ience.   20

¹ There is a space left for a large E, but only a little e is
written, as a guide to the capital-maker.   ² ! for C.   ³ 3 = y.
    POLIT. POEMS.   B

(6)

iij ares for iij Richardes þat bene of noble fames;
     A E. for Edward, men wote it is soo,
This ben the lettr[e]s of the iiij lordes names
     The whiche aH Englonde is myche bounden too.   24

(7)

A .3. for yorke that was manely & myghtfuH,
     The whiche Grewe be þe grace of god & grete reuela-
       cion,
Raynyng with Rewles[1] resenable and RightfuH,
     The whiche for oure sake hathe sofferde grete vex[a]-
       cion.   28

(8)

An .M. for marche, treue in eueri titeH & triaH,
Growinge be eistricion, that worthi and wis is,
Concayued in wedlocke, & comen of blode rialle,
Ioyning vnto vertu, devode of vices.   32

(9)

An S. for Salisbery, without any avision,
Riall in his reynyng, and riche in his Rente,
Brynging a man to a good conclucion,
Called for his wisdome patris Sapiente.   36

(10)

A Doble W. for Warwike, þat god be his gide,
     Who is called with þe comens their childe & þer
       deffence,
The boldest vnder baner bateH to a-bide,
     for þe righte of Englonde he dothe his deligence.   40

(11)

An F. for þe feterlock þat is of grete Substance,
     That hathe amendide many maters þorow his medi-
       acion;
In yrlonde & in walles, in englonde and in fraunce,
     He Reynyed with Rewelis of RiaH Repetacion.   44

---

[1] A long f with a stroke through it stands here.

(12)

An R. for the Rose þat is frische and wol nat fade,

    Bothe þe rote & the stalke þat is of grete honour*e*,

from normandie vnto norway þe leues do springe,

    from irlonde vnto Estlonde me reioise þat floure.   48

the White Rose
(badge of the
house of York),

(13)

An E. for þe egile þat grete worsħip hath wone

    Thorowe þe spredinge of his wengis þat neu*er*

        begane to flee,

There was neu*er* birde brede vnder þe stone

    More fortunable in a felde þan þat birde hatħ be.   52

the Eagle
(badge of the Earl
of Salisbury),

(14)

An R. for þe Raged staf[1] þat no man) may a-Skape,

    from scotlonde to Calles, þer*of* they stonde in Awe,

he is a stafe of stedfastne[s], bothe erly & latte

    To Chastes siche kaytifes as don ayenst þe lawe.   56

and the Ragged
Staff (badge of the
Earl of Warwick).

(15)

Nowe haue y declared you this lettr[e]s all xij

    Accordyng to their condisciones whereu*er* þei ride or

nowe thei be declared eche lorde be him self,   [goo[n] ;

    Their entent and purpos groundeth all in oon),   60

[leaf 135]
And all these

strive together

(16)

That is, for to distroy tresson, & to mak a treue triaħ

    Of theym that be-fawte & hurte vs all fuħ sore,

And for þe welfare of Edward Rex moste riaħ,

    That is þe verie purpos that we labure fore.   64

to destroy
treason,

for King
Edward's weal.

(17)

And nowe, my frendes in eu*er*i cost,

The grace and goodnes of þe holigost

    Kepe you in sted[fa]ste charite,

And after this life, bryng you & me   68

    vnto eu*er*-lasting Ioie ; amen, for charit[e] !

The Holy Ghost
keep you in Love,

and bring you to
everlasting Joy!

EXPLICIT.

[The poem on Women follows, which is printed in *The Wright's Chaste Wife:* 'Women), women), loue of women), make bare purs wi*th* some men).']

(Warwik)

[1] The Bere is bound that was so wild

    Ffor he hath lost his *ragged staffe.*

        Cotton Rolls, ii. 23, in Wright's *Pol. Songs,* v. ii. p. 222.

Edwardus, Dei Gratia.

[*Lambeth MS.* 306, *leaf* 136.]

<table>
<tr><td>Edward, chosen knight of God,</td><td>1</td><td colspan="2">A A A, Edwardeus Dai gracia,
    Sithe god hathe chose þe to be his knyʒt,
And posseside þe in thi right,</td><td></td></tr>
</table>

¹ A A A, Edwardeus Dai gracia,
    Sithe god hathe chose þe to be his knyʒt,
And posseside þe in thi right,

Edward, chosen knight of God,

honour Him!   Thoue hime honour w*ith* al thi myght,   4
         Edwardes, Dai gracia.

Oute of þe stoke þat longe lay dede²
He has made thee England's head,   God hathe causede the to sprynge & sprede,
And of al Englond to be the hede,   8
         Edwardes, Dei gracia.

Sithe god hathe yeuen the, thorough his myʒte,
Owte of that stoke birede in sight
White Rose of York!   The floure to springe, a Rosse so white,   12
         Edwardes, Dai gracia,

Thoue yeve hem lawde and praisinge,
Give praise to Him, then, virgin Knight!   Thove vergyne knight of whom we synge,
Vn-Deffiled sithe thy begynnyng,   16
         Edwardes, Dai gracia.

God save thy contenewaunce,
Forward, and exalt thy crown!   And so to prospede to his plesance
That eu*er* thyne Astate thou mowte enhaunce !   20
         Edwardes, Dai gracia.

France is thine: and so is Spain.   Rex Anglie & francia, y Say,
Hit is thine owne, why saist þou nay ?
And so is spayne, þat faire contrey,   24
         Edwardis, Dai gracia.

---

¹ The big initial is wanting, tho' a small one is put, as in the last poem.   ² MS. *lade day.*

Fy on slowtfuℲℲ contenewaunce
Where conquest is a noble plesaunce,
And Regesterd in olde rememberance, 28
    Edwardes, Day Gracia.

Fie on Sloth;
delight in War!

Wherefor, prince And kyng moste myȝti,
Remembere þe Subdeue of þi Regaly,
Of Englonde, frawnce, & spayn) trewely, 32
    Edwardes, Dai gracia.

Remember to
subdue thy
realm,

Edward, King!

EXPLICIT.

[A Recipe "For brekyng owte of scabbes & bleynes" follows.]

[MS. Lambeth 306, fol. 132. The heavy letters mark the red of the MS.]

THE RECEYVYNG OF KYNG EDWARD THE IIIJ[TH] AT BRYSTOWE.

First atte the comyng ynne atte temple gate there stode Wylliam co*n*quero*ur* w*ith* iij lordis, and these were his wordis

WeℲℲ-come, Edwarde, oure son) of high degre!
Many yeeris hast þou lakkyd owte of this londe:
I am thy fore fader, Wylliam of normandye,
To see thy welefare here thrugh goddys sonde.

Over the same gate stondyng a greet Gyaunt delyu*er*yng the keyes.

¶ **The Receyuyng atte temple Crosse next folowyng.**

Ther*e* was seynt George on horsbakke vppon*e* a tent fyghtyng w*ith* a dragon*e*, And þe kyng & þe quene on hygh*e* in a castell*e*, And his doughter benethe w*ith* a lambe. And atte the sleyng of the dragon*e* ther was a greet melody of aungellys.

[*Follows:* A medycyne for the pestylenee.]

For Jake Napes Sowle, Placebo and Dirige.

(A.D. 1450.)

[MS. Lambeth 306, fol. 51, in John Stowe's hand.]

HERE FOLOWYTHE A DYRGE MADE BY THE COMONS
OF KENT IN THE TYME OF THER RYSYNGE
WHEN JAKE CADE WAS THEYR CAPPITAYN.

(1)

In May, Jack Napes (the Duke of Suffolk) would go to sea.

¶ In the moneth of may whan gres growes[1] grene,

fragrans in there floures with A swet[2] savor,

Iake napis in[3] the see, A maryner for to bene, 3

with his clogge and his cheyne, to sell[4] more tresowr.

(2)

¶ suche A thynge[5] prykkyd hym, he axid[6] A confessowr:

nycolas of the towre seyd " I am redy here to se;"[7]

He was caught and beheaded. Sing his dirge!

he was holde so hard, he passyd the same[8] howre;

for Iake napes sowle, placebo and dirige. 8

(3)

[leaf 51, back]

¶ who shall execute ye fest of[9] solempnite?

Pray for him all bishops and clergy.

bysshoppis and lords, as gret reson is,

Monkes, chanons, and prestis, with al y^e[10] clergy,

prayeth for[11] hym that he may com to blys, 12

(4)

¶ And that[12] nevar such Anothar come aftar this!

Blessed be his killers!

his intersectures,[13] blessid mot[14] they be,

and graunt them[15] to reygne with aungellis!

for[16] Iake napys sowle, placebo & dirige. 16

---

[1] MS. Cott. Vesp. B. xvi, leaf 1, back, gresse growes.
[2] Flagrant in her flowres with swete
[3] wold ouer [4] seke [5] Swyche a payn [6] asked
[7] Nicolas said 'I am redi | thi confessour to be'
[8] holden so | that he ne pasade that [9] his exequies. | With a
[10] ch.. pr.. & other [11] pray for this Dukes soule | þat it might [12] let
[13] interfectours, [14] mighte [15] them for ther dede [16] and for

(5)

¶ "placebo," begynneth the bishop of hereforthre;[1]   These sing:
The Bishops of
"dilexi," quod ye bisshop of chester, "for my   Hereford,
Chester,
Avaunser;"[2]

"hew michi,"[3] seyd salysbery, "this game gothe   Salisbury,
ferforthe;"[4]

"Ad dominum cum tribularer," seyth ye abbot of   the Abbot of
Gloucester,
glocester.   20

(6)

¶ "dominus custodit," thus seyþ ye bisshoppe[5] of   the Bishop of
Rochester.
Rouchestre.

"leuaui oculos meos," seyþ frere stanbery,   Friar Stanbery,
["volaui."[6]]

"Si iniquitates," seyth ye bysshope of worcestre;   the Bishop of
Worcester,
for Iake napis sowle, "de profundis clamavi."   24

(7)

¶ "Opera manium tuarum," seyth ye cardinall wysely,   the Cardinal,
"hath wronge,[7] confitebor," for all Iake napis wis-
"Audiui vocem," seyd Ihesu crist[9] on hye.   [dome,[8]   and Jesus Christ.
[10] "Magnificat anima mea Dominum."   28

(8)

¶ Now to this dyryge most we nedys[11] come   Let us all come
joyfully, and sing
this Ioyfull[12] tyme, to say brevely,[13]   Jack Napes's
dirge.
ix spalmes (sic), ix[14] lessons, to say all & sum,[15]
for Iake napys sowlle, placebo & dirige.   32

(9)

¶ Executor[16] of this office, dirge for to synge,   These shall join:
The Bishop of
shall begynne ye bisshope of seynt as.   St. Asaph,

"varba[17] mea Auribus," seythe the abbot of Redynge,   the Abbot of
Reading.
for all our hope and Ioy[18] is come to Allas.   36

---

[1] Herforde   [2] Dilexi, for myn auauncement | saithe þe bisshop of Chestre
[3] me   [4] this gothe to ferre forthe;   [5] Abbot (om. thus)
[6] volavi is from MS. Cott. which omits 'meos'   [7] that brought forthe.
[8] alle this Napes reason.   [9] songe Allemightty god
[10] MS. Cott. prefixes 'And þerfore synge we'   [11] we gon &   [12] pascalle
[13] veryli.   [14] Thre psalmes & thre   [15] þat alle is and somme.
[16] Executors   [17] Verba   [18] Alle your ioye and hope

(10)

¶ " Convertere[1] d*omi*ne," for vs wantyth[2] grace,

thow[3] abbot of seynt albonys, full sorely synge ye :[4]

The abbot of the towre hyll, w*ith* his fate face,   39

tremelyth and quakythe,[5] for " d*omi*ne, ne in furore."

(11)

¶ M*a*ster watyr lyard schall sey[6] " nequando."

the abbes of seynt alborghe,[7] " d*omi*ne, d*eu*s m*eus, in*
     te sper*a*ui ; "

" Requiem et*er*nam, god graunte hem to,[8]

to sey[9] A patar nostar," [sai*þ*[10]] the bysshop of seynt
     davi.   44

(12)

¶ For the sowles of thes wyse and wurthy,[11]

Adam Molens, suffolke, s*ir* Robert Ros,[12] thes thre ;

And specyally for Iake napis sowlle[13] *that* evar was
     sly,[14]

for his sowle, placebo & dirige.   48

(13)

¶ " Rys vp, lord say, and[15] rede " p*ar*ce m*ihi* d*omi*ne,
     Nichil e*ni*m su*n*t dies mei," that shalt thou[16] singe ;

the bysshope of carlyyll seyth " credo videre[17]
     all[18] fals traytors to come to evyll[19] endynge."   52

(14)

¶ Dwelle thou shalt[20] withe grete mornyng*e*,
     Rede[21] " tedet a*ni*mam meam vite mee ; "

---

[1] MS. Cott. is wrongly read by Mr. Wright, Com*m*itere
[2] yet gr*a*unte vs   [3] Sai*þ*   [4] MS. Cott. omits *synge ye.*
[5] quake*þ* & tre*m*le*þ*   [6] syng*e*   [7] Abbot of Westmynstre.
[8] them all*e* to come to.   [9] *þ*erto   [10] From MS. Cott.
[11] soules *þ*at wise were & mightty.
[12] Suffolk, Moleyns, and Roos.   [13] in especial for Iac Napes
[14] wyly.   [15] vp, Say   [16] mei | *þ*ou shalt
[17] syng*is* Credo ful sore.   [18] To suych*e*   [19] come foule
[20] The baron of Dudley   [21] Redeth*e*

"Manus tue," danyell, thou shalt synge[1]

   For Iake napis sowle, placebo & dirige.[2]   56

(15)

¶ "Qui lazarum resussitasti," Treuilyan shall singe ;   Trevilian,

   Hungerford, "manus tue fecerunt me ;   Hungerford,

vby me abscondam, for dred this day ?"

   Iohn say, synge "dominus regit me."   60   John Say,

(16)

¶ "Nichyll mihi deerit," for owt that I can se ;

   "ad te domine levavi," Master somerset schall rede :   Somerset,

Iohn penycoke, "delycta Iuventutis mee,   John Penycoke,

   Allas, whythar may I fle for dred ?"   64

(17)

¶ "Dominus, illuminacio, help, for now is ned,"

   seyth mayster wyll say, "I trow it wyll not be :"

"credo videre," sir thomas stanle, take hede ;   Sir Thomas

   for Iake napis sowle, placebo & dirige.   68   Stanley,

[1] Who but Danyel, qui lasarum shal synge

[2] . . Iac nape . . . The Cotton MS. ends shortly thus, on
leaf 2, front :—

> ¶ Iohn Say redethe, "Manus tue fecerunt me."
> "Libera me," syngethe Trevilian | warre the rere,
> That thei do no more so. Requiescant in pace :
> Thus prayes alle Englond | ferre & nerre.
>
> ¶ Where is Somerset | whi aperes he not here
> to synge | Dies ire & miserie ?
> God graunte Englond | alle in fere,
> for thes traitours | to synge Placebo & Dirige.
>
> ¶ Meny mo þer be behynde | þe sothe for to telle,
> þat shall messes | oppon thes do synge.
> I pray som man | do rynge the belle,
> þat þese forsaiden | may come to þe sacrynge.
>
> ¶ And þat in brief tyme | without more tarienge,
> þat þis messe may be ended | in suyche degre,
> And þat alle Englond | ioyfulle may synge
> þe commendacioun, with Placebo & Dirige.

(18)

Thomas Kent,

¶ "In memoria et*er*na," seyth Mayster Thomas Kent,

"now schall owre treson be cornicled for evar ; "

Master Gerveyse,

"patar nostar," seyd mayst*er* Gerveyse, "we be all shent,

for so fals A company in englond was nevar."   72

(19)

the Abbot of Bermondsey,

¶ The abbot of barmundsey, full of lechery,

"Qua*n*tas ha*b*eo iniquitatys," take for thy lesson ;

Gabull (?) of the Chancery,

Gabull of the chancery begynyth "heu m*i*h*i* ! "

that is his preve bande, and detent of treso*n*).   76

(20)

the Master of St. Lawrence,

¶ "Homo natus de m*u*liere," seyth y*e* Mayst*er* of sent lawrence,

"repletus multis miseri*is*," and *tha*t shall he wayll

of Iake napes sort that hath do*n*) gret offence,

and ever whill be lyvyd, cheffe of his counceyll.   80

(21)

[leaf 52, back]
Stephen Shegge,

¶ "Ne recorderys," stephen shegge shall synge,

"quis m*i*h*i* tribuat for wichecraft," seythe stace ;

"Do*m*ine no*n* secu*n*du*m* actu*m* meu*m*, for then shall I hynge ; "

for Iake napys sowle, placebo & dirige.   84

(22)

Sir Thomas Hoo,
John Hampton,

¶ "Expectans exp*e*ctaui," seyth s*ir* thomas hoo,

"complaceat tibi," begynneth Io͞hn Hampton ;

"beatus qui intelligit, and dredit also,"

John Fortescue,

seyth Iohn fortescu, "all this fals treso*n*)."   88

(23)

¶ "sana, domine, oure wittes with reson,"

Lord Sudeley,

the lorde sudeley devoutly prayth,

"quem ad modum," desiderat y*e* lord stowrto͞n,

"sitiuit an*im*a mea," for him lyeth.   92

(24)

¶ The lord ryvers all onely seythe,   <small>Lord Rivers,</small>

  " Requiem eternam) god grawnt vs to se ;

A pater nostar ther must be in feyth,

  for Iake napis sowle, placebo & dirige."   96

(25)

¶ "spiritus meus attenuabytur," blakney shall begyn,   <small>Blakeney,</small>

  "pecantem) me cotidie," seyth myners ;   <small>Mynors,</small>

"pelle me consumptus carnibus to the nynne,"

  Robart horne, alderman, that shall be thy vers. 100   <small>Alderman Horne,</small>

(26)

¶ "Requiem eternam," for the respons,

  Phylip Malpas, be thow redy to synge ;   <small>Philip Malpas,</small>

It wexyth derke, thou nedyst A scons ;

  com forth, Iude, for thou shalt in brynge."   104

(27)

¶ " Quare de uulua eduxisti,"

  ser Thomas tudnam, that rede ye :   <small>Sir Thomas Tudnam, the</small>

Abbot of westmystar, com), stond by   <small>Abbot of West-minster,.</small>

  in thy myter & cope, & sey "libera me."   108

(28)

¶ A-rys vp thorp and cantelowe, & stond ye togeder,   <small>Thorpe and Cantelowe,</small>

  and synge 'dies illa, dies ire ;'

pulford and hanley *that* drownyd *the* duke of glocestar,   <small>Pulford and Hanley.</small>

  as two traytors shall synge "ordentes[1] a*nim*e."   112

(29)

¶ And all trew comyns ther to be bolde   <small>Let all true commons pray</small>

  to sey ' requiescant in pace,'   <small>that all false</small>

for all the fals traytors *that* engelond hath sold,   <small>traitors may rest in peace.</small>

  And for Iake napis sowlle, placebo & dirige. finis. 116

Amen)—writn owt of david norcyn his booke, by
         John stowe.

---

[1] MS. ordêtes. ? for *ardentes*.

Satirical Proclamation (? 1436).

(MS. Cott. Vespas. B. XVI. Fol. 5.)

I am King of all Kings,

TO alle you, I sende gretynge. Wot ye þat I am kyng of alle kynges, Lord of alle lordes, Souden

Steward of Hell,

Porter of Paradise,

of alle Surry, Emperour of Babilon, Steward of Helle, Porter of Paradise, Constable of Ierusalem, Lord of 4 Certoffis, þat is to say, lord of þe parties of þe world,

Cousin of Christ,

Cosyn to youre crist þat was nailed on þe rode. And if ye wol witen whi þat I am kynge of alle kynges, I lete you wite þat I haue vnder my lordship, of youre 8 cristen kynges, xxxvij kynges crowned. And whi þat I

and none is so worthy as I.

am lord of alle lordes,—semyng to me, þer is none so worthi as I am. And whi I am Emperour of Babilon:

I wedded the daughter of the Emperor of Babylon,

I lete you wite þat I wedded þe Emperourys doughtter, 12 which was Erle of Surry: Her fader died; wherfor I am Erle by her. And whi þat I am Stiward of

and govern all wicked spirits,

Helle: I lete you wite I haue alle gouernaunce of wicked mawmentries & wicked spirites. And whi I am 16

and keep the streams of Paradise.

Porter of Paradis: I lete you wite I am keper of þe Stremes of Paradis, whiche may no man come to but he haue my lordship, & gef me a gret tribut. And

I am Constable of Jerusalem and keep Port Joppa.

whi þat I am Constable of Ierusalem: I lete you wite. 20 þer may no man come to Port Iaffe but he gef me a gret tribut. And whi þat I am floure of alle þe worle:

I have Christ's Cross,

I may wel sai I haue þat cristen men prayn fore, þat is, þe holi cros þat your lord my cosyn died on, 24

and am his Cousin.

which ye may not haue without me. And þat I am

I was a Christian

cristes cosyn: I let you wite, I was cristen made, in Englond born, & for certeyn poyntes of lollerdy I [ne]

but turned Saracen,

my3t abide þer, & so I wende to Rome, & after to Rodes; 28 & þer I was with Sarasens, & turne to her lawe or be

ded. And for my *cu*rtesie I was put to þe Soudenys
house, & was made vssher of hall*e*; & þen died þe
Souden & his heire, And I wedded his wiff. & so I
4 was souden. & þen died my wiff; and I wedded þe
Emper*ou*rys doughtt*er*, & was Emper*ou*r bi here, &
bycome Souden of Surry. but I sende gretyng to
Henry kyng*e* of Engl*and*, þe frensh*e* wo*m*man sone. &
8 so be þat he wol wed my doughter, I wel becom
*cr*i*s*ten, & all*e* my meyne, And wol gef hy*m* iij Milions
of gold, And delyu*er*e hym þe holy cros, w*ith* al þe
Reliques in my kepyng; And I shal make hym
12 Emper*ou*r of xxxvij kynges *cr*i*s*ten, þat is, Anglond,
Frau*n*ce, Irland, Scotland, Denmark, norwey, portu-
gale, Cicile, Sipres, Spayn, Swhen, Sastel, Orsorial,
beme, hungry, Magon, Naples, Cschresy; And to stonde
16 w*ith* hym agaynst all*e* Cristen kynges. Writen in þe
yere of youre gret god, my cosyn. MCCCCxvj yere.

married the Souden's widow, and then the Emperor's daughter.

If Henry of England will wed my daughter, I will give him £3,000,000, and the Holy Cross, and make him Emperor of 37 Christian Kings, of whom I name 18.

Dated A.D. 1416.

[Mr. James Gairdner, of the Record Office, tells me
that 'Henry kynge of England, þe frensh womman son,'
can only mean Henry VI., born in 1421, son of Catherine, daughter of Charles VI. of France. Henry's
marriage with Margaret of Anjou, suggested by the
Earl of Suffolk in 1444, took place in 1445. Mr.
Gairdner therefore thinks the date of 1416 (the third
of Henry V.) a mistake of the copier of the MS. In
this Mr. G. E. Cokayne agrees, and would fix the date
at 1436, believing that " þe frensh womman son" would
not have been used after her death, in 1438. But the
difficulty is to settle what the Proclamation is intended
to satirize. The possession of Jerusalem, Joppa, the
Holy Rood, etc., the being Souden of Surre or Syria,
and the like, point to the Sultan. The Porter of
Paradise, the Cousin of Christ, the opposition to
Lollardy, might have been thought to hint at the Pope,
if the marriages (unless allegorical ones are alluded to)
did not prevent that. Professor Brewer suggests Antichrist, that is, the representative of the Antichristian
powers. The allu-ion to Lollardy may point to Sir
John Oldcastle, Lord Cobham's rising, for which he
was executed Dec. 25, 1417. "Curiously enough,
Henry III. was also King of England for some time
during the lifetime of his mother, a French woman;

but of course the text could not apply to so early a date, besides that the taking away from the date is a greater sin than adding thereunto. I am inclined to think the whole thing a satire by the party of Cardinal Beaufort on the poverty of, and want of any real power in, René, Duke of Anjou, titular King of Jerusalem, Sicily, Naples, Aragon, Valence, etc., etc., who had succeeded his brother Louis in all these and many other high-sounding titles in 1434, and was probably at that time displaying them to the utmost advantage in hopes of getting something more solid by so doing—which came to pass in 1444 and 1445 by the betrothal and subsequent marriage of his daughter Margaret with King Henry. Jerusalem, etc., were considered by René as belonging to him. Remember, too, this was *before* the conquest of the Eastern Empire in 1453.[1] Of course René's marriages do not apply. He married twice, but his first wife did not die till 1453. I have not time to go into the subject fully. Other points ought to be looked into—viz., Henry VI. was in his 23rd year, wished by the Duke of Gloucester to marry a daughter of the Count of Armagnac. Who was he? Could he be meant? I do not think so, because at that time Catherine was dead, and probably Henry would not be spoken of as the son of the Frenchwoman, it being usual for English kings to marry French princesses, and every king (excepting Edward III.) having done so from John downwards, though some had English wives as well. In 1425 John Palæologus II. was Emperor of the East, till 1448. What sort of man was he? He had probably many titles and (titular) kingdoms, and little else. I have not time to pursue him, liking René better."—G. E. C.]

[1] Constantinople was taken May 29, 1453, by Mahomet II., and Constantine XIII. (Palæologus) slain, with whom ended the Eastern Empire.—*Haydn's Dict. of Dates.*

15

Lydgate's Horse, Goose, and Sheep.

[Written after A.D. 1421: see note to l. 234, p. 25.]

(92 *stanzas; 77 in sevens, ababbcc; and* 15 *in eights, abab,bcbc;
with an Envoy "Don't despise your Neighbour."*)
From the Lansdowne MS. 699, *in the British Museum, collated
with the Harley MS.* 2251 (leaf 277, &c.) and *the Roxburghe
Club reprint of the black-letter copy of the poem.*

¶ Incip*it* Disp*utacio* int*er* Equu*m*, Auca*m*, & Oue*m*. [leaf 66, back]

A Disputation between a horse, a Sheepe and a Goose, [leaf 67]
for superioritie (*in a later hand*).

(1)

Ontrouersies / plëys & discordis   1 The old plan was
  Atween p*er*sonës / we*r*e it too or thre,
 Sought' out the grou*n*d / bi witnessis of recordis :
This was the costom) / of antiquyte ;
Iuges we*r*e sett / that hadde Auctor[i]te,   5 to settle disputes by Judges.
  The cas conceyved / stondyng*e* indifferent',
 Attwee*n*e parties / to yeue A Iugëment'.   7

(2)

¶ Parties assemblid / of hih or lowe degre,   8 Each party stated his case.
  Weren admittid / to shewen in senténce,
Grou*n*d of her*e* quarell / the lawë made hem fre
 Without excepcïou*n* / to come to Audience,
 Bi the p*r*esident / commau*n*did first' silence,   12
  Fredam yove / the parties nat to spare
 Bi rule of right' / ther grevès to declare.   14

Line 1 *pleys . .*] plees and al discorde HR. 2 *Atween . .*] Betwene . . bien yit of it, Bitwene . . were R. 3 *witnessis . .*] witnesse of Record*e* H, groundes be recordes R. 6 *cas*] cause H, caas R. 7 *Attweene*] Betweene HR. *A*] om. R. 8 *or*] and HR. 9 *Weren . . shewen*] They were . . shewe H, Weren . . shewen R. 10 *her*e *quarell*] theyr quarels HR. 13 *yove*] yeven H, yeue R. 14 *rule*] title HR.

(3)

¶ Vpon this matere / shortly·to conclude,   15

I lately saw a painting of a trial.

Nat yoore a-gon / as I rehersë shaH,

I fond to purpos / A similitude

Ful craftily / depeyntid vpon a waH :

Tweyn) sitt / in ther estat RoiaH,   19

The Lion and Eagle

The hardy **Leou**n / famous in al rewmys,

Themper̃iall **Egle** / pershyng the sonnë bemys. 21

(4)

were the Judges;

¶ These were the dreedful / RoiaH Iugis tweyne,   22

In ther estatë / sittynge I took keepe,

That herde the par̃ties / bi & bi compleyne,

the disputants were the Horse, Goose, and Sheep.

The **Hoors**, the **Goos** / & eke the symple **Sheepe**.

The processe was nat / to profounde nor deepe,   26

Off that debat / but cóntryued of a fable :

Which of them was / to man most profitáble.   28

(5)

[leaf 67, back] Each party urged its claim to be

¶ Ech for his par̃tie / proudly gan procede   29

Tenforce hym silf / bi record of scripture

In philosophie / as clerkis seen or rede,

The prerogatives / geven hem bi nature,

the most useful to man.

Which of these thre / to euery crëature   33

In **re publica** / availeth most to man).

For his par̃tie / then first the hors began) :   35

(6)

Equus

¶ " To procede breffly, & nat long to tarie,   36

First fro the trowthë / that I do nat erre,

The Horse askt what animal was so needful as he, in peace or war.

What beste is found / at al so necessárie

As is the hors / bothë nyħ & ferre,

Or so notáble / to man) in pees & werre ?   40

Line 16 *Nat*] Nought HR.   19 *sitt*] sette H, sittyng in estate R.   20 *Leoun . . rewmys*] Lyonne . . realmes H, The fierce lyon . . royames R.   21 *pershyng*] percynge H, percyng R.   22 *Roialle*] *om.* R.   23 *keepe*] goode kepe H, kepe R. 25 *& eke*] and eke H, & LR.   27 *that*] theyr HR.   28 *was / to man*] HR, to man was L.   30 *Tenforce*] To enforce H.   31 *In philosophie . . or*] By philosophres . . and HR.   32 *The . . goven*] This . . gyven H, The . . yeuen R.   34 *to*] a R. 36 *Equus*] The Horse H.   *long to*] HR, *om.* L.   37 *First*] HR, *om.* L.   *trowthe*] R, trowth LH.   38 *at al*] in al L, in alle thing R.   39 *bothe*] LR, bothe so H. 40 *in*] bothe in H.

Hors in cronyclis / wo-so looke a-riht᷄,　　　

Hav be savacion / to many a worthi knyht᷄.　42

(7)

¶ " Marcial prowessis in especïaH　　　43

God hath, bi hors / yovë to werreiour's—

Record of Alisandre / whoos hors BusifaH　　　Remember Alex-

Made hy*m* tascapë / many sharp[ë] shours :　　ander's horse
Bucephalus,

The golden char*e* / of oldë co*n*queroure*s*　　47

　Toward the tryumphe / for ther knyghtly deedis

　Conveied were / with fourë whitë steedis.　49

(8)

¶ " Remembre of Ector / the Troian chau*m*piou*n*,　50

Whoos hors was callid / whilom **Galathe** ;　　and Hector's
horse Galathe,

Vpon whos bak he pleyèd the leou*n*,

And oftë sithë / made the Grekis flee.

The stede of Perseus / was callid the **Pegasè**,　54　and Perseus's
steed Pegasus.

　With swift[ë] wengis, poetis seyn the same,

　Was, for swifftnesse / callid ' the hors of Fame.' 56

(9)

¶ " Eq*u*es, ab ' equo ' is seid of verray riht᷄,　　57　[leaf 68]

And **cheualer***e* is saide of cheualrye :　　A knight gets
his name from a

In Duche, a **Rudder** is a knyght᷄ ;　　Horse.

　Aragon tu*n*ge / doth also specifie

　Caualaro[1] / which, in that p*a*rtie,　　61

　　Is name of worship*e* / & took bigy*n*ny*n*ge

　　Off spooris of gold / & cheefly of rydynge.　63

Line 41 *looke*] redith*e* HR.　42 *Hav . . a*] Han saved many a ful H, Haue saved often many a R.　43 *prowessis*] prowesse HR.　44 *yove*] gyven H, yeue R.　45 *Record*e . .] ¶ Bukoyfal eq*uus* Alexandri.　Looke of Alisaunder . his hors Bukoyfal H.　46 *tascape*] escape from H, fro R.　47 *olde*] R, old LH.　48 *Toward . . for*] Towardis . . of H, Towarde for R.　*ther*] *om*. R.　49 *were*] LH, hit was R.　50 *Remembre*] Now H.　*of*] LH, *om*. R.　51 ¶ Galath*e* eq*uus* Hector*is* H, in margin.　53 *ofte . . made*] oft . . he made H, Full ofte sithes he made R.　54 *stede of P.*] persaus stede . was callid H, stede . . cleped R.　55 *seyn*] reherse H.　56 *Fame*] LR, name H.　58 *cheualere*] LR, cheuallice H. 59 *Duche, a Rudder*] whiche a Rider . callid H, Duche a rider is calld R (Hexham gives both *Rudder* and *Rider* in his Dutch Dict.).　60 *Aragon . . doth*] LR, Arragoners don H.　61 *which in*] LR, thurghout al H.　62 *took . .*] so toke hys gynnynge H.　*name*] LH, named R.　63 *of rydynge*] LR, Ridynge H.

[1] MS. Caualato, alterd to Caualaro, and with " Cavalero " in margin.

(10)

¶ " Thes Emper*o*ures / thes p*r*incis & thes ky*n*ges,   64

Whan thei been armyd / in bright' plate & mayle,

How could kings fight without horses?

Withouten hors / what we*r*e he*r*e mustrynges,

There brodë Baneres / & the*r*e riche app*a*raile,

To-fore ther Enmyes / to shew the*m* in bataile ?   68

Withouten hors / spere, swerde, no sheld*l*

Mihte litel a-vailë / for to holde a feeld*l*.   70

(11)

¶ " The hardy prikeris / vpon hors[ë] bak   71

Be sent to-forn) / what ground*l* is best to take,

In that ordynau*n*ce, that ther be no lak

Bi providance / the feelde / wha*n* thei shal make,

An hors wole weepë / for his maistir sake :   75

Chaucer put a brass Horse in his Squire's Tale.

Chau*n*ser remembrith / the swerd*l*, the ryng, the glas,

Presented wern) / vpon a stede of bras.   77

(12)

Zechariah saw 4 diversely-colourd horses.

¶ " Tween to hyllis / the p*r*ophete Zacarie   78

Sauh steedis foure / the first of he*m* was red,

In charis foure / the feeld to magnyfie ;

The secu*n*de was blak / it is no dreed ;

The thrydde was whight*e* / bodi, nek, & hed ;   82

The fourthe was dyuers / & eue*r*ichon were stro*n*g;

And to knyght'hood / alle these coulourë*s* long*e*. 84

(13)

[leaf 68, back]
These 4 horses typified Boldness, Soberness,

¶ " The red hors / was tokne of hardynesse,   85

Which Apperteneth / to euery hardy knyht' ;

The cole-blak hew / a sygne of sobirnesse,

Lines 65, 67 &c] or H.   67 &c] LH, or R.   69 *no*] or H, ne R.   70 *to holde*] LR, the conquest of H.   71 *The . . prikeris . . hors*] LR. These . . Rynne*rs* . . theyr hors H.   72 *Be . . toforne*] Bien . . afore H.   73 *In that*] In theyr HR.   74 *the . . shal*] how they the fielde shul HR.   75 with ' ¶ secu*n*dum Bartho*l*ome*u*m de proprietatibus rer*u*m ' in margin.   76 *Chaunser . . ryng*] Chawer . . the swerd . rynge R, Chauncier . . the rynge the swe*r*d H.   77 *Presented*] LR, Whiche presented H.   78 *to*] two HR. H has ' ¶ Montes erant &c. Zakarie .iij°.' in margin.   81 *it is no*] leevith withouten H.   83 *was . . were*] dyue*r*s and eche of hem was H, diue*r*ce of colours / wonder R.   85 *was*] LR, was there H.   87 *a*] LR, *om.* H.

Poraile oppressid / to helpe the*m* in ther right' ;
The mylk-whiht' steede / that was so glad of siht', 89
 Tokne that knyht'hod / trewly shuld ente*n*de,
 Holi chirche / & preesthod to deffende.   91

(14)

¶ " The many-fold coloures / to speke in gene*r*aH,   92
Been sondry vertues / & condicïou*n*s,
As the fower vertues / callid CardynaH
 Longy*n*g to knyhthod / tencrese ther hiH renou*n*s,
In re publica / callid the Chau*m*piouns,   96
 Treuthe to sustene / shewë he*m* siluen strong',
 Bou*n*de bi ther' ordre / to se no man have wrong'.

and the 4 Cardinal
Virtues, &c.

(15)

¶ " Withouten hors / Iustis ne turney, att aH   99
 May nat be holden, in werrë ne in pees ;
Nor in palestre / nor pleyes marcïaH,
 Yiff hors do faile / may come to no*n* encres,
Nor no ma*n*) sothly dar put hy*m* silf in pres   103
 Withouten hors / for short conclusïou*n*,
To atteyne the palme / of tryu*m*phal guerdou*n*. 105

But for horses,
no jousts or
tournaments
could be held.

(16)

¶ " Lower degrees / ther been of hors al-so,   106
 Do grett profite / to eue*r*y comou*n*te,
The plouH, the cart / myhtë no thyng' doo
 Withouten hors / dayly ye may see :
Tilthë were lost, ne werë hors parde ;   110
 The besi Marchant' / to his ávau*n*tage
Nar shippis & hors / coude make no cariage. 112

Without horses,
no plough or cart
could move.

Line 89 *of*] LR, a H.   *mylk-whight . . so*] LH, white mylke . . was R.   90
Tokne] Toknyth HR.   91 *Holi . . preesthod*] The chirche and pristhode, Holi
chirche maidens & wedewis holy H.   92 (in margin) ¶ Significant vi*r*tutes
diue*r*sas ad Miliciam pertinentes H.   93 *vertues*] vertuous   94 *As . . callid*]
And . . clepid H.   95 *Longyng . . hihe*] Longen . . to encresen theyr H, longyng . . tencrece their R.   97 *shewe hem siluen*] they ay to shewe hem H, &
shewe hem self R.   98 *to se no man*] HR, so no moor L.   99 *hors . . alle*]
horses . Ioustes ne turnal H, horse iustes ne tournaill R.   100 *holden*] holde
HR.   101 *nor*] no HR.   102 *do*] om. H.   103 *Nor*] Ne H.   *sothly*] LR, om. H.
silf] LH, om. R.   105 *palme of*] LR, om. H.   107 *Do . . to*] LR, To . . of H.
108 *myhte no thynge*] neyther my3hte nat H, ne carte myght nought R.   109
Withouten] H, Without L, With oute R.   110 *ne were*] ner we H.   *Tilthe*]
LH, Tillyng R.   *were*] LH, were we R.   111 *besi*] H, best L.   112 *Nar . .
hors*] Ner . . horses H.   *make*] LH, haue R.

(17)

[leaf 69]

The Horse.

¶ " The ship*e*, bi liknesse / is clepid an hors of tree 113

(Ful notably / who can vndirstond,)

To leden men / & carien ouer see

    As don these hors whan) thei ar*e* come to lond :

**Poor men use
little horses for
carrying corn.**
The poor man) / ladith vpon a lond   117

    His litel capil / his corn), his mele, to selle ;

      Whan) it is grounde / hors carye it hom from

        melle.   119

(18)

¶ " In Wyntir seson / for to make **bele cheere**, 120

**Horses carry fuel,
food, wine, &c.**
The hors is nedeful / wode & stuff to carie ;

Wyn), frute, & oyle / to servë thoruh the yeere

    Is brought to vynter*e*s / & to the appotecarie

    Divers draggës / & many a letuarie,   124

      Sondry bales / & shortly, al vitaill*e*,

      Off the cariágë / hors have the travaille.   126

(19)

**Horses drag
hay and oats to
granaries.**
¶ " Hey nor Otis / (playnly who list lerne,)   127

    May from the feeldis / nor the medewis grene

To the garner*e* / nother to the berne,

    Withouten hors / be caried, it is soene ;

    And to purpos / (I sei right as I meene)   131

      Ther is no best / (to rekne as I be-gan))

      So necessarie / as hors is on-to man).   133

(20)

**In August, horses
bring home the
sheaves of corn.**
¶ " **August** is a season / mery & glad,   134

    Whan eu*e*ry tre / with newë frut is lade,

With drauht of hors / the shevis ben hom lad :

Line 113 *bi*] in H, be R. *clepid*] LH, callid R. 115 *carien*] carye hem óuer
the see HR. 116 *hors . . are*] horsis they H, horse whan they R. 117 *vpon*]
eke in H, eke ledith in R. 119 *hom . .*] from the mylle H. *from*] om. L. And
whan it is grounden bringeth it fro ye melle R. 120 *bele*] the beal H, beal R.
121 *The hors is nedeful*] HR, Than is neede L. *stuff*] LH, turf R. 122 *vynteres*]
the vynter H. *appotecarie*] potecarye HR. 126 *the . . have*] LR, cariage horsis
han H. 127 *lerne*] to lierne H. 128 *feeldis nor*] fieldis . ne H, feldes nor (the
medes) R. feeld nor L. 129 *To . . to*] Vnto . . to H, To . . to R, To . . fro L.
130 *Withouten*] H, Without L. 131 *to . . as*] vnto purpos . . herk what H,
vnto pourpose I seye as R. 132 *began*] can H. *to*] LH, om. R.

That moneth past / the levis gynnë fade, *The Horse.*

Which made, in somer / a plesant' lusti shade : 138

What doon hors than / (to speke in wordis pleyn),)

The secunde crop / thei carie home Roweyn). 140

(21)

¶ " Bi draught' of hors / fro riveres & fro wellis 141   [leaf 69, back]
Horses also carry
water, lead, stone,
&c.

Bowges be brought' / to breweres for good ale ;

Leede, ston, & tymbre / cariage eek for bellis,

We brynge to chyrches / (of trouthe, this is no tale);

We lade cloth sakkis / & many a largë male, 145

And gladly someres / ar sent euyr to-forn)

With gardeviaundis / how myht' we be for-born)?

(22)

¶ " Ye prudent Iugis / the Egle & the leoun, 148   Judges,

What I haue saide / doth wisly advertise ;

Weieth this mater' / in your' discrecïoun,

Whedir Goos / or Sheepë (pleynly to devise)   judge whether
Goose or Sheep

Off ther naturë / may in any wise 152

(Iustly demyth / lat it nat be sparid,)   can be compared
to a Horse!

Vn-to an hors / be likned & comparid. 154

(23)

¶ "That I have told / is trouth, & no feynynge ; 155

No wiht' of reson / may a-geyn replie,

Goos nor Gandir / nór no Grene goslynge,   Let the Goose
speak.

But if he entre / the boundis of Envie :

Lat hir come forth / & say for hir partie." 159   *The Goose.*

    ¶ " Yis, trust me weel / for the[1] I wil nat spare,   ¶ Auca.

Lik as I fele / my verdite to declare : 161

Line 137 *gynne*] begynne to H, gyn to R.   138 *plesant lusti*] LR, lusti plesaunt H.   139 *What . . than*] Than what don hors H.   140 *home Roweyne*] of
Rowayne H, home of ryweyn R.   141 *fro . . & fro*] from . . from & H, fro . .
& R.   143 *for*] of H, caryage of bellis R.   144 *We*] horsis H. *of*] LH, in R.
145 *lade*] leede H, lede R.   146 *ar . .*] ever be sent aforn H, be sent to forne R.
147 *we*] hors H, horse R.   150 *Weieth*] LR, Wey H.   152 *may*] LR, mowen H.
153 *demyth*] LH, deme ye R.   154 *&*] LR, or H.   155 *no feynynge*] LR, nat
feyned H.   156 *may ageyn*] agenst it may HR.   157 *nór . . nor no*] ne . . ne
HR.   158 *he*] they HR.   159 *hir . . hir*] theym . . theyr H, her . . her R.
The Goose answers.   160 *Auca*] The Goose H. *trust me weel*] saide the goose
H, Ghoos yes truste me wel R.

        [1] MS. "the I" with I crost thro.

(24)

The Goose says:
You, poor horse,
are only on the
ground:

¶ " Where-as thou hast / vnto thi pasture   162

But oo place / to make in, thi repair'

It is me grauntid / pleynly by nature

I am in land,
water and air.

Tabide in thre / **lond, watir,** & ayer',

Now a-mong floures & grevis that been fair',   166

Now bathe / in riveres / swymme in many a pond,

For stormes & shoure / as drie as on the lond. 168

(25)

[leaf 70]

¶ " To myn entent / mo thyngës ye may seen)   169

As men expertë knowen / that been olde :

Wild geese flying
high foretell snow
and storms.

Whan) wildë gees, hiĥe / in the ayer vp fleen,

A pronostik / o snow & wedris colde

With her weenges / displayed & vnfolde.   173

Kalendis bryngë / pleynly for to seye

A-geyn wyntir / how men shal them purueye. 175

(26)

Goose-grease is
good for aches;

¶ " The grees of gandris / is good in medicyne,   176

With sundry gummës / tempred for the gout',

Diveres achis taswáge / & to declyne

In thextremytes / drawe the malice out' :

Goose-feathers
for arrows.

Fetheres of goos / whan thei falle or mout,   180

To gadre hem vp / heerdis hem delite,

Selle hem to flatcheres / the grey with the whihte.

(27)

¶ " Men plukke stalkes / out of my weengis tweyn), 183

Some to portraye, somme to noote & write,

Line 162 *as . . vnto*] that . . lo vnto H.   163 *But . . in*] LR, Only but oon . .
make H.   164 *It . . pleynly*] Yit is it to me I graunted H, Hit is graunted to
me.   165 *Tabide . . watir*] To abide . . in water land H, To abide on water . .
londe R.   166 *among . . been*] among . . grenys . . be R, on greues . amonge the
floures H.   168 *&*] or H, storme or R.   169 *ye*] LR, eke ye H.   170 *men ex-
perte*] R, men expert H, expert L.   *wele*] H.   171 *in . . fleen*] LR, vp in . .
flone H.   172, 173] H *and* R *transpose these lines,* H *leaves out* o, *has* frostis *for*
wedris, *and* theyr *for* her.   R has ' frosti.'   174 *Kalendis*] The kalendis H.
175 *Agayn . . shal*] Agenst . . shulde H.   *shal them*] sholde R.   177 *tempred*]
medled H.   178 *diveres . . taswage*] Sundry . . to swage H, Dyuerce . . to swa-
gen R.   179 *thextr . . drawe*] the extremytees to drawe H, . . to drawe R.   180
goos] ghees R.   *mout*] mowte HR.   182 *Selle hem*] LH, To selle to R.   183
stalkes] fethers H.

Whan Rethoriciens / han doon ther besy peyn〃

 Fressh Epistolis / & lettris to endite.

  With-out writyng[t] / vaileth nat a myte ; 187

  For, yiff pennys / & writyng[t] were a-way,

  Off rémembrau*n*cë / we had lost the kay. 189

(28)

¶ " Off Gees also / the deede is previd oft[t] 190

 In many a contre / and many a regiou*n*,

To make pilwes / & Fether-beddis soft[t],

 Of p*r*ovident men / plukkid of the dou*n* :

Thus, to make / a pleyn compa*r*isou*n*, 194

 As pilwes been to chau*m*bris ágreáble,

So is hard strauhë / litteer[r] for the stable. 196

Goose's down makes pillows and feather-beds.

(29)

¶ " The fymë of gees / & greenë gos[e]lyngis 197

 Gadred in May / among[t] the herbis soote

A-geyn〃 brennyng, scaldyng[t] / & many othir thy*n*ges,

 Tempred w*it*h oile & Buttir doth gret boote

Tasswage the peyne / that p*er*ceth to the roote ; 201

 But hors[ës] du*n*gë / as refus al-way

Is good for forneyssis, te*m*prid w*it*h clay. 203

Horse-dung only for furnaces.

(30)

¶ " A dedë hors / is but a fowle careyn〃, 204

 The ayr[r] Infectyng / it is so corrypable ;

But a fatt goos / whan〃 it is newë slayn〃,

 In disshis of gold / a morsel ágreáble,

Is sewid vp / attë kyngis table, 208

 Swy*m*myng on lyve / in watris cristallyn〃 ;

Tendre rostid / requeerith to have good wyn〃. 210

A dead Horse is good for nothing ;

but a roast Goose is servd at a king's table.

Line 188 *yiff*] if that H, yf R. 189 *we had*] LH, than were R. 193 *provident*] providence H, prudence R. 194 *Thus . . pleyn*] Lo thus to make a H. 196 *strauhe / litter*] strawe to litter H, strawe lytter R. 197 *goselynges*] HR, goslyngis L. 198 *the herbis*] LR, these erbis H. 199 *Ageyne*] Agenst H. *many*] LH, *om.* R. 200 *&*] or H. 201 *that*] H, *om.* LR. 202 *hors . .*] horsdunge as refuse . is cast away HR. 203 *forneyssis . . with*] furneys . . with white H, furneis . . with R. 204 *dede*] HR, ded L. *is*] is ne H. 205 *it*] HR, *om.* La, corrupable H, coruptable R. 206 *newe*] R, new LH. 207 *morsel . .*] LH, mussell greable R. 208 *sewid vp atte*] ser*v*ed vp at the H, seruid v*p*on a R. 210 *Tendre . . good*] LH, Tenderly . . haue R.

(31)

¶ "Through al the lond / of Brutis Albion),   211

    For fetherid Arwes / (as I rehersë can))

The best arrows are made with goose-feathers.

Goos is the best / (as in *com*parisoun,)

    Except' fetheris / of Pekok or of Swan):

And with bow and arrow, English-men have won great victories.

Bi bowe & Arwis / sith the warr' began,   215

    Have ynglysshmen) / as it is red in story,

On her enmyes / had many gret victóry.   217

(32)

¶ "Hors in the feeld / may mustre in gret pride,   218

    Whan) thei of tru*m*petis / here the blody soun;

When an Arrow pierces a War-horse, down he goes,

But whan) an Arwe hath *per*ced thoruh his side,

    To groun*d* he goth / & cast his maistir dou*n* :

Entryng' the feeld' / he pleyeth the leou*n* ;   222

rots; and only his skin and shoes are worth anything.

    What folwith aftir? / his cooreyn) sty*n*kith sore;

Sauf skyn) & shoon) / me*n* leve of hy*m* no more.

(33)

[leaf 71]

¶ "Mihty capteyns / & knyhtis in the feeld   225

Poitiers was won by the goose-featherd Bowmen.

    Makë her wardis / & her ordynau*n*ce :

First, men of Armys / with pollax, spere & sheeld,

    Sett in dew ordre / to have the gouernau*n*ce,

The capture of the French king at Poitiers was due to the Goose— the arrows.

Which at Peiters / toke the kyng*e* of Frau*n*ce.   229

    Thank to the goos / mote be yove of riht',

Which in that feeld' / so proudly took her flight'.

(34)

¶ "Slouth of my fliht' / for hasti necligence   232

    Of *pre*su*m*cion) / the goos was left bi-hynde,

Line 211 Side-note : ¶ auca petit Bachum, Mortua vina lacum.   *Through*]
Though La, Thurghe H, Thurgh R.   213 *as in*] LH, to make R.   214 *fetheris*]
. . *or*] the fethers . . . & H, fethers . . & R.   215 *bowe* . . *warre*] LR, Bowes . .
werris H.   216 *as it is red*] Remembrede is H, r. in R.   217 *her* . . *many*] theyr
. . many a H, Of their many a R.   218 *Hors*] LR, Horsis H.   *in*] LH, with R.
220 *an* . . *his*] LR, the . . the H.   *thoruh*] LH, *om.* R.   222 *the*] the fiers H.
224 *men* . . *hym*] of hym profiteth H, ther leveth R.   225 *Mihty*] These H.
226 *Make her* . . *her*] Maken theyr . . theyr H, Make their . . their R.   228
dew ordre] the Renges H, ordre dewe R.   230 *mote be yove*] must be gyve H,
most be youen R.   231 *that*] H, here La, the R.   233 *was*] LR, *om.* H.

Whan the famous / worthi duke of Clarence[1]

Rood on baiard / with his eynë blynde,—

Fliht' of my fetheris / was put out of mynde ;   236

And, for he sett / of me, that day no fors,

Ful litel or nouht' / availed hy*m* his hors.   238

The Goose.

When the Duke of Clarence left the Goose-arrows behind,

his Horse was no good to him.

(35)

¶ " Bookis old / remembren in sentence   239

Som tyme whan Romë / bi his foon was take,

The Capitoilë kept / with gret deffence :

Noise of a Gand*r*e / the Capteyn did awake ;[2]

Which thyng reme*m*bryd / thei sett vp for his sake,

In her' templis wondir wide & olde,

A largë ga*n*dre / forgid of fy*n* golde.   245

At a siege of Rome,

a Gander's noise saved the city ;

and a Golden Gander was set up in the temples

(36)

¶ " His wakir noise / was their savacïou*n*   246

Bi which the Capteyn) / ran vp to the wall :

Line 234 *worthi*] LH, & worthy R.   235 *eynë*] Ien H, eyen R.   236 *was put*] LR, that day H.   237 *of me that day*] LH, that day of me R.   238 *Ful . . nouht*] LH, So . . nought / what R.   239 *Bookis*] LR, The bookes H.   240 *Som tyme . . foon*] Whilom . . foomen H, Whilom . . foon R.   242 *did awake*] LH, dide wake R.   243 *thyng*] LH, *om.* R.   *thei sett vp*] LR, *om.* H.   244 *here templis*] theyr temple . so H, their temples, *om.* wondir . R.   245 *large*] LR, grete H.   *of*] LH, al of R.   246 *their*] they H, theire R, the L.   247 *ran vp to*] gate vpon H, ran vpon R.

[1] Thomas, Duke of Clarence (1388 ?—1421), second son of Henry IV., by his first wife, Mary de Bohun. . . After Henry V.'s marriage, he accompanied the king at his triumphal entry into Paris on Dec. 1, 1420. On Henry's departure for England at the end of Jan. 1421, Clarence was appointed Captain of Normandy and Lieutenant of France in the king's absence. Soon after, he started on a raid thro' Maine and Anjou, and advanced as far as Beaufort-en-Vallée, near the Loire. Meantime the Dauphin had collected his forces, and, being joind by a strong body of Scottish knights, reached Beaugé, in the English rear, on March 21. Clarence, on hearing the news, at once set out with his cavalry, not waiting for the main body of his army. He drove in the Scottish outposts, but was in his turn overwhelmed, and, together with many of the knights who accompanied him, was slain. His defeat was due to his own impatience, and his anxiety to win a victory which might compare with Agincourt. After his death the archers, under the Earl of Salisbury, came up and recovered the bodies of the slain (Cotton MS., Claud. A, viii., leaf 10 *a*). Clarence's body was carried back to England, and buried at Canterbury.—*Dict. Nat. Biog.*, lvi., 158, 159.

[2] The Grey Lag-Goose is one of the most wary and knowing of birds, yet the word 'Goose,' as applied to men and women, is a term of ridicule, and this notwithstanding that the bird is credited with having saved Rome ; neither can we forget that the Grey Goose feather winged the deadly cloth-yard shafts, which, on many a hard-fought field, against overwhelming odds, brought victory to the side of England.—1897, Dr. Henry O. Forbes in Butler's *British Birds*, iv. 58.

The Goose.
Thus, bi a Gandre / recurèd was the toun,

of the most royal
city of the world.
Callid of the world / Cite most Roiaħ,

Cite of Citees / that day most principaħ.   250

Did a Horse
ever do a deed
like this?
Was euyr hors / in bookis that ye can rede,

Pro re publica / that dide sicħ a deede?   252

(37)

[leaf 71, back]
In the *Knight
of the Swan*
romance,
when gold chains
were torn off chil-
dren,
¶ " In the book / of Chyvaler⁾ de Sygne,   [See the E.E.
                                                     T.S. text]

The stori tellitħ / (as in sentement,)

Ther were childre / of the Roiall ligne

Born⁾ with cheynes / whicħ, whan⁾ thei wern of rent,

they turnd to
Swans,
Thei turned to Swannës / by enchantëment,   257

and swam in the
river.
Took her⁾ fliht⁾ / (the cronycle is ful cleer⁾,)

And, as swannys / thé swomme in the Riveer⁾. 259

(38)

The French story
is true.
¶ " This story is ful Autentik / & old,   260

In frenssħ compiled / often rad & seyn⁾ :

The gold cup
made of the chains
Of thilkë cheynes / was made a cuppe of gold

Which is yit kept / as sommë folkis seyn,

now belongs to
the Hertfords.
And bi descent / it longith (in certeyn⁾,)   264

To the Herfordis / ye shal it fynde in dede

Ceriously / who list the storye reede.   266

(39)

Not long ago
a Lombard was
sorcerized into
a goose for 7
years.
¶ " And semblably / nat longë here-to-forn⁾,   267

(I telle this talë / as for my partie)

Ther was a man⁾, in Lumbárdy born⁾,

To a goos turned / bi craft of sorcerye,

A-bood so seuene yeer⁾ / (me list nat lye) ;   271

Line 248 *recured*] rekouered HR.   249, 250] H *transposes these lines.*   249 *the
. . most*] al the . . most excelent H, the world the cyte moste R.   251 *bookis*]
LH, book R.   253 *of*] LH, named of R.   255 *childre*] children HR.   256
whiche . . rent] whan they were from hem went H, and whan they were of rent
R.   257 *enchantement*] thenchauntement] H.   258 *cronycle*] LH, trouth R.
259 *as . . swomme*] right as . . swamme H, as . . swamme R.   261 *often . .*] ful
oft radde and sene H, oft red and seyn R.   262 *thilke*] HR, the L.   263 *as
somme folkis*] as that some folk H.   264 *in*] om. H.   265 *Herfordis . . it*]
Warewyk . . so H, herfordes . . so R, And to the herfordis . yif ye H.   266
Ceriously / who list] Ceriously who so liste R.   267 *And . . here*] LR, Right . .
ther H.   268 *as*] LR, here as H.   *my*] HR, this L.   270 *turned*] Itorned H, y
torned R.   271 *Abood*] Boode H, And so abode R.   *lye*] H, to l. LR.   for to l. H.

His writ fil of / tho stood he vp a man),

A-bood with the duke in seruyce of **Melan**. 273

(40)

¶ " And for he was / a man) of hih degre, 274

Born) of good blood / & notable in substaunce,

His kynrede yeuyth a goos / for ther leveré,

The seide merveile / to put in rémembraunce.

Peise alle these thyngis / iustly in balaunce, 278

And lat the hors leven his boost & roos,

To be comparid / with gandir or with goos. 280

(41)

¶ " Withynnë Rome / the Gandre was deified, 281

Set in ther' templis / of gret Affeccïoun

Bi senatoures / of costom magnyfied

As cheeff protector / & saviour' of the toun :

Lat hors & sheepë / lay her' bost a-doun, 285

But yiff the Ram), with his brasen belle,

Can for the sheepe / any bettir story telle." 287

(42)

¶ The sheepe was symple / loth to make a-fray, 288

Lik a beste / disposid to meeknesse :

The sturdy Ram / aduócat' was that day :

Be-for the Iuges / Anon) he gan hym dresse,

With an exordie / in latyn, this texpresse : 292

" **Veste purpurea** / O Egle, & thou leoun,

Induti sunt Arietes Ouium. 294

(43)

¶ " Off this notáble / Roiall hih scripture, 295

The blessed Doctour Austyn, as I reede,

Line 272 *tho . . vp*] than . . forthe H, than . . vp R.   273 *Abood*] Dwellid H,
And bode (in seruyce with the duke of melan) R.   275 *&*] LR, *om.* H.   276
for] LR, to H.   278 *these thyngis*] LH, tynges R.   280 *with . . with*] othir
with to gandir or La, to gander or to H, To make comparison with gander or
ghoos R.   283 *costom*] the toun R.   284 *savioure*] saver HR.   *the*] her R.   285
here] theyr H, their R.   286 *Ram*] LR, Ram here H.   287 *any*] som HR.   288
¶ The sheepe spekith *at side*] H, The ram speketh for the sheep R.   289 *Lik*]
Ful liche H.   290 *aduocat*] his vocate H, his aduocate R.   291 *Be*] To HR.
292 *in*] of R.   293 *O Egle, & thou leoun* ¶ *Ouis*] vt rectores gregum HR.   295
Roialle] and H.

The Ram.

As by manere / a gostly fayr Figure

says the chaste
sheep Mary

Off a chast sheepë / (thus he doth procede,)

Callid **Maria**, a maide / in thouhtᵗ & deede,   299

begat the Lamb
Jesus,

Brouhtᵗ forth the lambe / lambe of most vertu,

The lambe of grace / which is callid Ihesu.   301

(44)

¶ " Austyn callith / this lambe, in his estatᵗ   302

(Bi many-foldë / recorde of scripture,)

the Royal Lamb
who lay down his
life for man.

The roial lambe / of colour purpurat,

Which for mankynde / list passioun to endure,

Borñ of a maide / bi grace, a-geyn nature,   306

Whan he, bi mene / of hir humylite,

Took the meeke clothyng of ourᵖ humanyte.   308

(45)

[leaf 72, back]

¶ " Born bi descent / to be bothe preest & kyngᵗ,   309

Kyngᵗ bi successioun / fro Dauid douñ bi line,

Of purpil red / was his Roial clothyngᵗ,

The Lamb of God,

This **Agnus dei** / borñ of a pure virgyne,

Which wessh a-wey / all venym superfyne   313

who died for man
on Calvary.

On Calverie / whan he for man was ded,

With his pure blood / purpurat & red.   315

(46)

¶ " This Paschale lamb / withouten spot, al whihtᵗ, 316

Bi his passioun / in **Bosra** steyned red,

Which cam from **Edom** / lamb of most delite,

That yaff his bodi / to mañ in forme of bred

Was ever found in
Scripture so
solemn a figure of
Horse or Goose as
of the Paschal
Lamb ?

On sheerthursday / be-forñ ar he was ded.   320

Was euyr founde / afore this in scripture,

Off hors or goos / so solempne a Figure ?   322

Line 297 *As . . a*] H, Be manere gostly fayr La, Be a maner . . faire of R.
298 *chast . . doth*] meke shepe . thus doth he H, m. s. t. he doth R.   299 *Callid
. . deede*] *om.* H.   300 *the . . of*] a lamb that was H, a lambe R.   301 *is callid*]
namede is H, whos name was R.   302 and 296 *Austyn*] Augustyn R.   *his*] *om.*
R.   305 *to*] *om.* HR.   306 *ageyn*] agenst H, agayn R.   307 *bi*] bi the H, be R.
308 *Took the meeke*] List take the H, Toke the R.   310 *fro*] from H, fro R.
311 *purpil*] purpur H.   (316 The Lambeth MS. 306 begins here.)   318 *lamb . .
most*] this lamb . . grete H, this lambe of R.   320 *beforne ar*] to-fore or H, to-
fore R.   321 *euyr . . this*] there euer founde HR.

(47)

¶ "This lamb was Crist / whicħ lyneal doun cam; 323

Bi descent / conveide the peedegree

Fro the Patriarcħ / I-callid **Abraham,**

Bi Isaac, Iacob / & so doun to Iesse,

Whicħ, bi the vertu / of his humylite,   327

List to be callid the blessed Lord Ihesu,

For his hiħ meekenesse / lamb of most vertu. 329

This Lamb was Christ, descended from Abraham and Jesse,

and called for his meekness, the Lamb.

(48)

¶ "And to reherse / worldly comoditees   330

In re publica make no comparison;

Ther is no best / which, in aħ degrees,

Nouther Tigre / Olifant, nor Gryffon—

Al thyngës rekned / thoruħ euery region— 334

Doth so gret profite / hors, nor goos, nor swan,

As doth the **Sheep**e, vn-to the ese of man. 336

Of worldly goods

none profits so the Common Weal

as does the Sheep.

(49)

¶ "Lat be thI bost, thou / hors, & thi Iangelyng'! 337

Ley doun thi trapures / forgid of plate & maile !

Cast of thy brydyl / of gold so fresshe shynyng !

What may thi sadil / or boses the availe?

This gostly lambe / hatħ doon a gret bataile;   341

Bi his meknesse / he offred vp for man,

Clad in pure purpil / venquysshid hath Satan. 343

[leaf 73]

Horse! let be thy pride.

What avail thy bosses?

The Lamb has vanquished Satan.

(50)

¶ "The Goos may gagle / the hors may prike & praunce:

Neither of hem / in prowes may atteyne

For to be set / or put in rémembraunce

A-geyn the lamb / thouħ thei ther-at disdeyne:

For comon profite / he passitħ bothë tweyne,   348

The Goose may cackle, the Horse may prance,

but, for the common profit,

Line 323 *lyneal*] lineally HR.   *doun cam*] cam doun LH, cam R.   324 *Bi . . convaide*] LR, In . . conveyede . bi.   *the*] LH, de R.   325 *Icallid*] callid loo H. 328 *Lord*] LH, *om.* R.   329 *hiħ meekenesse*] mekenesse . . the HR.   330 *to*] LH, for to R.   333 *nor*] ne HR.   335 *nor . . nor*] goos ne HR.   339 *brydyl*] sadil HR.   340 *sadil*] bridel HR.   *boses*] bos LH, boces R.   342 *vp for*] LR, for H. 343 *venq . .*] LR, he venquyssede H.   344 *gagle*] cacle H, cakle R.   *may*] *om.* R.   345 *prowes*] LH, processe R.   347 *Ageyn*] LR, Agenst H.   *ther-at*] LH, *om.* R.

The Ram.

they are nothing
like the Lamb.

Weied & considred / thei be no thyng⁺ liche

To hym in valew / be-tween poore & riche.   350

(51)

¶ " Off Brutis Albion / his wolle is cheeff richesse, 351

Wool is England's
greatest wealth
(excepting corn),

In prys surmountyng / euery othir thyng⁺

Sauff Greyn & corn) : marchauntis al expresse,

Woolle is cheeff tresoure / in this lond growyng :

To Riche & poorë / this beeste fynt clothyng :   355

Alle Nacïouns / afferme vp to the fulle,

and none better is
in the world.

In al the world / ther is no bettir wolle.   357

(52)

¶ " Of sheepe al-so / comyth̄ pilet & eke fell,   358

From Sheep come
fur and skins,

Gadrid in thys lond / for a gret Marchaundise

Caried ovir see / where men may it seH :

The wollë skynnys / makith̄ men to rise

enriching men—

To gret richesse / in many sondry wise ;   362

The sheepe al-so / turnyth to gret profite,

furs black and
white,

To helpe of man / berith furris blak & white. 364

(53)

[leaf 73, back]
garments and
gloves against
the cold,
and parchment to
write books on.

¶ " Ther is also / made of sheepis skyn),   365

Pilchis & glovis / to dryve awey the cold.

Ther-of also / is made good parchëmyn),

To write on bookes / in quaiers many fold ;

The Ram) of Colcos / bare a flees of gold ;   369

The flees of Gedeon / of deuh̄ délectáble

Was of Maria / a Figure ful notáble.   371

Line 349 *Weied . . liche*] Considre it wele . be-twene pore and riche H, Weye
and considere betwene . . R.   350 *To . . riche*] To the lamb in valu . . they be
nothynge liche H, To hym in . . . liche R.   351 *Brutis . . his*] LR, Inglande the
wulle H.   355 *fynt*] fyndith H, fynde R.   356 *afferme*] affermen it HR.   357
the . . is] this . . nys H, the . . is R.   358 *pilet*] pelt H. Lm (Lambeth), pellet
R.   359 *in . . a*] to gydre . for H, in . . for R.   *Marchaundise*] in margin, later ;
tresoure dotted under for omission, in text.   360 *ovir*] bi H, over the R.   361
wolle . . makith] wullen . . causen H, wulle . . causen R.   363 *turnyth*] tourn-
ynge H, tornyth R.   364 *furris blak*] LR, both blak H.   365 *of*] of the HR.
366, 368] as in HR ; La transposes these lines.   368 *on . . in*] on . . and HR,
of . . & R.   370 *of . .*] with dewe delitable H, . . delectable R.   371 *ful notable*]
LR, delectable H.

(54)

¶ " His fleessħ is / natural restauracion) ;   372

As summe men) seyn) / aftir gret siknesse,

Rostid or sodyn / holsom is moton) :

Wellid with growel / phisiciens expresse,

Ful nutritiff aftir a gret accesse.   376

The sheepe al-so / concludyng doutelees

Of his naturë / louyth rest & pes.   378

Mutton is also
wholesome after
sickness,

and its broth after
great illness.

(55)

¶ " Of the sheepe / is cast a-way no thyngꞋ :   379

His horn for nokkis / to haftis goth the bone ;

To the lond / gret profite doth his tirdelyngꞋ ;

His talwe eke seruyth / for plaistres mo than on ;

For harpë strynges / his roppis serue echone ;   383

Of his hed / boilèd holle, with wolle & alł,

Ther comyth a gelle / an oynement ful Roialł ; 385

No part of the
Sheep is lost ;
neither horns,
bones, dung,

fat,

guts,

nor head, which,
boild, makes a
salve

(56)

¶ " For ache of bonys / & also for brosoure   386

It remedieth / & dooth men ese ful blyve ;

Causith men starkid / bonys to recure ;

Dede synnewis / restoriħ a-geyn to live.

Blak sheepis wolle / with fresh oil of olive—   390

These men of Armys / with charmys previd good,—

At a streight neede / thei can weel staunchë blood.

that cures aches,

and restores dead
sinews to life.

Black Sheep's
wool stanches
blood.

(57)

¶ " But to the wolff / contrárie of nature   393

As seyn auctours / it is the humble best,

Louyth no debat / for which eche crëature,

[leaf 74]
The Sheep, too,
loveth Peace ;

Line **373** *seyne*] LR, *om.* H.   **374** *sodyn*] LR, soode . right H.   **375** *Wellid*]
Boyled H.   **376** *accesse*] LR, sikenesse H.   **377** *doutelees*] doutelees L, douteles
R.   **378** *louyth*] lovithe ay H.   **379** *Of*] Of al H.   **381** *To the*] The H, To R.
tirdelynge] tyrtelyng R.   **382** *eke*] *om.* R.   **384** *his*] LH, whos R.   *boiled holle*]
boild La, boylede holle H.   **385** *an oynement*] H, an oynemet La, oynement R.
386 *ache*] LH, the ache R.   **387** *men*] H, *om.* LaR.   *ful*] als H.   **388** *starkid /
bonys*] stark ioyntes H, of starke Ioyntes R.   **389** *Dede . . live*] LaR, *om.* H.
390 *fresh*] *om.* R.   *oil of*] oyle HR.   **391** *previd*] LR, preve it H.   **392** *a . .
weel*] strayte nede . therwith H, . . . can wel R.   **393** *But to*] Vnto HR.   **394**
it . . humble] is this symple H, is this humble R.

The Ram.

For his party / he woldë lyve in rest.

wherefore, ye Judges,
Where-fore, ye Iugis / I hold it for the best,   397

since Peace is better than War,
Rem publica*m* / ye must of riht' preferre,

Alwey consideryng / that pees is bet tha*n* werre.

(58)

¶ " In this mater*e* / breffly to conclude,   400

Pees to p*r*eferrë / as to my devis,

Bi many an old / p*r*evid symylitude,

give the Sheep the prize,
Makith no delay / yeuyth to the sheep*e* the pris,

Of oon assent / sith that ye be wis :   404

and stop all war.
Lat al this werr*e* & striff / be sett a-side,

And vpon pees / dooth wit̄h the sheep*e* a-bide."

(59)

"No," says the Horse, "the
¶ " Nay," q*uo*d the hors / " your' request is wrong*e*, 407

Al thyng' co*n*siderid / me wer*e* loth to erre :

Sheep is the cause of war.
The sheep*e* is causë / & hath be ful long*e*,

Of new*e* stryvës / & of mortal werre :

The circu*m*stancis / me list nat to defferre :   411

For his wool the Duke of Burgundy
Thi wolle was cause / & gret occasïo*n*)

Whi the forsworn / and proude Duke of Burgo*n*)

(60)

attackt Calais;
¶ " Cam befor Caleis / with Flemy*n*ges nat a fewe, 414

Which yaff the sakkis / & sarpler'es of the tou*n*

To Gau*n*t & Brugis / his freda*m* for to shewe,

And of thi wolle / hiht' he*m* pocessïou*n* ;

But his boistous baistill*e* / first was bete dou*n* ;   418

He vnethe / escapid with the liff :

What but thi wolle / was cause of al the striff' ?

Line 396 *he wolde*] R, the sheepe wold*e* H, he wol La.   398 *must*] shuld*e* H, shold R.   399 *Alwey . . than*] . . better than R, Consideryng*e* alwey . the peas is bette the H.   401 *my devis*] LaR, myn advise H.   402 *an*] *om.* R.   403 *Makith . . yeuyth*] Make . . yeue R.   404 *sith . . be*] LaR, sithen . . bien H.   405 *al this*] H, al La, alle R.   407 *youre*] LaR, for youre H.   409 *and*] LaR, and so H.   410 *stryves*] HR, striff La.   411 *to*] *om.* H.   413 *the . . and*] H, that the proude LaR.   415 *sakkis . . of*] LaR, sarpluce . and sakkis in H.   417 *And . . hem*] Of thy wullis theyr gaf theym H, Of . . he hyght hem R.   418 *But*] *om.* HR.   419 *He*] Hym self HR.   420 *wolle*] wulles R.   *the*] this HR.

(61)

The Ram.

¶ " Wher richesse is / of wollë & sich good,　421　[leaf 74, back]

Men drawë thidir / that be rekëles,　　　　and where wool
　　　　　　　　　　　　　　　　　　is plenty, there
As Soudïoures / that braynles been, & wood,　reckless men
　　　　　　　　　　　　　　　　　　gather to plunder.
To gete baggagë / put hem silf in prees.

Thou Causist werre / and seist thu louest pees ;　425

And yiff ther were / no werrë nor bataille,　Without war, too,
　　　　　　　　　　　　　　　　　　great Horses
Lityll or nouht / gret horsis shuld availe."　427　would be no
　　　　　　　　　　　　　　　　　　good."

(62.　*The Goose*)

The Goose.

¶ " No," q*uod* the Goos / " nór my Fetharis white, 428　"Nor white
　　　　　　　　　　　　　　　　　　feathers," says
Withoutë werre / shuld do no*n* Avau*n*táge,　the Goose,

Nor hookid Arwis / profite but a lite.　　"nor arrows,

To mete our*e* enmyes / magre ther visage,

And fro*m* oure foomen / save vs fro*m* damáge,　432

Fliht' of my Fetheris / despite of sheepe echon,　which, despite of
　　　　　　　　　　　　　　　　　　Sheep, shall save
Shal vs defende / a-geyn) our' mortal foon)."　434　us from our foes."

(63)

The Horse.

¶ " Sothe," q*uod* the hors / " as in my inward siht', 435

Withouten werre / (be-forn) as I yow told),　" Without war,"
　　　　　　　　　　　　　　　　　　says the Horse,
We may nat save / nor keepë wele our' right',　" we cannot keep
　　　　　　　　　　　　　　　　　　our rights,
Our garisonës / nor our*e* castelis old.

But her*e* this sheep*ë* / rowkyng in his fold,　439　but for these the
　　　　　　　　　　　　　　　　　　Sheep cares not,
Set litiH stoor / of swerd or Arwis keene,　if he can feed on
　　　　　　　　　　　　　　　　　　the green.
Whan he, in pees, may pastur*e* on the greene. 441

(64)

¶ " Yiff it so stood / that neu*er* werrë were,　442　The Armourers'
　　　　　　　　　　　　　　　　　　craft would also
Lost wer*e* the craft / of thesë Armoreres.　be gone,

What shuld availë / pollax, swerd or spere,

Line 421 *Wher . . wolle*] . . . wulles R, There riches is of wullis H.　422 *that be*] whiche bien H.　*rekeles*] recheles R, rekles La.　424 *put*] LaH, they put R. *silf*] LR, forth H.　425 *Thou . . and*] Thus causest thou werre & R, Causist werre LaH.　*seist thu*] seystow H.　426 *yiff . . nor*] gyve . . nother H, yf . . ne R.　427 *horsis*] H, hors La, horse R.　428 *quod*] said R.　430 *hookid*] LaR, sharpe H.　431 *enmyes*] ennyes La, enemyes HR.　432 *foomen*] H, enmyes to La, them to R.　433 *despite*] LaR, faute H.　435 *Sothe*] R, Sithe H, Bothe La. 436 *Withouten*] H, Without La, With oute R.　*beforne*] to-fore H, afore R.　437 *save*] LaR, sawen H.　*wele*] HR, *om*. La.　439 *rowkyng*] H, vukyng La, ruckyng R.　441 *in pes may*] LaR, may in pease H.　442 *Yiff . . stood*] If it so were H. *neuer*] H, no LaR.　443 *these*] *om*. R.

Or these daggarës / wrouht¹ bi coteleres,

Bowës, crosbowës / arwis of fletcheres ?   446

These instrumentis / for the werre all wrouht¹,

Yif werrë stynt / they shuldë serue of nouht¹. 448

(65)

¶ " Her occupacioun / shold have non encres ; 449

Knyhthod nat flouren shuld / in his estat¹ ;

In euery contre / yiff ther¹ werë pees,

No man of armys shold be fortunat¹ :

I preve that pees / is grond of all debat,   453

For on five spookis / lik as on a wheel,

Turnyth al the world / who can considre weel. 455

(66)

¶ " Gyn first at pees / which causith most richesse,

& riches is / the originall of pride :

Pride causith / for lak of Rihtwisnesse,

Werre between Rewmys / look on euery side,

Hertis contrarye / in pees can nat A-bide : 460

Thus, fynally / (whoo can considre & see,)

Werre is cheff ground & cause of pouerte. 462

(67)

¶ " Pouert¹ bi werrë / brouht¹ to disencrese, 463

For lak of tresoure / than he can no more,

Sauff only this / he crieth aftir pees,

And, compleyneth / on the warris sore :

He seith, ' bi werris / he hath goodis lore, 467

Can no recure / but grutchyng & disdeyn,'

And seith he wold right fayn / have pees a-geyn.

(68)

¶ " Thus pride & richesse / to cónclude in a clause, 470

Betwene thextremytes / of pes & pouertee,

Line 446 *of*] R, or La, of the H.   447 *These . . all*] The . . al H, All these
Inst . . for the werre La, Alle . . is R.   448 *stynt*] were stint HR. *they shulde*]
shuld La. 449 *Her*] Theyr H, Their R. 450 *nat . . shuld*] ne shuld . flaure H,
shold not floure R.   454 *on . . on*] in . . spekis . . as is R.   455 *can considre*]
considereth R. 456 *most*] al H, *om.* R. 460 *can*] wil R. 466 *on*] LaR, vpon H.
467 *goodis*] his goodis HR. 469 *And, right*] H, *om.* La. *he*] LaH, the world R.
fayn] lief H. 471 *Betwene*] LaR, *om.* H. (Scan 'thextremytes' as 1 foot).

Off all debatis / & werrë, be cheeff cause ;
  And, sith wollis bryngith in greet plente
    Wher thei haboun̄de / (as folk expert may se),   474
      Than̄) may I seyn / (yiff men wole takyn keepe,)
      Werre is brouht¹ in / al only bi the sheepe.   476

(69)

¶ " Here is a gentil reson of an hors !   ¶ Ouis 477
  I trowë he be fallen / in a dotáge,   [leaf 75, back]
Which, of madnesse / bi wollë set no fors,   "Is the Horse
  Falsly affermeth / it doth non̄ ávaun̄táge,   mad," says the Sheep, "to say
    Vertuous plente / may do no damáge :   481   that Wool does no good ?
      Sheepe berith his wolle / I told so whan I gan̄),
      Nat for hym-silf, but for profit of man̄).   483

(70)

¶ " Divers comoditees that comen of the sheepe   484   The Sheep causes no wars.
  Cause no werris / what men Iangle or muse,
As in her² gilt / ¶ ye Iuges, takith keepe
  What that I sei / her Innocence texcuse !
    Of Coveitise / men may falsly mysvse   488   Men wrongly blame their benefactors.
      Her² bëenfatis / & wrongly hem attwite
      Of such occasioun̄s / where he is nat to wite.   490

(71)

¶ " What is the sheepe / to blamë in your² sight¹   491   Is the Sheep to blame because men shear him and fight for his wool ?
  Whan̄) she is shoorn̄) / & of hir flessh made bare,
Thouh folk of malice / for hir wollis fiht¹
  Causelees to stryve / foolis wil nat spare :
  Where pees restith / thér is al weelfare ;   495

Line 472 *debatis*] La R, delayes H.   473 *sith*] thy H, saith R.   475 *yiff*] yif that H, yf R.   477 *Ouis*] ¶ The Ram spekyth H, The shepe answereth R.   478 *trowe . . a*] trowe . . into som R, leeve he be fal . in grete H.   479 *wolle*] wullis H.   *no*] HR, so La.   480 *affermeth*] affermyng HR.   482 *wolle*] flees HR.   *so*] om. R.   482, 483 H has in margin : ¶ Non sibi, sed Reliquis, Aries sua vellera portat.   483 *Nat*] Nought H, Not R.   484 *Divers*] LaR, om. H (scan ' comoditees ' as 1 foot).   486 *her . . takith*] her take ye R, his . . taken H.   487 *texcuse*] LaR, to excuse H.   488 *mysvse*] vse H, muse R.   489 *Her . . attwite*] LaR, His . . bewite H.   490 *occasiouns . . he*] lewdenesse . . he H, occasions . . she R.   492 *she . . flessh*] he . . his flees H, she . . her flees R.   493 *hir wollis*] his wulle H, his wollis La, her wulles R.   494 *stryve*] LaR, deryve H.   495 *Where*] Where that H.

And sith the sheep*e* / louyth pes of Innocence,

Yeuyth to his p*a*rty / diffynytiff sentence."   497

(72)

¶ The Roial **Egle** / the **leon**) of assent,   498

Al thyng considerid / rehersid heer*e*-to-forn*)*

Of all these thre / bi good avisëment,

Of hors, of goos, of **Ram**, with his gret horn*)*,

Sauh in re pu*bli*ca / myht' nat be for-born*)*,   502

Bi short sentence / tavoydë al discorde,

Cast a meene / to sett hem at a-corde.   504

(73)

¶ This was the meene / tavoidë first the stryves,   505

And al old Rancour / with her hertis glade ;

Vse her' yiftës / & her' prerogatives

To that same eende / for which that thei wer*e* made,

Ware, with presu*m*pcioun / her bakkis be nat lade,

Vndevided / with hert(ë), will & thouht'   510

To doon her' office / as nature hath he*m* wrouht'.

(74)

¶ The hors, bi kynde, to lyvë in travayle,   512

Goos, with his gooslynges / to swymme in the lake,

The Sheep*e*, whoos wollë / doth so myche availe,

In hir pasturë grese / & mery make ;

Her' comparisou*n*s / bi on assent for-sake,   516

Al-wey reme*m*bryng / how god & natur*e*,

To a good ende / made eu*er*y creatur*e*.   518

Line 497 *Yeuyth . . party*] Yeue ye for his parte R.   *to his party*] for his part H.   (72) The lyon & egle yeuyng Iugement R.   498 *the leon of*] and the lyon of one R.   499 *toforn*] aforn H, beforn R.   501 *of Ram . . gret*] and Ram with croked' H, and ghoos / and the ram with his R.   502 *nat*] noun R.   *forborne*] LaR, forsworn H.   503 *tavoyde*] to avoyde H, to voyden R.   504 *Cast*] They cast H.   505 *tavoide first*] to awoyde al HR.   *the*] her R.   *stryves*] H, strif La, her striues R.   506 *al . . her*] of olde grucchynge with theyr H,R (less ' of '). 507 *Vse . . here*] To vse they gyftes and theyr H, Vse these ghyftes & thise R. 508 *same*] H, om. LaR.   *for*] to R, om. La.   *that*] om. H.   509 *Ware*] H, War La.   *her*] theyr HR.   510 *Vndevided with*] al . vndevided . in Vndeuoyded in R.   512 *lyve*] lyuen R.   513 *Goos . .*] The ghoos . . his La.   *to*] R, om. LaH. *his . . swymme*] their goselynges to.   514 *wolle / doth*] wullis . don H, wulles doth R.   515 *hir . . grese*] his . . gresen H, his . . grese R.   516 *Her*] om. H, Their R ('-parisouns' is 1 foot).   517 *Alwey . . &*] LaR, Remembrynge hem how god & eke H.   518 *To*] LaR, Til H.

(75)

¶ That noon of hem, to othir / shuld do no wrong⸍ 519 None who are

The ravenous wolf / the sely lambe toppresse ;

And thouh oon bé / more than an othir strong⸍, strong should
oppress the weak.

To the febler⸍ / do no froward duresse.

Al extorcioun / is groundid on falsnesse ; 523

Wiłł is no lawe / whethir it be wrong or riht⸍ :

Treuthe is put doun / the feeble is put to fliht⸍.

(76)

¶ Odious of old / been ałł comparisouns, 526 Comparisons are
odious ;

And of comparisons / is gendrid hatereede ;

Ałł folk be nat / of lik condicïouns,

Nor łik disposid / of thouht, wil, or deede ;

But this fable / which that ye now reede, 530 let him who has
most of virtue's
gifts share them
with his friends,

Contreuëd was / that who that hath grettest part

Off vertuous yiftis / shold with his freend depart.

(77)

¶ Thus ałł vertues / alloone hath nat oo man⸍ : 533 [leaf 76, back]

That oon lakkith / god hath yove a-nothir : one supplying
another's lack,

That thou canst nat / parcas a-nothir can⸍ :

So entircomon⸍ / as brothir doth with brothir ;

And if charite / gouerne weele the tothir, 537

And in oo clausë / speke in wordis pleyn⸍, and no man dis-
daining any other.

That no man shold⸍ / of othir ha disdeyn⸍.[1] 539

Line 519 *of hem*] H, *om*. LaR.   *no*] *om*. La.   520 *wolf*] HR, *om*. La.   521
And thouh] Although La.   522 *no froward*] LaR, none hard H.   524 *no*] now
R.   525 *put*] leyd R.   526 *comparisouns*] HR, coparisouns La.   527 *comparisons* . .] hem engendred bien fowle hateredis H.   *gendrid*] engendrid R.   528
lik] oon H, And alle . . lyke of R.   529 *or deede*] or dedis H, & dede R.   530
But . .] For whiche cause this fable that ye rede R, For whiche this fable.
whiche that ye redis H.   531 *that who that*] who that H, who R.   532 *freend
depart*] LaR, friendis part H.   533 *Thus*] As thus R.   *alloone* . . *oo*] LaR, oon
have no lyveng H.   534 *god*] nature HR.   535 *parcas*] LaR, parchaunce H.
536 *So* . .] Entercomen therfore R.   *doth with*] LaR, with his H.   537 *And if*
. . *tothir*] If . . Roother H, Yf . . rother R.   538 *And in oo clause*] Al in oon
vessel . . to H.   539 *of othir ha*] have . . of othir H.

---

[1] Below, a later hand has written "Amor uincit omnia." The Roxb. Club
reprint of 1822 has no envoy, but says, "Thus endeth the hors, the ghoos, and
the sheep."

¶ The Auctour makith a Lenvoie vpon alle the mateere be-fore said.

(78)

Understand the	¶ Off this fable / conceivith the sentence; 540
	At good leiser / doth the mateer see,
	Which inporteth gret intelligence
Moral of this Fable:	Yiff ye list takë / the moralite
	Profitable to euery comounte, 544
	Which includith in many sondry wise,
Don't despise your Neighbour!	No man shuld / of hih nor lowe degre,
	For no prerogatiff / his neighbore to despise. 547

(79)

Tho you're strong,	¶ Som man is strong / hardi as a leoun 548
	To byndë Beeris / or Booris to oppresse,
	Wher-as anothir / hath gret discrecïoun:
holy,	Som man hooly / liveth in parfitnesse, 551
or rich,	A-nothir besi / to gadre gret richesse;
	But with al this / tak heed of this emprise,
don't despise your neighbour!	No man presume / so hih his hornes dresse,
	For no prerogatiff / his neihbour to despise. 555

(80)

[leaf 77]	¶ Trappures of gold / ordeyned were for steedis; 556
Of sheep's wool	Sheepe in the pasture / gresen with mekënesse,
	Yit of ther wollis / be woven richë weedis,
are made soft pillows and feather-beds.	Of smothë doun / maad pilwis for softnesse, 559
	Fethirbeddis to sleepe, whan men dresse
	Toward Aurora / ageyn til thei arrise:
Don't despise your neighbour!	Rolle vp this problem / thynk what it doth expresse:
	For no prerogatiffe / thi neihbour nat despise. 563

(81)

	¶ The inward meenyng / to-forn as it is told, 564
	The hors is tokne / of Marcïal noblesse

The Auctour . .] ¶ The moralite of the hors, the goose, and the sheepe, translated by Dan Iohn Lidgate, H, in margin.   Line 540 *the*] this H.   544 *co-mounte*] comunalte H.   546 *nor*] or H.   547 *to despise*] despise La, to dispise H.   548–555] H omits.   557 *the . . gresen*] theyr . . to grace H.   558 *be woven*] bien wonder H.   560 *whan men*] on whan men hem H.   561 *ageyn*] H.   a gey La.   562 *what it*] it H.   564 *meenyng / to forne*] meanes . aforn H.

Witħ his hi belle / & bocïs brood of gold.

   Estat of Tirantis / the poraile doth opp*r*esse ;   567 Tyrants oppress
                                                the poor.

   The woolff in ffoldis / to sheepë doth duresse,

     Rukkyng· in ffoldis / for dreed· dar net arryse,

   Ye that han power / be war in yo*ur* hiħnesse,   Don't despise
                                               your dependants!

   For no p*r*erogatiff, yo*ur* sogettis to despise.   571

(82)

¶ As pronostatik / clerkis bare witnesse ;   572

   Botħ ware of pheb*us* / that erly cast his liht·,   After sun,

Of reyn, of stormis / of myste or of derknesse   come storm

   Shal aftir folwe / longe or it be nyht·,   575

   Signe of gret wyntir / whaȵ wild gees tak her fliht· and cold.

     Lik as nature / hir stou*n*dis can devise :

   Lat hiħ nor lowe / presumen of his myht·,   Don't despise
                                               your neighbour!

   For no p*r*erogatiff / his neihbour· to despise.   579

(83)

¶ Of mony strange vncouth simylitude,   580 By Esop's Fables
                                               of animals,

   Poetis of old / fablis haue *con*tryvid,

Of sheep*e*, of hors / of Ge*e*s, of bestis· rude,

   Bi which ther wittis / were secretly apprevid,   583 tyrants were
                                             reproved.

   Vndir covert / tyrau*n*tis eeke reprevid,

     Ther opp*r*essiou*n*s & malis to chastise

   Bi exanplis / of resou*n* to be mevid,   Don't despise
                                             the poor!

   For no p*r*erogatiff / poore folk to despise.   587

(84)

¶ Fortunës cours / dyuersly is dressid   588 [leaf 77, back]

   Bi liknessis / of many othir tale ;

Man, best, & fowle / & fisshis bee*n* opp*r*essid   In Nature,
                                            the great eat

   In ther nature / bi female or bi male :   591 the small.

   Of grettest fissħ / devourid been the smale,

     Which in nature / is a ful straungë guyse,

Line 566 *belle*] bellis H.   568 *ffoldis . . doth*] fieldis thc sheepe doth grete H.
569 *dreede*] feer H.   572 *As pronostatik*] H ; A pronostik La.   573 *cast*] castith
H.   574 *of stormis / of*] storme or H.   576 *wild . . her*] wielde . . theyr H.
577] H. leaves out.   578 *Lat*] Nat H.   582 *of bestis*] and bestis H.   583 *wittis
were*] witte was H.   584 *covert*] covert termes H.   586 *exanplis of reason*] example of reason . goodely H.   587 *poore folk*] thc poraile H.   589 *liknessis . .
othir*] liknes of many another H.   590 *Man*] Men H.   592 *grettest*] grete H (H
transposes lines 591, 592).

The Cuckoo kills
the Nightingale.

To seen) a kokkow / mordre a Nityngale,

An Innocent bird / of hattreede to despise.   595

(85)

¶ With this processe / who that be wroht' or wood, 596

Thynges contrarie / be founde in euery kynde :

The Churl hates
the Gentleman.

A cherl of berthë / hatith gentil blood :

It were a monstre / a-geyn nature, as I fynde,   599

That a gret mastyff should a leoun bynde ;

It's bad when
Beggars rise,
and despise their
neighbours.

A parlious Clymbyng / whan beggeres vp arise

To hih estat—merk this in your' mynde—

Bi fals prerogatives / ther neihbours to despise.

(86)

The climbing-up
of Fools

¶ Fals supplantyng / clymbyng vp of foolis,   604

Vnto chairës / of wordly dygnyte,

Lak of discrecioun sett Iobbardis vpon stoolis,

ruins a land.

Which hath distroied many a comounte ;   607

Marcolf to sitt / in Salamon-is see ;

What folwith aftir ? / nor resoun nor Iustise,

They despise their
neighbours.

Vn-Iust promocioun / & parcialite,

Bi fals prerogativis / the neihboures to despise. 611

(87)

What's the dif-
ference between
poor and rich
when both die ?

¶ Tweene riche & poore / what is the difference,   612

When deth approchyth / in any crëature,

Sauff a gay tumbë / ffresh of ápparence ?

The riche is shet / with coloures & picture   615

To hide his careyn / stuffid with fowle ordure ;

The poore lith lowe / aftir the comoun guyse,

Let this teach
you not to despise
your neighbour.

To techyn al proude / of resoun & nature,

For no prerogatiff / ther neihbour' to despise. 619

(88)

[leaf 78]

¶ Ther was a kyngë / whilom as I rede,   620

As is remembrid / of ful yore a-gon,

Line 597 *contrarie*] outrage H.   601 *parlious*] perilous H.   604 *vp*] om. H.
606 *Lak*] Looke H.   608 *Marcolf .. Salamon-is*] Marchol .. Salamons H.   609
nor .. nor] no .. no H.   610 *Vniust*] Iniuste H.   612 *Tweene*] Atwene H.
613 *any*] euery H.   615 *shet*] shitte H.   618 *proude*] prowde men H.   621 *of*]
of not H.

Which cast away / croune[1] & purpil weede,   [¹ ? MS.]
  Bi causë that he / knew nat bon fro bon,   623
  Of poore nor riche / hym sempte thei were al on,
    Refusid his crōūnë / gaɳ to aduertise
    Pryncis buried / in gold nor precious ston,
      Shuld, of no pompe / ther suggettis nat despise.

A King once gave up his Purple because he held rich and poor equal.

(89)

¶ This thyng was doon / in Alisandris tyme,   628
  Bothë autentik / & historiaꝉ;
Bood nat til nyht⁴ / left⁴ his estat at pryme;
  His purpil mantil / his garnement Roiaꝉ,   631
  Texemplifië / in especiaꝉ
    To Imperial powerᵖ / what perel is to rise:
    Who clymbitħ hihest / most dredful is his faꝉ.
      Beeth war, ye princis / yourᵖ sogetis to despise. 635

This was in Alexander's time.

Princes, be sure not to despise your subjects!

(90)

¶ Hiħ & low / wer maad of oo mateerᵖ;   636
  Of erthe we cam / to erthe we shal a-geyɳ;
Thees emperours / with diadémys cleerᵖ,
  With therᵖ victóries / & triumphes in certeyɳ,   639
  In charis of gold / lat hem nat disdeyɳ,
    Thouħ thei, eche day / of newe hem silf disguyse.
    Fortune is fals / hir sonne is meynte with reyɳ:
      Beth ware, ye pryncis / yourᵖ suggettis to despise.

From earth, all came; to earth, all shall go.

Princes! don't despise your subjects!

(91)

¶ Hed & feete / been necessary bothe;   644
  Feet beryn vp aꝉ / & hedis shal provide;
Hors, Sheep, & Gees / whi shuld thei bei wrothe,
  For therᵖ comoditees / tabreyden vpon pride?   647
  Nature, his giftis / doth dyversly devide,

Why should Horse, Sheep and Goose quarrel? Nature distributes his gifts diversly.

Line 622 *croune & purpil*] crowne and purpier H.   623 *bon . .*] boon from boon H.   624 *nor*] ne H.   625 *crounne*] corowne and H.   626 *gold nor*] glasse and H.   627 *nat*] to H.   628 *Alisandris*] Alisaunder H.   631 *garnement*] garnementis H.   632 *Texemplifie*] To exemeplifie H.   633 *perel . . rise*] H; powere . . arise La.   635 *Beeth . . to*] Eche man be ware . his neyghburgh H.   636 *mateere*] nature H.   638 H. leaves out.   640 *nat*] have no H.   643 *Beth*] Be H.   645 *beryn*] bere H.   647 *ta . . vpon*] to abrayden vp H.   648 *his*] theyr

He lasts well,
who doesn't
despise his
neighbour.

Whoos power' lastith / from Cartage into **Fryse** :

He lastith weel / that wisly can a-byde,

> For any prerogatiff/ his neihbour' to dispise.   651

¶ Conclusio.   (92)

[leaf 78, back]
Nature has set
each beast and
fowl its special
task;

¶ To beast & foule / Nature hath set a lawe,   652

Ordeyned steedis / in Iustis for the knyht',

In carte & ploult / stokkis for to drawe,

> Sheepe in the pasture / to gresë day & nyht',   655

> Gees to swymme / a-mong' to take ther fliht' ;

each man too:
so let no one
despise his
neighbour.

> Of god & kynde / to takë ther ffraunchise,

Yeuyng' exaumple / that no maner wiht',

> For no prerogatiff / his neihbour' shal dispise. 659

Explicit.

¶ Incipit quedam compilacio de Regibus Anglie.

THis myhti William / Duke of   Normandie,
  As bookis old[ë] / makë mencïoun, &c.

Line 649 *Frysc*] prise H.   654 *stokkis*] horsis H.   655 *grese*]
grase H.   657 *to take*] taken al H.

Rats Away.

[MS. Rawl. C. 228, fol. 113, fly-leaf. The writing on this page is very illegible.]

I comawnde alle þe ratons þat are here abowte,   *I order no rats to dwell here,*

þat non dwelle in þis place wi*th*-inne ne wit*h*owte,

thorgh þe ve*r*tu of ihe*s*u c*r*i*st* þat mary bare abowte,   *by virtue of Christ,*

þat alle c[re]aturs owyn for to lowte,   4

& thorgh þe ve*r*tu of mark, mathew, luke, an ion,—   *and the Four Evangelists,*

alle foure awangelys corden into on,—

thorgh þe vertu of sent ȝeretrude, þ*at* mayde clene,   *St. Gertrude*

  god gr*au*nte þ*at* grace   8

  þ*at* [non] raton dwelle in þe place

þ*at* her nanis[1] were nemeled in ;   *[1 namis?]*

& thorgh þe ve*r*tu of sent kasi   *and St. Kasi.*

þ*at* holy man   12

þ*at* p*r*ayed to god almyty, for skafhes[2]   *[2 for skathes.]*

þ*at* þei deden

hys medyn

be dayes & be nyȝt,   16

god bad hem flen & gon out of eue*r*y manesse syȝt.

d*omin*u*s* deus sabaot, emanuel, þe gret gods name,   *By the Lord God of Sabaoth,*

I be-tweche þes place from ratones & from alle oþ*er*   *Emanuel, I clear this place from rats, and all other shame.*

  schame !

god saue þis place fro alle oþ*er* wykked wytes

boþe be dayes & be nytes ! & in no*min*e p*at*ris &

  filii, &c.

[FOLLOWS : S 8.   GOOD MEDICEYN P*OUR* LE DROPESY, &c.]

Twelve Points for Purchasers of Land to Look to.

[*Fol.* 203, *col.* 1, *MS. Lambeth* 306.]

Who-so wylle be ware of purchassyng,
Consydre theese poyntes folowyng :—

.1. Fyrst, se that the lande be cleere,

.2. And the tytle of the sellere,

.3. That it stonde in no dawngeer

Of no womans doweere;

.4. And whethir the lande be bonde or free,

.5. And the leese or releese of the feoffe.

.6. Se that the seller be of age,

.7. And whethir it be in any morgage;

.8. Looke if ther-of a tayle be fownde,

.9. And whethir it stonde in any statute bownde;

.10. Consydre what seruyce longyth ther-to,

.11. And the quyterent that there-of owte shall goo :

.12. And yf thou may in any wyse

Make thy chartyr on warantyse

To thyne heyres & assygnes all-so,

This shall a wyse purchasser doo :

And yn tenne yere, if ye wyse bee,

ye shall a-geyne youre syluer see.

Marginal notes:

See that your land is free

from women's dower,

and from mortgage and entail.

Look to the quit-rent,

and have a conveyance in fee.

In ten years your land will bring back your purchase-money.

Like thy Audience, so utter thy Language.

TWO VERSIONS.

1. MS. Univ. Lib. Camb. Hh. 4. 12, leaf 82.

2. Harl. MS. 2255, leaf 1.

Lyke thyn Audience, so vttyr thy Langage.

(BY LYDGATE.)

[*MS. Univ. Lib. Camb. Hh.* 4. 12, *leaf* 82.]

(1)

I Counsell, what-so-euer thow be   1
  Off polycye, forsight, and prudence,

If thou wilt live in peace,

Yf yow wilt lyffe in pease and vnite,
  Conforme thiself and thynk on *this* sentence,   4
Whersoeu*er* thow hold[1] residence ;
  Among woluys be woluysch of corage ;

like thine audience utter thy language.

A leo*u*n w*ith* leonnys ; a lambe, for Innocence ;
  lyke[2] thyn audience, so vttyr thy langage.   8

(2)

¶ The vnicorne is cawght w*ith* maydyns song,   9
  By disposic*i*on, record of scripture ;

With cormorants, make thy neck long;

w*ith* cormerant*es* make thy nekke[3] long
  In pondys depe thy pray to recouere ;[4]   12

among foxes, be foxish.

Among foxys be foxische of nature ;
  Among rauenours[5] thynk for ávantage ;
w*ith* empty hand men may no hawk*es* lure,
  And like thyn audience, so vttyr thy langage. 16

(3)

With holy men, talk holiness;

¶ W*ith* holy men speke[6] of holynesse,   17
  And w*ith* a glotyn be delicate of thy fare ;[7]
W*ith* drownkyn men, do surfett*es* by excesse,
  And among wasters, no spendyng that þou spare ; 20

A. = Addit. MS. 34,360.   [1] That . . holdist A.
[2] And lyke A.   [3] nekke A, nek L.   [4] prayes to recure A.
   [5] Raveyers A.   [6] trete A.   [7] welfare A.

Lyke the Audience, so uttir thy language.

(*Harl MS.* 2255, *leaf* 1. 15 *Stanzas of eights   abab bcbc.*)

**Consulo, quisquis eris / qui pacis federa queris,
Consonus esto lupis / cum quibus esse cupis.**

(1)

I Conseyl, what-so-euyr thou be   1
     Off policye / forsight and prudence,
   Yiff thou wilt lyve in pees and vnite,
Conforme thy sylff / and thynk on this sentence   4
Wher-so-evere / thou hoold residence.
    Among woluys / be woluyssħ of¹ coráge,
Leoun with leouns / a lamb for Innocence,
   Lyke the audience / so vttir² thy languáge.   8

(2)

¶ The **Vnycorn** / is cauħt with maydenys song   9
  By dispocicioun / récord¹ of¹ scripture ;
With **Cormerawntys** / make thy nekkë long,
   In pondys deepe, thy prayës to recure ;   12
  Among ffoxis / be ffoxissħ of¹ nature ;
    Among ravynours / thynk, for ávauntage,
  With empty hand / men may noon haukys lure ;
   And lyke the audience / so vttir thy languáge. 16

(3)

¶ With hooly men / spekë of¹ hoolynesse ;   17
  And with a glotoun / be delicat of¹ thy ffare ;
With dronkë men / do surfetys by excesse ;
  And among wastours, no spendyng that thou spare ;

With wodcokk*es*, lerne for to dare;   21

with pillagers
sharpen thy
knife.
   And sharp thy knyfe w*ith* pilowrs for pilage;

like the market, so praysë thy chafare;[1]

   And like thyn audience, so vttyr thy langage.   24

(4)

¶ W*ith* an ottyr, spare ryuer none, ne ponde;   25

With ferrets, rob
rabbit burrows;
   w*ith* hem that fyrrettyth, robbe conyng herthys;[2]

A blode-hounde, w*ith* bowe and arow in honde,

Mawgre the wache of fosters and parkerrys.   28

[leaf 82, back]
with thy fellows,
spare not thy life.
like thy felishyp, spare no dawngers,

   For lyfe ne dethe, thy lyfe to[3] putt in morgage

Among knythys, squyrys, chanownys, monk*es*, frerys,

   like thy audience, so[4] vttyr thy langage.   32

(5)

Remember
Daniel's case,
¶ Daniel lay,[5] a prophet full notable   33

   Of god, pres*er*uyd in prison w*ith* lyouns;

Where god list spare, a tygre is not ve*n*geable,

No cruel best,[6] berys, nor grifonys;   36

and fear not to
be in caves with
dragons.
   And yf[7] thow be in cavys w*ith* dragownys,

   Remembre how Abacuk browght þe potage

So ferre to danyel, thorow many regionys;

   As case requirith,[8] so vttyr thy langage.   40

(6)

With wise men,
talk of Wisdom;
¶ W*ith* wise men talke of sapience,   41

   w*ith* philosophers speke of philosophye;

w*ith* schipmen, sailyng, that haf exp*er*ience,

In trobly sëys[9] how they schall hem guye;   44

with poets, of
poetry;
but be not pre-
sumptuous.
And w*ith* poetys talk of poe*t*ry;

   Be not pres*um*ptuose of chere ne of[10] visage,

But where thow cu*m*myst in any cu*m*pany,

   like thyn audience,[11] so vttyr thy langage.   48

---

[1] ware A.   [2] feret .. kunnynggers A.   [3] to *om.* A.
[4] so A, *om.* T.   [5] callid A.   [6] Nor no cruel bestis
[7] though   [8] Thus like thyn audience   [9] sees A.
[10] of, *om.* A.   [11] as case requyrith A.

With woodëcokkys / lernë for to dare ;   21
  And Sharpe thy knyff / with pilours, for piláge :
Lyke the markét / so preysë thy chaffare ;
  And lyke the audience / so vttre thy languáge. 24

(4)

¶ With an Otir / spare Ryveer noon, nor pond̓ ;   25   [leaf 1, back]
  With them that forett / robbë conyngerys,—
A bloodhou*n*d, with bowe & arwe in hond̓,—
  Mawgre the wacħ / of⸵ fosterys and parkerys.   28
  Lyke thy felaship / sparë no daungerys
    For lyff nor detħ / thy lyff put in morgáge
  Mong knyħtës, squyers / chanou*n*s, monkës, fryers :
    Like the Audience / vttir thy languáge.   32

(5)

¶ Danyel lay / a p*r*ophete ful notáble,   33
  Of⸵ god preservyd / in prysou*n* with lyou*n*s :
Where god lyst spare / a Tygre is nat vengáble,
  No cruel beestys / Berys nor Gryffou*n*s ;   36
  And yif⸵ thu be in Cavys with dragou*n*s,
    Remembre how Abácuk / brought the potage
  So ferre to Danyel / to many regïou*n*s :
    As caas requerith / so vttre thy languáge.   40

(6)

¶ With wysëmen / talkë of⸵ Sapience ;   41
  With philisóphres / speke of⸵ philosophie ;
With shipmen seyleng / that haue exp*er*ience
  In troubly sëis / how thay shal hem guye ;   44
  And with Poëtys / talke of⸵ Poetrye ;
    Be nat to presumptuous[1] / of cheer nor of viságe,
  But where thou comest in ony companye,
    Like the audience, so vttir thy languáge.   48

---

[1] 'presumptuous' stands for one foot.

(7)

¶ Thys lityll ditty concludyth in menyng,   49
Who that cast hym thys reule for to kepe,

In everything
conform to thy
company,

Mot conforme hym like in euery thyng,
Where he shall byde, vnto the[1] felyshype :   52
w*ith* wachemen wake, w*ith* sloggy folk*es*[2] slepe
w*ith* wode men wode, w*ith* frentyke men[3] sauage ;

and like thine
audience utter
thy language.

Renne w*ith* bestys, w*ith* wyldë[4] wormys crepe,
And like the[5] audience, vttyr thy[6] langage.   56

(8)

¶ Among all these, I counsell the[7] take hede   57
Where thow abydyst or rest[8] in any place.

[leaf 83]
But love God, and
fear to trespass
against Him.

In chefe, loue god, and w*ith* þi loue haf drede,
And be fereful, agayne hym to trespace :   60
w*ith* vertuose folk[9] encresë shall þ*i* grace ;
And viciose men[10] arn cause of gret damage ;
In euery feliship so for þ*i* self purchace
Where ve*r*tu regnyth, there[11] vttyr thi langage. 64

(9)

Be content with
little.

¶ Be payed[12] w*ith* litell, content w*ith* suffisance ;   65
Clyme not to hygh, thus byddyth[13] socrates,
Glad pouert is of tresours[14] most substance ;
And Catoñ seyth, is[15] none so gret encrese   68

Peace is of more
worth than
money.

Of worldly tresowr*e*, as for to lyve in pease,
Which among ve*r*tues hath þe vasselage ;

Diogenes told
Alexander

I takë record of[16] diogenes,
which to Alysaund*er* had thys langage :—   72

(10)

¶ Hys palace was a lytyl poore tonne,   73
Which on a whelë he gan w*ith* hym cary,[17]

to get from
between him
and the sun.

Bad thys emp*er*owr*e* 'ryde out of hys sonne,'
which[18] demyd hymself richar than kyng dary ;   76

[1] Thy A.   [2] men A.   [3] men A, *om.* C.
[4] wyld C, wielde A.   [5] thyn A.   [6] hys C, so vtter thy A.
[7] Among . . the A, Mong . . ȝit C.   [8] Restis A.   [9] man A.
[10] folk A.   [11] so A.   [12] pleased A.   [13] saith A.   [14] of tresoure is A.
[15] there is A.   [16] to recorde . the philosofre Diogenes A.
[17] with hym he dide A.   [18] MS. wihch

(7)

¶ This litel ditee / concludith in menyng,   49   [leaf 2]

  Who that cast hym / this rewlë for to kepe,

Not conforme hym / lyke in euery thyng

  Wher he shal byde / vnto the felashipe :   52

  With wachmen, wake / with sloggy folk*is*, sleepe ;

    With woodmen, wood / *with* frentyk folk, saváge ;

  Renne with beestys / with wildë wormys creepe,

    And like the audience / vtter' thy languáge.   56

(8)

¶ Mong allë thes / I counceyl yit take heed   ^{Verba trans-
latoris}

  Wher thu abydest / or reste in any place :

In cheef', loue god' / and with thy love ha dreed,

  And be feerful / a-geyn hym to trespace :   60

  With vertuous men / encrecë shall thy grace ;

    And vicious folk / arn cause of' gret damáge ;

  In euery Felaship / so for thy silf' purcháce :

    Wher vertu regnyth / thu vttir thy languáge.   64

(9)

¶ Be paied with litel / content with suffisaunce ;   65

  Clymbe nat to hih / thus biddith Socrates :

Glad pouert / is of' tresowr*es* most substau*n*ce ;

  And **Catou***n* seith / is noon so greet encres   68

  Off wordly tresour*e* / as for to live in pees,

    Which, among vertues / hath the Vasselage,

  I takë record / of' **Diogenees,**

    Which to **Alisaundre** / had this languáge :— 72

(10)

¶ His paleys / was a litel poorë tonne,   73   [leaf 2, back]

  Which, on a wheel / with hym he gan carye ;

Bad this Emperour' / ride out of' his sonne,

  Which dempt hym-sylf / richer' than kyng **Darye,**

kept w*ith* hys vesaile from wynd*es*[1] co*n*trary,   77
Where-in he maad daily hys passage ;

He cared not for princes,

Thys philosophre w*ith* pr*i*nces list not[2] tary,
Ne in their*e*[3] pr*e*sence to vttyr noo langage.   80

(11)

¶ A-twene theis tweyn a gret co*m*pariso*n* :   81
kyng alysaund*er*, he co*n*querryd a*ll* ;

though he lay in a tub;

Dyogenes lay in a sma*ll* dongeon,[4]
In sondre wedyrs which[5] turnyd as ba*ll* ;   84

and soon Fortune gave Alexander a fall.

Fortune to Alisaund*er* gaf a sodayne fa*ll* ;
The philosophre despised hys coig*n*age,
he thowght v*er*tu was more imp*er*ia*ll*,
Than   hys   aquayntance   w*ith*   a*ll*[6]   hys   prowd
langage.   88

(12)[7]

[leaf 83, back] Antony and Paul despised riches,

¶ Antonye and poule despised a*ll* richesse   89
lyuyd in desert of wilfu*ll* pouert ;

while Cæsar and Pompey brought cruelty about.

Cesar and pompey of martia*ll* wodnesse,
By theyr enuyose co*m*passyd cruelte,   92
Twene germany and affrik was gret en*m*yte ;
Noo co*m*p*er*ison twene good grayne and forage ;
Prayse eu*er*y thyng like to hys degre,
And like þ*e* audience, so vttyr þ*i* langage.   95

(13)

I saw a picture armed with virtues,

¶ I founde a liknesse depict vpon a wa*ll*,   97
Armyd in v*er*tues, as I walkyd vp and downe,
The hede of thre, fu*ll* solempne and roiall,
Intellect*us*, memórye, and resoune ;   100

with eyes and ears of discretion, mouth and tongue avoiding detraction,

w*ith* eyne[8] and erys of clere discrec*i*on,
Mowth and tongge avoydyng a*ll*[9] outrage,
A-gayne the vice of fals detracc*i*on,
To do no surfett in word ne in[10] langage ;   104

---

[1] vessel . from wynde most A.   [2] the prince . list nat to A.
[3] Not in his A.   [4] tonne A.   [5] Like s. w. A.
[6] his grete riches . for al A.   [7] This st. left out by A.
[8] yen A.   [9] to-avoyde al A.   [10] in A, *om.* C.

Kept with his vessel / fro wyndis moost cont*r*arye, 77
 Wherin he madë / daily his passáge.
This philisóphre / with pryncys lyst nat tarye,
 Nor, in the*r* presence / to vttre no languáge. 80

(11)

¶ Attwen thes tweyne / a greet comparysou*n* : 81
 Kyng **Alisaundir**ᴵ / he conquéryd al;
Diogenes / lay in a smal dongou*n*,
 Lyke sondry wedrys / which turnyd as a bal. 84
 Fortune to **Alisaundir**ᴵ / gaffᵗ a sodeyn Fal;
  The philisophre / disposed his coignage ;
 He thouħt vertu / was moor Impe*r*rial
  Than his acqueyntau*n*ce / with al his proud
   languáge. 88

(12)

¶ Antonye and **Poule** / dispisid al richesse ; 89
 Lyved in desert / of wilful poverte.
Cesar and **Pompey** / ofᵗ ma*r*cïal woodnesse,
 By the*r* Envïous / compassyd cruelte ; 92
 Twen **Germanye** / and **Affryk** / was gret Enmyte.
 No compa*r*isoun / twen good greyn and Forágc ;
 Preise euery thyng / like to his degre,
  And, lyke the Audïence / so vttir thy languáge. 96

(13)

¶ I fond a lyknesse / depict vpon a wal, 97
 Armed in vertues / as I walk vp and dou*n* :
The hed ofᵗ thre / ful solempne and Roial,
 Intellectus / **Memórye** / and **Resou***n*, 100
 With eyen / and Erys / ofᵗ cleer' discrecïoun :
  Mouth and tonge, avoiden al outráge
 A-geyn the vice / ofᵗ fals detraccïou*n*,
  To do no Surfet / in woord nor in languáge. 104

(14)

hand and arms

¶ Handys[1] and armys with thys discrecion, 105
Where[2] so man haf[3] force or febilnesse,

giving help,

Treuly to mene in hys affeccïon ;

following
Righteousness,

For[4] ffraude or fauour, to folow ryghtwisnesse ; 108
Entrailys, inward deuocïon with mekenesse.

far surpassing
Pygmalion's
image.

Passyng pigmalion, which grauyd hys ymage,
Prayd to venus, of louers chef goddesse,
To grant it lyfe and qwiknesse of langage. 112

(15)

May Christ make
such an image in
our conscience

¶ Off hole entent pray we to crist ihesu, 113
To qwik[5] a figure in owre conscience :
Reason as hede, with membres of vertu
A-forne rehersyd breuely in sentence, 116
Vndir support of hys magnificence.
Crist list so[6] gouerne owre worldly pilgremage,

that to His con-
tent we may utter
our language.

Twene[7] vice and vertu to set a difference,
To hys plesaunce to vttyr owrë[8] langage. 120

EXPLICIT.

[1] Handis A, Hand' C. [2] Whether A. [3] had A.
[4] from A. [5] quykene A. [6] so list A. [7] Atwene A.
[8] his A.

(14)

¶ Hand and armys / with this discrecioun,   105
  Wher'-so man hauë / force or Febilnesse,
Trewly to meene / in his affeccioun,
  For fraude or favour' / to folwe riħtwisnesse,   108
  Entrailes inward / devocioun with meeknesse
    Passyng **Pigmalioun**[1] / which graued his ymáge,
  Prayd to Venus / of' lovers / cheef' goddesse,
    To graunt it lyff' / and quyknesse of' languáge. 112

(15)

¶ Of' hool entent / pray we to Crist ihe*s*u   113
  To quyke a figure / in our' conscïence :
Reson as hed / with membris of' vertu
  A-forn rehersyd / breefly in sentence,   116
  Vndir support / of' his magnificence.
    Crist so lyst governe / our' wordly pilgrymáge
  Tween vice and vertu / to sette a difference,
    To his plesaunce / to vttren our languáge.   120
                                              Ex*plic*it.

        [1] 'Pigmalioun' stands for one measure.

[The next Balade of Lydgate's against false Bakers
and Millers is put in to fill the blank page at the back
of this, tho' it's only a fragment. It happens to be the
last leaf of this Harl. MS. 2255, and so, just handy.]

Put thieving Millers and Bakers in the Pillory.

[*Harl. MS.* 2255, *leaf* 137 *and last.*]

[*Harleian Catalog* ii. 594, on MS. 2255, art. 45. The conclusion of some Ditty (not now easily to be found out) in three Stanzas . . . These Stanzas plainly set forth the Punishment inflicted upon thievish Millers and Bakers, by putting them not only into the Tumbrell, as of old, but into Wooden Bastile, as Hudibras says, by which, in this place is not to be understood the Stocks, but a Superior and more Conspicuous Machine, called the Pillory.]

(1)

Put out the rogue's head.	¶ Put out his hed / lyst nat for to dare, 1
	But lyke a man / vpon that tour to a-byde,
Shy eggs at him,	For Cast of eggys / wil not Oonys spare,
	Tyl he be quaylled / body, bak, and syde ; 4
and gild his head.	His heed endooryd / and, of¹ verray pryde,
Put out his arms :	Put out his Armys / shewith abrood his face,
the holes are wide.	The fenestrallys / be made for hym so wyde,
	Cleymyth to been / a capteyn of¹ that place. 8

(2)

This bastile belongs to false Bakers.	¶ The bastyle longith / of¹ verray dewë ryght, 9
	To fals bakerys / it is trewe herytage,
	Severall to them / this knoweth euery wyght,
	Be kynde assyngned / for their sittyng stage, 12
	Wheer they may freely / shewe out ther visage
	Whan they take oonys / there possessïoun,
	Owthir in youthë / or in myddyl age :
Don't take 'em out of it.	Men doon hem wrong / yif¹ they take hym doun.

(3)

Let Millers and Bakers form a Guild,	¶ Let mellerys and bakerys / gadre hem a gilde, 17
	And alle of¹ Assent / make a fraternite ;
and build a Chapel under the Pillory.	Vndir the pillory / a litil Chapell bylde,
	The place amorteyse / and purchase liberte 20
	For allë thoo / that¹ of¹ ther noumbre be,
	What-evir it coost / afftir that they wende,
	They maÿ cleyme / be Iust auctorite,
There they should be hangd.	Vpon that bastile / to make an ende. 24
	Explicit, quod Lydgate /

(86) Proberbys of Howsholde-kepyng.

[*Lambeth MS.* 306, *fol.* 64 ; ? ab. 1530 A.D.]

THE DOCTRYNALL P*R*INCYPLIS & P*R*OVERBYS YCONOMIE, OR HOWSOLDE KEPYNG, SENT FRO*M* SAYNT BERNARDE, VNTO RAYMONDE, LORDE OF AMBROSE CASTELL*E*.

(1) Attende that if thy charg*is* of thy houce & thi Rent*is* be egaH, A soden chavnce may sone distroye the of yt.

(2) A Ruynoys houce is the state of a negligent man.

(3) The neglygens of a Ruler ys compared vnto a gret fyre bry*nn*y*ng* vp-an a houce.

(4) Peyse wisely the besynes & the purpose of them wich a*m*mynyste*r* thy goode*s.

(5) To hym that is in the wey of poverte, & not fully power, it is lesse shame to spare, than vtterly to fawle.

(6) It is wysdome, ofte to se thin owne goodis, how they ben*e* dysposid.

(7) Chargeabyl mariag*is* cawse hurte w*ith*oute wurshyp*e*.

(8) Charge or expense for chyvalrye is wurshypfuH.

(9) Charge for helpyng of frendys is resonabyl.

(10) Charge for helpyng of wasters ys but losse.

(11) Consyder the mete & the drynke of thy bestys, for though they hungyr, they aske not.

(12) Feede thi howce w*ith* groce, & not w*ith* delycate meete.

(13) The glotone onethis chaungyth hym before his deth.

(14) Glotony of a vyle neglygent ma*n* is but corruptio*u*n.

(15) Glotony of a besy ma*n* is to hym a solace.

(16) Feede thy howce at pry[*n*]cipalle festes, plentevosly, but not delycatly.

(17) Make a plee betwyx glotony and thy pursse. Nevyrthelesse be ware to which of thise two thow be advocate, or what sentens thou geue betwyx them, for glotony hath effectuaH wytnes.

(18) The pursse aH-so provith evidently for hyr, be cofrys & celerys wastyn*g*e.

(19) Thow demyst a-mysse a-gens glotonye, whan covetyse byndʒith or knyttith thy pursse.

(20) Covetyse shaH nevyr deme ryght be-twyx glotonye & the pursse, For ¹covetyse is distroyer of hym selfe.

(21) Covetise is not ellys, but evyr in powre lyving, and evyr to be a-ferde of poverte.

(22) The covytous man lyvith ryght wysli in him selfe, in that he lesith not, but kepith to othirs advayle. Bettyr it is, to kepe for othir, than to leese in hym selfe.

(23) In Plente of corne, desyre no derth ; for he that lovith it, is a dystroyer of power men.

(24) Sel thi corne at a lowe price, & not whan yt may not [be] bought of powre men : Not oonly to thy neyghbours, but aIlso to thyne enmyse, for litel pryce ; for ofte the enmy is easelyer ven-quysied w*ith* ser*u*ice than w*ith* stroke of swerde.

(25) Pride ageynste frende or neyghboure, is as a bath where men feer the thondyr strooke.

(26) Be ware of straungers while thou haste an enmye, & se weH to his wayes.

(27) Debylite of an enmye is no sure peace, but truce for a seasoñ.

(28) Iffe thou suppoce the sure whiH thou haste an enmye, thow puttyst thi sellfe in peryH.

(29) Be not curyous to wete or knowe what thin suspect wome*n* do. Thow shalte nevyr be curyd if thowe oonys knowe the cryme of thyne owne true wyfe.

(30) In heryng of othir mens wyfes, thow shalte aswage the sorwe of thyn owne.

(31) A nobyH and a wurshipfuH hert nevyr askyth of womens dedys.

(32) Thowe shalte bettyr chastise a shrode wyfe w*ith* myrthe, then w*ith* strokes or smytyng.

¹ leaf 64, col. 2.

(33) An olde commyn woman, if the lawe woulde suffyr, shulde be buryed quyke.

(34) A costefull clothe is tokyn of poverte.

(35) A sity garment is yrkesome to neybors.

(36) Pleace with thi dedys rathir than with thy clothis.

(37) A woman havyng clothis, & evir desyryng mo, lakkyth stedefastnes.

(38) Holde hym thy bettir frende, [1]that rather geuith his goodys, than hym whiche offerth the his persoone.

(39) Holde not [him] thy Frende that praysith the, present.

(40) Yiff thow cowncel thy frende, folowe reason, & not his plesure.

(41) Sey not to thy frende "do thus," but "me thynkyth thow mytyste do thus"; For yf ought fall a-mysse, thowe mayste soner be blamyd, than shuldyst be thanckyde yf thy councel avaylede.

Nota. Se what folowth to them that love mynstrels.

(42) A man that Intendyth to mynstrels, shall soone be weddyd to poverte, & his sonne shall hyte derisioun.

(43) Iff mynstrels pleace the, feyne as thow herde them, but thynke vppone a-nother.

(44) He that lawith at a mynstrels worde, gevith to hym a wedde.

(45) Rebukyng mynstrels ben well wurthy dethe.

(46) Instrumentis of mynstrelsy seldome doth pleace god.

---

(47) Put from the a proude servaunte, as hym that shulde be thy enemye.

(48) Allso repelle that seruavnte that vsith to blaundysh the.

(49) Wythstande the seruaunte that praysith the, for ellys he thynkyth the for to deceyve.

(50) Loue that servaunte as thy childe, that sone is ashamyde.

(51) Yf thou wilte bylde, let necessite induce the ther-to, and not luste of howsynge.

(52) Covetyse of byldyng, in bildyng is not lessid.

(53) Inordynat[2] bildyng causith hasty sale of placys.

[1] leaf 64, back.   [2] MS. In inordynat.

(54) A performyd towre & a baare cofyr make, ovyr late, the greate bilder wyse.

(55) Sel thyne howce to hym [1] that wyll geue moste.

(56) Bettir it is to suffyr greate hungyr than sale of patrymonye.

(57) Selle no parte of thyne heritage vnto thy bettyr, but for lesse pryce selle yt to thy subiecte.

(58) What is vsure, but venyme of patrymonye, and a lawfull thefe that tellyth ys entent.

(59) By right nought with felawshippe of thyne bettyr.

(60) Suffyr patiently thy power felowshippe, & coople the not to the strawnger.

(61) Evyr-lastyng god oonely ys sobyr yn plente & scarsnes of wynes.

(62) Drunkeshippe doyth ryght nought evynly, but whan yt ovyrthroughith.

(63) Yf thow felyst stronge wynes, fle felyshippe : seke slepe rathir than talkyng.

(64) The drunke man with wordys accusith his owne excesse.

(65) It besemyth not a yonge man to be A tasteoure of wynes.

(66) Fle & estchue A leche that is drunkelewe.

Nota.   (67) Be ware of that leche which by the woulde take experyens howe he myght hele a-nothir.

(68) Smale whelpes, leeve to ladyse & clerkys. [See *Wyclif*, E.E.T.S., 1880, p. 12.]

(69) Waker howndes been profitable.

(70) Howndes of venery coste more then they aveyle.

(71) Make not thy sonne, stuarde of thy goodys.

(72) Say not in thy selfe, ' what a-vaylith all doctryne, yf fortune lyste not to favoure ? ' I haue seene folys leevyng contyngence, accuse them-selfe infortunat, of whom the wyse man seledom complaynith.

(73) Wyse laboure & myshappe seldom mete to-gyder, but yet sluggednes & myshappe be seldome dyssevyrde.

(74) The slugge lokyth to be holpe [2] of god that commawndyth men to waake in the worlde.

(75) Peyse the eese of thyne expence with the laboure of thy getynge.

---

[1] leaf 64, back, col. 2.   [2] leaf 65.

(76) Commytte thyne age [to] thy god rather than to thy sonne.

(77) In dysposyng thy legatys [*sic*], pay firste thy servannt*is*.

Nota. (78) Co*m*mytte not thi soule to swych as loue thy p*er*sone, but rather to them which loue her owne sowles.

(79) Dispose thi goodys or sykenes take the.

(80) He that is a s*er*uaunt to sykenes, may no testament make.

(81) Free, theerfore, & in helth̄, make thowe thy testament.

(82) Here what thi chyldern wyħ doo aftyr thy deth̄. P*er*aventure thei seke departysion of ther heritage.

(83) If thi chylderne ben*e* gentilmeñ, it ys bettyr they be dyvydid in the worlde, then her heritage shulde be deuydide.

(84) Yff thi childryn be laborers, let them do as th[e]i wyħ.

(85) Yf thei be merchauntes, dyvision of heritage is bettyr than co*m*mvnion, that the infortune of oone hurte not the other.

(86) Iff the mothir of them seke to be maride, she doth folyly, and, woulde god, in-to the bewailyng of her, for her trespas, she myght be weddid to a yonge mane, For suche oone shulde sone caste her a-way & co*n*sume her goodes, and so oone cuppe of sorowe shulde be comvne to the*m* bothe.

[*Follows:* The list of Books proscribd on the 1st Sunday of Advent, 1531, p. 62.]

𝕿𝖍𝖊 𝕳𝖊𝖎𝖌𝖍𝖙 𝖔𝖋 𝕮𝖍𝖗𝖎𝖘𝖙, 𝖔𝖚𝖗 𝕷𝖆𝖉𝖞, &𝖈.

[*Lambeth MS.* 306, *fol.* 203, *col.* 2.]

THE LONGITUDE OF MEN FOLOWYNG.

Moyses .xiij. fote & viij ynches & di*midium*.

Cryste .vj. fote & iij ynches.

O*ur* lady .vj. fote & viij ynches.

Crystofer*us* .xvij. fote & viij ynches.

Kyng Alysaund*er* .iiij. fote & v ynches.

Colbronde .xvij. fote & ij ynches & di*midium*.

Syr Gy .x. fote. iij ynches & di*midium*.

Seynt thomas of Caunterbery .vij. fote saue a ynche.

Long Mores, a ma*n* of yrelonde borne, & s*er*uaunt to kyng Edward the iiijth .vj. fote & x. ynches & di*midium*.

[Printed in *Reliquiæ Antiquæ*, v. 1, p. 200, with Ey for Gy, and " half" for the contraction *di*.]

List of 30 Books Proscribed in 1531.

[*MS. Lambeth*, 306, *fol.* 65, *col.* 2.]

Memorandum, the firste sonday of Advent in the yere of our lorde Mᵗ fyue hundreth & xxxi^{th}, these Bokes folowyng' were opynly, at poules crosse, by the autorite of my lorde of london vnder his Autentycal seale, by the doctor that that day prechide, prohibite, and straytely commaunded of no maner of man to be vsed, bought, nor solde, nor to be red, vnder payne of suspencioun, and a greter payne, as more large apperyth in for-sayde autoryte.

The first boke ys this,

.1. The disputacioñ betwixte the fathyr and the soñ.

.2. The Supplicacioñ of beggars. [Extra Series XIII., E. E. T. Soc., 1871.]

.3. The Revelatioñ of^t Antechriste.

.4. Liber q*ui* de voti & novicio deo inscr*ibitur*.

.5. Pre Precaciones.

.6. Economica christiana.

.7. The burying of the masse *in* english, yn ryme.

.8. An Expositioñ in-to the vij^{th} chapt*er* to the Corinthians.

.9. The Matrimony of Tyndal*e*.

.10. A. B. C. ayenst the Clergye.

.11. Ortulus anime, in Englissħ.

.12. A Boke a-yenst saynt Thomas of Caunterbury.

.13. A Boke made by freer Roye ayenst the sevyn sacrament*is*.

.14. An Answere of Tyndal vnto *sir* Thomas Mores Dyaloge, yn englisħ.

.15. A Disputacion of Purgatorye, made by Iohn Fryth.

.16. The Firste boke of Moyses called Genesis.

.17. A pr*o*loge in the ij^{de} boke of moyses, called Exodus.

.18. A prologe in thyrde boke of Moyses, called Leviticus.

.19. A prologe in the iiij^{th} boke of Moyses, called Nvmeri. [leaf 65, bk.]

.20. A prologe in the vth boke of Moyses, called Detronomye.

.21. The Practyse of Prelates.

.22. The Newe testament in englissh, *with* a Introductioñ to the Epistle to the Romaynes.

.23. The Parable of the wyked ma*m*monde.

.24. The Obediens of A Chrysteñ man.

.25. A boke of thorpe or of Johñ Oldecasteħ.

.26. The Some of Scripture.

.27. The Prymer in Englissh.

.28. The Psalter in Englissh.

.29. A Dyalog betwixt the gentylman and the plowmañ.

.30. Ionas In Englissh.   And aħ other suspect bokes, bothe in Englissh and in laten, as weħ now pr*i*nted or that here-after shaħ be pr*i*nted, and not here afore namyd.

A Tale of Ryght Nought.

[*Egerton MS.* 1995.]

There was a man that hadde nought ;
There come theuys & robbed hy*m*, & toke nought :
He ranne owte, and cryde nought.
Why shoulde he crye? he loste nought.
Here **ys** a tale of ryght nought.

A Medicine to Restore Nature in a Man.

[*Lambeth MS.* 306, *leaf* 65, *back*, *col.* 2.]

Put three Chick-
ens in a coop.

Soak some wheat,

collect snails with
shells,

or black slugs,
and boil them
with the wheat;

then take out the
wheat,

and feed the
Chickens with it
and bread, and
the snail-water.

Eat a chicken
every two days.

Take iij Chekyns or .iiij. as ye lyke, & put them in a coope to feede, as I shaH teche you. Fyrste take a quantyte of whete, & put yt in clene watyr, & then gadyr a good quantyte of Snayles that beer howses on them, & put them therto as they be, shelles & aH; and yf ye canne fynde no soche snayles, thanne take blak snayles, and so thanne boyle aH these to-gyder, the whete & the snayles in water, w*ith* the shelles of them that haue shelles; & for lakke of them that haue shelles, boyle the blakke snayles. And whan it is weH boylid to-gedyr, th*en* take oute the whete by hym-selfe, & the watyr by hym-selfe, & caste awey the shelles & the corruptyon of the snaylles; And w*ith* that whete fede the checons, and w*ith* brede a-monge, And let them drynke of the watyr, & of none other watyr. And when ye be dysposyd, ete a Chekyñ, one day rostyd, And ij dayes aft*er*, a-nother, & so contynue as ye fynde yt doth you good.

Pr*o*batum est.

[*Ibid.*]

For to Dystroy a Wrang Nayle, otherwyse callyd a Corne.

Take wylde tansey, and grynde yt, and make yt neshe, & ley it therto, and it wyl bryng yt owght.

Of the Seats of the Passions.

[*Lambeth MS.* 306, *fol.* 118, *at foot.*]

The bones in a man ben in nombre .ij C. xvij. The
veynes ben .iij. C. lxv. The tethe in p*er*fyte Age
.xxxij. The mynde is in the Brayne. The vndyr-
stondyng in the fronte. The Ire in the gawle. Auaryce in
the kydney. Loue in the harte. Brethyng in the lownges.
Gladnes in the splene. Thought in the harte. Blode in
the body. Hope in the sowle. The mynde in the spyrit.
The harte in the mynde. The Feyth in the harte.
And cryst in the feyth. And whylth it noryssh the
body, it is cawlyd A*n*ima, the sowle. This worde
A*n*ima hath many significacions, for when it is in con-
templacyoñ, it is sayde a spyrit, **Spiritus**. And when
it savyrtħ, it is saide Reson or wytte, **Anim***us*. And
when it felith, it is sayde felyng, **sensus**. And when
it vnderstondyth, it is callyd mynde, **Mens**. And when
it demyth, it is called **Reson, Racio**. And when it
co*n*sentyth, it is callyd **wylle, Voluntas**. And when
it recordytħ, it is sayde **mynde, Memoria**.

Men have 217
bones, 365 veins,

32 teeth.

The Mind is in
the spirit.

Anima
means
spirit,
wit,
feeling,
mind,
reason,
will,
memory.

A Greeting on New Year's Morning.

[*Lambeth MS.* 306, *leaf* 136, *back.*]

(1)

Iuellis pricious cane y none fynde to Sell   1
    to sende you, my Souerein, þis newe yeres morowe,
wher-for, [for] lucke and good hanssell,
    my hert y sende you, & seynt Iohn to borowe,

    that an C yeres wi*th*outon) adue*r*ssit[e] & Sorowe   5
      ye mowe live : y pray to god þat ye so moote,
      And of all your Dessires, to sende you hastely bot.

(2)

Beseching you, Dere heret, as Enterly as y cane,   8
    to take en gre this poure gifte Onely for my sake,

as is the custome, & hath ben ma[n]y a Day,
    Oo frend to a-nother yeve and take.
Riche is it nat, grete boste of to make,   12

    Saue an hert is reme[m]bratyf to you in eu*er*i
      stound*e*
      the whiche pe*r*isschide ones, yet grene is þe wonde.

(3)

That it be youres, trewely it is my liste ;   15
    my possesioon and my parte þer-of y denye ;
and as towcheing to þis olde worlde called 'hadywiste,'
    Vnto my lives ende ful y Deffie.

palaman gafe his herte to emely ;   19
    He fuched it no better, ne repentide it les
      thanne y do of this gifte, god y take to witnes. 21

(4)

my purpos hathe ben longe my hert thus to chast,   22

  And til this yeres day y ne durst for schame.

men sei that no thinge is so free as gyfte,

  And to take it ayene y were fulle to blame ;   Never will I take it again

    But as in that deffaute y wille not lese my name, 26

      So that y yeue ones be yeve for euermore,

      For this hath loue and trouth y-lerned me þe lore,

        Euermore without chaung for eu*er*

        til body and soule parte and disseuer*e*.   30   till body and soul dissever.

To my Heart's Joy.

[*Lambeth MS.* 306, *leaf* 137.]

(1)

My heart's Joy ! My hertes Ioie, all myn hole plesaunce,   1
    whiche that y sarue, and schall do faithfully
    with treue Entente and humble obseruaunce
    you for to please in that y cane treuely,
May this verse and I   besechinge youe, this litil biH and y   5
    may hertely, with som plesaunce & drede,
find favour with you, the Flower of Beauty.   be Recomaundide moste specially
    vnto you, the floure of goodely-hede.   8

(2)

And yf ye liste to haue knoweliche of my part,   9
Though well in body, I am ill in heart   I am in hel, god thanked mote he be,
    as of body, bute treuely nat in herte,
till I see you.   nor nat schaH be til tyme y may you see ;
    but thynketh that y as trewely will be he   13
    that for youre Ease schaH do my pouer' & my3te,
    And schaH be your' Deffence in all aduerssite
    As though that y were dayly in your' sight.   16

(3)

I write no more to you, for lacke of space,   17
I pray the Trinity to keep you in all adversity,   but y beseche the holy trin[i]te
    you kepe and save, be sopporte of his grace,
    and be youre Deffence in aH aduerssite.
    go, litil bill, and say thoue were with me,   21
    this same day at myne vp-Ryssinge,
    where that y be-sought god of merci
    tho to haue my Souereiñ in his kepeing.   24

(4)

for I am only yours,   As wyssely god me save
    as y am onely yours,
and will be at all hours.   what payne so euer y haue
    And will be at all owres.   28

To my Lady Dear.

[*Lambeth MS.* 306, *leaf* 138.]

(1)

Frische flour of womanly nature,	1 Fresh flower, fair to see,
ye be full gentill and goodly one to se,	
And all so stedfaste as any criatur	
that is lyuynge in any degre,	
fullfyled' with all benyngnete,	5 fulfilled with all benignity,
And an Exsample of' all worthynes,	
And they that to you haue nessesite	
be gracious euer thorough your gentilnes.	8

(2)

But y am so bowndon), y may nat stert,	9 to you am I bound.
to you complaynyng in this manere,	
Besechinge you euer with myn enterly hert,	
And humbly also y you Requer,	I pray you
As that bethe onely withowten pere	13
of goodely-hede and of assuraunce,	
y that am yours, whethe[r] ye be fare or' ner,	put me not out of your Remembrance.
Reffuse me nat oute of' your Réme[m]braunce. 16	

(3)

Concedire, ladi dere, of' your pete,	17 [leaf 138, back] Consider my distress,
the highe complaynt of my desses,	
my gref and myn) aduerssite !	
ye be my bote þat may me best please ;	
schewe me your meke sprite in my desses,	21 and show your sweet soul to me.
for other louer' haue y none,	
And euer' y well be Redy youe for to plesse,	I am yours alone,
neuer none to haue bute you alone.	24

(4)

never to part till Death.

None but you, lady and maistras,   26

fro whos herte with lyue myn may no disseu*er*,

so faste it is lokyn̅ in þe locke of̄ stedfastnes

that in your s*er*uice it schaħ abide for eu*er*.

Cure me of my pains.

ye wete weħ my woo ye may recouer*e*;   29

my paynes to Rellis may non bute yee,

my lyfe And deth̅ lithe in you euer,

Right as it plesithe you to save or to flee.   32

I care but to please you.

lothe to offende ! so y may my lady pleas,

welcome payne, And Fie one esse !

[On the next folio (139), "Her begyneth the Retenewe of the
dowty kynge k Edward*e* the thirde, and howe he went to the
sege of Callis with his Oste," etc.]

Unto my Lady, the Flower of Womanhood.

[*Lambeth MS*. 306, *leaf* 137, *back*.]

(1)

That pasaunt Goodnes, the Rote of all vertve,   1
  whiche Rotide is in youre femynete,
whos stepes glade to Ensue.

  ys eueri woman in their degre !
  And sethe that ye are floure of bewte,   5
    Constreyned y am, magre myn hede,
    hartely to loue youre womanhede.   7

All are glad to follow you, the Flower of Beauty.

(2)

Your sade, Demewre, appert, goueronance   8
  Of eliquens prengnavnt sauns coloure,
So it Renyth in my Rememberaunce
  that dayly, nyghtly, tyde, tyme, and owre,
  hit is my will to purches youre fauoure,   12
    whiche, wilde to Crist I myght atteyn,
    As ye of all floures Are my Souerayn.   14

Your staid soft speech

runs so in my mind

that would to Christ I might attain your grace.

(3)

Whan Reste And slepe y shulde haue noxiaH,   15
  As Requereth bothe nature and kynde,
than trobled are my wittes aH,
  so sodeynly Renyth in my mynde
  your grete bewte ! me thynketh thaṅ y fynde   19
    you as gripyng in myn armes twey ;
    Bute whan y wake, ye Are away.   21

All night

my wits are troubled by your Beauty.

I seem to grip you in my arms, but you are gone.

(4)

Entirmet this with woo And gladnes,   22
　　bothe Ioye and sorowe in woo memoraƚƚ,

I seem to see your likeness, but it is fancy: for than me thynkithe y see your' likenes :
　　Hit is nat so, it is fantasticaƚƚ ;
　　the whiche my herte with þe swarde mortaƚƚ   26
and I shall die. 　　that nothinge is, saue uery Dethe,
　　my wette is thynne, so schortithe my breth.   28

(5)

[leaf 138] But, lady mine, Nowe, lady myn, in whomë Vertus Alle   29
　　ar Ioined¹, and also comprehendide,
as ye of¹ al women y call moste principaƚƚ,
think on my grief lette my gref¹ in youre herte be entenderde,
remember my love; love me again, as God and Nature will. And also my veri treue loue Rememberde,   33
　　And, for my treve loue, ayene me to loue,
　　As welethe nature, and god that setithe Above. 35

(6)

Go, verse, and tell her Go litiƚƚ bill, with all humblis,   36
　　vnto my lady, of womanhede þe floure,
how Troiles anew lies in distress— and saie hire howe newe troiles lithe in distreȝ
　　All onely for hire sake, and in mortaƚƚ langoure ; 39
　　And if sche wot nat whoo it is, bute stonde in erore,
her old love, loving her alone. 　　Say it is hire olde louer¹ þat loueth hire so trewe,
　　hire louynge a-lone, not schanginge for no newe. 42

EXPLICIT.

¹ The word looks like *loli* in the MS., but *u*, with the contraction for *er*, is written the same way at the end of *disseuer*
(p. 70, l. 26), showing that *lou*er is the right reading here.

Bewte will Shewe, thow Hornys be Away.

(A LITELLE SHORT DITEY AGAYNE HORNES.)

(9 stanzas of eights, *abab, bcbc.*)

[*MS. Univ. Lib. Camb. Hh.* 4. 12, *leaf* 84 *a, collated
with Harleian* 2255, *leaf* 6.]

(1)

Of god and kynd procedyth aH beaulte ;
   Crafte may shew a foreñ apparence,
But nature ay must haf þe soueraynte.
   Thyng countirfetyd[1] hath non éxistence ;
   Twene gold and gossomer is gret difference ;
     Trewë metaH requirith non alay ;
   vnto purpóse by clere experience,
     Bewtey wiH shewe, thow hornys be[2] away.

All true beauty is natural.

Counterfeits have no real existence,

and beauty needs no horns.

(2)

¶ Riche attyrys of gold and [of] perry,
   Charbunclys, rubeys of most excellence,
Shew in derknes lyght, whereso[3] þey be
   By their natural heuenly influence ;
   Doblettes of glasse yeue a gret euidence,
     Thyng countirfet wyl failen[4] at assay ;
   On thys mater, concludyng in[5] sentence,
     Bewte wyH shew, thow hornes be[6] away.

Gold and precious stones, carbuncles, and rubies, shine by their own light.

Glass counterfeits can be detected.

(3)

¶ Aleyn remembryght,[7] hys cómplaynt who[8] list see,
   In hys boke of famose eloquence ;
Cladd aH in flowris, and blossummys[9] of a tre,
   he saw Nature in hyr most excellence,

Remember how Aleyn tells us that he beheld Nature arrayed in a kerchief only,

---

[1] countirfet H.   [2] wer H.   [3] wher so H., whersouer C.
[4] faylen H., faile C.   [5] in H., no C.   [6] were H.
[7] remembryth H.   [8] who H., whoso C.   [9] blosmys H.

Vpon hyr hede a kerchef of valence,   21
None othyr riches of countyrfet aray ;

Texemplifye by kyndly prouidence,
Bewte wyꞁ shew thow hornys be[1] away.   24

(4)

¶ Famose poëtys of antiquite   25
In Grece and Troy, renowmyd[2] of prudence,

Wrote of qwene Helene, and Penolope,
Of Policene with hyr chast innocence ;

ffor wyfys trew caꞁ Lucrece to presence ;   29
That they were fayre, ther can no man say nay,
kynd wroght hem with so gret[e] diligence,

Theyr' bewte cowde shew,[3] thow hornys were cast
away.   32

(5)

¶ Clerkës record by gret auctorite,   33
hornys wer gyffe to bestis for diffence ;
A thyng contráry to feminite,
To be mad sturdy of résistence ;

But archwyfès,[4] eger in ther violence,   37
fferse as a[5] tigre forto make affray,
They haf despite, and agayne conscïence,
list not, of pride, theyre hornys cast away.   40

(6)   Lenvoye (H. *om.* C.)

¶ Noble princesse,[6] thys litell short ditey,   41
Rudely compilyd, lat it be none offence
To ȝowre womanly mercifuꞁ pyte,
Thow it be radd in ȝowr' audience.

Payse euery[7] thyng in ȝowre iust áduertence.   45
So it be no displesance to ȝowre pay,

Vndir support of ȝowr' pacïence,
Yeueth example hornes to cast away.   48

---

[1] wer H.   [2] remowmyd C., renoumyd H.   [3] bewte couthe H.
[4] arche wyves H.   [5] a *om.* H.   [6] pryncessys H.
[7] Peysed ech H.

(7)

¶ Grettest of vertues is humilite, 49   Solomon says,
    As Salamon sayth, soñ of Sapience,   humility is the
 greatest of
Most was accepted[1] to the deite.   vertues.

    Take hede here-of, gefe[2] to thys word credence,   Observe too how
    How Maria, who had a preeminence[3] 53   Mary, when she
 lay at Bethlehem,
      Aboue aH women, in Bedlem whan she lay,   wore no rich
 clothing, and bare
    At Cristis byrth, no cloth of gret dispence,   on her head only
 a kerchief, and no
      She weryd a keuerche; hornys were cast away. 56   horns.

(8)

¶ Of byrthë[4] she was hyghest of degre, 57   She was one to
 whom angels did
    To whom aH angelles did obedience,   obeisance;
Of Dauides lyne, which sprong out of Iesse,
    In whom aH verteu is,[5] by iust conuenience
Made stable in god by gostly confidence. 61
      a rose of price,
      This rose of Jerico, ther growith non such in May;   such as grows not
 in May;
    Pure in spirite, parfite in pacïence,   and all horns
 of pride she put
      In whom aH hornys of pride were put away. 64   away from her.

(9)

¶ Moder of Ihesu, myrrour of chastite, 65   [leaf 85]'
      Mother of Jesu,
    In word nor thowght that neuer did offence;   true pattern of
 virginity!
Trew examplire[6] of virginite,
    Hede-spryng and weH of parfite continence!
 Was neuer clerk, by retoryk or[7] science, 69   No clerk can re-
 hearse her virtues.
    Cowde aH hyr verteus réherse to þis day.
 Noble princesse,[8] of meke beniuolence,   Noble princess,
 take example by
    By example[9] of hyr, ȝowre hornys cast away. 72   her, and cast your
 horns away.

¶ Explicit.

[1] acceptyd H., accept C.   [2] yeuyth H.   [3] premynence H.
[4] birthe H., byrth C.   [5] vertues H.   [6] Trewe exemplaire H.
[7] nor H.   [8] Pryncessys H.   [9] Bexample H.

["This Ballad," says Mr. Halliwell (who printed it in his
edition of Lydgate's *Minor Poems*, p. 46-9), "has been printed
by Sir Harris Nicolas, and in the *Reliquiæ Antiquæ*. The
present version is from MS. Oxon. Laud. D. 31, N. 683, Bernard,
798; other copies are in MS. Rawl. Oxon. C. 86; MS. Bibl.
Coll. Jes. Cantab. Q. Γ. 8, fol. 27; MS. Harl. 2255; MS. Voss.
Lugd. 359; and the first four stanzas in MS. Harl. 2251." It
was reprinted in the Percy Society's *Satirical Songs and Poems
on Costume*, 1849, with a woodcut of a woman in a horned
bonnet on p. 52.]

The Parliament of Love.

[MS. Univ. Lib. Camb. Ff. 1. 6, leaf 51.   Handwriting of the
15th century.]

What so euyr I syng or sey,
My wyH is good too preyse here weH.

Now ȝee that wuH of loue lere,
I counseH yow þat ȝe cum nere ;
To teH yow now is myne entent,

Houth loue made late his parleament,   4
And sent for ladyes of euery londe,
Both mayde, and wyfe þat had housbonde,
Wythe gentyH wymmen of lower degre,
and marchauntz wyfes grete plente,   8
Wythe maidenes eke þat where theym vndre,
Of wyche there were a rygthe grete numbre.

And aH tho men þat louers were
They had there charge for too be there,   12
And when they were assembled aH,
(yf I the werre sothe sey schaH),
with-in a casteH feyre ande stronge,
And as y lokyd them amonge,   16

I sawe a ryȝth grete cumpany
of gentiH-wummen that were there by,
The whyche, as the custum was,
Songe a balad stede of the masse   20
For goode spede of thes folkys aH
þat where assemblede in the haH ;

and yf ȝe lyst ley too yowre ere,
Rygh[t] thys they songe, as ȝee schaH heyre.   24

" O god of loue ! wyche lorde hart and souereyne,
Send downe thy grace a-monge thys louerys aH,

Soo þat þey may too thy mercy ateyne.
At thys parlament most in Asspeciaŀl ;
as þou art oure Iuge, so be egaŀl
Too euery wygth þat louyth feythefully,
And aftyr hys dyssert grante hym mercy ! ”

28   lovers in this parliament may succeed as they deserve!”

And whan this songe was songe and done,
Then went these ladyes eueryschone
Vn-too A schambyr where they scholde
Take theire places, yong and olde,
like as þat they where of astate
For tescheue aŀl maner debate.
There sawe I first the goddesse of loue
In here see sitte, rigth ferre aboue,
And many othyr þat ther where.
yitt for too teŀl whom y sawe there,
It passit now rigth ferre my wytte ;
But, among aŀl, I sawe one sitte
whiche was the feyryst creature
þat euer was furmyd by nature ;
and here beaute now too dyscryvye
Ther can noo mannes vyttes alywe.
yett as ferre as y can or may
Of[1] here beaute sum-what too say,
I wiŀl applye my wittes aŀl ;
For here I am & euyr schaŀl
Too speke of schape and semelynessé,
Off stature & of goodlynesse ;
here sydes longe with myddyŀl smale,
here face weŀl coulord and not pale,
With white and rode ryth weŀl mesuryd ;
And ther-too schee was well emyred,
And stode in euery mannes grace,
This goodly yong and fresche of face ;
and too speke of condicion,
Coude noo man fynde in noo regioɲ

32   [leaf 52]
Then all the ladies took their places for the debate.

36

Venus sat in her seat far above.

40

One lady I especially noticed,

44

whose beauty no man's wit can describe.

48

But I must try and describe her if I can.

52

Her sides were long, her middle small, her face well-coloured,

56

[leaf 52, back]
and every man admired her.

60

[1] MS. Oof.

One of soo grete gentillnesse,
Of curtaise and lowlynesse,
Of chere, of port, and dalyaunce,   64
And mastres eke of aᴫ pleasaunce ;
Aᴫ-soo weᴫe of secretenesse,
The werray merroure of stedfastnesse.
Of onest merth sche cowde rith mosche,   68
Too daunce and synge and othre suche ;
Soo well assuryd in here hert,
That none il worde from here scholde stert.
And thus on here y set my mynde,   72
And left aᴫ othre thyng by-hynde
As touchyng too these louers aᴫ,
whysche on here causes fast kan caᴫ.
and for too teᴫ theire aᴫ cumplayntes,   76
In sothe too me the matire queynte is ;
For as too hem i toke none hede.
But in myne nowne[1] causes[2] to prosede,
I drowe me by [my] sylf allone,   80
And into a corner gan too gone,
And there I satte me downe a while,
A litle biᴫ for too compile
Vn-too thys lady wych was soo faire,   84
and in her doyng soo debonaire.
And if ye list too hyre & rede,
Theffect of whych was thus in dede :—

[*The little Song.*]

" O souereyn[3] prince of aᴫ gentillnesse,   88
      Too whom I haue and euyr-more schaᴫ bee
Trewe seruant with aᴫ maner humblenesse ;
      What peyne I haue or what aduersyte,
yett ȝee schaᴫ euyr fynde suche feyth on me   92
         þat I schaᴫ doo that may be your plesaunce,
      If god of his grace list me so a-vaunce.

Marginal notes:
- There was none so gentle, courteous,
- agreeable,
- and true.
- Gay she was, and danced and sang,
- and no ill word escaped her lips. On her I set my heart,
- and withdrew into a corner
- to compose a 'litle songe' to [leaf 53] my lady fair,
- which was to this effect,—
- "Sovereign Prince of all gentleness, whom I have ever truly served,
- whatever trial comes, you shall ever find me true.

---

[1] *Sic* in MS.   [2] *Sic* in MS.   Read 'cause.'
[3] MS. soueuereyn.

" And yow I pray, as lowly as I can,

    Too take my seruice if hyt myth yow please ;   96

And if ȝee list too reward thus yowre man,

    Than mygth hee say he were in hertis easee ;

    For by my trouth y wulde not yow displease   99

    For aħ the goode þat euer I hadde or schaħ,

    By my goode wille, what euer me be-faħ.   101

I pray you humbly, accept my service, and if you please to reward me, then my heart will be at ease.

" And if I haue seide any[1] thynge amysse   102

    Too pardoñ me I yow be-sech and pray ;

For as wischli as euer y cum too blisse,

    My will is goode what euer y write or say."

Pardon anything I have said amiss,

for indeed my will is good."

Go, thow litle songe, thow hast a blisfuħ day ;   106

    For sche þat is the floure of wommanhode

At her oown leyser schaħ the syng and rede.   108

Go, happy song, the Flower of Womanhood shall sing and read you.

[1] MS. my.

[*La Belle Dame sans Merci*, p. 80. See on this, Prof. Skeat's Introduction, Text, and Notes, in his pseudo-Chaucerian pieces, vol. vii. (1897) of his edition of Chaucer's Works, pages li.-lv., 300—326, 517—520, and H. Gröhler's earlier notice of Sir Richard Ros in *Englische Studien*, x. 206, and his dissertation "Ueber Richard Ros' mittelenglische ubersetzung des gedichtes von Alain Chartier, La Belle Dame sans Mercy," Breslau, 1886. Nichols, in his county history of Leicestershire, ii. 37, says that the Sir Richard Ros, who was presumably the poet, was born in 1429, and is known to have been alive in 1450, when he was 21 years old. The date of his englishing is probably about 1460. As the family of Roos or Ros were lords of Hamlake and Belvoir in N.E. Leicestershire, not far from Grantham in Lincolnshire, and Bourne, whence Robert of Brunne gets his name, Prof. Skeat (p. liii.) says there was something of a Northern element in Sir Richard's language, as shown by his ryme *longès* with *songès* in ll. 53–5, and his use of the Northern possessive pronoun *their*. This leaves little doubt that the Trinity manuscript's *awn* (ll. 455, 475, 608) for *own*—which Prof. Skeat adopts, no doubt from Thynne—is Sir Richard's own form of the word. The Harleian text of the poem, which I printed in our first issue of the *Polit., Rel. and Love Poems*, was copied from a MS. of which the leaves had been misplaced, as I found when comparing it with Chartier's French, at Prof. Skeat's request, on Jan. 21, 1895. He had none of the editions of Chartier, ab. 1490, 1526, 1527, 1617, etc., at Cambridge.]

𝕷𝖆 𝕭𝖊𝖑𝖑𝖊 𝕯𝖆𝖒𝖊 𝖘𝖆𝖓𝖘 𝕸𝖊𝖗𝖈𝖎

englisht by Sir Richard Ros from the French of Alain Chartier.[1]

[*MS. Ff.* 1. 6, *University Library, Cambridge* (U), *leaf* 117.]

[Collated with MS. R. 3. 19, Trin. Coll., Camb. (T),
and Harleian 372, leaf 61 (H).]

Prologe [*by Sir R. Ros, in* 4 *stanzas of Sevens, ababbcc.*]

(1)

Half in a dream	Halfe in a dreme, not fully well a-waked, 1
	The golden slepe me wrapt vndir his wyng
I rose,	yet nat[2] for-thy I rose,[3] *and* welny naked,
and suddenly remembered	All sodenly my-selfë Rémembryng
	Of a matér, leuyng all othir thyng 5
that I was bound	Which I schuld do, wi*th*outen more delay,
	ffor hem[4] þe which[5] I durst nat dysobbey. 7

(2)

to translate the	My charge was þis,[6] to *tr*anslat by *and* by, 8
	(All thyng foryif[7]), as part of my penaunce,
Belle Dame sanz Mercy, that Aleyn (Chartier), Secretary to the King of France, wrote. I stood a while	A boke callëd "la belle dame sans mercy,"
	which maister Alayn made, of Rémembraunce,
	Chefe secretary wi*th* the kyng of fraunce. 12
	And here-vpon, a while I[8] stode musynge,
	And in my-selfe gretly ymagynynge 14

(3)

	What wyse I schuld *p*erfourme þis said *pr*ocesse, 15
considering my want of skill, and, on the other hand, the strait command laid on me:	Consideryng, by go*d*e a-vysëment,
	Myn vnkonnyng *and* my gret[9] symplesse,
	And ayeynward, þe streyt co*m*maundëment
	which þat I hade ; *and* þus, in myn entent, 19
	I wasse vexid, *and* turnyd vp *and* doun ;
	yet att the last, as In conclusyoun,[10] 21

---

[1] Œuvres de M. Alain Chartier, 1617, p. 502. The heading
in H is "La Belle Dame sanz Mercy, translated out of French
by S*i*r Richard Ros." [2] UH not, *om.* T. [3] arose UH.
[4] hyr T, them H. [5] UT, to whom H. [6] UH, thus T.
[7] foryeuyn T, forgiven H. [8] I UH, *om.* T.
[9] UT, *om.* H. [10] HT, conclusy U.

(4)

I cast my clothës on, *and* went my way,—   22   [leaf 117, back]
     This forsaid charge hauyng in rémemb*r*aunce,—   so I put on my
     clothes, and
Til I cam to[1] a lusty grene valey   walkt to a lovely
     green valley, full
     fful of floures ; to se, a grete plesaunce ;   of flowers, fair
     to see.
     And so, bolded[2] w*ith* þair benyng suffraunce   26   And, by them
     made bold,
       That Rede[3] þis boke, touchyng þis[4] said matere,
       Thus I bygan,[5] iff h*i*t please yow to here :   28   I begin.

(5. *The Poem, in 50 stanzas of eights, ababbcbc.*)

Not long ago, Rydyng an[6] esy paas,[7]   29   Not long ago
     I fill in þought, of ioy full desperat,
W*ith* gret disease *and* payn, so þat I was   I was the most
     unfortunate of
     Of all louérs þe most vnfortunat,   lovers,
     Sith by[8] his dart most cruell, full of haat,   33
       þe[9] dethe hath[10] take my lady *and* maystres,   Death having
     slain my Lady.
     And left me sole, thus[11] discom*fort* *and* mate,
       Sore languischynge, *and* in way of distresse.   36

(6)

Then said I þus: h*i*t falleth me to cesse,   37   Then I said
     I must stop
     Eyþer to ryme, or dytes for to make ;   making ditties,
And I, seurly,[12] to make a fulle p*r*omesse
     To laughe no more, but wepe in clothës blake.   must laugh no
     more, but weep;
     My ioyfull tyme, alas ! now is h*i*t[13] slake,   41   my joyful time
     is gone.
       ffor in my selfe I fele no maner ease ;
     lat hit by[14] wryten, siche fortune I take,
       which neyther me, nor doth non other,[15] please.

---

[1] UT, into H.   [2] UH, voldyd T.   [3] UH, to Rede T.
   [4] UT, the H.   [5] begynne H.   [6] UH, on a T.
   [7] N'agueres cheuauchant pensoye,
     Comme homme triste & douloreux,
     Au dueil où il faut que je soye
       Le plus dolant des amoureux ;
     Puis que, par son dart rigoureux,
       La mort me tolli ma Maistresse,
     Et me laisse seul langoureux
       En la conduiste de tristesse.
         Œuvres de M. Alain Chartier, 1617, p. 502.
[8] UT, with H.   [9] UH, *om.* T.   [10] UH, Det hath fro me T.
[11] UH, thys T.   [12] UH, yet therw*ith* T.   [13] UH, hit is T.
[14] be H, by U (by is an allowable spelling, but apt to confuse
     a reader).   [15] UH, non other doth T.

(7)

Iffe h*i*t wer so,[1] my will or myn entent   45
     wer cónstreynëd a ioyfull thyng to wryte,
my penne couth neu*er* hauë[2] knolege what h*i*t ment ;
     To speke þerof, my tunge hathe no delyte ;
     And w*ith* my mouth, iffe I laugh myche or lyte,   49
        Myn yne schuld make a countynaunce vntrue ;
        Myn hert also wold haue þerof despyte ;
          the wepyng terës haue so large issue.   52

(8)

Thes seke louers, I leue þat to hem longes,   53
     whiche lede þair[3] lyfe in hope of állegeaunce,[4]
þat is to say, to make balade[5] or songes,
     Eu*er*yche of hem, as þei fele her[6] grevaunce ;

ffor sche þat wasse my ioy *and* my plesaunce,—   57
     whos soule, I pray god of his m*er*cy saue,—

Sche hath myn wyle, my hertës ordeynaunce,
     which lithe w*ith* hir vnder her toumbe in[7] graue.

(9)

ffro þis tym forthe, tyme is to hold my pees ;   61
     It weryth[8] me þis mater for to trete ;

lat other louers put hem selfe in prees ;
     Thair sesou*n* is ; my tym is now[9] for-yete ;

ffortune, by[10] strenght, þe forser hath[11] vnschete,   65
        Wher-in wasse sparde[12] all my worldely[13] Rychesse,
        And all þe goodys which þat I haue gete,
          In my best tyme of youth *and* lustynesse.   68

(10)

Loue hath me kept vndir his gou*er*naunce :   69
     Iffe I mysdid, god gr*a*unt me for-yifnesse !

---

[1] UH, so that T.   [2] neuer have U, haue no T, haue H, with 'neuer know' in margin. [Neuer = ne'er.]   [3] her HT.
[4] Fr. *allegement.*   [5] UH, baladys T.   [6] theyr T, þer H.
[7] in H, y T, & U. Which lyeth here, within this tombe ygrave. Skeat, from 3 MSS.   [8] werieth H.   [9] UH, nygh T.
[10] UT, with H.   [11] UH, hath the forser T.
[12] H, *margin : text* spradde ; sperryd T, spred U.
[13] H, wordely U.

Iffe I did well, yit felt[1] I no plesaunce ;
  hit caused neither ioy nor[2] hevynesse ;
ffor when sche dydë, þat wasse[3] my maistresse,   73   When my mistress died, all my welfare ceased.
  All my[4] welfare then made[5] þe sam purchasse ;
þe deth hath set my boundis, of wytnesse,[6]
  which for no thyng myn hert schall neu*er* passe.

(11)

In þis gret þought, sore trowbled in my mynde,   77   Thus in great trouble I rode alone,
  Allon þus rode I[7] all þe morow tyde,
Tyll, at þe last, hit happed me to fynde
  The place wher-In I cast me to a-byde,[8]
when þat I had no ferþer for[9] to ryde.   81
    And as I went, my loggyng to purvey,
Ryght sone I herd, but lytell me be-syde,   but soon I heard minstrels playing
    In a gardyn, wher mynstrells gan to play.   84   in a garden.

(12)

W*ith* þat anon I went me bakkermore ;[10]   85   I drew back,
  My selfe *and* I, me þought we wer Inow ;
But tweyn,[11] þat wer my frendis her-byfore,[12]   but two old friends saw me,
  had me espiëd, *and* I wot[13] not how.
    Thai cam for me : aweyward I me drow,   89
    Su*m*-what by force, su*m*-what by þair request,
That in no wyse I couthe[14] my selfe rescow,   and made me come in and
  But[15] nede I must cum In, *and* se þe fest.   92   see the Feast.

(13)

At my co*m*myng, the ladyse eu*er*ychon   93   [leaf 119] The Ladies bade me welcome,
  Bade me welcom, god wot, ryght gentilly,
And made me cher*e*, eu*er*ych by on *and* on,
  [16]A gret dele better þen I wasse worthy ;
  [16]And, of þair grace, schewd me gret courtesy   97   and showed me great courtesy,

---

[1] UH, fele T.   [2] UH, causeth no but T.
[3] whyche was T, that was H, þat wasse all U.
[4] HT, My gode U.   [5] UT, made then H.
La mort m'assist illec la bourne.   [7] H, I rode T, rode & U.
[8] UT, I purposid me to hide H.   [9] UT, forth H.
[10] Si me retray.   [11] UH, y. T.   [12] UH, tofore T.
[13] UH, wyst T.   [14] UH, cowde T.   [15] HT, bud U.
[16] These lines transferred in Trinity MS.

that I might not
mourn.

with good disport, by cause I schuld not morne.[1]

That day I bode[2] still in þair cumpany,

which wasse to me a gracyous soiourne.   100

(14)

Tables were
spread;

The boordës wér spred in ryght[3] lytell space ;   101

The ladyse sat, eche as hem semyd best.

the servants were
pickt men,

were[4] non þat dide seruyse[5] with-In þat place,

But chosen men, ryght of þe goodlyest ;

And sum þer were, paraunter[6] most[7] freschest,   105

and I saw judges,
sitting solemn,
regarding no one.

That saw þair Iuges syttyng full demure,

without semblant, oþer[8] to most or lest,

Not with standyng[9] þai had hem vndur cure.   108

(15)

One there was
who lookt as if
entranced,

Among all oder, on I gan aspye,   109

which in gret thought full often cam and went,

As on[10] þat had bene rauysched vttirlye,

In his langage not gretly dylygent ;

Hys countynaunce he kept with gret turement,   113

But his desir far passed his resoun,

his eye seeking
his Love at every
turn.

ffor euer his yie[11] went after his entent

ffull many a tyme, when hit wasse no sesoun.   116

(16)

[leaf 119, back]

To make gud chere, ryght[12] sore hym selfe he payned.[13]

And outwardly[14] he feyned gret gladnesse ;

They made him
sing,

To syng also, by force he wasse constrayned,

ffor no plesaunce, but[15] verrey schamfastnesse ;

but the tone of
his sadness came
unsought into his
voice.

ffor the compleynt of his most hevynesse   121

Cam to his voyce alway with-out request,

lyke as þe sown of byrdës doth expresse,[16]

when þai syng lowd, in fryth or in[17] forést.   124

---

[1] UH, mone T.   [2] UH, abode T.   [3] UH, full T.
[4] were H, wher U, Ther were T.   [5] UT, þat serued H.
[6] parauenture H.   [7] more T, *om.* H.   [8] UH, eyþer T.
[9] UH, But not . . T.   [10] UT, man H.   [11] ey T, yee H.
[12] UH, full T.   [13] he peyned H, payned U, he feynyd T.
[14] UT, outeward H.   [15] UH, for T.   [16] UH, doutles T.
[17] in UT, *om.* H.

(17)

Othir þer wer þat serued in the halle, 125
　But non lyke hym, as after[1] myn avyse ;
ffor he wase pale, *and* sumwhat lene *with*-all ;　　He was pale and
　his speche also tremlyd[2] in ferefull wyse ;　　lean, his speech
　　　　　　　　　　　　　　　　　　　　　　　　faltered,
And euer allon, but when he dyde seruyse. 129
　All blake he ware, *and* no deuyse but playn ;
Me þought by hym, as my wyt couth[3] suffyse,　and I saw his
　hys hert wasse no thynge[4] in his awn demayn. 132　heart was not
　　　　　　　　　　　　　　　　　　　　　　　　his own.

(18)

To feste hem all, he did his dilygence ; 133
　And wel he couth,[5] ryght as h*i*t semyd me ;
But euermor when he wasse in p*r*esence,
　his chere wasse do,[6] it wold non other[7] be :
his scolemaystres[8] hade siche autoryte, 137　His mistress had
　That, all the while he stode[9] still in þᵉ place,　such power over
　　　　　　　　　　　　　　　　　　　　　　　　him that he could
Speke couth[10] he nat ; but vpon her beaute　not speak, but
　he lokyd still, *with* Ryght[11] a pytous face. 140　only gaze on
　　　　　　　　　　　　　　　　　　　　　　　　her beauty.

(19)

W*it*h þ*a*t, his hede he tu*r*ned attë[12] laste, 141　[leaf 120]
　ffor to biholde þe ladies eue*r*ychon ;　　Others he might
　　　　　　　　　　　　　　　　　　　　　　　　turn to,
But eue*r* in one he sette his ye[13] stedfaste　but she drew back
　On hir, þe which his þought was most[14] vppon ;　his eyes.
And of his yen,[15] the shot[16] y knewe anon, 145
　Which federid was *with* right humble requestis.
Then to my self y seyd, 'by god allon,
　Sich on was y, or that y[17] sawe þese gestes.' 148

(20)

Out of the prees he went full esily, 149　He went out to
　To make stabill his heuy contynaunce ;　　recover his coun-
　　　　　　　　　　　　　　　　　　　　　　　　tenance,

---

[1] hym . . H, hym for soth to T, as after U.
[2] UH, he spake also tremblyng T.　　[3] UH, wyll cowde T.
[4] UH, then not T.　　[5] couthe H, cowde T.　　[6] UH, done T.
[7] UH, no bettyr T.　　[8] scole-maister UH, scolemaystres T.
[9] UH, that while he bode T.　　[10] coude H, cowde T.
[11] UH, ryght with T.　　[12] at the T.　　[13] ey T.　　[14] UH, euer T.
[15] yen H, eyen T.　　[16] UT, sight*e* H, [Fr. *trait*].
[17] or y that y U, I that there H, I or euer y T.

And wite ye wele, he sighëd tenderly

ffor his sorowes *and* wofull rémembra*un*ce.

Then in hym self he made his ordyna*un*ce,　153

　　And forth-w*ith*-all cam to bryng in the mes;

But, for to Iuge his[1] moste rewfull semblaunce,

God wot it was a petous entremes.　156

(21)

After dynér, anone they hem avaunsed　157

To daunce aboute, these[2] folkës eu*er*ychon;

And forth-w*ith*-all þis heuy lover[3] daunced,

　Sumtyme w*ith* tweyne, *and* su*m* tyme but w*ith* on:

Vnto hem all, his chere was after[4] on,　161

　Now here, now there, as fill by áuenture;

But eu*er* among,[5] he dr*ow* to hir allon,

　Which he most dredde,[6] of lyuyng crëature.　164

(22)

To myn avise, god[7] was his p*ur*uiaunce　165

When he hir chase[8] to his maystres allone,

If þat hir herte were sette to his plesa*un*ce

As moche as was hir beauteous p*er*sone;

ffor who þat eu*er* setteth[9] his trust vppon　169

　þe réporte of thair yen, w*ith*outen[10] more,

he myght be dede, and grauen vnder a[11] stone,

Or eu*er* she[12] shuld, his hertis ease restore.　172

(23)

In hir faylëd no thyng, þat y couthe[13] gesse[14]　173

O wyse nor other,[15] pryue nor apert;[16]

A garnyson[17] sche was of all goodnesse,[18]

To make a frounter[19] for a louers herte;

---

[1] UH, But to beholde with T.　[2] UH, the T.
[3] louer HT, *om.* U.　[4] UH, euer T.　[5] among HT, anone U.
[6] UH, louyd T.　[7] good H.　[8] UH, chose T.
[9] sett H, wyll set T.　[10] UH, such oon then w*ith*out T.
[11] *om.* HT.　[12] UT, he H.　[13] as I koude H, þat I cowde T.
[14] En la dance ne failloit riens
Ne plus auent ne plus arriere
[15] On vice ner othir H, In any wyse nether T.
[16] or perte H, ne perte T.　[17] UH, gramyson T.
[18] UH, goodlynesse T.
[19] Fr. *frontiere*, front rank (make an attack on).—Skeat.

Right ȝonge and fressh, a woman full couert ;   177
 Assured wele[1] hir port, *and* eke hir chere,
Wele[2] atte hir ease, wi*th*outen wo or smert,
 All vndirnethe the standart of daungere.   180

she was young, fresh, and well at her ease.

(24)

To se the fest, it weryd me full sore ;   181
 ffor hevy ioye dothe the herte sore[3] t*r*auaylle.
Out of the prees y me wi*th*drow therfore,
 And sette me down allon, behynde a trayll
ffull of leuès, to se, a gret me*r*vayll :   185
 wi*th* grene wythies ybounden[4] wundirly ;
 The leues were so thik, wi*th*outen fayll,
  That thoroughout myght no man me[5] aspye.   188

I withdrew from the press, and sat down behind a screen of leaves so thick that no one could see me.

(25)

To his lady he cam full curteysely,   189
 Whan he[6] þought tyme to daunce wi*th* hir a trace ;
Sith in an herber made full plesauntly
 Thei rested them, fro thens but lytill space ;
Nigh hem were non, a certeyn of compace,[7]   193
 But onely they, as fer as y couthe se ;
And safe[8] the trayll, there y[9] hadde chose my place,
 Ther was nomore betuyxt hem tweyne[10] *and* me.

[leaf 121]

The lady and her lover came and rested in an arbour, all alone,

with the leaf-screen between them and me.

(26)

I herde þ*e* louer sighyng wondir sore ;   197
 ffor ay þe ner, þe sorer it hym sought ;[11]
his[12] inward payn he couthe[13] not kepe in store,
 Nor[14] for to speke, so hardy was he nought ;
his leche was nere, þe gretter was his þought ;   201
 he mused sore, to conquere his desire,
 ffor noman may to more pen*au*nce be brought,
  þen in his hete to bryng hym to þe fire.   204

The Lover sighed,

but could not speak at first,

---

[1] UH, wele wi*th* T.   [2] UH, went T.
[3] sore the herte T, soore the hurte H.   [4] UH, ybounde full T.
[5] UH, man T.   [6] UH, he hy*m* T.   [7] UH, certeyn space T.
[8] saue HT.   [9] UH, there as T.   [10] UH, ij. T.
[11] UH, thought T.   [12] UH, whos T.   [13] UH, cowde T.
[14] ne HT.

(27)

þe herte began to swelle wit*h*yn his chest,   205

so anguisht was his heart,

   So sore streynëd for anguysh and for payn,

That all to pecis almost it to-brest,

   When bothe at ones, so sore it did constrayn ;

and his longing so restraind by shame.

Desire was bold, but shame it gan[1] refrayn ;   209

   þe ton[2] was large, the tother[3] was full cloos ;

No lytyll charge was leyd on hym,[4] certeyn,

   To kepe such ware,[5] *and* haue so many foos.   212

(28)

[leaf 121, back]

fful often tyme to speke, hym self he payned,[6]   213

   But shamefastnes *and* drede seid eue*r* ' nay ; '

But at last he addrest the Lady,

yit atte the last, so sore he was constreyned,

   When he full longe hadde putte it in delay ;

To his lady, right thus then gan he[7] say   217

   Wit*h* dredfull voys, wepyng, halfe in a rage,

" Black the day that I first saw you !

" ffor me was p*ur*ueied an vnhappy[8] day

   Whan y first hadde a sight of youre vysage !   220

(29)

My pain nearly kills me,

" I suffre peyn, god wot, full hote[9] burnyng,   221

   To cause my dethe, all for my trew se*r*uice ;

And y se wele, ye reche[10] therof nothyng,

and you take no heed of it,

   Nor take non hede of it in no kyns[11] wyse ;

But when y speke, after my best avise,[12]   225

but make game of me.

   ye set it at[13] nought, but make therof a game ;

And though y sue[14] so grete an entirprise,

   It peireth[15] not yo*ur* wurship nor yo*ur* fame.   228

(30)

" Alas ! what shuld be to you preiudice,   229

   yf þat a man do loue you faythefully,

To yo*ur*[16] wurship, eschuyng eue*r*y vice ?

Yet I am wholly yours,

So am y youres, and will be[17] verely ;

[1] can H, dyd T.   [2] UH, That oon T.   [3] UH, that other T.
[4] UH, on hym was leyd T.   [5] werre H.   [6] UH, feynyd T.
[7] UH, he gan to, T.   [8] UH, happy T.   [9] UH, sore T.
[10] UH, rek T.   [11] UH, therof hede in no man*er* T.
[12] UH, deuyse T.   [13] *om.* HT.   [14] UH, shew T.
[15] UH, apeireth T.   [16] UH, eue*r*y T.   [17] UH, shalbe T.

I chalange nought[1] of right, and resoun why,   233
   ffor y am hole submyt to youre seruyse ;   and in your
service.
Right as ye lyste it be, right[2] so will y,
   To bynde my selfe, where y was[3] in fraunchise.

(31)

" þough it be so,[4] þat y cannot deserue   237   [leaf 122]
   To haue youre grace, but alwey leue[5] in drede ;
yit suffre me you fór to loue and serue   Suffer me to love
   without magrè[6] of youre most goodlyhede ;   you,
Bothe feyth and trouth y yeue[7] your womanhede,
   And my seruise, without ayen-callyng ;
Loue hathe me bounde, withoutë wage or mede,   for love binds me
   To be your man, and leue all othir thyng."   244   to be your man
alone."

(32) LA DAME.

When this lady hadde herde all his[8] langage,   245   The Lady
   She yaf[9] answere full softe and démurely,   answerd,
Without chaungyng of Colour or corage,
   Nothyng in haste, but mesurabëly :   quietly,
   " Me thynketh, sir, your þought is[10] grete foly.   249   "You are very
foolish, for I shall
   purpose ye not your labour for to sees ?   never love you."
ffor thynketh[11] not, whils þat ye leue and[12] y,
   In this[13] matier to sette youre hert in pees."[14] 252

(33) LAMANT.

" þer may non make þe pees, but only ye,   253   The Lover said,
"You alone can
   Which ar the ground *and* cause[15] of all this war ;   give me peace.
ffor with youre yen þe letters writen be,   Your eyes and
pleasant look
   By which y am defied[16] and put a-fer,   made me put all
my trust in you."
youre plesaunt looke, my very lodësterre,   257
   was made heraud of thilke same[17] diffiaunce

[1] UH, shall nat T.   [2] euyn H, *om.* T.   [3] UH, am T.
[4] be so I cannot H, so be þat I can hit nat T.
[5] ay to lyve H, alwey lyue T, alwey to leue U.
[6] mauger H, mawgre T.   [7] yeue T, to gif H, ye U.
[8] UT, this H.   [9] yaf hym U, *om.* hym HT.
[10] your hert is T, ye doo fulle H.   [11] thynk ye, HT.
[12] ye . . and HT, I . . an U.   [13] UH, your T.   [14] UH, ese T.
[15] cause and grounde HT.   [16] UH, deferryd T.
[17] thilke same H, þe same U, thys saunce T.

which vtterly behight me to forbar[1]

Mi feythefull trust, *and* all my affiaunce."   260

(34) LA DAME.

[leaf 122, back] "To leue in wo, he hathe gret fantasie,   261

"A man must
have a great fancy
for woe who is put
out by a look.

And of his hert also hathe sliper hold,

That, only for byholdyng of an ye,[2]

Cannot abide in pees, as resou*n* wolde.

Other, or me,[3] yf ye liste to biholde,   265

Our eyes are made
for looking.
Why shouldn't
we use them?"

Oure yen[4] ar made to loke : why shuld we spare?

I take no kepe, nether of yong ne olde ;

who feleth smert,[5] y consayll hym by[6] ware." 268

(35) LAMANT.

"But since you
have caused me
so much pain,
why don't you
keep this in
mind?

"If it be so,[7] one hurt an other sore,   269

In his defaut þat feleth the[8] greu*au*nce,

Of very right a man may do no more ;

yit resou*n* wuld it were in rémembra*u*nce.

And, sith fortune nat only (by his chaunce)   273

hathe caused me to suffre all this payn,

Why do you
hold me in such
disdain?"

But yo*ur* beaute, w*ith* all þe sircumstaunce,

Whi list you[9] haue me in so grete disdeyn?" 276

(36) LA DAME.

"I neither dis-
dain,

"To yo*ur* pe*r*sone ne haue y non[10] disdeyn,   277

Nor neuer hadde, truly ; nor nought[11] will haue,

nor love you,
nor hate you.

Nor right gret loue, nor hatrede, in certeyn ;

Nor[12] youre consayll to knowe, (so god me saue !)

If such beleue[13] be in yo*ur* mynde y-graue,[14]   281

þat lytell thyng may do you gret plesaunce,

Pray understand
that I don't want
to trouble you."

you to begyle, or make[15] you for to rave,

I will not cause non[16] such éncomberaunce." 284

(37) LAMANT.

[leaf 123] "What eu*er* h*i*t be þat hath me[17] þis p*ur*chácyde, 285

Wenyng hath noght deseyued me,[18] se*r*tayne ;

---

[1] forbarre (loodsterre, aferre, werre) H.   [2] yee H, ey T.
[3] UH, ne T.   [4] yeen H, eyen T.   [5] UH, seketh harme T.
[6] be H.   [7] UH, so be T.   [8] the HT, no U.   [9] ye HT.
[10] UH, *om.* T.   [11] ner neuere H, ne neu*er* T.   [12] UH, Ne T.
[13] UH, conseyte T.   [14] UH, graue T.   [15] UH, mok T.
[16] noon H, no T.   [17] UT, me hath H.   [18] UH, *om.* T.

But feruent loue so sore me hath I-chasede,[1]
 That I,[2] vnware, am casten[3] in y*our* chayne;
 And sith so is, as[4] fortune lyste[5] ordayne,   289
  All my welfare is in y*our* handys falle,
  Inn éschewyng of more myschévous payne;
  Who su*n*nest dieth, his care is leste of alle."   292

"Ah, but I love you fervently, all my welfare is in your hands: and I had better die."

(38)   LA DAME.

" þis[6] sykenesse is ryght[7] esy to endure,   293
 But few peple h*i*t causeth for to dye;
But what þei meane, I know h*i*t[8] v*er*rey sure,
 Of mor comfórt to draw the remedye.
 Sych be þer now,[9] playnyng full pytouslye,   297
  That fele[10] (gode wote) not alþ*er*[11]-grettyst payne;
  And[12] iffe so be, loue hurt*es*[13] so grevously,
  lesse harme h*i*t were, wone sorouful, þen twayn."[14]

"Your illness won't trouble you much: few people die of that.

If it were real, why, one had better be ill than two."

(39)   LAMANT.

" Alas, madame! iffe þat h*i*t[15] myght you please,   301
 mych better wer,[16] by way of gentyllesse,
Of won sory,[17] to make twayne[18] well at ease,
 Then hyme to strye[19] *that* lyueth in destresse.
 ffor my desyr is noþ*er* mor ne lesse,   305
  But my s*er*uysse to[20] do, for y*our* plesaunce,
  In éschewyng al man*er* doublenesse,
  To make too Joys insted of won[21] grevaunce." 308

"No, surely; better put two in ease than destroy the one who suffers.

Make two joys instead of one pain."

(40)   LA DAME.

" Of loue I seke noþ*er* plesaunce nore[22] ease,   309
 Nor Ryght gret loue,[23] nor[24] ryght gret affyaunce.
þough ye be seke, h*i*t dothe me no thyng please;
 Also, I take none hede to y*our* plesaunce.

[leaf 123, back] "But I don't want any trouble about love, and don't care whether you're ill or happy.

---

[1] UH, hath me enbrasyd T.   [2] UH, *om.* T.   [3] UH, cast T.
[4] UH, hyt ys that T.   [5] UH, lyste so T.   [6] UH, The T.
  [7] UH, full T.   [8] it H, *om.* T.   [9] nought H, lew T.
[10] UH, faylen T.   [11] UH, all the T.   [12] Are UT.
[13] hurte H, hurt T.   [14] tweyne HT, wayn U.   [15] UT, I H.
[16] UH, hyt were bettyr T.   [17] UT, sorwe H ('sory' *in margin*).
  [18] UH, ij. T.   [19] stroye H, dystroy T.   [20] UH, I T.
   [21] oo HT.   [22] UT, ne H.   [23] Nor gret desire HT.
    [24] UH, ne T.

Chese who-so wyle, þair hertys to a-vaunce, 313

I am free, and am not going to put myself under any man's rule."

ffre am I now, *and* fre wyll I endure ;

To be Rulyd by mannys gouernaunce,

ffor erthly gode, nay ! that I you ensure." 316

(41) LAMANT.

"Love makes ladies

" Loue, which þat[1] ioy *and* sorow doth depart, 317

hath set þe[2] ladyes out of all seruage,

And largëly doth graunt hem, for þair[3] part,

lords and rulers,

Lordschip and rule of euery maner age.

The pore seruaunt noght hath of[4] ávauntage 321

But what he may get only of purcháce ;

and their lovers only homagers."

And he þat ones to loue dothe his omáge,

ffull often[5] tyme, der boght is the rechace." [6] 324

(42) LA DAME.

" Ladies are not such fools as to be taken in by pretty speeches.

" Ladyes beth not so symple (þus I mene), 325

So dulle of wyte, so sotyd[7] of folye,

That, for wordes which said ben of[8] þe splene,

In fayr langáge, paynted ful plesantlye,

Which ye *and* mo[9] holde scolys of[10] dailye,[11] 329

To make hem all[12] grete wondyrs to suppose ;

They can turn their heads, and shut their ears."

But sone thei cane, away her hedes[13] wrye,

And to fayr speche, lyghtly þair yerës close." 332

(43) LAMANT.

[leaf 124]

" þer is no man þat iangulith bysily 333

"The mere talker speaks not like the man laden with woe,

And sette[14] his hert *and* all his mynd þerfor,

þat be reason may playn so pytously

As he þat hath myche hevynesse in store.

Whose hede is hole,[15] *and* saith þat hit is[16] sore, 337

his fayned chere is hard[17] to kepe in mewe ;

---

[1] UT, *om.* H.   [2] UH, yow T.   [3] þar H, youre T.
[4] UH, hath noon T.   [5] ofte H, oft T.
[6] UT, dere his richesse boughte has H. O. Fr. *rachatz ;* Mod. Fr. *rachat,* redemption, ransom.—Skeat. ' *Rachapt,* a redemption, redeeming, rebuying, recovery of a thing sold, by paying that for which it was sold.'—Cotgrave.
[7] sottid H, dotyd T.   [8] UT are, *om.* H.   [9] UH, me T.
[10] UT, scoolys holden H.   [11] dulye U, dieulye *margin,* daily H.
[12] UT, of H.   [13] UT, þer hedys away H.   [14] UT, settith H.
[15] UH, nat sore T.   [16] UT, is nat T.   [17] UH, herde T.

But thoght, which[1] is vnfaynëd euermore,

   The wordẽs previth[2] as the warkẽs sewe."[3]   340

(44) LA DAME.

"Loue is sotyle, *and* hath a grete awayte,[4]   341

   Scharpe in worchyng, in gabbyng gret plesance,

And cane hyme venge of[5] siche as, by deceyte,

   Wold fele *and* know[6] his secrete gouernance;

   And makyth hem to abey[7] his ordynance   345

      By cherfull wayes,[8] as In hem[9] is supposed,

But when þei[10] fallen in-to[11] répentance,

   Then, in a rage, þeir councele is disclosed."   348

(45) LAMANT.

"Sith, for-as-mych as gode and eke natur   349

   hathe loue avaunced[12] to so hye degre,

Mych scharper is the poynte, þis[13] am I sure,

   yete[14] greueth mor the faute, wher-euer hit be.

Who hath no colde, of hete hathe no deyntye;   353

   þe tone for þe toder, axed is expresse;

   And of plesaunce knothe non[15] þe serteyntye,

      Bot hit be[16] wonen with thought *and* hevynesse."

(46) LA DAME.

"As for plesaunce, hit is not alway wone:[17]   357

   That you[18] is swete, me thynketh[19] a bytter payne;

ye may not me constrayn, nor yet ryght none,

   After your lust to loue,[20] þat is bot vayne.

To chalange[21] loue by ryght, was neuer[22] sayne,   361

   But hert assent, by-fore bonde or promyse;

ffor strenght nor force may not ataine, sertayne,

   A wylle þat stant enfeffyd in[23] franchyse."   364

---

[1] UH, that T.   [2] preven H, present T.
[3] shew T, sewe *margin*, shew H.
[4] UT, abaite H, *margin* awayte.   [5] UH, on T.
[6] UT, knowe & fele H.   [7] obeye H.   [8] weies H, wyse T.
[9] UT, hym H.   [10] UT, þat þei H.   [11] UH, vnto T.
[12] Skeat MSS. avaunced loue.   [13] UH, thus T.
[14] UT, hit H.   [15] noon H, not UT.   [16] be H, *om.* UT.
[17] on (one) H.   [18] UH, to you T.   [19] thynketh HT, thynke U.
[20] UH, lyue T.   [21] UH, shall T.   [22] UH, men T.
[23] in HT, on U.

(47) LAMANT.

" Ryght fayr lady, god mot[1] I never please,   365
　　Iffe I seche oþer ryght, as in þis case,
　But for to schew you playnly my disease,

　　And your mercy to[2] abyde, *and* eke your grace.

Iffe I purpóse your honour to defface,   369
　　Or ever dide, gode *and* fortune me schende,
　And that I never ryghtwysly[3] purcháce
　　On only ioy, vn-to my lyvës ende ! "   372

(48) LA DAME.

" ye and oþer, that sweere such othës faste,   373
　　And so condempne *and* cursen to and fro,

ffull sykerly, ye wene your othës laste
　　No lengur then the wordës beth[4] ago ;
　And gode, *and* eke his sayntës, laugh[5] also.   377
　　In siche sweryng þer is no stedfastnesse ;

And þes wreches þat haue ful trust þer-to,
　　After, þai wepe *and* waylen in destresse."   380

(49) LAMANT.

"he hath no corage of a man, truly,   381
　　That sechith plesaunce, worschip to despyse ;

Nor to be callyd forth, is not worthy
　　The erthe to toche the ayre in no-skynnes[6] wyse.
　A trusty harte, a mouth without fayntyse,   385
　　Thes ben the strenght of euery man of name ;
　And who þat laith[7] his faith for lytel príce,
　　he lesith bothe his worschip *and* his fame."   388

(50) LA DAME.

" A currysche hert,[8] a mouthe[9] þat is courteys,   389
　　ffull wel ye wote, þei be[10] not ácordynge ;
　yet faynëd chere ryght sone may þeim[11] apeyse,
　　Wher of malece is sete al her[12] worchynge :

---

[1] UT, myght*e* H.　　[2] UT, *om.* H.　　[3] rightwisly H.
　　　[4] UH, byn T.　　[5] UH, dysplesyn T.
　　[6] UH, ne the . . . no kyns T.　　[7] latith H, lesyth T.
[8] Fr. Villain cueur.　　[9] UH, among T.　　[10] UH, these byn T.
　　　[11] UH, they may T.　　[12] there H, theyr T.

ffull fals semblant þei bere, *and* trew semynge ; [1] 393
    þaire name, þaire fame, þair tongë̈s be bot [2] fayned ;
Worschip in heme is put in fórgetynge, [3]
    Noght répentyd, nor in no wyse *co*mplayned." 396

(51) LAMANT.

" Who thynketh ylle, no good may hyme be-fale : 397
    Gode, of his grace, grawnt yche mon his desert !
But, for his loue, among yo*ur* [4] thoughtë̈s alle,   "For God's love
    As thenke opon my wofull sorous [5] smert ;   think on the pain
                                                          and woe I suffer;
ffor, of my payne, whedre [6] yo*ur* tendre hert,   401
    Of swete pytë, be noght þer-wit*h* a-grevyde,
And iffe yo*ur* grace to me wer [7] discouért,   be gracious to me,
    Then, be yo*ur* meane, sone [8] schuld I be releuyde." and I shall soon
                                                          be cured."

(52) LA DAME.

" A lyghtsome hart, a folye of plesaunce,   405   [leaf 125, back]
    Ar myche better, the lasse whyle þei abyde ;
Thei make you thynk, [9] *and* bryng you in [10] a traunce ;
    But þat sykenes will sone be remedyde.   "Your illness will
Respyte yo*ur* thought, *and* put all þis a-syde ; [11] 409 soon be over; put
    ffull goode disportë̈s werith [12] men al daye ;   this nonsense on
                                                        one side.
To helpe nor hurt, my wille is not aplyde ;   I neither care
    Who trouthe [13] me not, I [14] let h*i*t pase awaye."   to help nor hurt
                                                          you."

(53) LAMANT.

" Who hath a byrde, a faukyn or a hounde,   413   "If a bird or a
    That folowith hyme for loue in eu*er*y place,   dog loves a man,
                                                        he cherishes it,
he cherische [15] hyme, *and* kepith hym [16] ful sounde ;
    Out [17] of his syght he wol hym [18] note enchace.   and doesn't drive
And I, þat sette my wyttë̈s, in this case,   417 it away;
    On you allon, wit*h*outen any chaunge,   but me, who love
                                                        you above all
Am [19] put vnder, myche forþer out of grace,   others,
    And lese set [20] by, þen oþ*er* þat be straunge." 420 you set less by
                                                          than you do by
                                                          strangers."

---

[1] UT, meuyng H (semyng *in margin*).   [2] UT, not H (but *in margin*).
[3] forgetyng T, foryeting H, for etynge U.   [4] UH, hys T.   [5] sorowe H.
[6] UT, where H.   [7] UT, be H.   [8] UH, *om.* T.   [9] thyng U, thynk H.
[10] UH, into T.   [11] UT, on side T.   [12] werieth*e* H.
            [13] trowith H, troweth T.   [14] HT, *erasure in* U.
    [15] cherisith*e* H, cherysseth T.   [16] UT, *om.* L.   [17] UH, But T.
        [18] hym UT, *om.* H.   [19] UT, And H (Am *in margin*).
                    [20] UT, sette lesse H.

(54) LA DAME.

"Though I am
pleasant to other
men I shan't be
so to you.

"Though I make chere to eue*r*y man a-boute,   421
　　ffor my worschip, *and* of myn a͝wne fraunchyse,
To you I nylle do so, wi*th*outen doute,
　　In e͗schwyng all mane*r* pre͞iudyse.

Love

　　ffor, wett you well,[1] loue is so[2] lytle wyse,   425
　　　　And in be-leue so lyghtly wyll[3] be broght,
will have his own
way and do as he
likes."
That he taketh, al at his awne devyse,
　　Of thyng (god wot) þat se*r*ueth hym of noght."

(55) LAMANT.

[leaf 126]

"Iffe I, by loue *and* by my trew se*r*uyse,   429
"Why should I,
for my true
service, lose the
favour you show
to strangers?
　　lese the good chere þat straungers haue alway,
Wher-of schuld[4] se*r*ue my trouth in any wyse
　　les þen to heme[5] þ*a*t come *and* go alday,
　　Which hold[6] of you no thyng, þat is no[7] nay ?   433
　　　　Also in you is loste, to my semynge,
Surely, love for
love is only fair."
All courtesy, which of[8] Resou*n* will[9] say,
　　That loue by[10] loue were lawfull de͗se*r*uynge." 436

(56) LA DAME.

"Ladies' favour
will not be bound
by any prayers,
"Courtesye is allied wondir nere   437
　　To[11] worschip, which hyme louyth tendurly ;[12]
And he will not be bound, for no prayere
　　Nor for no[13] yifte, I say you verely,
but distributes its
gifts as it will."
But his good chere depart ful large͞ly   441
　　　　Wher hyme lyke͗th, as his conseit wil falle :
Guerdou*n* constraynt, a yifte done thankefully,
　　Thes twayn[14] may not a-cord, nor neue*r* schale."

(57) LAMANT.

"I ask no reward,
"As for guerdou*n*, I seche[15] none in þis case ;[16] 445
　　ffor þat desert, to me it[17] is to hye ;
only your grace ;
Wherfor I asche[18] yo*ur* pardou*n* *and* your grace,
　　Sith me by-houyth deth,[19] or yo*ur* me*r*cye.

---

[1] ye well HT, you will U.   [2] UH, *om.* T.
[3] wil H, wyll T, wel U.   [4] shuld H, I schuld UT.
[5] hem H, theym T.   [6] UH, had T.   [7] non H, to no T.
[8] UH, of all T.   [9] UT, wolde H.   [10] for Skeat.
[11] UT, with H.   [12] UT, best & tendirly H.   [13] UT, *om.* H.
[14] UH, ij. T.   [15] UH, seke T.   [16] UH, place T.
[17] UT, *om.* H.   [18] ashe H, ax T.   [19] H, *om.* UT.

To yiue the good[1] wher h*i*t[2] wanteth, treulye,　449
　　That wer Resou*n*, *and* á[3] courteys manere ;
And to yo*u*r awn myche bettyr were worthy,[4]
　　þen to straungers, to schew heme louely[5] chere."

and Reason would
that you should
show it to me
rather than to
strangers."

(58)　LA DAME.

" What call ye good? fayn wold I þ*a*t I wyste !　453
　　That plesith on, an-oþer[6] smertyth sore ;
But, of his awn, to large is he þat liste
　　yiue myche, *and* lese all his goode fame þerfore.
On schuld not make a gr*au*nt, lytele nor more,　457
　　But þ[e] request were ryght wele ácordynge ;
yif worschip be not kept *and* set byfore,
　　All þ*a*t is lefte, is but a lytell thynge."　460

[leaf 126, back]

" What pleases
me, pains
another ;

and no grant
should be made
unless it were
sure to be accept-
able."

(59)　LAMANT.

" In-to þis world was neuer formyd non,　461
　　Nor vnd*ur* heven crëature[7] I-bore,
Nor neu*er* schall, saffe only yo*ur* parson,[8]
　　To whom yo*ur* worschip toucheth half so sore ;
But me, which haue no sesou*n*, les ne more,　465
　　of youth nor age, but styll in yo*ur* ser*u*yse,
I haue non yne,[9] no wyt, nor mouth in store,
　　But all beth[10] yiuen to þe same offyse."　468

" There is no
creature under
heaven to whom
your good name
is so dear as to
me.

I have no senses
that are not
yours."

(60)　LA DAME.

" A full gret charge hath he, wit*h*outen fayle,　469
　　þat his worschip kepyth in sykernesse ;
But in daunger he settyth his trauayle,
　　That feffith h*i*t wit*h* othyrs[11] bysynesse.
To hym þat longeth honneur *and* noblesse,　473
　　Vpon non othir schuld not[12] he awayte ;
ffor of his[13] awn, so mych hathë[14] þe lesse,
　　That, of othir, mych folouth the conseit."　476

" Each one's good
name is enough
for himself to look
to.

If he troubles
about others,
he has less of his
own."

---

[1] good H, god U.　[2] UH, that it T.　[3] UT, *om.* H.
　[4] UH, worth T.　[5] H, lowly T, lonely U.
[6] UH, and other T.　[7] UT, o creature H.　[8] persone H.
[9] yeen H, eyen T.　[10] But . . byn T, that ne alle ar H.
　[11] UH, other T.　[12] UH, *om.* T.　[13] UT, *om.* H.
　　[14] hathe he HT.

(61) LAMANT.

"your yen[1] haue set the prynte[2] which þat y fele[3] 477
  wi*th*yn myn herte, þat, wher-so-eue*r*[4] y goo,
If y do thyng þat sowneth[5] vnto wele,
    Nede must it[6] come from you, and fro no mo.
    ffortune will thus, þat y, for wele or wo,   481

        My lyfe endure, you*r* mercy ábidyng ;
    And very right, will þat y thynk also
        Of your wurship, aboue all other thyng."   484

(62) LA DAME.

"To you*r* wurship se wele, for þat is nede,   485
    þat ye spende not you*r* seasou*n*[7] all in vayn.
As touchyng myn, y rede you take non hede,

    By you*r* foly, to putte you*r*-selfe in peyn.

    To Ouercom is good, *and* to restreyn   489
        An herte which is deseyved folyly ;
    ffor wers it is to breke þan[8] bowe, certeyn,
        And better bowe, than falle to sodenly."   492

(63) LAMANT.

"Now, faire lady, thenk, sith it first began,   493
    þat loue hadde sette myn hert vndre his[9] cure,
It neuer myght, nor[10] treuly y ne can,
    None othir serue, whils y shall here[11] endure ;

    In most fre wise, therof y make you sure,   497
        which may not be wi*th*-drawe : this is no nay.
    I must abide all maner áuenture ;

        ffor y may nought putte to, nor take away."   500

(64) LA DAME.

"I holde it for no yifte, in sothefastnes,   501
    That one offereth, where þat it is forsake ;
ffor suche yifte is abandonnyng expresse,
    That, with wurship, ayen may not be take.

---

[1] yeen H, eyen T.   [2] UH, they*m* p*r*esent T.
[3] Fr. Voz yeulx out si empraint leur merche.
[4] where-sum-euer H.   [5] sowndith*e* H.   [6] UH, it must T.
[7] UT, ye you*r* sesoun spende not H.   [8] UH, the T.
[9] your H, *om.* T.   [10] I . . ne H, It not UT.
[11] UT, here I shal H.

he hathe an hert full fell,[1] þat list to make   505
   A yift lightly, þat put is in refuse ;
But he is wyse þat suche conseyt will slake,   *Cool your desires and save your*
   So þat hym nede nether stodie nor[2] muse."   508 *anxieties."*

(65) LAMANT.

" he[3] shuld not muse, þat hath[4] his seruyse spent   509   *"A lover must be anxious;*
   On hir which is a lady honouráble ;
And yf y spende my tyme to þat entent,
   yit atte the lest y am nat répreuáble   *and I am not worthy of reproof*
Of faylëd herte : to thynk, y am vnable,   513
   Or me mystoke whan y made this request,   *unless my request is mistaken."*
By which loue hathe, of entirprise notáble,
   So many hertis getyn bi conquest."   516

(66) LA DAME.

" yf þat ye liste do after my Counsayll   517   *"Let me advise you to seek a fairer Love who'll care for you.*
   Secheth fayerer,[5] and of more hier fame,
Which in seruice of loue will you prevayll
After your þought, acordyng to the same.
he hurteth both[6] his wurship and his name,   521   *You are now only damaging your reputation."*
   þat folyly for tweyn[7] hym-selfe will trobull ;
And also he leséth his after game,
   That surely cannot sette his poyntës double."[8] 524

(67) LAMANT.[9]

" This your Counsell, by ought þat y can se,   525   *[leaf 128]*
   Is better seid than done, to myn avise.
Though i beleue it not, foryif[10] it me ;
   Myn herte is suche, so hele[11] withoute fayntyse,   *"My heart is so true that I can*
That it may not[12] yeve credence, in no wyse,   529   *believe nothing which does not mean truth.*
   To thyng which[13] is not sownyng vnto trouth :

---

[1] Thynne (Sk.), hertis full fele UT, hurte ful fele H.
[2] UT, neuer to stody ne H.   [3] UT, Who H.   [4] hath HT, *om.* U.
[5] UH, ferther T.   [6] both HT, *om.* U.   [7] UH, ij. T.
[8] *After-game*, return-match . . . I believe l. 524 to mean, 'who cannot thoroughly afford to double his stakes.' To *set* often means to stake. The French is :—
     ' Et celuy pert le ien d'attente
       Qui ne scet faire son point double.'—Skeat, vii. 519.
[9] Fr.: Le conseil que vous me donnez.   [10] UH, foryeue T.
[11] hoole THU.   [12] TU, *om.* H.   [13] UH, thynke that T.

You will pity me."

Other Councell, it[1] are but fantasise,[2]

Saf of[3] your grace to shewe pitë and routhe." 532

(68) LA DAME.

"He is wise who can quit his folly when he likes;

" I holde hym wise, þat wurcheth folÿly,   533

And, whan hym list, can leue[4] and part therfro ;

But in konnyng he is to lerne, trewely,

þat wold hym selfe condit,[5] and cannot[6] so.

but he who will not take advice

And he þat will not after Conseyll do,   537

his sute[7] he putteth in desé[s]peraunce ;

must be set aside as dead."

And all the good, which[8] þat shuld fall hym to,

Is lefte as[9] dede, clene out of rémembraunce." 540

(69) LAMANT.

"Lady, I will love you while I live;

" yit will y sue this matier faythfully   541

whils y may leue, what-euer be[10] my chaunce ;

and if I die,

And if it happe þat in my trouth y die,

þat dethe shall not do me no displesaunce.

I'd rather die

But when þat y, by your full hard[11] sufferaunce, 545

Shall die so trewe, and with so gretë[12] peyne,

than live as a false lover."

yit shall it do me moche the[13] lesse grevaunce,

þen for to leue a fals louer, sertayn."   548

(70) LA DAME.

[leaf 128, back]

" Of me gete ye right nought, this is no fable ; 549

"Well, you'll get nothing from me; I don't care for you.

I nyll[14] to you be nether hard nor streyght ;

And right wil nat, nor maner Custumáble,

To thynke ye shuld be sure of myn conseyt.

If you want sorrow, you'll get it."

Who secheth sorow,[15] his be[16] the reseyt.   553

Other Counceyll can y not fele nor se ;

Nor for to lerne, y cast not to awayte :

Who wyll therto, late hym assay, for me."   556

[1] other counsail it H, others counsayles hit T, hit om. U.
[2] UH, fantasyes T.   [3] of HT, om. U.
[4] And . . leue UH, when he can leue T.
[5] conduyte H, condute T.   [6] cannat HT, canno U.
[7] UT, suerte UH (sute in margin). [8] goodys T, good which H.
[9] UH, all T. [10] UH, what oon by T. [11] UT, your harde H.
[12] UT, grete a H. [13] UT, moche H. [14] ÜH, wyll T.
[15] UH, sorowys T. [16] is by H ('his bi' margin), by T.

(71) LAMANT.

" Ones must it be[1] asaied, þat is no nay,[2] 557
 w*ith* suche as be of reputacïou*n*
And of trewe loue the right deuoyr[3] to paie,
 Of fre hertis, getyn by due Raunsom ;
 ffor fre will holdeth this opynyon,   561
  þ*a*t it is grete dures *and* discomfort
 To kepe an hert in só streyt a presou*n*,
  þ*a*t hathe but on body for[4] his disport." 564

"When a free heart has been won, the winner should honourably pay love's dues,

otherwise it is great hardship on the lover."

(72) LA DAME.

" I knowe so many Cases[5] meruelos,   565
 That **y** must nede, of resou*n*, thynk certeyn,
þ*a*t suche entre[6] is wondre perelous ;
 And yit wele more, the comyng bak ageyn ;[7]
 Good or wurship therof is seldon seyn ; 569
  Wherfore y wil not make none suche aray,
 As for to fynde a plesaunce but bareyn,
  When it shall coste so dere, þ*e* first asay." 572

"That would be dangerous work to begin, and more to rid.

I will not try it."

(73) LAMANT.

" ye haue no cause to doute of this matiere,[8] 573
 Nor you to meve w*ith* non suche fantasise
To putte me far all[9] out, as a straunger ;
 ffor youre goodnes can thynk[10] and wele avise,
 þ*a*t y haue made a prefe[11] in eu*er*y wise, 577
  By which my trouth sheweth open evidence :
 Mi long abidyng *and* my trew ser*u*ice
  May wele be knowe by playn experience." 580

[leaf 129]

"You should not treat me as a stranger,

for you know well my continued truth."

(74) LA DAME.

" Of very right, he may be called trewe,[12] 581
 (And so must he be take in eu*er*y place)
þ*a*t can deser*u*e, and let as he ne knewe,
 And kepe the good, yf he it may p*ur*cháce.

"He is true

who deserves favour, and keep it when got ;

---

  [1] UH, it must be T. [2] Fr.: Vue fois le fault essayer.
[3] UT, duetes H. [4] UH, to T. [5] UT, caases H (causes *margin*).
[6] UH, entent T. [7] bak ageyn H, abak certeyn U, bak certeyn T.
   [8] Fr.: Vous n'auez cause de douter. [9] all, *om.* T.
  [10] thynk H, thynke T, thyng U. [11] prese U.
    [12] Fr.: Il se peut loyal appeller.

but there's no
truth in merely
praying."

ffor who þat prayeth or sueth in any cace[1]   585
   Right wele ye wot, in[2] þat no trouth is preued :
Siche hathe ther bene, and[3] are, þat geteth[4] grace,
   And lese it sone, whan they it haue acheuyd." 588

(75) LAMANT.

"If truth makes
me love, and be
rejected,

" yf trouth me cause, bi vertu souerayn,   589
   To shewe good loue, and all-wey fynde contráry,
And cherissh þat at[5] slethe me with þe payn,

this is good, as
pity will come at
last and comfort
me."

þis is to me a louely aduersarie.
   when þat pite, which longe aslepe dothe tarye,   593
     hathe set þe fyn of all myn hevynesse,
   yit her comfort, to me most necessarye,
     Shuld sette my wille more sure in stabilnesse."

(76) LA DAME.

[leaf 129, back]
"The sorrowing
lover cannot think

" þe[6] wofull wight, what may he[7] thynk or say ?   597
   þe contrarie of áll ioye and gladnesse.
A seke body, his thought is all away[8]

of those who feel
no sorrow,

ffro hem þat fele no sorow nor sekenes.
   þus hertis[9] bene of dyuerse besynes   601
     which loue[10] hathe putte to right gret hynderaunce,

and he forgets
truth too."

   And treuthe also put in foryetfulnes,
     when they so sore begynne to sigh askaunce." 604

(77) LAMANT.

"He who turns to

"Now god defende, but he be hauëles[11]   605
   Of all wurship or good þat may befalle,

evil any favour

þat to the wurst turneth, by his lewdenes,
   A yift of grace, or ony thyng atte all

that his lady
vouchsafes him

That his lady[12] vouchesaf vppon hym calle,   609
   Or cheryssheth[13] hym in honorable wyse !

deserves more
than double
death."

In þat defaut, what-euer he be þat fall,
   Deserueth[14] more, then dethe to suffre twyse." 612

---

[1] UH, place T.   [2] in, *om.* T.   [3] and H, an U.
[6] UH, getyn T.   [5] that H.   [6] UH, A T.   [7] ye UT, he H.
[8] UH, bodyes thought is alwey T.   [9] hurtes H. Skeat.
[10] loue UH, *om.* T.   [11] De tous soit celuy deguerpiz.
[12] his lady H, this lady U, ys T.
[13] cherysshe TH, cheryssheth U.
[14] Deserueth H, Derserueth U.

(78) LA DAME.

"There is no Iuge yset of[1] suche trespáce,   613
   By which, of right, one may recou*er*ed be ;
One curseth faste, an-other dotbe manáce,
   yit dieth non, as fer as y can se,
  But kepe her cours all-wey, in one degre,[2]   617
    And eue*r*more[3] there labo*ur* dothe encrece,
  To brynge ladise, bi their grete[4] sotelte,
   ffor othirs gilt, in sorow and disese."   620

"Ah, one man curses, another threatens, but none die,

yet all try new tricks to bring ladies into trouble."

(79) LAMANT.

" All-be-h*i*t[5] so, on do so gret offence,[6]   621
   And be not dede, nor put to no Iuyse,
Ryght wele I wot, hym gayneth no deffence,
   But he must ende in full myschéuous wyse,
  And all þat eue*r*[7] is gode will hym despyse ;   625
    ffor falshode is so full of cursydnesse,
  That highe[8] worschip may[9] never haue ent*er*prise
   Wher h*i*t rayneth, *and* hath the wylfulnysse." 628

[leaf 130]

"If I were to be false and change,

all good men would despise me."

(80) LA DAME.

" Of[10] that haue þei[11] no gret fere now of[12] dayes, 629
  Siche as wyll[13] say, *and* maynten h*i*t þer-to,
That stidfast trouth is nothyng for to preyes[14]
   In hem þat kepe h*i*t longe, for weile or wo.
þaire bysy hert*es* passen to and fro,   633
   þai be so wele reclaymed to the lure,
  So well lorned hem[15] to w*ith*-holde also,
   And all to chaunge, when loue schuld best endure."

"Oh, don't be afraid of that,

there are plenty of changes now-a-days."

(81) LAMANT.

" When won hath sett his hert in stable wisse,   637
  In siche a place which is boeth gude *and* trewe,

"When a man has once fixt his heart,

---

[1] UH, on T.   [2] on*e* degre H, oo degre T, ordre U.
[3] euermore UT, euere newe H.   [4] grete UT, *om.* H.
    [5] Though hit be T, Al be it H.
   [6] Fr.: Combien qu'on n'arde ne ne pende, p. 518.
   [7] euer UH, *om.* T.   [8] theyr T, her H.
   [9] may U, *om.* T, shall H.   [10] Yef T, Off H.
[11] þei haue T, haue þei H.   [12] a TH.   [13] wyll T, wel U, wil H.
    [14] preys H.   [15] hem H, theym T, & U.

he should not
change, but
ever be true.

he schuld not flytte, bot do forth his seruyse

Alway, with-outen[1] chaunge of any newe.

As sone as loue by-gynneth to remew.[2]　　641

All plesaunce goth anon, in letel space :

For me, I'll never
alter while I live."

As for my party, þat schal I[3] eschewe,

Whils þat my[4] sowle abydythe in his place."

(82)　LA DAME.

[leaf 130, back]

"To loue trewly, ther as ye oght of ryght,　　645

"That is well
enough when you
are loved again,
but you have
made a mistake
with me, and had
better give up at
once."

　ye may not be mysse-taken, dout[ë]lesse,

Bot ye be fowle deceyued in your syght,

　By lyghtly vndurstandyng, as I gesse ;

yet may ye wel repeale your bysynesse,　　649

　And to resoun, some-what haue átendaunce,

myche better þen to abyde, by fole[5] symplesse,

　The feble socour[6] of desesperaunce."　　652

(83)　LAMANT.

"Reason and
good advice are
set aside in love."

"Resoun, councell, wysdam, and good avyse　　653

　Bene vndur loue a-restyd[7] euerychone,—

To which I can acord in euery wyse ;—

　ffor þai be not rebell, bot still as[8] stone ;

Their will and myne ar[9] medeled al in won,　　657

　And þer-with bownden with so stronge a cheyne,

That, as in hem,[10] departyng shal be none,

　But pytë breke the myghty bonde a-tweyn."　　660

(84)　LA DAME.

"Who loueth not hym-selfe, what-euer he be,　　661

　In loue he stant[11] for-yet in euery place ;

"If you'll not
pity yourself,
you'll get pity
from no one else.

And, of your woo, if ye haue no pyte,

　Othirs pyte be-leue not to purcháce,[12]

But bethe fully assurèd in this case,　　665

I mean to have a
better man.
Don't hope for
favour from me."

　I am al-ways vndur on ordynaunce,

To haue better : trysteth not after grace,

　And al þat leueth,[13] take to your plesaunce."　　668

[1] without the T, withoute H.　　[2] renew T, remewe H.
[3] UT, For my party, al H, that I shal H.　　[4] my T, the UH.
[5] sole T, foly H.　　[6] UH, socours T.　　[7] UH, arestyn T.　　[8] UH, as a T.
[9] myne ar T, mynd as U, myn ben H.　　[10] theym T, heuen U, hem H.
[11] UH, standeth T.　　[12] purches UH.　　[13] UH, loueth T.

(85) LAMANT.

" I haue myn hope so sure *and* so stedfast,[1]   669   [leaf 131]
    That sich a lady schuld not faile pyte ;

But now, alas, it is schit vp so fast,

    That daunger schewth on me his cruelte.

And iffe sche se þe[2] vertu fayle in me   673

    Of trew seruyse, þen sche to faile also

No wondir wer ; but þis is the seurte,

    I must suffre, which way þat euer hit[3] go."   676

"I did hope that you would be pitiful, but now all hope is gone.

One thing only is sure, that I must suffer."

(86) LA DAME.

"leue[4] this purpos, I rede you for yo*ur* best ;   677

    ffor, lenger that[5] ye kepe hit þus in vayn,

The les ye gete, as of yo*ur* hert*ës* rest,

    And to reioisse hit, schal ye neuer attayne.

When ye abyde goode hope, to make you fayne,   681

    ye schal be founde a-sotyde[6] in dotage

And in the ende, ye scháll know for sertayne,

    That hope schall pay þe wrecches for þer wage."[7]

"I do advise you give this matter up:

for never can you win my love."

(87) LAMANT.

"ye say as fallyth most for yo*ur* plesaunce,   685

    And yo*ur* power is grete ; al þis I se ;

But hope schall neu*er* out of my Rémem*bra*unce,

    By which I felt so grete adue*r*syte.

ffor when nature hath set in you plente   689

    Of all goodnes, by vertu and by[8] grace,

He[9] neu*er* assembled hem, as semyth me,

    To put pyte out of his dwellyng place."   692

"But I must hope

that when Nature set all goodness in you,

he never left out Pity."

(88) LA DAME.

" Pyte of ryght ought[10] to be resonáble,   693

    And to no wyght of gret disáuauntage :[11]

Ther as is nede, hit schuld be[12] profytáble,

    And to the pytous, schewyng no domage.[11]

[leaf 131, back]
" Pity must be reasonable ;

---

[1] Fr.: I'ay mon esperance fermee.   [2] that T, the H.
[3] I T, it H.   [4] Loue T, Leve H.   [5] UH, the lenger T.
[6] UH, bounde assured T.
[7] þer wage H, your wage T, your waye U.   [8] UH, hygh T.
[9] He UT, Ne U.   [10] oweth T, aught H.
[11] disauauntaye . . domaye U.   [12] by U, be HT.

and if a lady were
to let pity lead
her love astray,
it would turn to
deadly hate."

Iffe a lady will do so gret outráge   697
    To schew pyte, *and* cause her awn debate.
Of siche pyte comyth dispytous Rage,
    And of þe loue also ryght dedly[1] hate "   700

(89) LAMANT.

"To comfort the
comfortless would
add honour to
you;

" To coumfort hem þat lyue[2] all coumfortles,   701
    That is non harme, but worschip to yo*ur* name ;
But ye, þat bere an hert of syche dures,
    A fair body I-fo*ur*myd[3] to the same,

but this cruelty
will defame you

Iffe I durst say, ye wyn all þis diffame   705
    By cruelte, which sittyth you full ylle,

unless Pity dwell
in your heart."

But iffe pyte, which may al þis atame,[4]
    In yo*ur* hye hert may reste *and* tary stylle."   708

(90) LA DAME.

"Am I to be
blamed because I
won't do what a
man who says he
loves me, wants
me to?

" What-eu*er* he be þat saith he loueth me,—   709
    And p*ar*aunt*er* I leue[5] þat hit be so,—
Ough[t] he be wroth, or schuld I[6] blamyd be,
    Though I did not as he wold haue me do ?

If I gave in to
him,
I should be miser-
able afterwards,
and repent it then
too late."

Iffe I medlyd w*ith* siche, or othir mo,   713
    h*i*t myght be called ' pyte man*er*-les ;'
And aftirward, iffe I schuld lyue in wo,
    Then to repent h*i*t were to late, I gesse."   716

(91) LAMANT.

[leaf 132]

"O marble heart!

" O marbre[7] hert, *and* yet mor hard[8] ; p*ar*dyc,[9]   717
    Which m*er*cy may not perse,[10] for no labo*ur*,
mor strong[11] to bow then is a myghty tre,
    What vayleth[12] you to schew so gret rygo*ur* ?

would you rather
see me die for
your amusement
than give me
some comfort?"

please it you mor, to se me dye þis oure   721
    By-for yo*ur* yne,[13] for yo*ur* disport *and* play,
Then for to schew some co*m*fort or soco*ur*
    To respyte dethe, which chaseth me alway ?"   724

---

[1] UH, dewly T.   [2] UH, byn T.
[3] And a fair body formed. Thynne, Skeat.
[4] may . . attame H, may not al þis attame U, all this may attame T.
[5] UH, beleue T.   [6] wrother schuld I T, wroth or I schuld U.
[7] marbil H, marble T.   [8] UH, mor hardyr T.
[9] Ha ! cueur plus dur que le noir marbre.   [10] parte T, perce H.
[11] UH, stronger T.   [12] UH, avayleth T.   [13] eyne T, yeen H.

(92) LA DAME.

"Of yo*ur* disease ye may haue á-legeaunce;[1]   725
  And as for myn, I lat h*i*t ou*er*-schake.[2]

"Your disease can soon be cured; mine is nothing.

Also, ye schall not dye for my plesaunce,
  Nor for yo*ur* hele[3] I cane no suerty make.

It would give me no pleasure to see you die;

I wyll[4] not hate myn hert for o*þer*[5] sake: 729
  Wepe þei, laghe þei,[6] or syng, þis[7] I warant,
ffor this mater so wele to[8] vnd*ur*-take,

and none of you shall be able to make a boast about me."

  þat none of you schall make þ*er*-of avaunt."   732

(93) LAMANT.

"I can no skylle of song: by god allone,   733
  I haue mor cause to wepe in yo*ur* prese*́*nce;

"I cannot sing.

And wel[9] I wote, avaunter am I none,
  ffor c*er*taynly,[10] I loue better sylence.

I will not boast.

On schuld not loue by his hert*is* crede*́*nce,   737
  But he wer suer to kepe h*i*t secretly;
ffor ávaunter is of no reuerence

No one should love who cannot keep it secret."

  When þ*at* his tonge is his most enemy."   740

(94) LA DAME.

"Male-bouche in court hath gret comaundëment;   741
  Ech man studith to say the wurst he may.

[leaf 132, back]

Thes fals louers, in þis tyme now prese*́*nt,
  Thai s*er*ue to bost, to Iangle as a Iay.

"Scandal is much about now, and false lovers chatter like jays.

þe most secret wylle wele þ*at* su*m* man[11] say   745
  how he mystristed is on su*m* partyse;[12]

Wherfor, to ladyse what men speke or p*ray*,[13]

What men say to women should never be believed."

  It schuld not be byleuyd in no wyse."   748

(95) LAMANT.

"Of good *and* yll, schall be, *and* is alway;   749
  the world is sich; þe erth it is nat playn.

"There are bad as well as good in the world,

Thay þ*at* be good, the preef schewth eu*er*y day,
  And othir-wyse, gret vylany, s*er*tayn.

---

[1] allegeaunce T, allegeance H.   [2] UH, slake T.
[3] UH, lyfe T.   [4] UH, wold.   [5] othyrs T, othirs H.
[6] UH, or laghe T.   [7] UH, thus T.
[8] weel to H, wyll I T, wele I U.   [9] wel T, wele H, wil U.
[10] UH, in certeyn T.   [11] men TH.   [12] UH, in .. parte T.
[13] UH, wherfor these louers whatsoeu*er* they say T.

but the talk of the bad should not be held to sully the good."

Is hit reson, þough on his tonge distayn,   753

   with cursyd spech, to do hym-selfe a schame,

þ*at* such[1] refus schuld wrongfully remayn

   Vpon the good, Renomyd in þair fame?"[2]   756

(96) LA DAME.

"When those who have made good resolves hear that faults will soon find pardon,

" Sich as be nought, when þai her[e] tydyngs newe,

   That eche trespace schall lyghtly haue pardon,

Thai þ*at* p*ur*pósith[3] to be goode *and* trewe,

   (Wele set by noble disposicïoun

     To cóntynue in goode condycïoun)   761

they will be the first to go astray."

   Thai ar the first þ*at* fallith[4] in damáge,

And full frely þair hert*ës*[5] ábandone

   To lytell fayth, w*ith* soft *and* fair[6] langage." 764

(97) LAMANT.

[leaf 133]

" Now know I welle, of v*er*rey s*er*taynete,   765

"Then, though a man be true, he is to be ruined because ladies have neither justice nor pity.

   Though[7] on do trowly, yit[8] shal he be schent,

Sith all man*er* of Iustyce *and* pyte

   Is banyscht out of á ladys entent.

I can nat se but all is at o stent,[9]   769

Vice and virtue fare alike."

   þe good, þe[10] yll, þe vyce, *and* eke v*er*tu.

Sych as be good, schall haue the punyschment

   ffor the trespace of hem þ*at* beth vntrewe." 772

(98) LA DAME.

"I have no power to injure any one,

" I haue no power, you to do[11] greuaunce,   773

but I mean to keep clear of men.

   Nor to punysch[12] non oþ*er* crëature ;

But, to eschewe þe more encoumberaunce,

They are snares,

   To kepe vs from you[13] all, I holde h*it* sure.

ffals semblant hath a vysage full demure,   777

and ladies must keep a good look out."

   lyghtly to cache þ*e* ladyse in a-wayte ;

wherfor we must, iffe þat[14] we wyll endure,

   Make ryght good wache : lo ! þis is my conseyt."

---

[1] such T, suche H, sich*ur* U.   [2] UH, renewyd in his name T.
[3] purpose T, purposen H.   [4] fall T.   [5] UT, theym H.
[6] UT, faire & softe H.   [7] Though TH, Iff U.   [8] yet H, ye T.
[9] a stent T, oo stente H.   [10] and TH.
[11] UH, to do you T.   [12] UH, promyse T.
[13] you H, yow T, yois U.   [14] UH, *om.* T.

(99) LAMANT.

"Sith þat, of grace, o goodly word allone   781
    May noght be hade, but alway kept in store,
I pele[1] to gode, (for he may her my mone,)
    Of þe duresse which greuythe me so[2] sore.

and of pyte I playne me fordermore,[3]   785
    which he foryat, in all his ordynaunce,
Or ell*es* my lyfe to háue endid by-fore,
    which he so sone put out of Rémembraunce."   788

"Since you will give me no grace,

I appeal to God against your hardness."

(100) LA DAME.

"Myn hert, nor I, haue done you no[4] forfait,   789
    By which ye schuld co*m*playne in any kynde.
Ther hurtyth you[5] no thyng but your[6] conseyt :
    Be Iuge yo*ur*-selfe ; for so ye schall h*it* fynde.

Ons, for alwey, lat þis synke in yo*ur* mynde :   793
    Thát ye desir, schall neu*er* Reioysed be.
ye noye me sore, in wastyng all þis[7] wynde ;
    ffor I haue sayd ynoghe, as semythe me."   796

[leaf 133, back]

"I have never given you any pledge whatever,

and, once for all, your desire shall never be gratified.

You annoy me terribly with all your talk."

(101)

This wofull man rose vp in all his payn,   797
    And so p*ar*tyd, w*ith* wepyng[8] countynaunce ;
his wofull hert, all-most itt brast a[9]-twayn
    ffull lyke to dye, forth walkyng[10] in a t*r*aunce,
And said, "now, deth, com forth![11] thi-selfe avaunce,
    Or þat my hart for-yet his p*r*opirte ;
And make schortyr[12] all þis wofull pena*u*nce
    Offe my po*ur* lyfe, full of adu*er*syte !"   804

On this the woeful man departed broken-hearted,

calling on Death to take him.

(102)

ffro thens he went, bot whid*ur* wyst I noght,   805
    Nor to what part he drow, in sothfastnese ;
But he no mor wasse in his[13] ladyes thought,
    ffor to the daunce anon sche gan her dresse.

The lady went on dancing again.

---

[1] UH, speke T.   [2] which . . . so UH, that . . me T.
[3] furthermore T, further*e*-more H.   [4] noo H, *om.* T.
[5] UH, Then T.   [6] your TH, ys U.   [7] UH, of yo*ur* T.
[8] UH, heuy T.   [9] it brest in H, brast in T.
[10] H, walkyng forth UT.   [11] UH, deth come forthe and T.
[12] UT, shorte H.   [13] his UH, *om.* T.

And afterward,—on[1] told me þus expresse,—   809

Her lover tore his hair

He rent his here, for anguysch *and* for payn,
And In hym-selfe toke so gret hevynesse,

and died.

That he wasse dede wit*h*-In a day or twayn.   812

(103) LENVOY.

[leaf 134]

ye trew louers, þis[2] I be-seche you all,   813

All ye true lovers, keep clear of such affairs as this.

Syche ávauntou*rs*, fle[3] hem in euery wyse,
And as peple diffamyd, ye hem call,
ffor þai, trewly, do you gret p*r*eiudyse.
Refuse hath mad, for all sich flate*r*yse,   817
Hys castels strong, stuffyd wit*h* ordynaunce ;
ffor þai haue hade long tyme, by þair offyce,
The hole cuntre of loue in obbeisaunce.   820

(104)

And ye ladies, be

And ye, ladyes, or[4] what a-state ye be,   821
In whome worschip hath chose his dwelly*n*g place,

not so cruel as she

ffor godd*es* loue, do no sich cruelte,
Namly to hem þat haue[5] dese*r*uyd g*r*ace.
Nore[6] in no wyse ne folow not[7] the t*r*ace   825

who is rightly named La belle Dame sans Mercy.

Of hyr, þat her is namyd[8] ryght-wysly,
Which by Reson, me semyth in þis case,
May be called "la belle dame san3 mercy."   828

Explicit.[9]

(105. Sir R. Ros's Envoy, in 4 Stanzas of sevens, *ababbcc*.)

God give this book fair way,

Go, lytell boke ! god send thè good passáge !   829
Chese well thy way ; be[10] symple of man*er* !
Loke thy clothyng be[10] lyke thy pylgrymage,
And specyally, lete þis be[11] thi prayer ·

and may those who read it correct its faults,

Vn-to hem all[12] þat thè wull rede or her,   833
'Wher þou art wronge, after þair helpe to call,
Thè to corecte in any parte or all.'   835

---

[1] on UH, and T.   [2] UH, thus T.   [3] UH, sle T.
[4] UH, of T.   [5] haue UT, *om*. H.   [6] Ner H, Ne T.
[7] ye not HT.   [8] UH, is namyd her T.   [9] UH, *om*. T.
[10] be TH, by U.   [11] be H, be in T, by U.
[12] all UT, *om*. H.

(106)

Pray hem also, with thyn humble seruyse,   836

   Thi boldënes[1] to pardon in þis case;   *and pardon my boldness,*

ffor els þou art not able, in no wyse,

   To make thi selfe a-pere[2] in any place.

    And forþermor, by-seche hem, of þair grace,   840

      By þair fauour and supportacïoun,   *taking kindly this rude translation,*

      To take in gre þis Rude translacioun.   842

(107)

The which, got wot, standith full destytute   843   *destitute of eloquence and metre.*

   Of eloquence, of metre, and of[3] colours,

Lyke as oo[4] best, naked, with-out refute,

   Vpon a playn tabyde[5] all maner schours.

    I can no mor, but aske of hem socours,   847   *I ask help of those who asked me to write it.*

      At whos request you wer mad[6] in þis wyse,

      Comaundyng me with body and seruyse.   849

(108)

Ryght þus I make an end of þis processe,   850

   By-sechyng hym þat all hath in baláunce,   *God grant that no true man be vexed now like our Lover:*

That no trew man be vexid, causëlesse,

   As þis man wasse, which is of Rémembraunce;

    And all þat do þair faithfull óbseruaunce,   854

      And in þair trouth purpóse hem to endure,   *but may all fare well!*

      I pray god send[7] hem bettyr áventure.   856

    Explicit la bell dame saunce mercy.[8]

[1] boldenesse H, boldnes U.   [2] appere TH.
      [3] of H, *om.* UT.
[4] a H.   Wilde as a Harl. 372, Ff. I. 6, Camb. Univ.—Skeat.
   [5] to abyde T, to bide H.   [6] made was H.
      [7] sende H, sun U.
[8] T, *om.* U, Qui legit, emendat scriptorem, non reprehendat H.

A Hymn to the Virgin Mary to preserve King Henry.

[Lambeth MS. 306, leaf 177, back.]

(1)

Blessed Mary,	O blessed mary,[1] the flowre of vírgynite !
	O quene of hevyn Imperyall !
Empress of Hell!	O empres of hell, and lady of chastyte !
	To thè obey all aungels celestyall !
God entered thee	For the hevynly kyng enteryd thy close vírgynall, 5
	Man to redeme from dedely synne,
to get heaven for man.	That, by his deth, hevyn he myght wynne. 7

(2)

Hail,	Hayle, bryght starre of Ierusalem ! 8
Rose of Jericho!	Heyle, ruddy roose of Ierico !
	Heyle, clerènes of bethlehem !
All sinners go to thee for aid.	To thè all synners do go,
	Mercy callyng, and besechyng to & fro, 12
	Them to dyrect in this stormy se,
	As thou art parfyte rodde of Iesse. 14

(3)

O Gate of Paradise!	O clerè porte of paradyse ! 15
	O spowse of Salamoñ so eloquent !
	O quene of most precyous pryce !
	Thou art a pyller of feyth excellent !
My tongue cannot express thy brightness.	My townge is not suffycïent 19
	Thy clerènes to comprehende,
	Yf euery membre a tunge myght extende. 21

[1] 'mayde,' alterd to 'mary.'

(4)

Heyle flece of gedioñ, w*ith* vertu decorate ! 22 Hail,

  Heyle plesaunt lyly, most goodly in bewty ! lovely Lily !

Heyle towr*e* of Dauid & vyrgyn immaculat !

  Redres mans sowle from aℏ mysery, Save men from
        misery,

  That he may enter the eternal glorye. 26

    As thou art cyte of god, & sempiternal throne,

    Here now, blessyd lady, my wofuℏ mone. 28 and hear my
        moan.

(5)

O plesaunt olyue w*ith* grace circundate ! 29 O pleasant Olive !

  O lemyng lawmpe, in light passyng nature !

How greatly is thy name glorificate !

  To the geuyth p*r*aysynges euery creature !

  As thou art goddys modyr & vi*r*gyn pure, 33

    Graunt to man the blysse eternaℏ Grant man eternal
        bliss.

    When he passith thys lyfe terrestryaℏ ! 35

(6)

Heyle virgyn mary s*u*rmountyng clere tytan ; [col. 2] 36 Hail, Virgin
        Mary !

  Syttyng in hevyn most t*r*iumphantly !

Heyle blasyng starre w*ith*owte peere !

  I beseche the as thou art moder of me*r*cy,

  To p*r*eserue nobyl kyng herry 40 Preserve King
        Henry !

    And aℏ hys holy realme,

    As thou bare Iubyt*er* In bethleem. 42

EXPLICIT.

[The Wright's Chaste Wife follows, though headed by "A medycine for the tothe ache."]

Trentale Sancti Gregorii.

[*Brit. Mus. MS. Cott. Calig., A ii., leaf* 86, *back, col.* 2, *and MS. Lambeth* 306, *leaf* 110.]

[The B. Mus. text is rather earlier than the Lambeth, and is therefore printed here, the chief variations of the Lambeth MS. being put in the notes. See an earlier version in *Minor Poems of the Vernon MS.*, E. E. T. Soc.]

This noble story was written by a Pope about his mother;	[1] A nobull story wryte y fynde, A pope hit wrote to haue yn mynde Of his modur, (& of her lyf)	
who was held to be a holy	That holden was an holy wyfe,[2] Of myrthes sadde, &[3] mylde of mode,	4
and good woman,	þat alle men held[4] her holy & gode, Bothe deuowte &[5] mylde of steuen	
worthy of heaven.	þat alle men helde her wordy[6] heuen ; So holy as she was holde of name, Alle men were gladde of her fame, But as holy as she holden was,[7]	8
But the Devil	þe deuell browȝth her[8] yn a foule cas, He trifeled her so[9] with his trecherye	12
made her lustful,	And ledde her yn lust[10] of lecherye : For with lust of lecherye he her[11] begylde	
and she conceived a child.	Tyll she hadde conceyued A chylde.[12] And al so priuely she hit[13] bare That þere-of was no man ware. And, for no mon shuld wyte of þat[14] case, A-none as þe chylde born was,	16 20

[1] A Writt men ffynt, A fayre storye, The Pope hit wrote, Seint gregorye   [2] That al men helden an holy housewyffe   [3] So sade of maneres, so   [4] Alle men helden   [5] Bonoure devoute so.   [6] gesshed hire worthy to   [7] Also holy as she was   [8] The Fende it felde   [9] And travailde hir   [10] into synne   [11] That luste of loue hir so   [12] So ffer that she was with childe.   [13] So privily ner the lees she her   [14] witte her

The chylde she slowȝ & wyryede,[1]

And pryuely she hit[2] byryede.

As soon as it was born, she killed it, buried it secretly,

þer[3] was she combred yn a carefull case,

And vnshryuen þer-of she was ;[4]   24

She ne tolde no[5] preste her priuyte,

For she wolde holy holden be.[6]

and never confessed her sin to a priest.

Efte sones she fell in[7] þe same case

Ryȝth as beforn her be-tydde[8] was.   28

For she was comen of hyȝ parage,[9]

Of gentyll[10] kynne & worþy[11] lynage ;[12]

þerfore she wolde not her synne[13] shewe,

Nor yn schryfte hit be[14] knowe,[15]   32

And so here[16] dedes were not a-spyed ;

But afturwarde sodenly[17] she dyed.

Afterwards she died suddenly,

When she was seyn so sodenly[18] dye,

Men hoped she was yn heuen hye ;[19]   36

They helde her[20] so holy & deuowte,

þat of here deth þey made[21] no dowte,

But sykurly men wende y-wys[22]

þat she was worþy[23] heuen blys.   40

and men hoped she had gone to heaven.

Then aftur with-Inne a shorte[24] tyme,

Vpon a day soone aftyr pryme,

The pope, as he at his massë[25] stode,

Vpon his modur he hadde þowȝt[26] goode,   44

Prayng to god with conciens clere

[leaf 87, col. 1] But one day as the Pope was at Mass,

he prayed God to

---

[1] Be the necke the child she wriede.   [2] And a-none the childe she
[3] Thus   [4] She shewed neuer shryfte þerof, alas!   [5] She tolde neuer
[6] L. transposes this and the line above, and adds,
     Alle folke were fayne of hire name,
     So holy she was holdene, and of gode fame.
     Twyes
[7] hir felle the   [8] as hit be-forne   [9] price   [10] Riche   [11] gentille
  [12] L. adds, Hir sonne was Gregory the pope ;
     Men helden hir holy with alle her hope.
   [13] durste she no shryft   [14] lest be schreft hir case were
  [15] L. adds, So shame maketh men to hide ther shryffte,
     And lese the grace of god alle-myght,
     And sethen to lyve synfully,
     And fallen to dethe sodeynly.
[16] This womans   [17] And sothely afterward   [18] softly   [19] fulle hie
[20] helden hire   [21] men had   [22] wenden witterly al to wysse   [23] sett in
  [24] Ther after . . . litelle   [25] Her Sonne the pope at the mas
    [26] And of his moder hee trowed but

tell him the truth
about his mother;
and suddenly a
great darkness
came over him,
The soþe to knowë as hit were ; [1]

And sodenly, yn myddës his [2] masse,

þer þrowȝ to hym sucħ a [3] derkenesse   48

þat he lakkede ner [4] þe dayës lyȝt,

For hit was [5] derkë as mydnyȝt ;

In þat derkenes was [6] myste among.

which stank,
     Aħ a-stonyed he stode, so hit stongke ; [7]   52

Be-syde he loked vnþur hys lere ;

and from it came
a gruesome thing
In þat derknes a þyng þrew hym [8] nere,

A wonþurfuħ [9] grysely creature,

like a fiend,
Aftur a fend fyred with aħ her' feture, [10]   56

Aħ ragged & rente, boþe elenge & [11] eueħ,

as horrible as any
devil,
As orrybuħ [12] to be-holde as any [13] deueħ :

Mowthë, facë, [14] eres & yes,

all aflame.
Brennede aħ [15] fuħ of brennyng lyes.   60

[16] He was so agast of þat grysyly goste,

That yn a swonyng he was almoste ;

He conjured the
spectre
He halsed hit, þorow [16] goddes myȝte,

That þe fende he putte to flyȝte, [17]   64

And be þe vertu of hys blode

That for mankynde dyed on Rode,

to tell him why
it came
" Sey me sykerly þe soþë [18] soone

What þou hast [19] yn þis place to done :   68

to trouble him
at Mass.
What ys þy cause þou cursed [20] wreche,

Thus at masse me for to [21] drecche ? "

The ghost
answered,
" I am thy
mother."
     þe gost answered with drury [22] chere

" I am þy modur þat þe beere,   72

þat for vnschryuen dedes so [23] derne

In byttyr paynes þus y brenne."

---

[1] L. omits lines 45, 46.   [2] the myd   [3] drewe to him a grete
[4] That blacked alle   [5] And was alse   [6] And in the derknes a
[7] L., Stonyed he was of a stynche fulle stronge.
     Ther-of so gresely he was a-gaste
     That in swonyng he was alle-moste.
[8] Amiddes the derknes that þat drewe on   [9] wonder
[10] But as a ffende was hir feture   [11] So ragged so rent and also   [12] dredfulle
[13] helle   [14] and nose   [15] Flammynge   [16–16] He asked fullyche bi
[17] That alle deuelis shulde drade by right   [18] Sey thou me the sothe wel
[19] Whate hate thou   [20] the cause that þu weked
[21] Thus me at masse do der and   [22] drery   [23] *om.* so

Then sayde[1] þe pope, "alas! Alas!

Modur, þis ys to me[2] a wondur case.   76

A! leef[3] modur! how may þis be

In such paynes[4] þe for to se?

For alle men wende y-wys[5]

That þou hadde bene wordy[6] heuen blys,   80

And fulł good[7] þat þou were

To praye for vs þat ben[8] here.

Sey me, modyr, with-outen fayne

Why art þou put to alł þis payne."   84

    She sayde, "sone, sykerly[9]

I shalle þe telle þe causë why :

For y was not such as y semed,

But mychë[10] worsë þen men wened ;   88

I lyuede in lustes[11] wykkydly in my lyfe,

Of þe whyche y wolde me not[12] shryfe ;"

And[13] tolde hym trewly alł þe[14] case

Fro þe bygynnyng how þat[15] hit wase.   92

   [16]The pope lette teres a-down Renne,

And to his modyr he sayde þen,[16]

"Telle me now, modur, for[17] loue of mary flour,

If any þyng may þe help or[18] sokour?   96

[19]Bedes, or masse, þy penaunce to bye,

Or ony fastyng þy sorowe to aleye ;

What crafte,[20] or caste, or any oþur þyng

The may help, or be þy Releuyng." [19]   100

" My[21] blessed sone," sayde she,

"Fulł welł y hope þat hit may[22] be ;

Syker & saf myзth y[23] be welł,

[1] Tho answerd   [7] My moder this is   [3] Alas   [4] A-Raye
[5] Men wendyne witterlyche I-wis   [6] were worthi to haue
[7] fulle welle with god   [8] leven   [9] my sonne sothefastlye
[10] Butt wecked and   [11] I synned   [12] durste me neuer   [13] She   [14] her
[15] From one tille other as   [16—16] L. omits these lines.
[17] Sey me, moder, for   [18] Yf oughte the may save and
[19—19] Wheþer fastynge or pennaunce may þee alegge,
    Bedis or masses thi peynes to brygge,
    With cost, and crafte, and other thinge
    To the be helpe of Any savynge.
[20] ?MS. ; may be ' curste '   [21] My dere   [22] welle y-holpen y myght
    [23] Holpen and savide y myghte

<small>if any one would sing 30 Masses for me on ten Chief Feasts:</small>	Who-so trewly wolde take a[1] trenteⱦ Of ten chef festës of[2] þe ȝere, To syng for me yn[3] þis manere,	104
<small>3 at Christmas,</small>	Thre masses of crystys natyuyte,	
<small>3 at the Circum- cision,</small>	And of þe xij day[4] oþur þre,	108
<small>3 at Mary's Puri- fication,</small>	Thre of our ladyes puryfycacioun,	
<small>3 at the Annunci- ation,</small>	And oþur þre of her Annunciacioun,	
<small>3 at Christ's Re- surrection,</small>	Thre of crystes gloryous Resurreccioun,	
<small>3 at His Ascen- sion,</small>	And oþer þre of his hyȝ Ascencioun,	112
<small>3 at Pentecost,</small>	And of pentecoste oþur þre,	
<small>3 on Trinity Sunday,</small>	And þre of þe blessed trinite,	
<small>3 at Mary's As- sumption,</small>	And of our ladyes Assumpcioun, oþur þre,	
<small>and 3 at her Nativity.</small>	And of here Ioyfuⱦ natiuite þre ;	116
	These ben þe chefë[5] festës ten	
	That sokour þe sowles þat ben fro heuenn.[6]	
<small>These Masses</small>	" Who so[7] sayth þese masses with-out fayle,	
	For synnfulle sowles þey shalle[8] a-vayle ;	120
<small>[leaf 87, bk., col. 1] said in one year deliver a soul from torment;</small>	Alle A[9] ȝere, with-outen) trayne, They delyuere a sowle[10] out of payne.	
	Lette say þese masses be ȝour hestes	
	With-Inne þe[11] vtas of þe[11] festes ;	124
<small>but with them should be said the prayer,</small>	And he þat shaⱦ þese masses do, Sey[12] he þer-with þis oryson also,	

[1] vnder-toke a trewe   [2] of alle   [3] on
[4] Epuphanie. L. compresses the next eight lines into four long ones.
[5] tho ilke   [6] That souerenly socouren synfulle men   [7] Whate preeste
[8] To . . . they shulden myche   [9] In one   [10] Delyuer sowles   [11] euery
[12] Shalle sey . . too. For the next four lines the Lambeth MS. (fol. 112) reads :

Trewly with-owtene ony were
Euery day thorowe-oute the yere ;
Do hem it to saye euery daye,
Or he that dothe thes masses to saye,
Whoso wille knowe this orisoun clene,
Hit is in Englisshe this myche to mene :
Oracio, ' Deus qui es nostra Redempcio '
"God, that arte oure verray Redempcioun,
To owre Sowlis sothefast saluacioun :
That chesest, alle oþer londis be-forne,
The lond of hest, in to be borne,
And thi dethe suffrest in that same,
Delyuere the Soules from helle blame !
Brynge hem oute of the fendis bonde,
And that londe out of hethen men honde !
And that pepille that levith not on the,
Throwe thi vertue a-mendide may be,

' Deus qui es n*os*tra Redempcio'

W*ith* alle þe oþ*ur* þat longen þer-to." 128

The pope was gladde here-of i*n* fay,

And to h*i*s mod*ur* þen gon he say,

" Modyr," he sayde, " þis shaH be[1] do,

For y am most bounde[2] þerto ; 132

Thou were[3] my mod*ur*, I was[4] þy sone ;

Thys same ȝere h*i*t shaH be done ;[5]

God gr*au*nte me gr*a*ce to[6] stonde i*n* stede

Aȝeyns alle þe syn*nus* þat eu*ur* þou dede ; 136

I co*m*maunde hooly, my[7] moder dere,

þ*at* þ*i*s tyme twelfmoneþ þou to me apere,

And hooly to me þy state þou telle,[8]

That how þou fare y may wyte wel*le*."[9] 140

" My sone," she sayde, " y woH yn fay ;"

And w*ith* þat worde she wente her' way.[10]

Day by day[11] þe ȝere gon passe,

The pope for-ȝate neu*ur*[12] h*i*s masse 144

The samë dayes þat were a-syned,

To helpe h*i*s mod*ur* þat was[13] pyned ;

And toke þe orysons aH-way þer-to

Ryȝth as she bad hym for[14] to do. 148

xij moneþ aft*ur*, as he at masse[15] stode,

W*ith* gr*e*t deuocioun & holynesse gode,[16]

At þat samë tyme fuH RygHt[17]

He sawe a fuH swetë[18] sygHt : 152

A comely lady dressed[19] & dygHt,

That aH þe worlde was not so[20] bryȝt,

Comely[21] crowned as a qwene,

And all*e* that trustyn on thi m*er*ce,
Lord, save hem all*e* for thi pite !"

[1] will*e* y [2] I am a man moste holdynge [3] artte [4] am
[5] To synge these masses y shall*e* not shonne [6] me moder the
[7] pray the holiche [8] Holiche thi state to me thowe shewe
[9] faryst I mowe it knowe [10] she vansshed*e* awaye [11] So day from day
[12] lete neu*er* to say [13] was soo [14] As his moder praide hi*m*
[15] That time a twelmothe at the masse he
[16] Holy in pr*a*yers, with devociou*n*s gode [17] And in the same tide a-plight
[18] wonder*e* sely [19] so dressyd [20] all*e* the place of hir shone
[21] Comly and

and led by 20 Angels.	Twenty Angellys her' ladde[1] betwene. 156
	He was so Raueshed[2] of þat sygħt
	That nyȝ[3] for Ioye he swoned[4] Rygħt ;
He fell down before her, and said,	He feħ down flatte by-fore[5] her' fete,
	þat deuowtly teres wepynge[6] he lete, 160
	And[7] grette here with a mylde steuen,
"Virgin Mary,	And sayde þere,[8] " lady, qwene of heuen,
[leaf 87, bk., col. 2]	Modyr of Ihesu, mayde[9] marye,
have mercy on my mother."	For my modyr, mercy I crye." 164
	[10]At þat worde, with myldë chere
The lady answered, " I am not Mary,	She hym answered on þis manere,
	" Blessed sone,[10] I am not she
	Who wenest þou[11] þat I be ; 168
	But certes,[12] as þou seest me here,
but thy mother,	I am þy modyr þat þe bere,
	That here by-fore,[13] þou wystë weħ,
who was worthy of hell,	I was wordy payne yn heħ,[14] 172
	And now y am such[15] as þou seest here,
but now from thy prayers shall enjoy heaven's bliss.	þorow help of þe[16] vertu of þy prayere ;
	Fro derknesse I dresse to[17] blyssë clere ;
	þe tyme be blessed þat y þe bere ! 176
	And, for þe kyndenesse of[18] þy good dede,
	Heuen blysse[19] shaħ be þy mede.
And all those who have Masses sung shall save themselves and their sinning friends.	And alle þo þat leten þese masses be[20] do,
	Shaħ saue hem self & oþur[21] mo ; 180
	þus may þey helpe her' frendes alle
	That Reche-lesly yn synnë falle :
Preach this, my son."	Therfore, sone, þis story þou preche ;
	And almyȝty[22] god y þe be-teche." 184
	[23]At þe endyng of her wordes euen)

---

[1] Two Angilles helden hir hem   [2] was y-Ravesshede   [3] Allemoste
[4] felle downe   [5] to-for   [6] Devoute teres ther   [7] He   [8] *om.* þere
[9] mylde   [10]—[10] Do way, she saide   [11] Ne whom þu wenest   [12] sothe
[13] Be-forne y ferde   [14] Right foule as a deville of helle   [15] I Am nowe swiche
[16] and   [17] derknesse in to   [18] and, sonne, for   [19] Sovereyn Ioye
[20] this massys this
[21] haue hem selfe and the soules.   L. omits the next two lines.
[22] My dere sonne
[23]—[23] When she hadde this saide A-none,
The Angelle to hevyn with her con gone :

An Angeⱡ her ber yn to heuen :

In-to þat placë god vs sende,

To dwelle w*ith* her w*ith*-outeꝺ ende !   188

¶ Thys ys þe vertu, y þe telle,[23]

Of seynt gregory trenteⱡe ;

But who so wyⱡ do h*i*t trewely,[1]

He mostë do more sykurly :[2]   192

þe p*r*este þat þe masse shaⱡ[3] synge,

At eche feste þat he doþ h*i*t mynge,[4]

He moste say w*ith* good deuociouꝺ,

Ouer[5] Eueꝺ þe *com*mendacyou*n*,   196

Placebo & dyryge[6] also,

The sowle to brynge out of woo ;

And also þe salm*is*[7] seue*n*ne

For[8] to brynge þe sowle to[9] heuen ;   200

Among oþ*ur* p*r*ayeres þey ben[10] good

To brynge sowles[11] fro helle f[l]ode,[12]

For eu*er*y psalme qwencheth[13] a sy*n*ne

As ofte as a man þoth he*m*) my*n*ne.[14]   204

Loke[15] w*ith* good deuocyon þou hem[16] say,

And to alle halewes þat þou[17] pray,

To[18] helpe þe w*ith* aⱡ her' my3te

The sowle[19] to brynge to heuen bry3ht   208

There euur ys day, and neuur ny3ht ;

Cryst gr*a*unt vs parte of þat ly3ht ![20]

Loke þese[21] ben sayde alle in fere

Then an angel bare the Pope's mother into heaven.

Such is the power of St. Gregory's Trental.

But the priest who sings the

Mass should say the Commendation the eve before, the Dirge too,

and the 7 Penitential Psalms,

for every Psalm quenches a sin.

[leaf 88, col. 1]

He should pray also to all the Saints,

To that place god vs sende
That wonneth in blysse with-owten ende !
Now haue we herd fayre and wele
The vertus (of Seint Gregories trentall*e*)

[1] parfitely   [2] therto trewly   [3] shall*e* this trentall*e*   [4] dothe mynde
[5] Eu*er*y   [6] & the direges he most sey   [7] spalmes   [8] That helpeth
[9] till*e*   [10] For A-monge all*e* other they beth*e*   [11] the soule
[12] flode L. (*fode*, Cott., is offspring, person).   [13] dothe quynche
[14] Any man dothe them be-gynne. L. adds:
And with gode Devocion seith þe*m* to the ende,
Then may the soules to hevyn wende ;
Therfor*e* this Salme haue ye in thought ;
The xv Salmes for-yete ye nought ;
The letany also ye haue in mynde,
Loke thou leve hit not be-hynde.
[15] *om*. Look   [16] hit   [17] hallowu*n* ther-w*ith* to   [18] Pray hem to
[19] soules   [20] vs grace to se that sight   [21] þis

and say all these prayers every day in the year.	Euery day yn[1] þe ȝere ;	212
	Neuer a day þat þou[2] for-gete,	
	These to say þou ne[3] lette ;	
And in the octave of every feast	Also in þe Vtas[4] of euery feste	
	Al so longe as hit doth[5] leste—	216
	Viij^te dayis men) callen þe Vtas—	
the priest must	þe preste moste say in his masse,	
	(A nobull orysoun) hit ys holde,)	
say the Collect I spoke of first, and after the first orison,	þe colette þat fyrst y of tolde ;	220
	And aftur þe fyrste orysoun),	
	þer ys an-oþur of gret Renoun)	
	þat to þe sowle ys wonþur swete,	
the Secret;	Menne calle hit þe ' secrete.'[6]	224
and after Mass	When þe preste hath don[7] his masse,	
	Vsed,[8] & his hondes wasche,	
	A-noþur oryson he moste say	
	þat yn þe boke fynde he may,	228
the Post Communion.	þe ' post comen '[9] men don hit calle,	
	That helpeth sowles out of þralle ;	
If this be done,	And þat þis be don at eche a feste	
	As þe trentall speketh[10] moste & leste ;	232
assuredly the soul will be brought from hell to endless joy.	Then may þou be sykur & certayne[11]	
	To brynge þe sowle out of[12] payne	
	To endeles Ioye, þat lasteth aye,	
	þat god dyed fore on good fryday.[13]	236
May God bring us to everlasting joy in heaven ! Amen !	To þat Ioye he[14] vs brynge	
	þat ys in heuen with-oute endynge !	
	Pray we alle hit may so[15] be,	
	And say Amen for[16] charyte !	240

EXPLICIT. [SENT GREGORYS TRENTALLE, L.]

[HERE AFTER FOLOWETH MEDCYNES OF LECHECRAFTE, FOL. 114 L. 'Vrbanitatis' follows in Calig. A ii. : printed in *Babees Book*, E. E. T. Soc., Orig. Ser. No. 32.]

[1] thorowe   [2] And euery day loke thou not   [3] This is to say loke thou not
[4] In the evtas   [5] they do
[6] L. has the side note, *Secret*[*um.*] *Omnipotens sempiterne deus.*   [7] sacred
[8] And vsid   [9] L. side note, *post communionem.* *Deus cuius nomine* (?).
[10] That . . . speketh of   [11] fulle serteyne   [12] sowles oute of her
[13] He vs graunte that for vs Dyed on gode Frydaye.   [14] god   [15] that hit so
[16] Amen, Amen per

The Adulterous Falmouth Squire.

(A STORY OF TOO SKWYRYS THAT WERE BRETHERN, THE WYCHE
DWELLYD HERE YN YNGLOND, YN THE TOUNE OF FAL-
MOWTHT, YN DORSETSCHERE ; THE TONE WAS DAMPNYD
FOR BREKYNG OF HYS WEDLOK, THE TOTHER WAS SAUYD.—
Lambeth MS. 306, leaf 110 : in a 16th century hand.)

PROLOGUE.

From MS. Ashmole 61, *fol.* 136.

SIR WILLIAM BASTERDFELD'S WARNING.

All crysten men þat walke by me,   Christian men!
Be-hold *and* se þ*i*s dulfull syȝht !
It helpys not to calle ne cry,
For I ame dampned, a dollfole wyȝht. 4 I am damned.
Some tyme in Ingland duellyng*e*—
Thys was trew w*ith*-outen lesyng*e*—
I was callyd s*ir* Wylli*a*m Basterdfeld, knyȝt ; I was Sir William
Be-were be me, both kynge *and* knyȝht, 8 Basterdfeld.
And amend ȝou whyle ȝe haue space,
Fore I haue lost eu*er*-lastyng*e* lyȝht, I have lost ever-
And þ*us* of m*er*cy cane I gete no g*ra*ce. lasting bliss;
When I was now as ȝe be, 12
I kepyd neu*er* oþ*er* lyffe,
I spendyd my lyffe in vanyte, for I spent my
I[n] veynglory, bate, *and* stryffe ; life in vain-glory
Grete othes w*ith* me w*er* fulle ryffe ; 16 and swearing,
I had no g*ra*ce me to amend,
I sparyd noþ*er* meyd ne wyffe, and spared neither
And þ*at* hath brouȝt me to þ*i*s ende. maid nor wife.
I hade no hape whyll I was here 20

I did not repent	Forto a-ryse *and* me repent,
	Tyll þat I was brouȝt on bere ;
till it was too late,	Than was to late, ffore I was schente.
	All-wey w*ith* þem I ame aweyde, 24
and I shall burn for ever in hell.	In fyre of hell I schall eu*er* be brente ;
	Alas ! þis world hath me deseyuede,
	For*e* I had no gr*a*ce me to amende.
I spent my life in lechery,	In lechery I lede my lyfe, 28
	For*e* I hade gode *and* gold at wylle ;
	I scleuȝe my selue w*ith*-outene knyffe,
gluttony, and sloth.	And of glotony I hade my fylle ;
	In sleuth I ley, *and* slepyd stylle. 32
	I was deseyued in a reyste,
I was slain,	A dolefulle deth þat dyde me kylle ;
	Than was to late off had-I-wyste.
	Thus ame I lappyd all a-boute ; 36
and am now gnawed by toads and snakes.	W*ith* todys *and* snaks, as ȝe may se,
	I ame gnawyn*e* my body a-boute.
	Alas, alas ! full wo is me,
	It is to late, it will not be ! 40
I sinned with women great and small,	I knaw welle women, m*or and* myn*n*e,
	For*e* hy*m* þat dyȝed for*e* ȝou *and* me,
	Aryse, *and* rest not in ȝo*ur* syn*n*e !
	For*e* when I was in my flowres, 44
and was as gay as a bird on brier; but now I suffer sharply for it,	Than was I lyȝht as byrd o*n* brere ;
	Ther*e*-for*e* I suffer*e* scharpe schoures,
	And by þat bergayn*e* wonder dere,
	And byde in peynes many *and* sere ; 48
	Ther*e*-for*e* þ*us* I make my mone.
and no prayer can help me.	Now may helpe me no pr*a*yer*e*,
	I have no gode bot god alone.
Woe be to them who will not be-ware by me!	Wo be þei, who so eu*er* þei be, 52
	And haue þer v wytt*es* at wylle,
	And wyll not be-w*er* be me,
	And knaw gode thing*e* fro þ*e* ylle.
[leaf 136, back] Let not the poor want,	The pore, for*e* faute late þem not spylle ! 56
	And ȝe do, ȝo*ur* deth is dyȝht ;

Ʒoure fals flessch ʒe not fullfylle,

Lost *with* lucyfere fro *the* lyʒht.

or you will die for it.

In delycate mete*s* I sette my delyte,

And myʒhty wynes vn-to my pay;

60 I delighted in delicate dishes,

That make þ*is* wormys *on* me to byte,

Th*er*-fore my song is well-y-wey!

and now worms bite me.

I myʒht not fast, I wold not p*r*aye,

64 I would not pray;

I thouʒt to amend me *in* my*n* age,

I droffe eu*er* forth fro dey to dey,

There-fore I byde here *in* þis cage.

I put off amendment;

therefore I burn in everlasting fire—

Thys cage is eu*er* lastynge fyre;

68

I ame ordeynd þer-in to duelle;

It is me gyue*n*, fore myn*e* hyre,

Eu*er* to bryn*e* in þe pytte of helle.

in the pit of hell,

I ame fet*er*yd w*ith* þe fende*s* selle,

72 fettered as a beast in a stall.

There I a-byde as best in stalle;

There is no tonge my care can*e* telle,

Be-were ʒe haue not sych a falle!

Be ware by me.

Alas þat eu*er* I borne was,

76 Alas that I ever was born!

Or moder*e* me bore! why dyde sche so?

For I ame lost fore my trespas,

And a-byde in eu*er*-lastynge wo;

I am in woe for ever,

I haue no frend, bot many a fo.

80

Be-hold me how þat I ame tou*r*ne,

Fore I ame rente fro tope to to;

and torn from top to toe.

Alas þat eu*er* I was borne!

Gode broþ*er*, haue me *in* mynd,

84 Good brother, think on thy death

And thinke how þ*ou* schall dyʒe all wey,

And to þi soule be not vn-kynde,

Remenbyre it boþe nyʒt *and* dey!

night and day.

Besyly lokë þat þou p*r*aye,

88 Pray Heaven's King

And be-seke þo*u* heue*n* kynge

To saue þe *on* þat dredfull dey

to save thee on the Day of Reckoning,

That eu*er*y man schall gyffe rekeny*nge*;

Fore þ*er* no lorde*s* schall fore þe pray*e*,

92 when no lords

Ne Justys, noþ*er* no man*e* of lawe;

or man of law

There charte*r* helpys þe not þat dey,

can help thee,

nor any plea.	There pletyn*e* is not worth an hawe.
God grant thee and every man to know himself!	God gyue þe *grace* þi selue to know, 96 And eu*ery* man*e* in hys degre !
Farewell ! The horn blows for me.	Fare wele ! I here an horn*e* blow, I may no leng*er* byde w*ith* þe.

The Story.

(*From MS. Lambeth* 306, *fol.* 107—110 (*sign l.* 3—6, *which has no Prologue*).

Take heed to my talking!	**M**An, Frome[1] myschefe thou þe A-mende, 100 And to my talkynge thou take gode hede,
Keep from the seven Sins.	Fro synnes vij thou the defende, The leste of a*ll* is for to drede ; For of the leste y wi*ll* you speke, 104 And for to fabi*ll* I wi*ll* you noug*ht* ;[2]
God will be avenged on him who breaks his wedlock,	Be warë, man*n*, god wi*ll* hi*m* wreke Off hi*m* that is cause, spowsode to breke.[3] The first Sacrement that eu*er* god made, 108 That was wedlok, in gode faye ; Kepe[4] thou hit[5] wi*th*-outë dred,
which lasts till the judgment day;	For hit lastith ti*ll*[6] domes daye. For his bonde we may a*ll* breke,[7] 112 His owne worde, and[8] we wi*ll* halde,
for death shall come to all,	To[9] deth*e* comë that sha*ll* wreke,[10] And be cast in claye fu*ll* colde.[11]
and the greatest kings shall lose their crowns.	The grett*er*[12] kynge of a*ll* the worlde 116 By som*n* cause his Crowne may for-gone,— I take witnesse of olde and yenge,[13] Off kynge Sacre and kynge Salamond*,[14] Off Davit[15] that made the Sauter booke,[16]— 120
[leaf 107, back]	Criste of[17] hym his crowne con*n*[18] take.[19]

---

[1] MS. Ashmole, fro   [2] fro hell I wyll you tech   [3] his teching do breke
[4] Be-leue   [5] þat   [6] þat schall last to   [7] This line omitted.   [8] if
[9] Tyll   [10] all shall werke   [11] vs all in cley to fold   [12] gretyst
[13] kyng rycherd   [14] And kynge faber*e* and Absalome   [15] And kynge Dauyd
[16] Add, "For synne þat he dyde w*ith* bersabe"   [17] fro   [18] he
[19] Add, "Thus holy wryte tellys me"

The grettest Clerke that Euer thou seste,

To take hym vnder heuen cope,[1]

He may neuer take order of preste, 124

But he haue licence[2] of the pope,

And he be getten in bawdre,[3]

Or ellis a bastarde he be borne,—

This cause I tell well for the,[4]— 128

The order of preest-hode[5] he has forlorne.

The[6] begger at the townës ende,

To hym wedlok is as fre

As to the Ricchest kynge or quene,[7] 132

For all is but one[8] dignyte.

Man), yf thou wist whate it were

To take a-noþer then thi wyffe,

Thou wolde[9] rather suffre here[10] 136

To be quycke[11] slayne with a knyffe;

For yf thou take a-noþer manes wyffe,

A wronge aire[12] thou moste nedis gett¹

And this (*sic*) thou bringest iij sowles in stryfe, 140

In hellë fyre to bren[13] and hete.

But write thes thingës in thine[14] herte

That felis the[15] gilty in this case,

With shryfte of mouthe and pennaunce smerte, 144

They wene ther blis for to vmbrace,[16]

But and thei dye a sodeyne dethe

With-outen shrefte or penaunce,[17]

To helle they gone[18] with-outen lese,[19] 148

For thay can chese none oþer chaunce.

A gode Ensampill[20] y will[21] tell;

To my talkynge ye[22] take gode[23] hede,

In Falmowthe[24] this case be-fell. 152

Thirty wynter be-for[25] the dethe

---

[1] This line (not in Lambeth MS.) is from MS. Ashmole. [2] leue
[3] vowtry [4] Thus I canne well telle to ye [5] preste [6] And the
[7] þe ryall kyng of kyne [8] a [9] woldyst [10] it [11] Omitted.
[12] eyere [13] ly [14] wreches thinke in þer [15] fele þem [16] vn brace
[17] repentans [18] go [19] lete [20] sampull [21] þou inserted.
[22] tale if ȝe [23] Omitted. [24] felamownte [25] senne

the Black Death, dwelt two brothers,

Ther dwellyd two breþeren in a[1] towne,

By on) Fadir and moder goten and borne,[2]

Squiers thei were of gret Renowne,   156

the elder of whom had a lovely wife,

[3] As the story teH[4] me by-forne.

The elder broþer had a wyfe,

The fairest woman) in any[5] londe,

but he lived a cursed life,

And yett he[6] vsid' a cursid' lyfe,   160

And brougħt his[7] soule in bitter bonde ;

and had every woman he could,

He Rougħt not whate woman) he toke,

So liteH he sett by his spoushode,[8]

till the devil crooked him.

To[9] the deviH caught him in his[10] croke,   164

And witħ grete myschefe marked his mede.[11]

One day both Brothers were slain ;

Thes two breþeren) vpon) a daye

With Enmyse were slayne in figħt' ;

the elder went to Hell,
and the younger to Paradise.

The elder to hellë[12] toke the waye,   168

The yonger to paradicë brigħt' ;[13]

And this was knowen) in sothefastnes ;[14]

Herken),[15] sires, whate y wiH[16] saye !

Take gode hede bothe more and lasse,   172

For godis loue ber this[17] a-waye !

The elder left a son

The elder broþer hade a Sonne to[18] clerke,

WeH of fyftene wynter of age ;[19]

He was wyse &[20] holy in[21] worke,   176

and heir,

To[22] hym shulde falle the Eritage.

For his Fader he made grete mone,

a good child,

As fallis a gode childe euer[23] of kynde ;

Eiche[24] nygħt' to his Fadir grave wolde he gone,   180

To[25] haue his soule in SpeciaH mynde.[26]

who prayed

Thus he prayed' bothe day and nygħt'

To god and to his modir dere,

to know where his father was.

Off his Fadyr to haue a Sigħt',   184

To wytt[27] in whate place that he[28] were.

---

[1] þe   [2] getyne   [3] This line follows line 154 in MS. Ashmole.   [4] tellys
[5] all þat   [6] Omitted.   [7] hyre   [8] wyffe   [9] Omitted.   [10] A
[11] And marked his mede with, etc.   [12] helle he   [13] ry3ht   [14] sothnes
[15] Herkyns   [16] schall   [17] this tale   [18] a   [19] fully xv 3ere of Age
[20] ry3ht   [21] in hys   [22] Tho   [23] sone   [24] Euery   [25] For to
[26] in minde   [27] Omitted.   [28] he in

The childe that was so nobiłł and wise
Stode at his Fadir graue at eve ; [1]
Ther come in [2] oone in a white Surplice,
And priuely toke him by the sleve,
And saydł, " Childe, come on witħ me, [3]
God [4] hase herde thi prayer ;
Child, thi Fader thou shalt see,
Where he brenys [5] in hellë fyre."
He led him to A comly hiłł,
The Erthe openedł, and in thay yode ; [6]
Smoke and fire ther con [7] oute falle ; [8]
And many gostis glowinge on glede, [9]
In peynes stronge, and troubiłł witħ-alle. [10]
Ther he sawe many Sore turment,
How saules were putt in grete pyne ; [11]
He sawe his Faþer how he brentt,
And by the membrys how that [12] he henge ; [13]
Fendis black [14] witħ Crokis kene
Ṙent his body fro litħe to lytħ. [15]
" Child, þu comyste [16] thi Fadir to sene,
Loke vp nowe, and speke him witħ." [17]
" Alas, Fadyr, how standis [18] this case
That ye bene in this peynës stronge ? "
" Sonne," he said, " y may sey alas
That euer y dił thi moder wronge,
For she was bothë fayre and gode,
And also bothe tresti and trewe.
Alas ! y am [19] worssë than wode
Myn ownë balë for to [20] brewe."
" Fadir, [21] is ther no [22] Saint in hevyn
That ye were wonte to haue in mynde,
That myght you helpe [23] oute of this payne, [24]

188

192

196

200

204

208

212

216

[leaf 108, back]

An Angel in white
came to him,

told him he

should see his
father in Hell-
fire,

and then took him
into Hell.

The son saw
spirits in torment,

and his father
burning,
hung up by his
sinning members,
and torn by fiends
with sharp hooks.

The father repents
of his sin against
his fair, good wife,

[1] *grauys graue*   [2] Omitted.   [3] Come onne chyld and go witħ me
[4] For God   [5] bryneth   [6] he in ȝede   [7] gan þer   [8] welle
[9] saules glo-wand in glede   [10] This line omitted.   [11] py[n]inge
[12] Omitted.   [13] hynge   [14] bold   [15] fader fro lyth to leme   [16] conets
[17] with him   [18] stand   [19] was   [20] þer I dyde   [21] Wheþer   [22] any
[23] lowse   [24] prison

[leaf 109]   Our lady mary, or some gode frende ? "

and says that no
saint or angel can
rid him of his
pain,

" Sonne, aH the saintes that bethe in hevyɲ),

Nor aH the Angilles vndir the trinite,[1]   220

For to redde me[2] of this payne

They haue no power for to helpe[3] me.

not if every blade
of grass were a
priest to pray for
him;

Sonne, and[4] euery gresse were a preeste

That growiҺ vpon goddis grownde,   224

Off this paynes[5] that thou me seste

Canne neuer makë me vnbounde.

and his son, when
made priest, must
never pray for him
for seven whole
years

Sonne, þu shalt be a preeste, y wote it wele ;

Onys or this day seveɲ) yere—   228

Att' messe ne[6] matynes, mett' ne[7] mele,—

Thou take me neuer in thi prayer :

Loke, Sonne, þu do as Y the saye !

lest he should
increase his pains,

Therfor y warne the wele before,   232

For euer the lenger[8] þu prayes for me

My paynes shaH be more and more.

Fare wele," he saide, " my derë Sonne,

The Fadir of hevyɲ) be-teche y the,   236

but he must warn
all against break-
ing their wedlock.

And warne euery man, where-so þu come,

Off wedlok to brekë,[9] ware to be."

The Angel then
takes the son up

The AngiH be-ganne þe child to lede

Oute[10] of that wrechidly[11] wone   240

In-to a forest was longe in brede ;

The sonne was vp, and brigҺt' it' shone.

to a fair Mansion
with crystal gates

He led him to a fayre Erbere,[12]

The yatis[13] were of clene Cristalle   244

That to his sigҺt' were passyng' fayre.

And as[14] brigҺt' as any beralle ;

The wallys semed of' gold brigҺt',

WiҺ dorrys that were higҺ and longe,[15]   248

whereon they
hear Angels,
[leaf 109, back]

Thay harde vpon the yatis on higҺ,[16]

Mynstralsy and Angelle[17] songe :—

---

[1] skye   [2] one oure space oute   [3] to lyst me   [4] if   [5] peyne   [6] At
          [7] ne At   [8] more   [9] brekynge   [10] Sone oute   [11] wrechyd
               [12] arbour   [13] pathys   [14] als   [15] dores and with tourys strong
                         [16] hyht   [17] with Angelles

The pellycan and the papynjaye,

pelicans,

The tymor and the turtiłł trewe,

252 turtle doves,

An hondered thousande in[1] her laye,[2]

The nyghtyngale witħ not*is* newe.

and nightingales
sing.

On a grene hiłł he sawe a tre,[3]

And on a hill a
tree,

The Savoure[4] of[t] hit[t] was stronge & store,

256

Pale it was, and wanne of ble,

wan

Lost[t] hit had bothe[5] frute and floure.

A Ruthefułł[6] sigħt[t] that child con) see,

And of that[t] sigħt[t] he had grete drede,

260

"A ! dere[7] lady, howe may this bee,[8]

The blode of[t] this tre bledis[9] so rede ?"

and bleeding:

The Angiłł saide, " childe,[10] this is the tree

That God, Adam, the frute for-bede,

264 the Tree for-
bidden to Adam
in Paradise,

And therfor drevyn oute was hee,

And in the Erthe his lyfe to lede.

In the same place ther yn feste it blede,[11]

Grewe[12] the appiłł that Adam bote,

268

And that was thorougħ Evys rede

And the deviłł of hełł, fułł wełł y wote.[13]

Whan Any Synfułł comys here in,

which bled afresh
whenever a sinful

As þu sest nowe here[14] witħ me,

272 person came near
it.

For vengeance of that cursyd Synne,

The blode wiłł Ranne[15] oute of[t] the tre."

He ladd*e* him forthe vpon) a[16] playne,

Then the Angel
takes the son to

He was ware of a pynacle pigħt[t],—

276 a shining tent,

Suche on) had[17] he neu*er* sayne,[18]—

Off clothes of gold burneyssħed[t] brigħt[t];

Ther-vnd*er* sate a crëature

and there he sees
a man whom

As[19] brigħt[t] as any Sonnë beme,

280 angels honour,

Angillis[20] did[t] him grete honoure ;

"Lo, childe,"[21] he saide, " this is thy neme ;

even his Uncle,
in Heaven,

Ther, Faþ*er*[22] broþ*er* thou may senne in heuen,[23]

[1] on [2] rewe [3] an hylle [4] fauour [5] hat þe [6] reufull [7] god
[8] le [9] lokys [10] Omitted. [11] For in the place ther thou seys it spred
[12] Grow [13] it knewote [14] chyld [15] ryuneth [16] þe [17] saw
[18] none [19] Als [20] The angell [21] son [22] Thy feyr [23] Omitted.

In heuen[1] blissë with-oute Ende ;   284

where his father
might have been
had he kept truly
his wedlock.

So myght¹ thi Faþer hauë[2] bene

And he to wedlock¹ had ben kynde,

But[3] therfor he has getten) him helle

Endles in the[4] depe dongeon)   288

Ther euer more for to dwelle ;

Fro that place is þer no[5] Redempcion)."

Leave then thy
misdeeds, man,

Man), from myschefe thou[6] þe a-mende,

And þu may sitt full[7] safe from care :   292

From dedely synne thou[8] the defende,

and go to bliss.

And stryghte to[9] blisse thi soule shall fare.

EXPLICIT.

[10] A story of too skwyrys that were brethern, the whyche
dwellyd here yn ynglond, yn the towne of Falmowtht,
yn Dorsetschere ; the tone was dampnyd for brekyng
of hys wedlok, the tother was sauyd.[10]

HERE FOLOWITH SENT GREGORIS TRENTALL*E*.[10]

[1] heuen*s*   [2] well a   [3] Omitted.   [4] þa*t*
[5] i*n* helle is no   [6] Omitted.   [7] all   [8] god   [9] And vnto
[10]—[10] These words are in a later hand.

Ihesu, Mercy for my Mysdede!

A DEUOYT MEDITACIONE.

[*Trin. Coll. Cambridge, B.* 10, 12, *leaf* 53. *Date of MS.
about* 1450.]

[22 *stanzas of eights, abab, cdcd.*]

(1)

Ihesu, mercy! mercy, I cry :
   myn vgly synnes þou me forgyfe.
þᵉ werlde, my flesch, þᵉ fende, felly
   þai me besale both strange & styfe ;
I hafe ful oft to þaim consent,
   & so to do it is gret drede ;
I ask mercy *with* gud entent ;
   Ihesu, mercy for my mysdede !

> Jesu, forgive me my sins!
>
> The world, the flesh, and the devil,
>
> 4
>
> I have oft consented to them.
>
> 8   Jesu, mercy!

(2)

þe werlde thurgh his fals couetyse,
   þᵉ fende *with* pryde, wreth, ire, envy,
I hafe, ihesu, bene fylde oft sythys,
   my flesche *with* slewth & lychery,
And oþere many ful gret synnes :
   with repentance, ihesu, me fede,
for euere my tyme opon me rynnes :
   Ihesu, mercy for my myse-dede !

> Pride, wrath, sloth, and lechery have filled me.
>
> 12
>
> Feed me with repentance.
>
> 16   Jesu, mercy!

(3)

Turne not þi face, ihesu, fro me,
   þof I be werst in my lyfynge ;
I ask mekely mercy of þe,
   for þi mercy passes al thynge.
In þi fyue woundes þou sett my hert,
   þat for mankynde on rode walde blede,
& for þi dede vgly & smert,
   Ihesu, mercy for [my¹] myse-dede !
               ¹ Omitted in MS.

> Turn not Thy face from me ;
>
> meekly I ask mercy.
>
> 20
>
> Set my heart in Thy five wounds,
>
> 24   and have mercy on my sins.

(4)

To þi lyknes þou has me made;
    þe for to lufe þou gyfe me grace!
þou art þe lufe þat neuere [1] sal fade;
    mercy I ask whils I hafe space.   28
I tryst ihesu of forgyfnes
    of al my synnes, þat is my crede;
I me betake to þi gudnes;
    ihesu, mercy for my myse dede!   32

(5)

Als touchande grace, bot ask & hafe:
þus has þou het in þi beheste,
þarfor sum grace on þe I crafe;
    with outen grace I am bot beste,   36
& warre þan beste defyled with syne;
    þou graunt þat grace may in me brede,
þat y [2] þi lufe, ihesu, myȝt wynn:
    Ihesu, mercy for my myse dede!   40

(6)

Al worldely lufe is vanite;
    bot lufe of þe passes al thynge.
þar is no lufe with outen þe;
    & þe to lufe I aske syghynge.   44
Ihesu, me graunt lufe þe forthy,
    & in þi law, ihesu, me lede.
þat I myslufede, I aske mercy:
    Ihesu, mercy for my mysdede!   48

(7)

It is of þe for to forgyfe
    alkyn tryspas both more & mynn;
It is of me, whyls I here lyfe,
    or more or lesse ilke day to synne,   52
And of þe fende to duell þer in:
    þou gyfe me grace to take gud hede
þat I þi lufe, ihesu, myght wynne!
    Ihesu, mercy for my myse dede!   56

         [2] Inserted in a different hand.

Marginal notes:

Give me grace to love Thee;
[1 leaf 53, back]

I trust Thee for forgiveness,

and yield myself to Thy goodness.

I crave Thy grace;

without it I am but a beast;

with it I may win Thy love.

Thy love passes all things.

Grant it to me,

and have mercy on me for my misdeeds.

It is Thine to forgive sins,

it is mine to commit them.

Give me grace to love Thee.

Mercy, Christ!

(8)

Dispyce me noȝt, swete lorde ihesu,
  I am þᵉ warke of þin aghen hende,
þof I hafe bene to þe vntrew ;
  Ihesu, þou kan me sone amende ;   60
þou has me made to þi lyknes,
  thurgh synne I hafe loste heuenly mede ;
Now, lorde, I aske of þi gudenes,
  Ihesu, mercy for my myse dede !   64

Despise me not,

for my unfaith-
fulness.

Thou madest me
like Thee,

have mercy on
me.

(9)

þow walde be borne for synful man,
  for syn þou take no wreke on ¹me.
[.   .   .   .   .
     .   .   .   . *no gap in MS.*]   68
My comforth be þi harde passione ;
  Ihesu, þer of hafe I gret nede ;
For synne þou graunt me contrycione :
  Ihesu, mercy for mysdede !   72

Take no venge-
ance for my sin.
[¹ leaf 54]

Let Thy sufferings
be my comfort,

and grant me re-
pentance for my
transgressions.

(10)

After my dedes þou deme me noȝt ;
  after mercy þou do to me ;
If þou me deme als I hafe wroght,
  in bytter payns I drede to be.   76
My lyfe to mende, & hafe mercy,
  my lorde ihesu, þou be my spede,
luf þᵉ, & drede, þat syttis on hy :
  Ihesu, mercy for my myse dede !   80

Judge me not
according to my
deeds ;

but help me to
mend my life

and love Thee.

(11)

If I had done ilke cursed warke,
  & alken synnes wer wroȝt in me,
þou may þaim sleke, als is a sparke
  when it is put in myddes þᵉ see ;   84
& þar may no man sleke my myse
  bot þou, ihesu, of þi godhede ;
when þou wouchesafe, þou sone forgyfese :
  Ihesu, mercy for my mysdede !   88

Thou canst
quench my sins

like a spark put
in the sea;

vouchsafe me Thy
mercy.

(12)

Who sal þe loue in fynyal blyse
  bot trow mankynde & aṅgels fre?

Restore me to the
heritage I have
lost

Myne heretage forsoth þat is:
  thurgh gude lyfeynge & grace of þe,   92
þou me restore vnto þat blyse;

through frailty of
my nature!

  beholde frelete of my manhede
þat makes me oft to do of myse:

Mercy, Jesu!

  Ihesu, mercy for my myse dede!   96

(13)

Thou desirest not
man to sin,

þo[u] wil no dede of synful man:
  þus says þou, lorde, in haly wryt;

but to turn and
amend.

Ful wele wote þou coueytis þan
  he turne his lyfe & sone mende it: 100

Give me Thy grace

þou gyfe me grace my lyfe to mende,
  beswylede in synn als wyckede wede;

and love for ever.

graunt me þi lufe with outen ende:

Mercy, Jesu!

  Ihesu, mercy for my myse dede!   104

(14)

Thou art my God,

þow art my god, I þe honour;
  þou art þe sone of maydyn & moder,

[leaf 54, back]

help me!

In my dysese þou me succure
  þou art my lorde, þou art my brother;   108

Thou shalt judge
me when all
people shall arise.

þou sal me deme, my cryatour,
  when vp sal ryse euere ilke a lede.
Mercy, ihesu, my sauyour!

Mercy, Jesu!

  Ihesu, mercy for my myse dede!   112

(15)

þou helpe me, lorde, in my dysese,

Thou helpedst
Susan in her
trouble;

  þat walde susan helpe in hir tyme;
Ful gret clamour þan gon þou pese
  when scho acusede was of crime.   116

put too my soul
at ease!

þou sett my saule, myn hert, in ese,
  þe fende to flee & his falshede,
& soferandely þe for to plese:

Jesu, mercy!

  Ihesu, mercy for my mysedede!   120

(16)

In my baptym I mayde beheste

  þᵉ for to serue lelely & wele ;

Of þi seruyse oft hafe I seste,

  w*ith* syₙnes thowsandes serued vnsele ;   124

Bot þi mercy nedes moste be sene

  þ*er* moste syₙn is & wyckededede ;

þᵉ moste synful I am, I wene ;

  Ihe*s*u, mercy for my myse dede !   128

My baptismal vow

I have not kept,

but Thy mercy is seen where most sin is.

Have mercy on me!

(17)

For synful man walde þou be borne ;

  for ryghtwys not þou wil recorde ;

when man had syₙnede, he was forlorne,

  & þan hi*m* kyndely þou restorde ;   132

þ*o*u sufferde paynes corōnde w*ith* thorne,

  nakede w*ith* outen cloth or schrede,

w*ith* mykel sorue þi body torne :

  Ihe*s*u, mercy for my mysdede !   136

Thou wast born for sinful man,

and sufferedst pain and thorns.

Jesu, have mercy on my sins!

(18)

þou art my hope, my way ful sure,

  ay lastande hele, both streng[t]h & pese ;

þou art pyte þat ay sal dure ;

  þou art gudenes þat neuer sal sese ;   140

þou art clennes, both mylde & mure ;

  me þᵉ displese, ihe*s*u, for bede,

Als þou was borne of virgyne ¹pure :

  ihe*s*u, mercy for my myse dede.   144

Thou art my hope and my salvation.

Prevent me from displeasing Thee. [¹ leaf 55]

(19)

þ*o*u byddes ilke man ȝelde gud for ill*e*,

  not il for il to ȝelde agayne ;

þan I beseke þe þat þou wil

  gr*a*unt me m*er*cy in stede of p*a*yne !   148

þ*o*u me forgyfe, & mercy gr*a*unt,

  & in my saule þou sawe þi sede,

þ*a*t I may, lorde, make myne au*a*unt :

  Ihe*s*u, mercy for my myse dede !   152

As man should return good for evil,

grant me mercy instead of punishment.

(20)

Bot, worthy lorde, to þᵉ I cry,
   & I in syne stande obstynate;
þarfore þou heres noȝt me forthy,
   þou wil noȝt here me in þat state.   156

þou gyfe me grace lefe my foly,
   & fe[r]uently þᵉ lufe & drede,
þan wate I wele I get mercy:

   Ihesu, mercy for my myse dede!   160

(21)

Noght euere-ilke man þat cales þᵉ lorde
   or mercy askes, sal hafe þi blise,
his consciencȝ bot he remorde,

   & wirke þi wil, & mende his lyfe.   164
to blyse sal I sone be restorede
   if I my saule þusgates wil fede;

Of þi mercy late me recorde:
   ihesu, mercy for my mysedede!   168

(22)

I me betake to þi mercy
   þat mercy gyffes to synful men;
þou kepe me, lorde, for I sal dye,
   & wot neuere whore, ne how, ne when.   172

In þi hote lufe me graunt to brene,
   & þat lesson trewly to rede;

Mercy þou graunt! amen! amen!
   Ihesu, mercy for my myse dede! Amen! 176

Alya Cantica.

[*Trin. Coll. Cambridge, B.* 10. 12, *leaf* 55. *Date of MS.*
about 1450.]

[5 *stanzas of eights, abab, abab.*]

(1)

Ihesu, þi name honourde myȝt be

 wiþ al þat any lyfe is in.

Nou, swet ihesu, als þou made me,

 þou kepe me ay fro dedely synne !   **4**

Ihesu, þᵉ sone of mary fre,

 þe ioy of heuen þou graunt me wynne ;

My saule, ihesu, take I to þe

 when my body & it sal twynne.   **8**

Jesu, keep me

ay from mortal sin,

[leaf 55, back] and grant me the joy of heaven.

(2)

Ihesu, þi name in me be sett

 als þou art kynnge & lorde of lyght,

& graunt me grace ai bett & bett

 my lyfe to mende & lyf ay ryght.   **12**

Ihesu, þi sydes wiþ blode war wett,

 & dulefully for me war dyght ;

þou kepe me oute of syne & dett,

 now, swete ihesu, ay moste of myght !   **16**

Set Thy name in me ;

grant me grace to mend my life,

and keep me out of sin.

(3)

Ihesu, þi name is hegh to neuen,

 & ȝit I, katyfe, cry & kall,

Ihesu, me helpe & brynge to heuen

 wiþ þᵉ to won my synful sall.   **20**

Myghty ihesu, þou here my steuen

 als þou me boght when I was thrall,

& forgyfe me þᵉ synnes seuen,

 for I am gilty in þaim all.   **24**

Jesu,

help me to heaven to dwell with Thee,

and forgive me the Seven Sins.

(4)

Jesu, my love,

Ihesu, my lufe & my lykynge,
  for euere more blyste mot þou be.

my darling,

Mi lufely lorde, my dere darlynge,
  ful wer me [fayne[1]] myght I þe se.   28

make me sing
'A lovely King
is come to me.'

Ihesu, my lorde, þou gar me synge
  a lufely kynge is comen to me ;

My trust is all in
Thee.

My swete swetnes of alkyn thynge,
  my hope & tryste is al in þe.   32

(5)

Help me evermore
at need ;

Ihesu, me helpe euere more at nede,
  & fro þe fende þou me defende ;

fix my soul in
love of Thee :

þou sett my saule in lufe & drede,
  & al my myse þat I may mende.   36

Ihesu, þi blude þat þou walde blede,
  fro þis fals lyfe or þat I wende

wash away my
sins, and grant
me endless bliss.

þou wesche a way al my mysdede,
  & graunt me blyse without outen ende.   Amen.

[1] Omitted in the MS.

𝔚𝔥𝔦 𝔞𝔯𝔱 𝔱𝔥𝔬𝔴 𝔉𝔯𝔬𝔴𝔞𝔯𝔡 𝔰𝔦𝔱𝔥 𝔍 𝔞𝔪 𝔐𝔢𝔯𝔠𝔦𝔞𝔟𝔩𝔢.

[5 *stanzas of eights, abab, bcbc.*]

[MS. Univ. Libr. Camb., Hh. iv. 12. leaf 85 *a*; handwriting
of the 15th century. In every case a stroke is drawn over the
final *on*. Sometimes the preceding *i* is omitted, in which case
it is here inserted in italics.]

In cruce sum pro te, qui peccas; desine, p*r*o me,
Desine; do veniam; dic culpa*m*, ret*r*aho pena*m*.

(1)

¶ "Vpon a crosse naylyd I was for the,
  Soffred deth to pay thy rawinson;[1]
Forsake thy synnë for the loffe of me,
  Be répentant, mak playne co*n*fessïon.   4
  To contrite hert*is* I do remissïon;
    Be nat dispayryd, for I am not ve*n*geáble;
  Gayn gostly enmys thynk on my passion;
    Whi art thow froward, sith I am me*r*ciáble?   8

I, Christ, died for thee;

forsake thy sin,

for I forgive all contrite hearts.

(2)

¶ "My blody wound*is* downe raylyng by thys tre,
  loke on hem well, and haf co*m*passïon;
The crowne of thorne, þ*e* sper*e*, and nailys thre
  Percyd hand and fote of indignac*i*on,   12
  Myn hert ryuen for thy redempcïon;
    lat us tweyn in thys thyng be greáble,
  loffe for loff, by iust conuencïon;
    whi art thow froward, sith I am me*r*ciáble?   16

Look on My wounds,

My riven heart!

Why art thou froward?

[1] or, rawmson

(3)

I pitied Peter

[leaf 85, back]

and Thomas.

I am kind

and merciful.

¶ " I had, on petyr and magdaleyne, pite
    For the gret constrent of there contricion ;
Gayne thomas Indès incredulite,
    he put hys [hand]¹ depe in my side adowne ;   20
    Rolle up thys mater, graue it in thy reson ;
        Sith I am kynd, why art þou so vnstable ?
    My blod, best triacle for thy tran[s]gression ;
        Whi art thow froward, sith I am merciáble ?   24

(4)

Think on My
humility,

and love ;

My blood spilt
drop by drop

as balm against
thy spirit's
poison !

¶ " Thynk, a-gayne pride, on myn humilete ;
    Ren to scole, record weH thys lesson ;
Gayn fals enuy, thynk on my charite,
    My blode aH spilt by distillacïon ;   28
    whi did I thys ? to safe the fro prisoune ;
        afforne thyn hert, hang thys lityll table,
    Swetter than bawme gayn aH gostly poyson ;
        Be þow not froward, sith I am merciáble."   32

(5)

"Lord, we are
mindful of Thy
death,

grant us Thy
mercy,

for Thy Mother's
sake!"

¶ " lord, on synfuH knelyng on ther knee,
    Thi deth remembryng of humble affeccion,
O ihesu, grant of thy benignite,
    That tho .v. wellys ple[n]teuose of fuyson,   36
    Callyd thy .v. wowndis by computacion,
        May wach in vs aH surfetis réproueáble.
    Now, for thy moders meke meditacion,
        At hyr request, be to us merciáble."   40

EXPLICIT.

NOTES.—L. 11, *Nailys Thre*, because one was put through the
two feet, and one through each hand. L. 19, *Thomas Indes* :—
Thomas was said in old legends to have preached in India ; see
"The Complaynt of Criste" in this volume, l. 58, and *Piers
Plowman* (vol. ii. p. 405, l. 13283), "Thaddee and ten mo :
with *Thomas of Inde*."

¹ A word is here lost.

Incypyt the Stacyons of Rome.

[Cott. Calig. A. ii. leaf 83, and Lambeth 306, leaf 152, back.
The text, to line 553, is that of the Cotton MS. : the
readings of the Lambeth MS. are in the notes.]

He þat wyłł hys sowlë[1] leche,
Lysteneth to me, and y wołł ȝou teche.
Pardon ys þe sowlë[2] bote,

At gretë Rome þer ys þe Rote : 4

Pardon, yn frensh a worde hit ys,[3]
Forȝeuënesse of synnes y-wys.
The[4] Duches of troye þat sum tyme[5] was,
To Rome she come with grete pres ;[6] 8
Of hyr came Romyrus[7] & Romulus
Of whom Rome ys cleped ȝyt y-wys :[8]
Hethen hit was, & cristened[9] nowȝt
TyŁł petyr and paule hadde hit bowȝt, 12
Wyth golde, syluere, ne[10] with good,
But with her' flesh &[11] her blode,
For þer þey suffrede bothë dethe,[12]
Here sowles to savë fro þe qweþe.[13] 16

In Rome Y shałł ȝou steuene
And honþred kyrkes fowrty and seuen ;
Chapelles þer ben many mo,
Tenne þowsand & fyfe ; also 20
A-bowte þe wałł, to & fowrty,
Grete towres þre hondredde & syxty,
Fowr & twenty gret ȝates þer be
Pryncypałł ouur oþur, y tełł þe. 24

Pardon is the
soul's cure, and
its root is in
Rome.

The Duchess of
Troy begat
Romyrus and
Romulus,

from whom Rome
was named,

and Peter and
Paul converted it.

In Rome are 147
churches,

and 10,005
chapels.

About the 42 walls
are 360 towers,

and 24 chief gates.

[1] wolle be his soullis [2] sowelys [3] Pardon, A worde in trouthe is
[4] A [5] whilom there [6] moche solace. [7] Remus [8] clepyd thus
[9] Rome was hethene, and crystene [10] Neydur with syluer, neydur
[11] and with [12] to be dede
[13] to save her soule from the qweede. L. omits the next eight lines.

¶ At seynt pet*ur* whe shall be-gy*n*ne

To telle of pardon þ*at* slaketh[1] sy*n*ne :

A fayr mynstyr men may þe*r*[2] se,

Nyne and twenty grecys þer be ;[3]   28

And al so ofte[4] as þ*ou* gost vp or downe,

Begy*n*neth of gode[5] deuocyou*n*

Thow sha[l]t haue at eche a gree,[6]—

Man or wo*m*mon whepur þou bee,—   32

Seue*n*ne ʒere of[7] pardon,

And þ*er*-to goddes benysou*n* ;[8]

Pope Alyxand*ur* h*i*t gr*a*unted at Rome,

To man or wo*m*man þ*at* ded*ur* come.   36

A-boue*n*ne þe grece, as þou shalt gone,

Stondeth a chapell hy*m* self a-lone,

In þe whycħ song petur h*i*s fyrst masse,

As þe Romayn*i*s seyn, more & lasse.   40

As often as þou wylt þyd*ur* come,

Seue*n*ne þowsand ʒer þou getest of p*a*rdon ;

And as mony lentones mo

Eu*er*y day ʒyf þou wylt þed*ur* go.   44

In þat mynster may þou[9] fynde

An houn*þ*red[10] Auters by-fore & be-hynde ;

And when þe[11] Auters halowed were,

xxiiij[12] ʒere, & so mony lentones more[13]   48

He ʒaf & gr*a*unted to[14] pardon,

And ther-to goddes[15] benesou*n*.

A-mong þe auters vij þer be

More of gr*a*ce &[16] dyngnyte :   52

The Auter of þe Vernake ys þat on,[17]

Vpon þe Ryʒth hond as þou shalt gon ;

---

[1] the pardon þ*at* quenchithe   [2] there þou myght
[3] xxxix Auters there be spesyally.   [4] As ofte   [5] Be cause of
[6] shalt . . degree.   [7] to
[8] And of thy synnes Remyssyon. The next two lines are,
Pope Alysaund*ur* grauntythe all and some
to all theyme that thydd*ur* come ;
and the next eight lines are omitted.
[9] þou mayste   [10] fowre score   [11] Alle the   [12] xviij   [13] le*n*tt*i*s by-foore
[14] of   [15] crystys   [16] moste of grace and of   [17] is one

¹The secounde, yn honour of our lady ys ;

The þrydde, of seynt symon y-wys ;

The iiij, of seynt Andrew þou shalt haue ;

þe .v. of seynt gregour, þer he lys yn graue ; ¹

The syxte, of seynt leon þe pope,²

There he song masse yn his cope ;

Of þe holy crosse þe seuennyþ ys,

In þe whych no wommon cometh ywys.

At eche on of þese Auteres þere

Is euery tyme, of pardon vij ȝere,

And as mony lentones mo

To aH þat wyH depur goo,

At þe hyȝ Auter þer petur ys done,

Pope gregory graunteth a pardon

Of synnis for-gyffenne & oþes³ Also,

Seuenne & twenty ȝere⁴ he ȝaf þer-to,

Fro holy þorsday yn-to⁵ lammes

Is⁶ euery day more & lasse,

Fowrtene⁷ þowsand ȝere.

To aH þat cometh to þat mynstere⁸

⁹On our lady day þe Assumpcioun

Is a þowsand ȝer of pardon,

On seynt petur & powle day

þat⁹ mynster was halowed, as¹⁰ y say,

þen ys þer xiiij¹¹ þowsand ȝer & le[n]tons¹² þer-to,

& þe þrydde part of þy¹³ penauns vndo.

When þe vernacuH shewed ys,

Gret pardon for soþe þer ys,¹⁴

Fowr þowsand ȝere, as y ȝou¹⁵ telle,

II. Our Lady's,

56 III. St. Simon's,

IV. St. Andrew's,

V. St. Gregory's,

VI. Pope Leo's,

60

VII. that of the
Holy Cross.

At each you get
7 years and
64 7 Lents.

At the high-altar
you get pardon
68 of sins

for 27 years,

and from Holy
Thursday to
72 Lammas

14,000 years,

and on the
Assumption of the
Virgin 1000 years.

76

On Peter and
Paul's day you
get 14,000 years of
pardons and
Lents, and are let
80 off one-third of
your penance.

[lf, 83, bk., col. 2]
When the Ve-
ronica is shown,
the residents in
the City get 4000

---

¹⁻¹ þe secunde is symonde & Iude, þou myght haue,
there of seynt gregorye there he is grave.
the iiij^te of oure ladye I-wys,
of whome the covent syngithe messe ;
the fyvithe of seynt Andrewe is.

² leo papa I-wys. L. omits the next seven lines, and transposes the eighth
and ninth, reading *doo* for *done*, to ryme with *also*.   ³ for-yeett and odur
⁴ MS. ȝef ; L and vij yere. Lambeth has, 'And vij ȝere he grauntythe therto.'
⁵ vnto   ⁶ *om.* Is   ⁷ there is xiiij   ⁸ to alle men that comys there
⁹⁻⁹ Of seynt Martyn the xviij daye this   ¹⁰ as *om.*   ¹¹ is vij   ¹² lenttis
¹³ þy *om.*   ¹⁴ is there I-wys   ¹⁵ thre thowesande yere the

years' pardon;
To men þat yn þe cyte[1] dwelle ;   84

outsiders 9000 years;
And men þat dwellen be-sydwarde,[2]
ix þowsand ȝer shaȜ be here[3] part ;

sea-crossing visitors 12,000 years,
And þou þat passen[4] ouur þe see,
xij þowsand ȝere ys graunted þe ;   88
And þer-to þou shalt haue more,[5]

and one-third of their sins forgiven. In Lent all pardons are doubled.
þe þrydde parte forȝeuenesse of þy sore.[6]
    In lenton ys more[7] grace ;
[8]Eche pardoun ys dowbled yn þat[8] place.   92

In that place are many holy bones,
In þat place þer be done
Holy bonës mony on,

of Peter, Paul,
Of petur, powle, & saynt[9] symon,

Gregory, Leo,
Seynt Iude,[10] gregour, and leon,   96

St. Petronilla,
[11]Seynt parneȜ þat holy vyrgyn,

St. Sythe,
And seynt Sythe[12] þat þoled[13] pyne,

and others
And mony mo þer are yn fere[14]

dear to Christ.
þat to Ihesu beth[15] leue & dere :   100
[16]No mon kan þe soþë say.

Pass we over four miles to St. Paul's.
þerfore passe we forth an oþur way[16]
To seynt powle, as y wene,
Fowr myle ys holden[17] be-twene ;   104
In þat place[18] ys grette pardon,
And of many synnis[19] remyssyoun ;

Saul was his first name,
Sawle was his nome[20] by-fore,
Syth þe tyme þat he was bore ;[21]   108
Heþen he was, & cristened noȝth,[22]
TyȜ criste hit putte yn[23] his powȝth ;

till Ananias christened him.
And þat holy mon Ananyas[24]
Crystened hym þorow[25] goddis grace,   112

---

[1] to hem that in Rome   [2] And they that were thyddyrwarde   [3] is theyre
[4] yff thowe passe   [5] shalt wynne   [6] For-yevenes of aȜ thy synne.
[7] lent that holy   [8]—[8] is dowbylde in eche place beethe Idoone   [9] Iude and
[10] and of sent   [11] L. inserts,
    Seynt Iohn and seynt Boneface,
    Proscesse and Martyn in that place.   See 171/841.
[12] sythi L, sythe C.   [13] suffyrde   [14] bethe I fere   [15] been to cryst
[16]—[16] Nowe passe we forthe in oure waye
    that we mowe the sothe saye
[17] been   [18] waye   [19] of synnes   [20] name
[21] frome that tyme he was I-boore   [22] he was hethen and crystyn nought
[23] hit in   [24] an holy man Amas   [25] by

And called[1] hym paule, petur brodur,
þat eche of hem shuld[2] comforte oþur;
And yn þe worshyp of þat[3] conuercyoun
ys graunted a M[lle][4] ȝere of pardon,   116
And at þe feste of his day
Two[5] Mlle ȝere haue þou may.[6]

On chyldermasse day yn[7] cristemasse
Is iiij Mlle ȝere to[8] more & lasse;   120
[9]And on seynt Martyn, þe viij day,
That mynster was halewed as y ȝou say,
Ther ys xiiij þowsand ȝere, & lentones þer-to,
And þe þrydde part of þy penauns vn-do.[9]   124
And ȝyf þou be þere aH þe ȝer,
Eche a day[10] yn þat mynster,
[11]Thow shalt have as moche pardon
As þou to seynt Iame wolde gon.[11]   128

¶ Her may we no lengur be;[12]
To saynt Anastase moste we;[13]
Two myle þer ys[14] be-twene,
Of fayr way & of clene;[15]   132
And eche a day ȝyf þou wolte trace,[16]
Seuenne Mlle ȝere þer þou hase;[17]
And þer-to shalt þou have also
The þrydde parte of þy penaunce vn-do.   136
Pope vrban, þat holy syre,
So rewardeth men for here[18] hyre;
Tho þat ben shryuen & verry[19] contryte,
Of aH here synnes he maketh[20] hem qwyte.[21]   140

Marginal notes:

In honour of his conversion you get 1000 years' pardon, and on his Festival 2000 years.

On Childermas Day you get 4000 years;

[leaf 184] at Martinmas

14,000 years, and Lents, and one-third of your penance excused. A year's daily visit to St. Paul's is as good as a pilgrimage to St. James's.

Next we go 2 miles to St. Anastasius's,

and for a daily visit there you get 7000 years' pardon, and one-third of your penance off.

If you are contrite, you are quit of all your sins.

---

[1] clepyd   [2] Ech one of them to   [3] In that Ilke   [4] Is an hundyrde
[5] A   [6] I the saye   [7] at   [8] Be xl. yere more   [9—9] omitted   [10] soneday
[11—11] thowe hatt pardone all and some
as thowe to seynt Iamis had gon & comyn.
[12] nat longe dwelle   [13] of seynt Austyn must I telle   [14] I holde
[15] Fulle fayre wayes and a green   [16] crave
[17] viii. Ml yere þou myghttis have.   L. omits the next two lines.
[18] hathe rewardede men her   [19] yf men be shreffe and   [20] alle Synnes god make
[21] L. inserts,   to alle thoo that ar Redye
In alle þe festis of oure ladye,
of pere, powle, and seynt Iohn,
Evangelystis baptysyde, & many one,
of mary mawdelyn, and kateryne,
Seynt Marget, Annes þe holy vyrgyne

Pope siluest*ur* ʒaf[1] to pylgrymes
That þyd*ur* come yn þere[2] tymes,
Penans broken, & othes also,
H*i*s holy help he putte[3] þer-to ;   144
Wrathyng[4] of fad*ur* & mod*ur*, ʒyf h*i*t be,
In goddes name he for-ʒeueþ h*i*t þe,
So þou smyte not w*ith* þyn[5] honde ;
Ryʒth so h*i*t ys, I vnþerstonde.[6]   148

Before the door
is the stone that
St. Paul was
beheaded on,
Be-fore þ*a*t[7] dore stondeth a stone,
Seynt powle[8] hedde was layde þer-on ;
A trayt*ur*[9] smote of h*i*s hede
W*ith* a swerde þat þer-by ys[10] layde ;   152

whence three
wells sprang
Ther sprong welles þre,—
Who so ys þer*e*, weħ may h*i*t[11] se,—
Of watyr boþħ fayr[12] & good,

that heal the sick.
Me*n*ne & wy*m*men haue þer boote.   156

The Virgin's first
chapel,
Scala Cæli,
is there, close by.
In þat place a chapeħ ys,
' Scala cely ' called h*i*t ys,[13]
' Laddere of heuen ' men clepeþ h*i*t
In hono*ur* of *our* lady, be my wytte.[14]   160

[leaf 84, col. 2]
[15]Ther ys two chapelles of h*er* more,
As me*n*ne in Rome tellys þore ;[15]

In it are the
bones of 10,000
Martyrs
Manye ys þe holy bone[16]
That vnþ*ur* þe hyʒ awter ys done ;[17]   164
Ten þowsand Marteres, w*ith* hono*ur*,

slain in Tiberius's
time.
In þe tyme of tyberye[18] þe e*m*pero*ur*,
They suffred deth aħ yn Rome,[19]
Her sowles yn[20] heue*n*ne for to wone.[21]   168
þ*er* men may helpe boþe[22] qwykke & dede,

thre thowesande and fyffty yere
of penau*n*ce ben for-yevyn there ;
Syluestre and gregory and od*ur* moo,
pope Nicholas confermethe thoo.

[1] gregorye   [2] comyth by dyu*er*s   [3] hande of helpe he doþe   [4] Wrathe
[5] So that þou smyttyst hym nat w*ith*   [6] And thus hit is to vndyrstande   [7] a
[8] powelys   [9] tyrau*n*t   [10] swerde there is   [11] L. his C, comythe there he may
[12] In that watyr that is ffresche   [13] celi I-clepyd I-wys   [14] hit is sett
[15—15] the seconde chapell*e*, I telle the,
In the name of her þer þou myght see
[16] boowe   [17] that on to the Auters men dothe vowe   [18] In tyme of tybyan
[19] Suffyrde dethe alle and some   [20] to   [21] come   [22] *om.* boþe

As clerkes yn her[1] bokes Rede;

[2]Who-so syngeþ masse yn þat chappeH

For any frend, he loseþ hym fro heH,

He may hym brynge þorow purgatory y-wys

In-to þe blys of paradys,

Ther sowles abyde tyH domis day

In mychë Ioye, as y ȝou say;

And iij Mlle ȝer ar grauntcd more

Of holy popes þat have ben þore:

And syx popes graunted þat þanne

That lyen at seynt sebastyan,

Pope vrban, siluester, & benet,

Lyon, Clement, confermed hyt.

¶ Passe we forth on our ȝate[3]

To saynt marye Annuncyate;[4]

Two myle ys bytwene,[5] y vnþurstonde,

But þey be somdele large &[6] longe.

Ther[7] ys wryten, as y ouȝ say,

Of owr lady yn þe[8] way,

Down she come with angelus

To a brodur of þat hows,[9]

And sayde to hym þat, eche manne

That out of dedely synne þydur camme,[10]

Fro þe fyr[11] of heH she wold hym shylde,

As she was mayden & modur mylde.

[12]And þis pardon papes han graunted

To hem þat ben verry Repentaunt:

Fyfe hondereth ȝer of pardon,

And þer-to goddes benyson.[12]

¶ To fabyane & bastyane moste[13] we,

Thyþur haue we mylës þre.

172

176

180

184

188

192

196

200

A mass sung there for any friend looses him from hell;

and 3000 years' further pardon have been granted by six Popes.

Let us next visit St. Mary Annunciate, two long miles off.

Our lady came

to a Brother of that house, and told him that whoever came there, she would save from hell;

and Popes have granted to repentant men 500 years of pardon.

We pass on, 3 miles,

---

[1] *om.* her [2-2] forty and viij popys grauntythe than that lyethe at seynt Bastyan; pope syluestre, Orban, and benett, seynt leo, and clement, confermythe hit.

[3] nowe passe .. with devocyon [4] Annunciacyone [5] there be [6] L. omits *large* & [7] that [8] that [9] A downe she come in to þat place, to a frere, by goddis grace.

[10] woulde come [11] frome fyre [12-12] omitted in L. [13] sebastyan passe

[leaf 84, back]
to St. Fabyan and
Sebastian,

An Angell from heuenne þydur[1] kamme

To seynt gregory, þat holy manne,

where an Angel
appeared to St.
Gregory,

As he songe masse at þe[2] Aweter

Of seynt fabyane, þat[3] holy martyr,   204

and said the light
of heaven and
remission of sins
were there.

And seyde, ' her yn þys place

Is ly3th[4] of heuen þorow[5] goddis grace,

And of mony synnes Remyssyoun ; '

Gelasius too gave
40 years' pardon
and Lents.

And fowrty 3er of pardon,   208

And also mony lentones[6] mo,

Pope Gelacyus 3af[7] þer-to.

The pardons are
equal to St.
Peter's

As moche pardon ys there

As yn[8] saynt petur mynstere,   212

on account of the
holy bones.

By cause of[9] þe holy bones

That were buryed þer[10] at ones.

Peter's and Paul's
lay for 500 years
before they were
found.

And þer lay petur & powle vnþur[11] grounde

Fyfe[12] hondred 3er er[13] þey were founde ;   216

And aftur-warde,[14] þorow goddes grace,

They wer founden yn þat place[15]

As þey Aw3të[16] for to be.

[17] Pope pelagyus, y telle þe,   220

Each of six Popes

(Of syxe popys telle y wyll,

On aftur an oþur, as hit ys skyll,)[17]

Gregory, Syluester, þer ben[18] þre ;

Alysaunder & nycholl, þer ben fyue ;   224

Honoryus was þe sixte whyll he was alyue.[19]

gave 1000 years of
pardon to all who
are shriven there.

Eche on hem 3af hys grace,

A þowsand 3er yn þat place,

To all þat þer[20] bene   228

Of dedely synnë shryuen clene ;

---

[1] om. þydur   [2] sange at an   [3] of Sebastyan the   [4] is in this place lyght
    [5] by   [6] as many lenttis   [7] glasius hathe grauntede   [8] is at
    [9] that is for   [10] alle   [11] There petur and poule laye vndur   [12] vij
    [13] afore   [14] than   [15] L. inserts, lf. 155, In tyme of glasius the pope,
                        with-owten dowte this is hepe,
                        and than with grete devosyon
                        they were broughte to Rome towne,
                        And worshupped with gret solempnyte.
[16] oughte wele   [17—17] Of odyr popes I telle the,
                        And so forthe of odyr three,
                        pope Gelasius as hit is see.
[18] and syluester this is   [19] H. the sixte in his lyue   [20] tho that there haue

For ellis[1] hit may not his sowle vaylen,
Of deedly synne but he be shryuen.[1]

A lytyH besyde þou may[2] go,   232   Near stands a chapel where 46 Popes' bodies lie,
There standes a chapeH yn a Roo ; [3]
Six[4] & fowrty popes somtyme were
Verrey marteres, & lyen)[5] þere,
Eche of hem ȝaf his benyson : [6]   236   and there you get forgiveness of all the sins that you ever sinned
Of aH þe synnes þat þou haste done
Synne þou yn to þe[7] worlde kom,   [If. 84, bk., col. 2]
Forȝeuenesse hast þou þer a-non,
AH hit[8] ys forȝeuen þe ;   240
So harde y a clerke say þat þer hadde[9] be.   (as I heard say).
And ȝyf þou dye dydurward,[10]   And if you die there, you shall have heaven's bliss.
Heuenne blys shaH be þy part ;
[11]Thow shalt go as derk as nyȝt,   244
And þerfore þou most haue condeH lyȝt,[11]
For vnþur þe erþe þou most wende,
þou shalt not see[12] be-fore ny be-hynde ;
For þydur fledde mony a[13] man,   248
For drede of deth to saue hem,
And suffred payne[14] harde & sore,
In heuen to dwelle for euur more,
¶ To þe palme wyH we goo,[15]   252   Then we go to the Palm (*i. e.* foot-sole).
'Domine quo uadys,' men clepe hit so,   Peter about to leave Rome, through fear of death, met Jesus,
And þer mette petur[16] with Ihesu,
And sayde, "lord, wheþur[17] wylt þou ?"
Cryste Answered to petur þo,   256
"In-to Rome," he sayde, "y[18] go,   Who told him He was going to Rome to die anew on the Cross ; which rebuke strengthend Peter
Efte to dye on[19] Rode for þe,
For[20] þou dredest to dye for me."
"Lorde," he sayde, "mercy y cry,   260

[1—1] thy soule may nought lyve
But thowe of dedly synne be shryue
[2] be-hynde þou myghte   [3] standythe . . . woo   [4] thre   [5] that lyythe
[6] L. inserts, There is playne Remyssyon, and leaves out l. 239, 'Forȝeuenesse,' etc.
[7] Sythe in to this   [8] that   [9] and alle odyr that there   [10] thyddyr-warde
[11—11] But þou must haue candyllyghte
Or ellis þou goest as derke as nyghte.
[12] see L., *om.* C.   [13] holy   [14] Suffyr paynes   [15] Now weende wee to þe palmete
[16] there petur mett   [17] whyddyr   [18] A-yeen I wylle   [19] on þe   [20] Petyr

to return for martyrdom.
To take þe deth[1] y am Redy."

A print of His foot is still to be seen on a marble stone;
Ther ys ȝette a syne of his[2] fote
On a marbull stone þer as[3] he stode ;

and you get 1000 years' pardon every day you are there.
[4]Eche a day, a þowsand ȝer   264
Of pardon þou may haue þer ;
¶ In a stone ys wryten, gret pardon
Ther ys, of synnis Remyssyoun

On the Festival of St. John of the Latin Gate
At seynt Iohn þe porte latyn   268
Is a chapell fayr & fyn ;
At þe feste of his day

you may, in his Church there, recover a soul from purgatory, and get 500 years' pardon for every day you pray.
A sowle fro purgatorye wynne þou may ;
And euery day, ȝyf þou wylt craue,   272
Fyfe hondred ȝere þer may þou haue,
He þat goth yn-to þat place
Where he yn oyle soden was,
The power ys of crystis graunt   276
To hem þat be verry Repentaunt.

[leaf 85]
At St. Thomas's Church if you give alms
¶ At[4] saynte Thomas of ynde
A kyrke þou may þer[5] fynde ;
Putte to[6] þy honde with[7] Almesdede   280

you shall have great reward
(And þou shat haue[8] gret mede,)
To helpe hem þat ben there
In þe[9] holy lond or elles where,

in others' prayers
Nyȝte & day to[10] pray for the   284
For þe help of the[11] charyte ;
Of mony popes þat þer haue[12] be
Thys pardon ys graunted clene to þe,[13]

---

[1] to dye for the   [2] crystis   [3] Vppon the marble there
[4—4] that stoone is vndyr An Awter
Palysyd with Iren and stele,—
that is for drede of stelynge,
that no man shoulde hit A-way bryng ;—
As offt as thowe comyst thare,
xl thowesande yere þou hast thare.
At seynt Iohn porte latyne
Soulys þou myghte brynge owte of pyne
In the daye of the feste of hym,
As þou shalt fynde hit wryttyn,
In honowre of . . . . .
[5] fayre place þou mayst   [6] thyddyr   [7] of   [8] shalt have þerfor
[9] this   [10] they   [11] For help of thy   [12] And . . þat hathe
[13] graunttyd thee

Fourtene Mlle ȝer & somdeH[1] more,　288

And þe þrydde *parte* forȝeuenys of[2] þy sore.

[3]Ther ys gret *pardon* y-wys

Wher þe stacyones cleped ys ;[3]

Pope bonyface *con*fermed aH,　292

And[4] eu*ur* more laste h*i*t shaH.

To saynte IoH*n* lat*ro*nense[5] moste we,

A whyle ther for[6] to be,

To telle of *pardon* þat ys þore :　296

In aH Rome ys no more

Then[7] ys þ*er* gr*a*unted of Ih*e*su cryste,

þorow[8] þe *pray*er of IoH*n* þe eu*au*ngelyste

And say*n*t IoH*n* þe baptyste also,　300

To aH þat þydur wyH[9] goo.

For sumtyme was a[10] emp*erour*

That loued[11] Rome w*ith* grete honou*r*,

' Kyng[12] *con*stantyne ' men dede hy*m* calle　304

Bothe yn bour & yn halle ;[13]

In mahounde was aH[14] h*is* þowȝtH,

For why, on cryste he leued[15] nowȝtH :

A meseH we fynde he[16] was　308

TyH[17] cryste sende hy*m* bett*ur*[18] grace.

Pope syluester gon hy*m* preche,[19]

Crystes lawë for to[20] teche ;

þ*er* leued he weH[21] yn goddi*s* sone,　312

And a cryste*n*[22] mon he wolde be-come ;

He dyde[23] hy*m* crystene, as y ȝ*ou* telle,

And þ*i*s myracuH h*i*t[24] be-felle :

þe wat*ur* wysh a-way h*is*[25] sy*n*ne,　316

and more than
14,000 years'
pardon, and re-
mission of one-
third of your sins.
The Stations are
productive of
great pardon.

At St. John
Lateran is pardon
to be had as great
as anywhere else
in Rome,

through the
prayers of the
St. Johns,

For the Emperor

Constantine

was a pagan and
unbeliever,
and a leper till
Christ healed
him.

Pope Sylvester
converted him

and baptized him,

and the water
washed away his
sins

[1] xiij M[1] yere and　[2] sevenythe part of all*e*

[3—3] Pope gregore, Alysaundyr, & Vrban,
All*e* thre grauntede than
the *pardon* that is so grete,
the ' stacyons ' men clepe hit.

[leaf 156]

[4] For　[5] laten*e*　[6] And a whyle there　[7] there

[8] L. omits þorow, and transposes the Johns.　[9] hem that thedyr　[10] An

[11] levyd in　[12] *om.*　[13] he was A sterne man w*ith* alle

[14] In many thyng*is* he sett　[15] In Ih*e*su cryste belevyd he　[16] that he

[17] But　[18] of his　[19] leche　[20] And of crystes lawe hym

[21] And than he be-levyd　[22] Cryst*is*　[23] lett　[24] hym

[25] that the watyr hym washed of

and his disease.	And[1] aH þe fylthe þat he was Inne.[2]
[leaf 85, col. 2]	Then speke[3] þe emperour
	To pope syluester with gret[4] honour,
On this, he confessed his errors,	" Syluester," he sayde,[5] " goddys klerke, 320
	I may se now,[6] þat ere was derke ;
	My mys-beleue blyndede[7] me
	That y myȝte not þe mote[8] se
	Of goddes myȝth & his werkes ; 324
promised to become God's clerk,	Now[9] y wyH be-come one of his clerkes."
	[10]Then þanked he criste with gret honour,
	Kyng constantyne, þat emperour ;[10]
gave up his palace	" My place,[11] syluester, y ȝeue þe to[12] honde ; 328
	Of me þou shalt hit vnþerfonge,
for a church,	And make þer-of goddys hows,
	For y wyH þat hit be þus ;
	I wyH hit leue[13] with aH my myȝtes, 332
	For y woH be on of goddis knyȝtes ;[14]
	And when þou haste so do',[15]
and asked Sylvester to give a great blessing to all who came to it.	Ȝefe þy grete benesoun[16] þere-to,
	To aH þat wyH[17] þydur come 336
	To honour[18] crystë, goddis sone,
	And saynt Iohn þe euaungelyste,
	Petur, powle, & Iohn þe[19] baptyste."
Sylvester said they should be purified from all sin	Pope syluester, þen sayde he,[20] 340
	" Of petur, powlë,[21] & of me,
	They shaH be clene of synne & pyne[22]
	As cryste clensed[23] þe of þyne,
	And as þe fylthe feH þe fro,[24] 344
	As clene of synne shaH be aH þo[25]
	Of aH maner kyn of synne[26]

[1] of   [2] his body with-in. L. adds:
for meselle he was, as l seyde ere,
And afftyr, fayre man and clere
[3] seyde   [4] *om.* gret   [5] holy Fadyre   [6] that I may see   [7] blent
[8] ne mytht the soothe   [9] *om.* Now   [10—10] omitted.   [11] palys
[12] in-to thy   [13] hym love   [14] And pray to been his owne knyght
[15] I-doo   [16] thy blessyng   [17] men that   [18] worshepe
[19] and poule seynt Iohn   [20] the p. s. sayde aye   [21] of poule
[22] be purgyd clene of synne   [23] sporgyd   [24] alle thy fylthe fylle frome thee
[25] Clene of syn shulle they bee   [26] fylthe

That dwelleth þe[1] sowle *with*-Inne." — in their souls.
[2]Pope boneface telleth þ*is* tale, — This is Pope Boniface's tale.
And y telleyth forth *with*-outen fayle.
H*it* were no nede to no mon yn crystyante — Therefore there is no need to go to the Holy Land or Jerusalem
To passe yn[2] to þe holy lond ou*ur* þe see,
To ier*usa*lem nor to seynte kateryne,
To bryngë sowlës out of[3] pyne; — to rescue lost souls.
For þ*er* ys pa*r*don[4] *with*-owten ende;
Well h*is* hy*m* þat þyd*ur* may wende!
Pope boneface telleth more — Boniface tells of more pardon.
Of mykyll pa*r*don þ*at* ys þore:[5]
Who-so comeþ to þe chapell of Ion baptyst,[6] — [lf. 85, bk., col. 1] At St. John the Baptist's chapel in this church
That dere ys to Ih*es*u cryste,
And hathe ony[7] deuocyon,
That þyd*ur* wyll go[8] *with* oryson, — whoever prays may be cleansed from sin.
þorow h*is* p*ra*yer þey may be cla*n*sed of sy*n*ne,[9]
What tyme þey entre þe chapell[10] *with*-In;
[11]Pope boneface maketh hem clene
Of all sy*nn*is þ*at* þey in bene.
In þ*at* mynster þ*at* ys so hende, — In that minster are 4 doors,
Fowr dores shalt þ*o*u fynde;
As sone as þ*o*u be In at one, — and if you pass through each, the sins you pray against are all remitted.
And passes þowr[12] eu*er*ychone,
Plener Remyssyon may þ*o*u haue
Of all þe sy*nn*is þ*at* þ*o*u wylt craue.[11]
¶ Reliquies[13] þ*er* ben mony on, — Relics are there:
In worshyp of c*ri*st & of sey*n*t Iohn:
In þe Roofe[14] ouyr þe popes see,
A saluator may þ*o*u see,[15]

[1] that noone shall*e* dwell*e* her
[2—2] the pa*r*done of Sylvester, Euery dele
the poope gregorye confermythe wele,
Boneface the pope seyde this tale;
yff men wyst grete and [s]male
the pardon that is at Rome,
they wold sey in theyre doome
hit were no neede for the
[3] men to helle [4] pa*r*done is there [5] of odyr pa*r*done in his lore
[6] To Iohn Evangelyste [7] goode [8] And comythe thyddyr (leaf 157)
[9] By oure poope wee purgythe his synne [10] he comythe the chirche
[11—11] omitted. [12] *for* þrow [13] Relykes [14] A chapell*e* [15] is, I tell*e* thee.

1. A Saviour not painted by hand of man,	Neu*ur* peynted w*ith* hond of mon,	376
	As men yn Romë[1] tellë kon :	
that came when the church was consecrated.	When syluester halewed þat[2] place,	
	H*it* aperede þorow[3] goddës *grace.*	
2. The table of the Last Supper.	[4]A tabuⱨ þer ys, þat[5] meṅ mey se	380
	That cryste made on h*is* monde,[6]	
	On shereþorsday[7] when he breke brede	
	By-fore þe tyme þat he was dede :	
	" To here of þ*is*,[8] h*it* doth ȝou gode,	384
	H*it* ys my flesh and my blode ;	
	When ȝe shaⱨ here me not[9] fynde,	
	H*it* shaⱨ[10] ȝou kepe fro þe fende."	
3. The two tables of stone written on by Christ and given to Moses.	Also þer beṅ two tabeles, y vnþ*ur*stonde,[11]	388
	That c*ri*ste wrote on w*ith* h*is*[12] honde,	
	And toke[13] þe lawe to moyses	
	To[14] kepe þe pepuⱨ yn godd*is* pece.[15]	
4. Aaron's rod.	A[16] ȝerde of aaron þat was[17] gode,	392
	H*it* turnede[18] watyr yn-to blode,	
	Aṅd fro blode to[19] wat*ur* a-gayn,	
	To shewe þat þey were goddes[20] meṅ.	
[lf. 85, bk., col. 2] 5. Angels' food. 6. Part of the five loaves, fishes, and fragments that Christ fed 5000 men with.	Angelles mete, þey seyn[21] þer ys ;	396
	[22]Also of þe fyue loues & of þe fesħ,	
	And Releue þat leued aft*ur* hem,	
	That c*ri*ste feed w*ith*, fyfe þowsand men*e*.[22]	
7. Four pillars of brass	Fowr pylers of bras þer bene strong,[23]	400
	That have stondeṅ þer fuⱨ longe,[24]	

[1] As the story   [2] þat holy   [3] stoode there by
[4] L. inserts :   A nodyr chappell*e* is in house,
                  there-in been Relyk*is* precyouse :
    [5] the tabylle there-in   [6] Maundee   [7] Shrofe thursday
  [8] And said "etythe one of hit   [9] me nat here shall*e*   [10] I wol*e*
         [11] Above An Auter made of tree
             lyche A tabyll*e*, I tell*e* thee ;
             vndyr the Awter, An Arche of stoone,
             w*ith* holy Relykys many one.
[12] wrought w*ith* his owne   [13] tolde   [14] the   [15] his pepull*e* for to holde in pease
    [16] The   [17] is   [18] he turnyd the   [19] in to   [20] goode   [21] fulle sothe
         [22]–[22] And fyve lovys and ij ffyshys
             w*ith* whiche cryste ffed v thowesande men,
             xij baskett*is* full*e* of Releeffe lefft then ;
             Ho-so is there, the sothe may see.
[23] there bee.   [24] A-boute the hyghe Auter stande ;
             they been styffe and stronge

Ther ben none suche yn aḻḻ[1] Rome ;
Wonþur hit ys how þey þedur come :
But vaspasyon þat holy[2] kyng,   404   brought by Vespasian and Titus from Jerusalem.
And tytus his sone þat was so ȝyng,[3]
From ierusalem he[4] dede hem come
In-to þe holy place of Rome.

    Ther ben þe[5] chaynis of saynt Iohn   408   8. The chains St. John was bound with, and the cup they gave him poisoned drink from.
When[6] he was bownden, & myȝt not gone ;
And þe vesseḻ þat þey ȝaf hym drynke In,[7]—
Moche[8] þe more was her pyne ;[9]
He dronke hit vp, hit[10] greued hym nowȝt,   412
For yn Ihesu[11] was aḻḻ his powȝth ;—
[12]And a kerteḻḻ of þat manne   9. A kirtle of the man then raised from death.
That fro deth was Reysed þan.[12]

    Ther be þe[13] clopis of Ihesu criste,   416   10. Christ's clothes.
And þe askes of[14] Iohn þe baptyste ;   11. John the Baptist's ashes.
[15]Also þe cloth þat Ihesu gan lede   12. The table-cloth of the Last Supper.
Hys dyssypeles on to fede,
* And a serke þat our lady gon make   420   13. A Shirt the Virgin made for Christ.
† For her swetë sonës sake ;
§ Of þe blood & watyr also   14. The Blood and Water out of His side.
‡ That out of cristis syde gan go ;
And mylke of marye þe vyrgyne,   424   15. The Virgin's milk.
And a foote of marye Magdeleyne,[15]   16. Mary Magdalen's foot.
And þe clopis þat criste was wonden[16] In   17. Christ's grave-clothes.
When he shulde dye[17] for mannis syn ;
‖ [18]And of þe flesh of his cyrcumsyce ;   428   18. Christ's fore-skin.
Men hit holde yn grete pryse.

    Of petur & powle þe heddys ben þere,   19. The heads of Peter and Paul,

---

[1] *om.* alle   [2] Vaspasius the nobylle   [3] tutus his sone yonge   [4] *om.* he
[5] ij   [6] where-with   [7] the venym was in   [8] alle   [9] synne
[10] of hit and   [11] on cryste
[12—12] of A curtylle of Seynt Iohn
that iij men frome þe dethe a-Ryse be-goone
[13] Of the   [14] of the asshis of seynt
[15—15] And of the clothe that cryste wypyd on foote & hande
On schroffethursday his Dissypyls to foonde
[16] wrapped   [17] was ded
[18—18] §of bloode and watyr also there is
‡that owte of crystis syyde gon goo I-wys ;
* And the shyrte that our ladye made

Welle closed a-bowte þe hyȝ Auter;

When þe heddis shewed shaⱡⱡ be,   432

Then ys þer pardon gret plente,

As mych pardon y-wysse

As when þe vernacuⱡⱡ shewed ys;

And þat ys graunted certaynly   436

Of pope Vrban & of gregory.

Ther ben oþur Relykes mony on[18]

In worshyp of criste & of seynt Iohn.[1]

¶ Her may we no lengur be;   440

In-to þe popes halle mostë[2] we;

In þat halle, þre dores þer be;

Eche a day open þou may hem se;[3]

[4]As ofte as þou gost þorow ony of hem,   444

And þou be of synnë clene,

And enterest þorow any of hem þre,[4]

Fowrty ȝer of pardon ys graunted to de.[5]

¶ [6]The pope Vrbane, y ȝou say,   448

In lenton þe fyrst þoresday,

Shewede petur & powle heuedes two

By-fore þe Romanes and oþur mo,

And graunted a hondred ȝere of pardon   452

Seuen myle abowte Rome towne;

And also mony lentones mo,

That same tyme he ȝaf þer-to;

† for hyr swete sonnys saake;
‖ of Ihesu cryste the Syrcumsyse;
  of the cloþe of seynt Iohn bapetyse,
  and odyr Relykys many oone
[1] L., leaf 129, inserts :
    On the mynyster ende iij durrys there bee—
    Whan thowe art there, þou mayst see;—
    As offt as thy be opynnyd to thee,
    And þan passithe thorowe ony of hem thre,
    pleyne Remyssyon þou myght have
    of alle thy Synnys, yf þou wolte hit crave.
      [2] pase   [3] they stonde opyn vnto thee
[4—4] As offte as þou passyste one of hem
    And entyrst by A-nodyr A-yeen,
    And passythe euery of the three,
        [5] xl yere is grauntyd thee
[6—6] Nowe pase wee to sancta sanctorum swythe,
      that mannys hart makythe blythe.

There ys no man now y-bore, 456

Nor hys fadur hym be-fore,

That of þe heddës haue a syȝth — but by God's grace only were the heads seen.

At þat¹ tyme, but be grace of god almyȝt.

Ther ys a chapell of gret pardon 460 — In the chapel Sancta Sanctorum is much pardon.

And of mony synnis Remyssyon,

Menne calle hit sancta sanctorum ;

In þat chapell shall no womon² com.⁶

Ther-yn ys A saluatowr 464 — In it is a figure of the Saviour

To whom men don gret³ honour,

The whyche was sent to our lady — sent by Christ to the Virgin

(Whyle þat she was her⁴ vs by)

From her' sone þat ys a-bouen, 468

Aftur þe tyme of his⁵ ascencion. — after His Ascension.

⁷Ther may no wommon entre þor — No woman may go into Sancta Sanctorum on account of Eve's sin.

By-cause of her þat synned sore ;

She browȝt vs alle to þe qwede 472

Tyll cryste on crosse suffered dede :

Euery day, seuen þowsand ȝere — Every day 7000 years' pardon and full remission of sins are to be had.

Of pardon þou may haue þere ;

And also, ȝyf þou wylt craue, 476

Plener Remyssyon þou may haue. — [leaf 86, col. 2]

   * At þe chappell of þe Rode — The Holy Rood chapel is called

Is an offrynge fayr & gode,

---

¹ The letter over the þ is blurred.
² 'wo' put over line in a later hand.   ³ yee shalle do
         ⁴ in eorthe   ⁵ affter his
   ⁷⁻⁷ the hedys of petyr & poule beþe there,
      wele I-closyd vndyr An Awter ;
      And odyr Relykys many one
      been closed in Iren and in stoone.
      who-so is poope of Roome,
      the keyys þer-of with hym dothe nome
      that no man may hem see
      But he hym sellfe in presence bee.
      In that chapelle, yf þou wolte craue,
      vii Mˡ yere þou myghtest haue,
      And so many lenttis more
      yff thowe be screffe,⁷ þou mayste haue soo ;   [¹ shriven, A.S.
      And yett theere is grauntyd therto   [leaf 158, back]   *bescrifen,* con-
      the thyrde parte of pennaunce vndo.   fessed, Som.]
   * the pardone of holy Roode chyrche,
      whiche is the name of þe seyde kyrke,—

Jerusalem [The
Basilica of Santa
Croce in Gerusa-
lemme].
It was built by
St. Helena.
The holy Con-
stance, Constan-
tine's daughter,

† Men calle hyt Ier*u*s*a*lem ;   480

‡ Sey*n*t Elene latte make hem.[7]

Constance, þe holy wo*m*mon,

Of kyng co*n*stantyne she kam ;

Hys þow3t*u*r[1] she was, & þat was sene,   484

For, þorow þe p*r*ayr of seynt Elene,

made it in honour
of the Holy Cross.

That holy place she[2] madë thus

In hono*u*r[3] of þe holy crosse.

Sylvester hal-
lowed it,

[4]Pope syluester h*i*t halewede þo,   488

And gret p*a*rdon he 3af þer-to ;

For eche[5] sonday yn þe 3er,

and every Wed-
nesday you get
2005 years'
pardon.

And eche[6] wedenesday, 3yf þou be þer,

[8]Is two þowsand & fyfe 3ere,   492

And yche a day, on hondered ys þer.[8]

Its relics are :

§ Relykes þer be mony & fele :

1. The Sponge of
gall and vinegar
offered to Christ.

[9]The sponge of galle & of eyse‖

That þe Iewes profered cryst to[9]   496

When[10] he sayde " scicio " ;

2. A Nail He was
nailed to the cross
with.

‖ [11]And a nayle, whe*n* Ihe*s*u c*r*i*s*te was

Don on þe Rode for our trespas.[11]

† Ier*u*s*a*lem, men clepe hit sertayne,
‡ Saynt Elyn hit made w*it*h noble mayne,
§ And put there-in Relekys fele,
   As I can shewen swythe wele ;
   hit was her house and her socoure
   god to serve withe honowre.
   for eche day in that mynystre,
   of p*a*rdoune is xxviij yere ;
   Also as many lentt*i*s moo
   Certenly is grauntyd þerto,
   At the hye Awter shalt þou have Also
   fourty yere, and lentt*i*s moo,
   for Anastace, cesar the martyr,
   Bothe were buryed*e* there.
     [1] doughtt*er*   [2] he   [3] worshupe
[4-4] Transposed, and put after scicio (spelt *sissio*), l. 497. [L. *sitio*, I thirst.]
      [5] E*u*ery   [6] *om.* eche
[8-8] An hundyrde yere myght þou have
   of p*a*rdone yff þou wylt hit crave
[9-9] that is there for sothe to tell*e*
   Whan . . . profyrde to drynk thoo
       [10] Whan that . . Sissio
[11-11] And yeet moore I wole the tell*e* :
   there is A coorde In one chapell*e*,—
   Ane highe in the Roofe hit is doo,   [leaf 159]
   for no man shoulde come þer-too.—
   that ylke coorde, they sey hit is,

And yn þat cherche[1] ys also

Of þe crosse þat he was on[2] Ido,

And of þe tre þat þe þeues henge on[3] by

That of *his* sy*nnis* askede[4] mercy ;

[5]And a tityꝲ of syr pylat,—

He may h*i*t Rede þ*at* ys[6] þer-at,—

" Thys ys Ihe*s*u of na3areth,

Kyng of Iewes, þat þolede[7] deth ; "

The tytyꝲ ys honged, y wyꝲ not[8] lye,

By[9] a crosse þat ys hy*m* bye,[10]

In þe maner of a bowe[11]

In þe myddes of þe kyrke, y trowe ;[12]

In þat maner h*i*t ys do[13]

For no man shulde come þer-to.

¶ Of more pa*r*don y wyꝲ 3ou[14] say

That at seynt laurence ys eche[15] day ;

Seuen þowsand 3er, & lentones[16] þer-to,

And þe þrydde parte of þy penau*n*s vndo.[17]

Pope pelagyus,[18] þat holy man,

That chyrche to halowe fyrst[19] be-gan,

And gra*u*nted þer-to hys pa*r*don[20]

And also goddes[21] benyson,

Thorow pr*a*yres of two martires[22]

Steuen & laurence þat þer lyes.[23]

500   3. A piece of
Christ's cross,
and

4. of the Penitent
Thief's cross.

504   5. The Title
written over the
cross by Pilate :

' This is Jesus
the King of the
Jews ; '

508   and it hangs like
a bow by a cross
in the middle of
the church.

512

At St. Lawrence's,
every day you can
get 7000 years'
516   pardon, and Lents
too,

[leaf 86, back]

520

through St.
Stephen's and
St. Lawrence's
prayers.

w*ith* whiche cryste was led to þe crosse I-wys ;

‖And A nayle that smyte cryst Ih*esus*

whane he Suffyrde Dethe for us ;

And the hede of seynt vynsent ;

the clothe of bapetyse whan he was brent.

      [1] the chirche hit   [2] god was

[3] the crosse þat þe theefe hyng hym   [4] whan he cryed, Lorde

[5] L. inserts : the tethe Also there been of seynt blase,

                And odyr Relykys many oone,

                I cannat telle hem everychone.

[6] made hit Red þat was   [7] suffyrde   [8] hyde w*ith*-owten

   [9] In   [10] hangithe hye   [11] In ma*ner* of A bowe for-soothe

       [12] menystre Rooffe   [13] I-doo   [14] I yowe

       [15] of seynt lawerens þat ylk   [16] w*ith* lentt*is*

[17] L. inserts : In tyme off the Emp*er*oure

             kynge constantyne of grete honoure

           [18] honorius   [19] halowed and

[20] the pa*r*doone he gra*u*ntyd to all*e* Anoone   [21] there-to his

   [22] the holy marter   [23] Seynt st. and seynt l. þat be there

[1]And vnþur þe awter ys made a stone,   524
There a-bowte þey may gone :

In the altar is a hole :

An hole on þis awter þou may fynde ;
Knele down þer with good mynde,

put your head in, and you'll smell a sweet smell of bodies whose souls are with God.

Putte yn þy heed or þy honde,   528
And þou shalt fele a swete gronde,
A swete smelle of bodyes þat þer be,[1]
Here sowles be with god in trinite.

If you are at St. Lawrence's every Wednesday, you can free a soul from Purgatory.

[2]And ȝyf þou be þer aꝇ þe ȝere,   532
Eche wednesday yn þat mynster,
Thow may haue, of cristes powere,
A sowle to drawe out of purgatory fyre.[2]

St. Simplicius,

¶ At seynt sympyꝇ, fawstyne, & betrys,[3]   536
That ben aꝇ martyres of[4] cryste.

the Pope,

Seynt sympuꝇ, pope of Rome he[5] was,
And god hym sente a fayr grace ;

put 700 holy bones

Seuen hondred holy[6] bones   540
He gedered, but not[7] at ones,

in his church,

And yn þat chyrche he dede hem graue,
For ho-so seke hem, his sowle he may saue ;[8]

and gave 5000 years' pardon to all who are shriven and visit it.

And he ȝaf pardon to alle þo   544
That be shryuen & þydur wyꝇ[9] go,
Fyfe þowsand ȝer[10] & more
Thorow prayeres of hem þat lyen[11] þore.

[1-1] A-bowte the Awter þou shalt goone ;   [leaf 159, back]
At every ende þou shalt fynde—
knele there-to yf þou be hende,—
A swete smelle, thoowe hit be derke,
(thorowe grace of crystis owne werke,)
of bodyes that there beryed be
[2-2] Who-so wole dwelle in halle,
And go eche Daye to seynt lawrence mynstyr,
he may there delyuer with orysone
A sowle owte of purgatory presone.
[3] In the chirche of fastyine, simple, beatrice
[4] be very Martyrs of Ihesu
[5] in Roome
[6] vj M¹ [= 6000] holy mennys
[7] gadyrde to gedur alle
[8] Sykyr he was that they were savede. (*Sowle* is in a later hand.)
[9] *om.* wylle   [10] vij M¹ yere of pardoon
[11] lygg

¶ ¹With-owte þe kyrke of Iulyan²　　　548　Outside St.
Julian's is a
Ther ys wryten yn a stone　　　　　　　　　stone, saying

That honoryus, þat holy pope,

That kyrke³ halewede yn his⁴ cope ;

And six⁵ þowsand ȝere he ȝaf to pardon　552　that 6000 years'
pardon is given
To aH þo þat þydur wyH come.⁶　　　　　　to all who go
there.

.;. Explicit þe staciones of Rome .;.

[Here the Cotton MS. ends, but the Lambeth MS. (leaf 160)
continues.]

In the menyster of⁴ þat holy preste　　　At St. Eusebius's

that is dere to Ihesu cryste,

Eusebius is there name,—　　　　　　　556

to teH of hym hit is goode game,—

hit is wryttyn in A stoone

' I wole the halowe or I goone,'

that pope gregory with his hande　　　　560　Pope Gregory

that chirche halowed, I vndyrstande,

and yave pardoun, I yowe saye,　　　　　gives 100 years'
and 40 days'
A C yerys and fourty daye　　　　　　　pardon.

and there-to mo I wole yowe telle　　　564

to Abate the peyne off helle.

And In the chyrche of seynt Iulyan　　　At St. Julian's are
his cheekbone,
there is his chykk, and tethe þer-one ;　　and a thorn stuck
in Christ's head,
A thorne thyrlyd in crystis hed,　　　　568

when he suffyrde for us to be ded,

And odyr Relykys many and dere ;　　　and other relics :

¹ Cott. MS. With-owte owte.　L. inserts :
　　　Whane he was dede, þer was he grave ;
　　　Cryste his soule kepe and save!
　　　A stoone doþe stande in þe weye
　　　By-twyx the chyrche and martyrs twey,
　　　Seynt Iulyan and seynt vrban,
　　　there was men and women,
　　　In that stoone wryttyn is
　　　grete pardoone, soothe I-wys,
　　　Euery daye in the yere
　　　vij thowesande yere þou myght have there.
² chirche of seynt vyuyen (lf. 160, bk.)　³ this chirche
　　　　　⁴ A　　⁵ thre
　　⁶ And there-to goddis benysone
　　　lastynge for euer-more
　　　to alle men that been there.

the pardon is 700
years.

Go thyddyr and haue vij C yere.

Anodyr chyrche for-soþe there is,   572

At St. Matthew's

of seynt Mathewe worshupe I-wys,

In the Riȝht' hande as þou shalt goone

to the chyrche of seynt Iohn͛ :

is an arm of St.
Christopher's,

An hole Arme of seynt *Christ*ofre, godd*is* knyght, 576

[In a chiste right there is dyght,]

In that same chyrche hit is I-doo,

And grete *par*done yeve thertoo,

on which Christ
stood when the
Saint carried him.

for cryste hym͛ selffe there-on͛ stoode,   580

whan he bare hy*m* on͛ the Floode.

[leaf 160, back]

In the chirche of uyȝht' and modeste,

At St. Vitus and
Modestus you get
one-fourth of your
sins forgiven,—

there men͛ mowe have, moste & leste,

the iiij^te parte of' for-yevenes of syn͛,   584

what tyme he comythe þe chirche w*ith*-in͛.

7000 Martyrs lie
there,—

vij M^1 martyrs lyggythe there,

As hit is wryttyn͛ in that mynystre ;

In tyme of' Emp*er*oure Anthony[n]e   588

that tyrant was, and' paynyme ;

and lose one-
seventh of your
sins.

this is the vij parte of þy synne ondoone.

At St. Mary the
Greater

At seint mary maioure

Is A chirche of grete honowre ;   592

As the hye Aut*er*, hit is seyde,

are buried Mat-
thew,

there is the body of mathewe leyde :

In the chyrche, Anodyr partye,

and St. Jerome,
who was brought
from Damascus,
and put before
a place

lyethe seynt Ierome sykerlye ;   596

frome the Cyte of Damase,

¹he was brouȝht' in-to þat plase ;

by-foore A plase he was pyȝht',

called the Præ-
sepe (boards from
the Manger of the
Nativity).

' precepe ' men clepe hit.   600

vppon his graue lyethe A stoone,

And A crosse is leyde there-one ;

A-bowte that stoone A grate there is

of Irne stronge made I-wys.   604

At the chapel of
St. Agas,

In that plase is A chapeⱶ

of seynt Agas, þou wott hit wele ;

¹ A long initial letter which looks like I, stands before *he*.

x yere of *par*done is grauntyd there,
lygyng there-to evyr-more.

608

ten years of par-
don are to be had.

A lytyH clothe lyethe there too,
of whiche cryst was fyrste in do
of his modyr, whan͢ he was bore
to save man that was for-lore.

Its relics are,
1. The cloth Christ
was put in after
His birth;

612

of his Flesche the Syrcumsyse,
Men hit holdythe of grete pryse ;
And of the hey, more and lasse,
that cryste lay on͢ by-fore þe asse.

2. His foreskin
when circum-
cised;

[leaf 161]
3. the hay He lay
in before the ass;

616

An arme is also there
of seynt thom[a]s the marter,
and A party of the brayne of his hede
At caunterbury there he was dede,

4. an arm, and

5. a bit of brain of
Thomas à Becket;

620

And Rochet that is goode,—
hit was sprongyn *with* his bloode—
which he had one whan he was take
for alle holy chirche-is saake.

6. his rochet;

624

And An Image sykurly
wondyr fayre of oure ladye ;
seynt luke, whyles he was in londe,
woulde haue payntyd hit *with* his hande ;

7. an Image of
Our Lady,
(see p. 172, ll.
886—9),
which St. Luke
was about to
paint,

628

And whane he hade ordeyinyd hit soo,
alle his colourse there too,
he founde An Image alle Redy,
Neuer noone syche in eorthe he sy,

but when his
colours were all
ready,

he found one
painted by Angels'
hands.

632

with Angell*is* hand*is*, & nougH͞t' *with* his :
the story in Roome wyttnessithe this,
that is wryttyn every dele
At the hye awter in A tabyH.[1]

636

there is *par*doone, men may see,
of many popys þ*a*t there hathe bee ;
vppon the chyrchë halydaye
A M[1] yere of *par*don þ*o*u may,
And there-to, yff þ*o*u wylt more,
the thyrde parte of alle þy lore,

On the Church's
holy day you may
have 1000 years'
pardon,
and one-third of
your loss [perdi-
tion ?],

640

---

[1] MS. In a tabylle at, etc.

and 700 years.

And vii C yere there-too ;

wele is hym that thyddyr may goo. 644

At every feast of Our Lady

In eche feste of oure ladye,

to þat graunttythe seynt gregorye ;

you get 100 years' pardon and Christ's blessing,

he yaffe therto A C yere of pardone,

And therto crystis benysone. 648

and from her Assumption [leaf 161, back]

In owre ladijs day Assumpsione,

There is than grete pardone ;

till Christmas

frome þat fest tyll Ihesu was bore,

No daye shall be for-lore ; 652

you get as much as for 15,000 years' penance.

there is xv M¹ yere

of penaunce þou shuldyst full-fyll here.

Anodur chyrche also there is,

At St. Puden-tiana's

'Pudencyam' hit is clepyd I-wys ; 656

An holy woman I fynde she was,

All full-fyllyd by goddis grace :

one-third of your sin is forgiven.

the thyrde parte of þy synne

for-yevenes ther þou myght wynne. 660

In St. Priscilla's churchyard adjoining,

A chyrche-yerde is there too

of seynt presell, men clepe hit soo.

Seynt gregory tellythe [us]

that in þat yarde & in þat house 664

are buried 3000 bodies,

Ben beryed many of thoo,

thre thowesand with-owten moo ;

and for each a year and a Lent of pardon are to be had.

for eche body þou myght tell

O yere and o lent þou myght spell 668

of pardon is grauntyd to þe

By prayer of hem þat there bee ;

for seynt petyr & seynt poule, þat some tyme were,

Bothe were harborowed there. 672

At the chapel *Sancti Pastoris*

A lytyll chapell yeet there is,

I-clepyd 'titulus pastoris ; '

As þou comyst at the chyrche-is ende,

that chapell þou shalt fynde ; 676

The pope of Rome þat was than,

St. Pius [or per-haps in reality St. Peter]

seynt peius the holy man,

the bapetystore there he founde,

and holowed [*sic*] hit w*ith* his honde ;　　680

one Easter

And vppon An estyr daye—

As I te𝔢 yowe nowe I maye—

Syxty soules and꞉ xviij there-to,

converted 78 souls
to Christianity.

to Crystyn-dom he brou𝔤ht꞉ thoo.　　684

Of praxed, the holy woma𝔫,

[leaf 162]

a𝔢 the sothë te𝔢 I ca𝔫,

A thowesande bodyes w*ith*-owten moo,

At St. Praxed's
are 1300 martyrs'

And iij hundyrde there-too,　　688　bodies buried,

In þ*at* place burye𝔡 shee—

her sowelys bethe w*ith* cryst so Fre—

that suffyrde dethe in þ*at* tyme

Of the empe*r*oure Anthony[n]e.　　692

pope Innocent, for love of he𝔪,

and for them a
year and 40 days'
pardon are grant-
ed and one-fourth
of your penance
is respited.

graunte[de] tho to a𝔢𝔢 me𝔫

O yere, and xl dayes there-to,

And the iiij parte of penaunce vndo.　　696

And there is of the pyllur A party

A part of the
pillar Christ was
bound to is there.

that cryste was bounde to sykyrly ;

And yff þ*ou* come in lent to chyrche,

In Lent you get
double pardon.

Double pa*r*doone þ*ou* myg𝔥t꞉ wyrche.　　700

there lyethe bodyes of sylvester & seynt marty𝔫,

Sylvester and
Martin are buried
there.

the story of Rome wytnessi𝔥e hit myne.

Anod*ur* Day in the yere

On the day of St.
Peter,

of seynt petre men clepy𝔥e there　　704

Ad[1] vincula i𝔫 londe,

Ad Vincula,

lammasse day þ*ou* vndyrstonde,

Lammas Day,

wha𝔫 pet*ur* was bounde w*ith* Irnys grete,

when he was
bound in irons,

As wee in oure bok*is* Reede,　　708

that daye is grete pa*r*doone,

is great pardon,
remission of
all sins ;

of alle thy synnys remyssyou*n* ;

And꞉ every day, yff þ*ou* wolt crave,

and every day
you can get 500
years' pardon,

fyve hundyrd yere there þ*ou* myg𝔥t꞉ haue,　　712

And꞉ so many lentt*is* moo

and Lents.

pope gelasius haþe grauntyd þerto.

¶ there is a pese of the Roode

The relics are :

[1] MS. And

1. A piece of
Christ's Cross.
2. St. Martin's
bed,

that cryst was on do for oure goode,   716

And the bed[1] of seynt Martyne,

An holy man þat tholyd pyne ;

in which no man
may lie.
[leaf 162, back]

In that bed shaH no man lye,

for he wole not þat hit be seye,   720

Ne touche-hit *with* no manis hande,[2]

for hit is prevy, I vndyrstande.

Suche bed of penaunce I not no moo,

In the Church
of the Twelve
Apostles,

to A plase of[3] the postyll*is* twoo—   724

cryste us kepe owte of[4] woo !—[4]

(built by Constan-
tine, destroyed
by heretics,

fyrste of[4] constantyne hit was sett,

And sytheñ) herytyk*is* done hit bett ;

and rebuilt by
Pelagius and
John,)

Pelagius and pope Iohñ),   728

    they dede hit Rere vp Anone,

      And yave there-to grete p*a*rdoone,

for there lyetĥe many A seynt of grete Renowne,

lie St. Philip
and James,
St. Eugenia,

phylype and Iacobe in shryne,   732

Sent eugenie þe holy vyrgyne,

St. Sabasabinus,

Seint sabasabyne, wrote wee fynde,

Thomas's cloak,

And the tabarde of thom*a*s of Inde :

St. Blasius's arm,
etc.

An arme of seynt blase is there,   736

And odyr relykys many and sere.

You may get here
2000 years'
pardon,

two thowesande yere, yf þou wolt crave,

Eche day there mygĥt[4] þou have,

and double on
each Apostle's
day.

And on eche Apostyll*is* day   740

this p*a*rdoon is dowbyld, I the saye.

At St. Bartholo-
mew's 1000 years'
pardon.

  At seynt bartylmewe þou my3te have

A thowesande yere yf þou wolte crave ;

there lyetĥe his bodye on þe hye Auter :   744

wele is hym that comytĥe there.

At St. Mary
Rotunda,

  at seynt mary Rotounde

there is A chyrche fayre I-founde ;

there is wryttyn, I yowe saye,   748

on a Sunday in
May

In o sonday that is in maye ;

---

[1] MS. hed   [2] This line is repeated after the next.
[3] MS. of of   [4] Seemingly l. 725 should follow 723, and
be followed by a line like 'Now lat us forthe goo.'

whan the soneday is I-come,
there is fułł Remyssyone,

is full remission
of sins.

And eche daye in the yere

752

grete pardon þou myght have there :
Agrypa ded hit make
for sabillis & neptuno-is sake ;

Agrippa built it
for Sabille's and
Neptune's sake

Modyrs they were of cursyd men,

756 [leaf 163]
[really Mars and
Jupiter],

And false fendis folowed hem.
he yave hit name of pantheoŋ ;

and called it the
Pantheon,

In ałł Romë was syche noone ;
A fygur they made of golde Reede,

760 made a golden
image

More than god they gan hit drede ;
' Neptune ' clepyd hit was I-wys ;

called Neptune,

to leve there-one they were nat wysse ;
An hye on the tempyłł hit satt,

764 set it high up on
the temple like a .
cat,

And lokyde forthe lyke A katt,
vppon the Rooffe in an holle
hit brent as hellë cole :

but it burnt up,

vppon his hed A covert of brasse ;

768 and its brass hat

to seynt petyr blowen hit was

was blown to St.
Peter's.

with A wynde of hełł, I trowe,
for no man myght hit thedur throwe ;
there standythe [hit,] I tełł thee,

772

by-fore the mynyster dor þou myght hit see ;
the Rofe is opyn there he stoode ;
there stondythe, and doþe no goode.

A nd the pope boneface

776 Pope Boniface

was fułł-fyllyd with goddis grace ;
In hym selfe he was dismayed
that mannys soule was so betrayed :
to the emperoure Iulius sone he came,

780 asked the Em-
peror Julius for
this
[Phocas, A.D. 609.]

that was forsoþe A wele goode man ;
" that tempyłł," he sayde, " graunt hit me,
I the praye for seynt charyte,
that men clepe pantheoŋ, I leve,

784 Pantheon:

that mannys soule hit doþe greve."
he seyde, " take hit euery dele ;

he gave it him.

that þou hit have, me lykythe wele."

And the fyrst day of novemb*ur*,　　　788

pope boneface w*ith* hartë tendyr

the pepuℋ of Rome ded calle,

And bade assemble in his halle,

In pantheon aℋ in-same,　　　792

for to chaunge þat ylkë name

In honowre of oure ladye,

and aℋ halowen þat bethe þ*er*-bye ;

this was noster dame la Rounde,　　　796

In pantheon fyrste I-founde ;

And sange hys mase þat ylkë daye,

And yave grete par*d*one, I yowe saye,

And comawndyd all crysty*n*) me*n*)　　　800

that daye to halowe, for love of he*m*)

that bethe i*n*) hevy*n*) w*ith* swete I*h*es*us*,

Nigℏt' and day to praye for us.

And on the morowe he be-hett also　　　804

that men shoulde to chyrchë goo

to pray*e* for hem that ded bee,

that cryste on hem have pyte,

And one us wha*n*) wee dye ;　　　808

Ame*n*), saythe aℋ for charyte.

At seynt mary transpedian

there been ij pyllurs made of stoone,

to whiche petyr and poule bounden were　　　812

when thé levyd in eorthë there.

there they stonde, I tellë thee ;

wha*n* þou ᴀrt there, þou mayste he*m* see ;

Eche day, yf þou comyste there,　　　816

foure hundyrd yerë þou haste there.

At seynt Speryte hospytall*e*,

there men mowe haue, gret and smalle,

vij yere of pardoune,　　　820

the vij^te parte of penaunce ondone.

At seynt Iamys vppon the flome

Be thre hundyrde yere of par*d*onne,

And so many Lentt*is* moore

for-sothe ben I-grauntyd there.

    Att seynt mary tryst-iuere

thowe shalt have sevyn yere :

two well*is* there bethe, I tell thee,

that sprynggythe oyle, there men may see,

that ylk nygħt' þat cryst was boore

to save man that was for-loore.

    At sesyle, the holy marter,

thowe mygħt' have A C yere.

    At seynt petyr and poullys preson)

thowe myght have grete pardonne,

two thowesande yere, I tell thee,

Eche day yf thowe there bee.

thorowe the vertu of her orysune

A well spronge there in prisune,

wi*th* whiche wat*er*, baptysyd were

processe and martuman, cryst*is* dere.

    A t seynt mary la noue þou mygħt' haue

        an hundyrde yere if þou wolt craue.

        at the chirche of seynt Alext

there wee mowe have, moste & leste,

two thowesande and ij C yere,

eche day yf þou comyst there.

    At seynt cosme and Demiave

iij hundyrd yere þou mygħt' have.

    At the chyrche of seynt eustace

there men mygħt' fynde A wele fayre place ;

there lyethe he and' his wyffe,

and his ij sonnes, wi*th*-owttyn stryffe,

two thowesande yere þou mygħt' have

eche Daye yf þou wolte crave.

    nowe passe wee to þe saluator

to whome men dothe grete honowre.

A fygur of god' þou mygħt' see,

his face, his crowne, I tell thee ,

there mygħt þou have A M^1 yere ;

---

824   and Lents.

[leaf 164]
At St. Mary
Trastevere 7
828   years' pardon.
Two wells that
spout oil on
Christmas day
are there.

832   At St. Cecilia's
100 years' pardon.

At St. Peter and
Paul's Prison

836   2000 years' pardon
every day.

840

At St. Mary
Nova, 100 years
pardon.

844   At St. Alexis'

2200 years.

848   At St. Cosmas
and Damian's,
300 years.

At St. Eustace's

852

2000 years'
pardon.

856   Here [*or*, At the
Church of San
Salvadore] is an
image of the
Saviour giving
1000 years'
pardon,

860

Eche day yff thowe be there,

[leaf 164, back]
and 630 years off
your time in hell.

Syx hundred and xxx^{ty} mo, I the teH,

for to Abate the peynys of heH.

At St. Cecilia's
100 years' pardon.

 at seynt Sysely the holy marter,   864

there thowe myght haue A C yere.

the Mawdlene there, I teH thee,

whan þou Art there þou mygĥt see.

At a chapel near
St. Peter-ad-
Vincula

 Be-sydes petre-Ad-vincula A chapeH is 868

of A Saluator worshupte Iwys,

where he delyd his tresoure

to save holy chyrchis honoure :

you get 2000
years' pardon.

of pardon) ij thowesande yere   872

thowe myght have whan þou art there

At each of St.
Jerome's, Gre-
gory's, Ambrose's,
Austin's,

 At the chyrche of iiij Doctours fyne,

Ierome, gregory, Ambrose, & Austyne,

At eche chyrche yff þou wylt craue[1] 876

1000 years'
pardon.
At St. Lawrence's

A thowesande yere, þou[2] mygĥt hit haue.

 At seynt lawrence in Damace

there shalt þou fynde A feyre place :

Eche day, yf thowe come there,   880

500 years' pardon.

thowe mygĥt have v C yere.

At St. Mary
Ara Cœli,

 At seynt mary Rochelle

there is many greses, I wete wele ;

2000 years and
more.

there is ij thowesande yere & more 884

to hem that wole thyddyr goo.[3]

Here is an image
of Our Lady made
by St. Luke.

there is An Image, I vndyrstonde,

of oure ladye þat Lewke wrougĥt with his honde,

I-closed alle withe syluer clere,   888

I-payntted Abowte withe colours dere ;

Minorites live
there.

there dwellythe Frere menowrse,

And servyn owre ladye with honowrse.

At St. Mary Merle
[de' Miracoli ?]

 At seynt Mary Merle bethe dwellynge 892

Frere prechourse to Rede and synge :

you can get 1000
years' pardon.

Sykyrly there þou myght have

A M[1] yere, and þou hit crave.

At St. Andrew's

 At seynt Andrewys holy chyrche sykyrly 896

  [1] MS. haue [2] MS. yf þou [3] For *forc* or *fare*.

Been yeerys grauntyd fuⱨ fourty,

And seynt gregory *pur*chased syche grace,

what maɴ or womaɴ is buryed in þ*a*t plase,

yf he beleve in god & holy chyrche also,　　900

he shaⱨ not be dampned for nougħt þat he hatħe doo,

But be saved frome the payne of heⱨ :

this is the sothe that I the teⱨ.

yf þ*o*u tryste no þyng to me,　　904

oɴ the chyrche-dore þou mayst hit see.

*par*done is there myche moore

than I have Reseyned[1] here byfore,

And that I shaⱨ w*ith* aⱨ my mygħt⸴　　908

there-off wryte boþe day & nygħt⸴,

By gode that was of mary boore

to save mankynde þat was for-loore,

Graunt vs parte of this *par*doone,　　912

And there-withe gyve us his benysone !

[leaf 165]
40 years' pardon.

Believers buried
there

shall not be
damned, however
they have sinned,
but shall be saved.

If you don't
believe me, you
can see it on the
church door.

Of the rest of the
pardon I shall
write day and
night.

Christ grant us
part of it, and
His blessing !

EXPLICIT þE STACIONS OF ROOME.

[Follow : A Medecyne for the Pestylens, etc., The maner to
kepe haukes, etc.]

[1] *resigno*, I reveal, disclose.

Gaude, Flore Virginali.

(Lambeth MS. 306, *leaf* 133.)

(1)

Hail, flower of
Virginity,

Gaude, the flowre of vi*r*ginyte,
In hevyn thow hast a p*r*incipalite
    Off worship and honowre ;
Thi blys is more in dignite   4

above all saints
and angels !

Then alle the saynt*is* that euer may be
    Or aungelis in hevyn towre !
            Gaude, flore vi*r*ginali !

(2)

Hail, God's
spouse,

Gaude, goddys spouse so deere !   8
Was there neu*er* sonnye day so cleere
    Nor of so grete lyg͡ht !

brighter than sun
in heaven !

There myght neu*er* son shyne heere
As thow fyllist heuyn empere   12
    W*ith* bemys that ar so bryg͡ht !
            Gaude, sponsa cara dei !

(3)

Hail, Queen of
Heaven,

Gaude, vessel of ve*r*tue & grace,
I-Crowned quene in that place   16
    Where thy sonne is kynge !

whom all angels
worship !

Angels alle in his p*r*esence
Ar vndyr thyn obedyence,
    And do the worshippynge !   20
            Gaude, splendens vas vi*r*tutu*m* !

(4)

Hail, Mother of
God,

Gaude, modyr and mayden fre,
Throw the bonde of charyte
    To god so holy and knytte,   24

whose every
prayer He grants !

That what so eu*er* thi askyng be,
Alle the holy trynite
    Ful goodly gr*a*untyth the hitte.
            Gaude, nexu caritatis !   28

(5)

Gaude, frute of allë flowres !
For who so euer the honowryth
  With preyour nyght or day,
The fadyr of heuyn, of his godhed   32
He graunt them to ther mede
  The blysse that lastyth aye !
      Gaude, mater mis*eror*um !

Gaude
mater
miserorum.
(MS.)

(6)

Gaude, the modyr of cryst iesu,   36
So gracyous and ful of vertu,
  That, for thi holynesse,
So highe arte nowe in dignite !
Thowe sitteste next the trinite   40
  In grete honowre and blysse.
      Gaude, vi**rgo, mat**er *Chri*s**ti** !

Hail, mother of
Christ,

who sittest next
the Trinity !

(7)

Gaude, mayden clene and pure,
Euyr beynge secure and suere   44
  That these yoies seuyñ
Shalle neuer swage nor sesse,
But euermore endure and encresse
  While god regnyth in heuyn.   Amen.   48
      Gaude, virgo, mater pura !

Hail, maiden
pure,

whose seven Joys
shall never cease.

Amen.

Script*us* A*nn*o D*omini* 1508 p*er*
D. T. Mylle.

Regina Celi Letare.

[*Lambeth MS.* 306, *leaf* 132, *back.*]

[The thick letters mark the red ones of the MS.]

Regina celi letare. alleluya.
quia quem **meruisti portare.** alleluya.
resurrexit sicut dixit. alleluya.
ora pro **nobis deu**m. alleluya.   4

In ista antiphona **alleluya** accipitur iiijᵒʳ diuersis
modis. **Primu**m alleluia. lauda deum creatura. **Secundum.** salus. vita. lux. **Terciu**m. saluum me fac deus.
Quartum idem est. quod pater, et filius, et spiritus
sanctus.   9

Regina   celi   le - ta - re !
Queen of heaven,   Quene of hevyn, make thou myrth !
alleluya ! lauda deum cr[e]atura !   12
praise God.   And prayse god wyth alle thy myght !
quia **que**m **meruisti portare.**
Of thee He took His birth.   For of the. he toke   his byrth.
alleluya. salus vita   lux.   16
That is, heele, lyfe, and lyght.
resurrexit,   sicut dixit ;
He rose from death.   he rose from deth ; so sayde he.
alleluya ! Saluum me fac deus !   20
Saue vs, god, in nedë moste !
ora pro nobis deum !
Pray for us.   Pra for vs the trynyte !
alleluya ! pater et filius et spiritus sanctus,   24
Fader, and sonne, and holy goste.

Quia Amore Langueo. (PART I.)

(THE VIRGIN'S COMPLAINT BECAUSE MAN'S SOUL IS WRAPT IN SIN.)

[Lambeth MS. 853, ab. 1430 A.D., page 4.]

[8 stanzas in eights, *abab bcbc*, except st. 1, *abab bcbd*.]

(1)

IN a tabernacle of a tour,
  As y stood musynge on þe moone,
A crowned queene, moost of hono*ur*,
  Me þouȝte y siȝ sittinge in trone.   4
Sche made hir cómpleynt bi hir oone,
  For ma*n*nis soule is wrappid in sy*n*ne :¹
  " Y may not leeue mankynde a-loone,
    Quia amore langueo.   8

As I gazed at the moon, methought I saw a Queen on a throne,

lamenting because man's soul was wrapt in sin.

(2)

I loke for loue of man, my broþ*ir*,
  I am his avoket² on eue*r*y wise,
I am his moder, y can noo*n* oþir ;
  Whi schulde y my dere child dispise?   12
  ¶ þouȝ he me wraþþe i*n* diue*r*se wise,
  þoruȝ freelte of fleisch be falle me fro,
  ȝit muste y rue til þat he rise,
    Quia amore langueo.   16

[page 5] She said, "I am his advocate and mother,

why should I despise him tho' he falls from me?

I languish with love.

(3)

I abood & abide w*ith* greet longynge,
  I loue & loke wha*n*ne ma*n* wole craue,
I pleyne me for pitee of pinynge ;
  Wolde he aske me*r*ci, he schulde it haue ;   20
  Seie to me, soule, y schal þee saue ;

I wait and long for the time when

he will ask mercy!

¹ The ryme should be in -o, as in the other stanzas.
² Alterd by a later hand to 'advoket.'

he never prayd,
but I forgave him.

Bid me, child, & y wole goo ;
Praiedist me neu*e*re, but y forgaue,
Quia amore langueo.   24

(4)

For him I was
made Mother of
Mercy.

Moder of m*e*rcy y was for þee made :
Who nediþ mercy but þou a-loone ?

I am more glad
to give than he
to ask ;

To ȝeue grace & m*e*rci y am more glade
þan þou to aske ; whi nyst þou noon ?   28

[page 6]

¶ Wha*n*ne seide y nay ?   tel me to who*m* !
Neu*e*re ȝit to freend ne foo !

and when he asks
not, I moan.

Wha*n*ne þou askist not, þan make y moo*n*,
Quia amore langueo.   32

(5)

O wrecche, in þis world y loke on þee

I see him sin day
by day in lust and
pride.

Wha*n*ne y se þee trespase day bi daye,
Wiþ leccheri aȝen my chastite,
W*it*h pride aȝen my meeke a-ray.   36

But still my love
awaits him ; anger
is away.

¶ My loue abidiþ þee ; yra is a-way ;
Mi loue þee calliþ, & þou stelist me fro ;

Sue to me, sinner,
I pray.

Ȝit sue to me, sy*n*ner, y þee pray,
Quia amore langueo !   40

(6)

My son was
beaten for thee ;

My sone was outlawid for þi sy*n*ne,
His body was beten for þi trespase,

that pricks my
heart.

Ȝit p*r*ickiþ it my*n* herte þat so nyȝ my ky*n*ne
þat so schulde be disesid, a sone, a-las !   44

He is thy father,

¶ Mi sone is þi fader, his moder y was,

and died for thee.
But yet with
love I languish
for thee.

He soukide my pappis ; he loued þee so,
He is deed for þee ; my*n* herte þou has,
Quia amore langueo.   48

(7)

[page 7]
To bring thee
to heaven
my son died,

¶ My sonë deedë for þi loue,
His herte was persid w*it*h a spere
To bri*n*ge þi soule to heuene a-boue,
For þi loue so diede he here.   52

¶ þerfor þou must be to me moost dere,
    Siþen my sonë loued þee so ;
þou praiest to me neuere but y þee here,
    Quia amore langueo.   56

(8)

My sone haþ grauntide me, for þi sake,
    Euery merciful praier þat y wole haue ;
For, he wole no veniaunce take
    If y aske mercy for þee, but þat y schal haue.   60
¶ þerfor axe þou merci, & y schal þee saue,
    With pitee y rue vpon þee so,
I longe for mercy þat þou schuldist craue,
    Quia amore langueo."   64

Quia Amore Langueo. (Part II.)

(OR CHRIST'S COMPLAINT FOR HIS SISTER, MAN'S SOUL.)

[16 stanzas of eights, *abab bcbc*.]

Lambeth MS. 853.

[Follows the last poem, seemingly as a continuation.]

(1)

IN a valey of þis restles mynde
   I souȝte in mounteyne & in myde,
Trustynge a trewe loue for to fynde.
   Vpon an hil þan y took hede;   4
   ¶ A voice y herde—& neer y ȝede—
     In huge dolour complaynynge þo,
   " Se, dere soule, how my sidis blede,
     Quia amore langueo."   8

[page 8]

(2)

Vpon þis hil y fond a tree;
   Vndir þe tree a man sittynge,
From heed to foot woundid was he,
   His hertë blood y siȝ bledinge:—   12
   ¶ A semeli man to ben a king,
     A graciouse face to loken vnto;—
   I askide whi he had peynynge,
     He seide " quia amore langueo."   16

(3)

I am true loue, þat fals was neuere;
   Mi sistyr, mannis soule, y loued hir þus;
Bi-cause we wolde in no wise disceuere,
   I lefte my kyngdom glorious.   20
   ¶ I purueide for hir a paleis precious;
     Sche fleyth, y flolowe, y souȝte hir so,
   I suffride þis peynë piteuous
     Quia amore langueo.   24

Quia Amore Langueo.

(From the Song of Solomon.)

[16 stanzas of eights, *abab bcbc.*]

[MS. Univ. Lib. Camb. Hh. 4. 12, leaf 41 *b*.   Handwriting
of the latter half of the 15th century.]

(1)

IN the vaile of restles mynd
　　I sowght in mownteyn & in mede,
trustyng a treulofe for to fynd :
　　vpon an hyll / than toke I hede ;　　　　　　　4
　　a voise I herd / (and nere I yede)
　　　　in gret dolo*ur* complaynyng tho,
　　　　" see, der**ë** soule, my syd**ë**s blede
　　　　Quia amore langueo." [1]　　　　　　8

In the vale of Restless Mind I sought for a true lover;

I heard a voice upon a hill;

(2)

¶ Vpon thys mownt I fand a tree ;
　　vndir thys tree / a man sittyng ;
from hede to fote / wowndyd was he,
　　hys hert blode I saw bledyng ;　　　　　　12
　　A semely man / to be a kyng,
　　　　A graciose face / to loke vnto.
　　　　I askyd hym / how he had paynyng,
　　　　he said, " *Quia amore langueo.*"　　16

and found a man [Christ] sitting under a tree, and bleeding.

I askt him whence his pain.

(3)

¶ I am treulove / that fals was neuer :
　　my sist*ur*, mannys soule, I loued hyr thus ; [2]
By-cause I wold on no wyse disseuere,
　　I left my kyngdome gloriouse ;　　　　　20
　　I purueyd hyr a place full preciouse ;
　　　　she flytt / I folowyd / I luffed her soo ;
　　　　that I suffred thes payn**ë**s piteuouse
　　　　Quia amore langueo.　　　　　　24

He said, It is for love of My sister, man's soul;

for whom I suffer because I languish with love.

[1] Solomon's Song, ii. 5 and v. 8 (Vulgate).　　[2] Sol. Song, iv. 9.

(4)

[page 9]

My fair spouse, & my louë briȝt,
  I saued hir fro betynge, & sche haþ me bet;
I cloþid hir in grace & heuenli liȝt,
  þis bloodi scherte sche haþ on me sette,   28
    ¶ For longynge of loue ȝit wolde y not lett;
    Swetë strokis axë þese; lo,
  I haue loued hir euere as y hir het,
    Quia amore langueo.   32

(5)

I crowned hir wiþ blis, & sche me with þorn;
  I ledde hir to chaumbir, & sche me to die;
I brouȝte hir to worschipe, & sche me to scorn;
  I dide her reuerence, & sche me vilonye.   36
    ¶ To loue þat loueþ, is no maistrie;
    Hir hate made neuere my loue hir foo,
  Axë me no questioun whi,
    Quia amore langueo.   40

(6)

Loke vnto myn hondis, man!
  þese gloues were ȝoue me whan y hir souȝte;
þei ben not white, but rede & wan,
  Onbroudrid with blood my spouse hem brouȝte.   44

[page 10]   ¶ þei wole not of, y loose hem nouȝte,
    I wowe hir with hem where-euere sche go;
  þese hondis for hir so freendli fouȝte,
    Quia amore langueo.   48

(7)

Merueille nouȝte, man, þouȝ y sitte stille;
  Se, loue haþ sched me wondir streite,
Boclid my feet, as was hir wille,
  With scharp naile, lo, þou maiste waite.   52
    ¶ In my loue was neuere desaite,
    Alle myn humours y haue opened hir to,
  þere my bodi haþ maad hir hertis baite,
    Quia amore langueo.   56

(4)

¶ My faire love and my spousë bryght,

    I saued hyr fro betyng / and she hath me bett ;

I clothed hyr in grace / and heuenly lyght,

    this blody surcote she hath on me sett ;   28

    for langyng love, I wiłł not lett,

        swetë strokys be thes, loo ;

    I haf loued euer[1] als I hett,   [1 MS. ouer]

        Quia amore langueo.   32

(5)

¶ I crownyd hyr w*ith* blysse / and she me w*ith* thorne,

    I led hyr to chambre / and she me to dye ;

I browght hyr to worship / and she me to skorne,

    I dyd hyr reuerence / and she me velanye.   36

    to love that loueth / is no maistrye,

        hyr hate made neue*r* my love hyr foo ;

    ask than no moo questions whye,

        but *Quia amore langueo.*   40

(6)

¶ loke vnto myn handys, man !

    thes gloues were geuen me / whan I hyr sowght ;

they be nat white / but rede and wan,

    embrodred w*ith* blode / my spouse them bowght ; 44

    they wyłł not of / I lefe them nowght,

        I wowe hyr / w*ith* them / where eue*r* she goo ;

    thes handes fułł frendly for hyr fowght,

        Quia amore langueo.   48

(7)

¶ Maruełł not, man, / thof I sitt styłł,

    my love hath shod me / wondyr strayte ;

she boklyd my fete / as was hyr wyll

    w*ith* sharp nailes / węłł thow maist waite !   52

    in my love was neuer dissaite,

        for all my membres I haf opynd hyr to ;

    my body I made hyr hertys baite,

        Quia amore langueo.   56

Marginal glosses:

[leaf 42]

I saved my love from beating, and she wounded Me thus.

I have ever lovd her as I promist.

I was kind to her, and she scornd Me;

but her hate has not made Me her foo.

Behold, O man, My hands;

they are bleeding and pallid;

I woo her with them ever.

[leaf 42, back]

My love hath fastend my feet with nails;

I made my body her heart's bait.

(8)

Ιn my side y haue made hir neste ;
  Loke in ! how weet a wounde is heere,
þis is hir chaumbir, heere schal sche reste,
  þat sche & y may slepe in fere.   60
    ¶ Heere may sche waische, if ony filþe were,
      Heere is sete for al hir woo ;
    Come whanne sche wole, sche schal haue chere,
      Quia amore langueo.   64

(9)

[page 11] Ι wole abide til sche be redy,
  I wole hir sue if sche seie nay ;
If sche be richilees, y wole be gredi,
  And if sche be daungerus, y wole hir praie.   68
    ¶ If she wepe, þat hide y ne may,
      Myn armes her hired to clippe hir me to ;
    Crie oonys ; y come : now, soule, asay,
      Quia amore langueo.   72

(10)

Ι sitte on þis hil, for to se fer,
  I loke into þe valey, my spouse to se ;
Now renneþ sche a-wayward, ȝit come sche me neer,
  For out of my siȝte may sche not flee.   76
    ¶ Summe wayte hir prai to make hir to flee,
      I renne bifore, and fleme hir foo ;
    Returne my spouse aȝen to me,
      Quia amore langueo.   80

(11)

Fair loue, lete us go pleye !
  Applis ben ripe in my gardayne,
I schal þee cloþe in a newe aray,
  þi mete schal be mylk, hony, & wiyn.   84
[page 12]!   ¶ Fair loue, lete us go digne,
      þi sustynaunce is in my crippe, lo !
    Tarie þou not, my faire spouse myne,
      Quia amore langueo.   88

(8)

¶ In my syde / I haf made hyr nest,

  loke in me / how wyde a wound is here !

this is hyr chambre / here shaH she rest,

  that she and I may slepe in fere.   60

    here may she wasshe / if any filth were ;

      here is socour for aH hyr woo ;

    cum if she wiH / she shaH haf chere,

      Quia amore langueo.   64

The wound in My side is her nest;

here may she wash herself.

(9)

¶ I wiH abide / tiH she be redy,

  I wiH to hyr send / or she sey nay ;

If she be rechelesse / I wiH be redy,

  If she be dawngerouse / I wiH hyr pray.   68

  If she do wepe / than byd I nay ;

    myn armes ben spred to clypp hyr to ;

  crye onys, "I cum !" / now, soule, assaye !

    Qui amore langueo.   72

I will wait till she be ready.

My arms are out-spread to embrace her.

(10)

¶ I sitt on an hille / for to se farre,

  I loke to the vayle / my spouse I see ;

now rynne she awayward, now cummyth she narre,

  yet fro myn eye syght she may nat be ;   76

  sum waite[1] ther pray / to make hyr flee,

    I rynne tofore / to chastise hyr foo ;

recouer my soule / agayne to me,   [1 MS. "make," corrected in margin to "waite."]

    Quia amore langueo.   80

[leaf 43]
I sit on a hill' [Calvary] to see far.

Some await their prey, but I run to chastise her foe [Satan].

(11)

¶ My swete spouse / wiH we goo play ;

  apples ben rype in my gardine ;[2]   [2 Sol. Song, iv. 16.]

I shaH clothe the in new array,

  thy mete shaH be / mylk / honye / & wyne ;[3]   84

now, dere soule, latt us go dyne,   [3 Sol. Song, v. 1.]

    thy sustenance is in my skrypp, loo !

tary not now / fayre spousë myne,

    Quia amore langueo.   88

Come, spouse, into My garden;

thy meat shall be milk, honey, and wine;

tarry not!

(12)

Iff þou be foul, y schal þee make clene ;
  If þou be sijk, y schal þee hele ;
If þou moorne ouȝt, y schal þee meene ;
  Whi wolt þou not, faire loue, with me dele ?   92
  ¶ Foundist þou euere loue so leel ?
    What woldist þou, spouse, þat y schulde do ?
  I may not vnkyndeli þee appele,
    Quia amore langueo.   96

(13)

What schal y do with my fair spouse,
  But a-bide hir of my gentilnes
Til þat sche loke out of hir house
  Of fleischli affeccioun ? loue myn sche is.   100
  ¶ Hir bed is maade, hir bolstir is blis,
    Hir chaumbir is chosen ; is þer non moo.
  Loke out on me at þe wyndow of kyndenes,
    Quia amore langueo.   104

(14)

[page 13] My loue is in hir chaumbir : holde ȝoure pees,
  Make ȝe no noise, but lete hir slepe :
My babe, y wolde not were in disese,
  I may not heere my dere child wepe.   108
  ¶ With my pap y schal hir kepe.
    Ne merueille ȝe not þouȝ y tende hir to ;
  þis hole in my side had neuere be so depe,
    But quia amore langueo.   112

(15)

Longe þou for loue neuere so hiȝ,
  My loue is more þan þin may be ;
þou wepist, þou gladist, y sitte þee bi,
  ȝit woldist þou oonys, leef, loke vn-to me !   116
  ¶ Schulde y alwey fedë þee
    With children mete ? nay, loue, not so !
  I wole preue þi loue wiþ aduersite,
    Quia amore langueo.   120

(12)

¶ yf thow be fowle / I shall make [thee] clene,
  if thow be seke, I shall the hele ;
yf thow owght morne / I shall be-mene,
  spouse, why will thow nowght wi*th* me dele ?   92
  thow fowndyst neuer / love so lele ;
    what wilt thow, sowle / that I shall do ?
  I may / of vnkyndnes the appele,
    Quia amore langueo.   96

If thou be foul, I will make thee clean ;

what wilt thou, O soul of man, that I shall do ?

(13)

What shall I do now wi*th* my spouse ?
  abyde I will hyr*e* iantilnesse,
wold she loke onys / owt of hyr howse
  of flesshely affecc*i*ons / and vnclennesse ;   100
  hyr bed is made / hyr bolstar is in blysse,
    hyr chambre is chosen, / suche ar no moo ;
  loke owt / at the wyndows of kyndnesse,[1]
    Quia amore langueo.   [1 Sol. Song, ii. 9.]   104

[leaf 43, back]

O that she would look out of her house of flesh !

Her bed, her bolster, is in heaven.

(14)

¶ Long and love thow neu*er* so hygh,
  yit is my love more / than thyñ may be ;
thow gladdyst / thou wepist / I sitt the bygh,
  yit myght thow, spouse / loke onys at me !   108
  spouse, shuld I alway fedë the
    wi*th* childys mete ? / nay, love, / nat so !
  I pray the, love, wi*th* aduersite,
    Quia amore langueo.   112

Though thou love much, yet I love more.

Must I always feed thee, O spouse, with child's meat ?

(15)

¶ My spouse is in chambre, hald ȝowre pease ![2]
  make no noyse / but lat hyr slepe ;   [2 Sol. Song, ii. 7 and viii. 4.]
my babe shall sofre noo disease,
  I may not here my dere childe wepe,   116
  for wi*th* my pappe I shall hyr kepe ;
    no wondyr / thowgh I tend hyr to,
  thys hoole in my side had neu*er* ben so depe,
    but *Quia amore langueo.*   120

My spouse sleeps; wake her not;

My love shall suffer no discomfort:

no wonder though I tend her.

(16)

Wexe not wery, myn ownë wijf!
 What mede is it to lyue euere in coumfort?
In tribulacioun y regne moore rijf
 Ofttymes þan in disport.   124

[page 14] ¶ In wele & in woo y am ay to supporte;
 Myn ownë wijf, go not me fro!
þi meede is markid whan þou art mort,
 Quia amore langueo.   128

(16)

¶ Wax not wery, myñ owne dere wyfe,
  what mede is aye to lyffe in comfort?
for in tribulac*i*on, I ryñ more ryfe
  ofter tymes / than in disport;   124
  In welth, in woo, eu*er* I support;
    than, derë soule, go neu*er* me fro!
  thy mede is markyd, whan thow art mort,
    in blysse; *Quia amore langueo.*   128

Finit.

[leaf 44]

What reward is it to live in comfort always in this life?

Thy true reward is after death, in heaven.

The Complaynt of Criste.

[*Lambeth MS.* 306, *ab.* 1460–70 A.D., *leaf* 145, *written in* 8-*line stanzas, though to l.* 135 *it is in* 12-*line ones.*]

(*Christ's First Complaint against Man.*)

(1)

This is the comepleynt off god
  Fro man) to man) that he haþe bouȝte,

  And thus¹ he seyethe to here Ateynt,

"My people, why
art thou so cold
to Me

 "Myne owne pepull, what haue yee wrought' 4
that thowe to me Art so feynt,
  And I thy love so sore have sought'?
In) thyn Answer no thyng þou peynte
  to me, By-cause I knewe þy þought'. 8

(2)

Who have done
all for thee,

"Haue I nat Do alle that me oughte?
have I lefft ony thynge be-hynde?
why wrathyst þou me? I greve þe nought';
  why arte thowe to thy Frende onkynde? 12

have made thee
like to Me,

I shewed thè Love; and that was seene
  whane I made thè lyke to me;

putting all My
works in thy
power!

On erthe my werkis bothe quyk & grene,
  I put hem) vndyr in thy poweste. 16

(3)

I delivered thee
from Pharaoh,

"And frome pharos (that was so keene)
  Of egypt' I delyuerd' thee,
I kyllyd hym) and his by-deene.

I dried the Red
Sea for thee,

  the Red see for the in) to flye, 20
I bad that hit drye shouldë bee;

[leaf 145, back]

  I seassid' the water and the wynde,
I lede the ouer, and made þe Free:
  why art thowe to thy freende onkynde? 24

Goddis owne Complaynt.

"WHI ART THOU TO THI FREEND VNKINDE?"

[*Lambeth MS.* 853, *ab.* 1430 A.D., *page* 81, *written without breaks.*]

(*Christ's First Complaint against Man.*)

(1)

This is goddis owne complaynt
    To euery man þat he haþ bouȝt,
And þus he seiþ to hem ataynt,
    "Myne ownë peple, what han ȝe wrouȝt,   4
¶ Þou þat to me art so faynt,
    And y þi loue so fer haue souȝt?
In þine answere no þing þou paynt
    To me; for whi, y knowe þi þouȝt.   8
    ¶ Haue y not doon al þat me ouȝt?
    Haue y left ony þyng bihynde?
    Whi wraþþist þou me? y greue þee nouȝt;
    Whi art þou to þi freend vnkinde?   12

(2)

I schewid þee loue, & þat was sene
    Whanne y made þee lijk to me;
On erþe my werkis [1]boþe quycke & grene,   [1 page 82]
    I putte hem vndir in þi poste.   16
And fro farao—þat was so kene—
    Of egipt y delyuered þee,
I killid him & hise bidene.
    Þe reed see atwo to flee   20
    ¶ I bad, þat drie it schuldë be;
    I ceessid þe watir & þe wynde,
    I ledde þe ouer, & made þee free:
    Whi art þou to þi freend vnkinde?   24

(4)

"And xl yere in wyldurnesse,
    w*ith* angels foodë I thè Feed;
Into the londe of grete Ryches,
    to schewe thè love, there I thè led.   28
to do thè more of kyndenes,
    I toke þè kyndely, and nothyng dred,

I lefft my[1] myght, ant toke mekenes,   [1 MS. my my]
    And my harte bloode for thè I bled.   32

(5)

"Thy soule to save, this lyffe I led,

    I bounde my selffe, þe to onbynde,
thus w*ith* my woo thy ned*is* I spede;
    why art thowe to thy frende onkynde?   36

for the in paradyse I ordeynnyd A plase;
    fuH Rychë was thyn énfeftment;
howe myght þou me þus dispyse ony more,
    than to breke my comaundement,   40

(6)

"And to synne In vij Maner wyse,
    and to myne Enemy so soone Assent?
he put the Downe, thowe myghttyst nat Ryse;
    thy strenkythe, thy wytt, A-way is went!   44
poore, naked, shamed, and shent,

    that Frendeshype myghttest þou nat fynde,
But me that on the Roode was Rent;
    why art þou to thy freende onkynde?   48

(7)

"Man, I love the! whome Lovyst thowe?
    I am þy frende; why wolt þou feyne?

I for-yave, and þu me slewe:
    ho hath dep*a*rtyd oure lowe A tweyne?   52

Turne to me! by-thenke the howe

    thowe haste go mys! come home Agayne!

And thowe shalt be as welcome nowe
    As he that synne neu*er* ded fayne.   56

(3)

And fourti ȝeer in wildirnes
   Wiþ aungelis fodë y þee fedde ;
Into þe lond of greet richesse,
   To schewe þe louë, y þee ledde.   28
¶ To do þe more of kyndënes
   I took þi kinde, and noþing dredde,
I lefte my myȝt, & tooke meekenes ;
   Myn hertë blood for þee y bleed.   32
   ¶ Thi soule to saue, þis lijf y ledde ;
     I boond my silf, þee to vnbinde ;
   þus with my wo þi nedis I spedde ;
     Whi art þou to þi freend vnkinde ?   36   [Page 83]

(4)

For þee y ordeyned paradijs ;
   Ful riche was þin enfeffëment ;
How myȝtist þou me ony more dispise,
   þan to breke my cómaundement,   40
¶ And synne in seuene maner of wise,
   And to myn enemy so soone assent ?
He putte þee doun, þou myȝtist not rise ;
   þi strengþe, þi witt, awei is went !   44
   ¶ Pore, nakid, schamed, & schent,
     þat frendschip myȝtist þou noon fynde
   But me, þat on þe roode was rent ;
     Whi art þou to þi freend vnkynde ?   48

(5)

O Man, y loue þee ! whom louest þou ?
   I am þi freend ; whi wolt þou feyne ?
I for-ȝaf, & þou me slouȝ :
   Who haþ departide oure loue a tweyne ?   52
¶ Turne [1] to me ! biþinke þee how   [1 Page 84]
   þou hast goon mys ! come hoom ageyne !
And þou schalt be as weel-come now
   As he that synne neuere dide steyne.   56

(8)

" Wayte what ded̴ Mary Mawdeleyne,

And what I seyd to thom*a*s of Inde;

I graunte the blysse, why lovys þou peyne ?

why art þou to thy Frende onkynde ?   60

of A Frende the fyrstë preffe

Is love, & drede, & nought̴ displease.

there was neu*er* thyng to me so leffe

As mankynde that nought̴ may peasse.   64

(9)

" For the I suffyrde grete repreffe :

In hygh̴e hevyn thy soule to easse

I was on-hanged as A theeffe ;

thowe dedest the deede, I had þe disease.   68

thowe canst me neyd*ur* thank nor pleasse,

Ne do goode deede, ne haue me in mynde ;

I am thy leche in thy Disease,

thowe cannyst me nowd*ur* thanke nor pleasse,[1]   72

(10)

" Ne do goode deede, we have in) mynde,[1]

I am thy leche in thy diseasse,[1]

Why art thowe to þy Frende on)-kynde ?

vnkynde,—for thowe kyllyd thy lorde,   76

And eu*er*y day þou wounedyst hym) newe,

for thowghe wee ben brought̴ to oone Acorde,

In) co*u*unaunt, wreche, þou art one-trewe,

And Redy also to Resorte,   80

(11)

" To folowe vyces and sle vertu ;

Al̴l Rybawdry thowe canste reporte,

And Day by daye hit to Renewe ;

[*No gap in MS.*]   84

And redy also to pursewe

the poore peepul̴l w*ith* sleyght̴tt*is* blynde ;

thowe shalt owte of this worlde remeve ;

why art thowe to thy Frende onkynde ?   88

¶ Waite what y dide to marie maudeleyne,
    And what y seide to thomas of ynde ;
I grau*n*te þee blis, whi lovest þou peyne ?
    Whi art þou to þi freend vnkinde ?   60

(6)

Of a freend the first[ë] preef
    Is loue wiþ drede, & nouȝt displese.
þere was neu*ere* þing to me so leef
    As ma*n*kinde þat nouȝt may pese.   64
¶ For þee y suffride greet repreef :
    In hiȝ heuene, þi soule to ceese,
Y was an-hangid as a þeef ;
    þou dedist þe dede, y hadde þe disese.   68
    ¶ þou canst me neu*ere* þanke ne please,
       Ne do no good dede to haue me in mynde ;
    Y am þi leche ¹in þi disese,   [¹ Page 85]
       Whi art þou to þi freend vnkinde ?   72

(7)

O vnkinde ! for þou haste slayn þi lord,
    And eu*er*y day þou wou*n*dist me newe,
For þouȝ we ben brouȝt to oon acoord,
    In couenau*n*t, wrecche, þou art vntrewe,   76
¶ And redy also to resorte
    To folewe vicis & flee vertu ;
Al ribaudie þou canst reporte,—
    Woo is hi*m* þat þi wraþþe may not eschewe !—   80
    ¶ And redi also to pursue
       þe poore peple w*ith* sleiȝtis blynde.
    þou schalt out of þis world remewe,
       Bi-cause þou art to þi freend vnkinde.   84

(12)

tempting Him,

"The devyll me tempttyd neuer but thrye,
  But þou me temptyst frome day to daye

with curses, to take vengeance.

whythe cursyng affter vengeaunce to crye,
    to styr my wrathe þou wylt assaye,   92

Thou wouldst be-
tray me worse
  [leaf 146, back]
than Judas did,

thowe woledyst, and ony woulde me by,
  Wele worsse than Iudas me be-traye ;
at my werke þou haste e[n]vye ;
    that wele ne woo is to þy paye.   96

(13)

and bind Me too,
hadst thou power
o'er Me as I o'er
thee.

"And thowe me myghttyst, as I þe maye,
  wele byttyrly thowe woldyst me bynde ;
I for-yave, and þou seyest nay,
    why arte thowe to þe frende onkynde?   100

And yet I bought
thy love full dear:

I have boughtᵗ thy love full dere :
  Onekynde ! why for-sakis þou myne ?

I gave thee My
heart and blood.

I yave the myn hart & bloode in Fere
  Onkynde ! why wolt þou nat yeve me þyne ?   104

(14)

Unfaithful
homager, thou
servest my foe ;

"Thowe art on-kyndë homagere,
  for with my Fo þou makest me fyne ;
thowe servyst me with febull chere ;
    to hym thyn hart wolte fully enclyne.   108
And I am lorde of blysse and pyne,
  and alle thyng may I lousse & bynde,

but whilst thou
dost I will shut
thee out.

Ayenst the wole I my yatis tynde
  All whyle þou arte to þy frende onkynde.   112

(15)

Man, think
whence thou
camest:

"Man ! by-thenk the what þou Arte,
  fro whens þou come, & wheder þou mone,
for thowȝe þou to-day be in hele & quarte,

how I may put
thee down!

    to-morowe I may put þe A-doune.   116
lett mylde mekenes melt in þyn hart,

Have pity on My
sufferings,

    that þou Rewe on my passyone,
with my woundis depe and smarte,
    with crosse, naylys, spere, & crowne.   120

(8)

Þe deuel me temptide neuere but þrie ;
  But þou me temptist from day to day
Wiþ cursynge, aftir venieaunce dooþ crie ;
  To stire mi wraþþe þou wolt a-saye ;   88
¶ þou woldist, & ony wolde me bie,   [Page 86]
  Weel worse þan iudas me bitraie ;
At my werk þou hast enuye,
  þat weel ne woo may þee noon paye.   92
    ¶ For & þou ouer me myȝtist, aſ y ouer þee may,
      Weel bittirli þou woldist me bynde :
    I forȝaf, & þou seiest naye ;
      þus y am freend, & þou vnkynde.   96

(9)

I haue bouȝt þi loue ful dere :
  Vnkinde ! whi forsakist þou myn ?
I ȝaf þee myn herte & blood in fere ;
  Vnkinde ! whi nyl þou ȝeue me þin ?   100
¶ þou art an vnkynde omagere,
  For with my foo þou makist þi fyn ;
þou seruest me with febil chere ;
  To him þin herte wolt hooli enclyne.   104
    ¶ And y am lord of blis & pyne,
      And al þing may y lose [1]& bynde,   [[1] Page 87]
    Aȝen þee wole y my ȝatis tyne,
      Al þe while þou art to þi freend vnkynde.   108

(10)

Man ! biþinke þee what þou art,
  From whens þou come, and whidir þou art boun !
For þouȝ þou to-day be in hele & qwart,
  To-morewe y may putte þee doun.   112
¶ Lete mylde & meekenes melte in þin herte,
  þat þou rue on my passïoun,
With wide woundis depe & smerte,
  Wiþ crosse, nailis, spere, & crowne.   116

(16)

and yield thy Will
wholly to Me.

"Let god and discressione
 thy wyll holy vp to me sende :
thowe hast wyttys & Reasone,
  And yff þou wylt, þou mayst be kynde."   124

(*Man's First Answer.*)

¶ " A ! lorde, A-yeenst the wee wole nat plette,
 for as þou wouledyst, hit is, and was,

Lord, we have de-
served hell fire.

And wee have deservyd hellë hete,
  But nowe wee yelde us to thy grace.   128

(17)

[leaf 147]

Chastise us for
our sins,

"Wee wole boowe, and thowe shalt bete,
 And Chastice us, lorde, for oure trespase,
And lett mercy for vs entrete

but let no fiends
chase our souls.

 that neuer no feondis oure soweles chase.   132
A ! blysfull lady, fayre of face,

Mary! help us!

 helpe ! for wee been fer be-hynde ;

Alas for our un-
kindness !

that wee nowe with weepyng crye ' alas,
  for that wee were to oure frende onkynde.' "   136

EXPLICIT [in a later hand. The Manuscript goes right
  on with the continuation, really a separate Poem.]

(18)
(*Christ's Second Complaint.*)

Thus oure gracius god, prince of pyte,
 whos myght, whose goodenes, neuer by-gan,
 at whose wyll all by-hovythe to bee,
  Compleynnyng hym thus to synfull man :   140

My people,

" Myne owne pepull, Answer me,
 Excuse thy selffe yf þou can :

why servest thou
Satan ?

what haue I trespassyd vnto the ?
  thowe for-sakyst me, þou servyst Sathan.   144

¶ Lete drede & good discresïou*n*
  þi wil holli up to me send :
þou hast fyue wittis & reasou*n*,
  And if þ*ou* wolt, þou maist be kynde."   120

(11)

(*Man's First Answer.*)

A ! lord, aȝens þee wole we not plete,
  For as þ*ou* wolt, it is, & was ;
We han deserued hellë hete,
  But now [1] we ȝeelde us to þi grace.   124   [1 Page 88]

¶ We wole*n* bowe, & þou schalt bete,
  And chastice us, lord, for o*ure* trespace,
And lete m*er*ci for us entrete,
  þat neu*er*e no feendis oure soulis chase.   128
  ¶ A ! blissid lady, fair of face,
    help ! for wee be fer bihynde ;
  þat wee wiþ weepynge mou*n* crie, alas !
    For that we were to o*ure* freend vnkinde."   132
      A-M-E-N.
    ["Iff þou wole be wul w*ith* god " follows.]

𝕮𝖍𝖗𝖎𝖘𝖙'𝖘 𝖔𝖜𝖓 𝕮𝖔𝖒𝖕𝖑𝖆𝖎𝖓𝖙,

" MAN, MAKE AMENDIS OR þOU DIE."

(otherwise called the Remorse of Conscience.)

(12)

(*Christ's Second Complaint.*)

Thus o*ure* gracious god, p*r*ince of pitee,   God | [Page 193]
    whos miȝt, whos goodnes, neu*er*e bigan,
At w*h*os wil al bihoueþ to be,
  Compleyneth hi*m* þus to synful man :   136
" Myn owne peple, answere ȝe me,
  Excuse þi silf if þat þ*ou* can :
what haue y trespasid vnto þee
  þat þou forsakist me, & seruest sathan ?   140

(19)

I loved thee so,

"Mane! suche A loue to the I hade!
  this worllde in vj dayes whan I wrougħt',

I made thee last
that thou mightest
want nothing;

thaw was the last thyħg that I máde
  By-cause I woulde þou wantyd nougħt'.   148
what thyng the mygħt' helpe or glade,
  [2 *lines wanting in MS.* . . . .

. . . .]

to thy be-hoffe alle forthe is brougħt'.   152

(20)

I gave thee power,

"More-ou*er* I yave the suffraunt[e]
  that alle Best*is* shoulde bowe þe vntyH;
I made the also lyke to me,

and Free-will

And yaffe the connyng¹ of Fre wyH,   [¹ MS. *comyng*]
me to serve, that thowe mygħt see,   157

to choose the good
and leave the ill.

god chese the goode, and leve the yH.
I ax no thyng Agayne of the

Then serve Me!

But be my² servaunt, as hit is skyH.   [² MS. *thy*] 160

(21)

But thou dost
not;

"But vnto this, takys thowe no tent
  thowe wyrchyst A-waye fuH onkyndely,
Aloone one-lefully that love is lent;
  thy hart be-holdythe nat hevyw one hye,   164

thou never once
saidst thanks.
[leaf 147, back]

For alle the goodenesse I have the sente,
  The lyst nat onys to saye gram*er*cye.

Repent before
thou diest!

In tyme comyng lest þou Repent,
  Maw! make Amend*is* or þou dye."   168

(22)

(*Man's Second Answer.*)

A crysten soule conseyvyd w*ith* synne
    Resceyvyd in consyence þis compleynt;
  he fyH downe flatt w*ith* dulfuH synne,

Lord, mercy;

And seyd, "lorde, m*er*cy, souerayne seynt!   172
I, moste vnkynde wreche of mankyn*ne*,

I acknowledge
my treachery
and sin.

I knowelege I aw thy traytur atteynt;
this wykkyd lyffe that I lyve iw,
  I may hit nat frome þy knowyng glent: 176

(13)

¶ " Man ! such a loue to þee y hadde !   [Page 194]
   þe world in sixe daies whanne y it wrouȝt,
þou were þe laste þing þat y maad,
   By-cause y wolde þee wantid nouȝt.   144
Whát þing myȝte þee helpe or glade,
   What þat þou nedidist durst nouȝt be souȝt ;
Foul, fische, al þing, þee to glade,
   To þi bihoue al was forþ brouȝt.   148

(14)

¶ " More-ouer y ȝafe þee souereynte
   þat alle beestis schulde bowe þee vntille ;
I made þee also lijk to me,
   And ȝaf þee kunnynge and free wille,   152
Me to serue þat þou myȝtist se,
   To chese þe good, and leue þe ille.
Y aske no þing aȝen of þee
   But be þi souereyn, as it is skille.   156

(15)

¶ " But vnto þis, takist þou no tent,
   But wriþist awey ful vnkindely,
On loue onleefful þi loue is lent ;
   þin herte biholdiþ not heuen an hiȝ,   160
For of al þee good y haue þee sent,   [Page 195]
   þou list not to seie oonys ' gramercy.'
In tyme comynge lest þou repente,
   Man ! make Amendis or þou dye."   164

(16)

(*Man's Second Answer.*)

A Cristen soule conceyued with synne   Man.
   Receyued in conscience þis compleynt ;
Fallyng doun flat with doolful dynne,   167
   And seide, "lord, mercy, moost souereyne seynt !
I, moost vnkynde wretche of mankynne,
   Y knouliche y am þi traitour atent ;
þis wickid lijf þat y lyue ynne,
   Y may it not from þi knowynge gleynt :   172

(23)

" I want word*is* and Also wytte,

    of thy kyndenes to carpe A clawse ;

Aᴌ that I haue, þou gave me hytt

    Of thy goodenesse w*ith*-owteᴅ cause ;   180

thowe I have grevyd the, anᵈ do yettᵗ,

    thowe thy benefitt*is* nougᷣtᵗ w*ith*-drawes ;

I haue deserved to haue heᴌ pytt,

    So haue I levyd Ayenst thy lawes.   184

(24)

" but, lorde, þou knowest mannys febullnes,

    howe Freᴌ he is, and haþe beeᴅ aye,

for thowȝe the sowle have thy lyknesse,

    Maᴅ is but lothesum eorthe anᵈ claye,   188

In synne conseyued, anᵈ wrechchydnes,

    Anᵈ to the soule Rebeᴌ Alleweye.

furst A maᴅ growys As A gras,

    Anᵈ Afftyr-warde welkythe as flowre or hay   192

(25)

" sithe maᴅ is thaᴅ so freᴌ A thyng,

    And thy power so grete in kynde,

this worlde, man, aye twynkelynge

    thowe maye distroye, noone may defende,   196

w*ith* that god me*r*cy wole meenge,

    and to my soule gostely þou sende ;

Sore me Repentythe my mys-levyng ;

    Mercy ! lorde ! I wole A-mende."   200

(26)

(Christ's Third Complaint.)

" **M**an, I sende the bodyly helth̄e

    that thowe shouldyst spendᵈ hit in my se*r*vyce,

    fayrenes and Also feturs fele :

But, maᴅ, what doste þou w*ith* aᴌ this ?   204

thowe doestᵗ the delytys of þe devyᴌ ;

    thy delyte is to me to dispyse ;

thowe levyst A lecherous lyfe one-lelle ;

    frome yere to yere þat lyst nat to A-Ryse.   208

(17)

¶ " I want wordis and also witt ;
  Of þin kindenes to carpe oon clause ;
Al þat y haue, þou ȝaue me it
  Of þi goodnesse, wiþ-outen cause ;   176
þouȝ y haue greued þee, & do ȝitt,
  þou þi benefetis not wiþdrawis ;
I haue deserued hellë pitt,
  So haue y lyued aȝens þi lawis.   180

(18)

¶ " But, lord, þou knowist *mannis* febilnes,   [Page 196]
  How freel he is, & haþ ben ay,
For þouȝ þe soule haue þi lijknes,
  Man is but wlatsum erþe and clay,   184
In *synne* conceyued & wretchidnesse,
  And to þe soule, rebel alwey.
First a ma*n* grow*ith* as doo*þ* a gras,
  And anoo*n* after welew*ith* as flou*ris* of hay.   188

(19)

¶ " Siþen ma*n* is þan so freel a þing,
  And þi power, lord, is so fer ykend,
þis world, is an iȝës twynkeling
  þou maist distroie, noo*n* may defende.   192
Wiþ þi riȝt, lord, m*er*cy mynge,
  And to my soule goosteli salue þou sende !
Sore me repe*n*tiþ my mys-lyuynge,
  For, merciful lord ! y schal amende."   196

(20)
(*Christ's Third Complaint.*)

" A Man, y ȝaf þee bodili hele
    , *þat* þou schuldist it spende i*n* my s*er*uice,
Fairnesse also, and feturis fele :
  But, ma*n*, what doist þou wit*h* alle þeise ?   200
þou doist þe delicis of þe deuel :   [Page 197]
  þi delite is me to dispise ;
þou lyuest a letcherouse lijf vnleel ;
  From ȝeer to ȝeer þou list not rise.   204

(27)

Thou studiest dress,

"Thowe stodyest affter more Araye,

And makest gret cost on) clothyng,

to make the semely, as who shoulde saye

as if to amend the making of thee.

thowe cowdest Amend[e] thy makyng.   212

thowe cannyst' Dyght' the Rychely day by day

to steere the peopull to synnyng,

thy wrechchyd wyll þou folowyst alle daye ;

what ende syn) hathe, thowe thenkyst nowght.[1]   216

(28)   [1 The rhyme requires *no thyng.*]

Think what vengeance came for lechery in Noah's time,

"In noyes tyme, by-cause of synne—

for lechery In Especyall—

what vengeaunce cam) þan) to mankyn) !

Save viij persowenys they were drowenyd alle.   220

and on Sodom and Gomorrah.

Of sodome and gomer the ought' to meene,

howe I made fyre and brymston) falle

frome heven) on men) that bade there-in) ;

for synne were distroyed boþe grete & smalle.   224

(29)

Thinkest thou My might is less than it was then ?

"Man, wenyst thowe my myght' be lesse

than) hit was than), or ellis I

hathe nat as mychë wykkydnesse

As whan I smote so spiteously ?   228

But yett I wyll thy fawtes Redresse,

I am merciful now ; make amends ere thou die !

thoowe I nowe sparë for my mercy ;

Man, thenke vppon) my Ryght'wysnes,

And make A-mendis or that þou dye."   232

(30)

(*Man's Third Answer.*)

I know sin must be punished,

"I wott wele, lorde, þou Ryghtfull arte,

And þat synne mut be ponysshed need ;

but Thy mercy exceeds my misdeeds.

But o thyng holdythe hope in) myn) harte,

that mercye passithe my mysdede ;   236

[leaf 148, back]

I knowë wele I may nat with-starte,

I have so doone, I ought' to dreede.

I have not served Thee ;

With beaute and with bodyly quarte

to servë the I toke noone heede.   240

(21)

¶ " þou studiest aftir nyce aray,
 And makist greet cost in cloþing
To make þee semeli, as who schulde say
 þou cowdist ameendë my making.   208
þou atirist þee richeli day bi day,
 To stire þe peple to synnynge ;
þi wrecchid wil þou folewist alway ;
 What eende synne haþ, þou þinkist no þing   212

(22)

¶ " In noes tyme, by-cause of synne—
And for letcherie moost in special—
What veniaunce came þanne to mankynne !
 Saue .viij. persoones, drowned were al.   216
On sodom and gommor þou ouȝte to mynne,
 How y made fier & brymstoone falle
From heuene on men þat abood þerynne ;
 In synne were distroied boþe greet & smal.   220

(23)

¶ " Man, wenest þou now my myȝt be lesse   [Page 198]
 þan it was þanne ? or ellis y
Hate not so mychë wickidnesse
 As whanne y smoot so spiteuoseli ?   224
But ȝit y wole þi fautis redresse,
 þouȝ y now spare for my mercy ;
Man, þinke vpon my riȝtwijsnesse,
 And, man, make amendis or þou die."   228

(24)

(Man's Third Answer.)

" I Woot weel, lord, þou riȝtful art,
  And þat synne mote be ponyschid neede ;
But oon þing holdiþ in hope myn hart,
 þi merci passiþ my mysdeede ;   232
I knowe weel y may nat with-start ;
 I haue so doon, me ouȝte to drede.
With bewte & with bodily qwart
 To seruë þee, y took noon hede.   236

(31)

"I haue mysspendyd my yonge age
   In synne, and wantonnehed also,
I have been slowe and lovyd outerage ;

   A gloton, A lechur, I was bothe to.   244
I am worthy noon odyr wage

   But for to dweH in eendeles woo ;
Alas ! why haue I been so outerage,
   And servyd the fende þat was my Foo ?   248

(32)

¶ " But, lorde, iɳ holy wrytt Rede wee
   that þou for-sakyst no wrechchyd wygħt'
that leuythe his syɳ and turnytħe to the,

   And I to the turne have tygħt.   252
ffuH prowde and RebeH haue I beeɳ,
   But I wele meke me to my mygħt',

frome hens forwarde I purpose me
   A-yenst myɳ ownë flesche to fygħt'.   256

(33)

" My Flesche to fellë I wole faste,
   My louys to traveH I wole sende,
And thorowe thy grace I am nat A-gast',

   what sorowe or sykenes to me þou sende,   260
to suffyr whyle my lyffe wole laste ;
   for vttyrly to this Entent,
to ponysche þat I haue trespassed,
   Mercy, Iħesu, I wole Amende."   264

(34)

(*Christ's Fourth Complaint.*)

"Maɳ, I haue sende þe syluer & gollde,
   And alle the weltħe within þy woone,
to susteyne the and thyɳ houssolde,

   And with the Resedewe many one   268
tho mygħttyst þou haue yonge and olde
   that been diseassyd and woo-by-goone ;

My servauntis suffyr hunger and colde,
   Releffe of the yeet haue I noone.   272

(25)

¶ " I haue myspendid my ȝong age
  In synne, & wantownesse also ;
Y haue be slow, and loued to rage ;
  A glotoun, a letchour, y was boþe two.   240
I am worþi to haue noon oþir wage   [Page 199]
  But for to dwelle in eendelees woo ;
Alas ! whi haue y ben outrage,
  And serued þe feend þat was þi foo ?   244

(26)

¶ But, lord, in hooli writt rede we,
  þat þou forsakist no wretchid wiȝt
þat leueþ his synne & turneþ to þee ;
  And y to turne to þee haue tiȝt.   248
Full proud and rebel haue y bee ;
  But y wole meeke me in my siȝt ;
From hens forward, y purpose me,
  Aȝen myn ownë fleisch to fiȝt.   252

(27)

¶ " My fleisch to feble, y wole faste ;
  Mi boonis to traueile y wole bende ;
And þoruȝ þi grace, y am not agast,
  What sorewe or sijknes to me þou sende,   256
To suffre whilis my lijf may laste ;
  For vttirli to þis y wole entende,
To ponysche þat y haue trespast ;
  Mercy, ihesu ! y wole amende."   260

(28)

(Christ's Fourth Complaint.)
" **M**An, y haue sente þee siluer and goldc,   [Page 200]
  And al þe welþe wiþinne þi woon,
To susteine þee and þin householde ;
  And with þe residue, manye oon   264
þou myȝtist han holpe, ȝong & oolde
  þat ben disesid and woo-bigoon ;
My seruauntis suffren hungir & coolde,
  Releef of þee ȝit haue þei noon.   268

(35)

but thou givest with a heavy heart,	" yff þou yeve for my love A ferthẏng,
	thowe doest hit w*ith* An hevy harte ;
	In almys dar þou Do nothyng
fearing to fall into poverty.	for Drede þou fallë in pou*er*te, 276
	In word*is* and in vayne spekyng,
	what-eu*er* þou wastyst, mery þou arte ;
	Of suche I wole haue Rekenyng ;
But at Doomsday	A Domys day þou shalt not starte. 280

(36)

thou shalt give account,	" than shalt þou yeve A-counte full strayte,
	howe thowe come by thy goode, eche dele,
	whed*ur* w*ith* trouthë or Dyssayte,
	And howe þou spendyst hit, evyll or wele. 284
	Noone odyr grace than afftyr wayte :
and as thou hast wrought, so shalt thou fare.	As þou haste wrougħt, so shalt þou fele.
No pounds then will profit thee,	what shall than) prophyte þi gowne p*ur*fylled ?
	Poundes and markes of the I peele. 288

(37)

but a pure conscience,	" A clene conscyence shall þat daye
	More pr*o*phyte be, & more sett bye,
	than all thy muke and alle þy moneye
	that eu*er* was, or shall be vndyr þe skye. 292
and no pleas.	than wole nat helpë plete nor playe,
	for ar Rigħt-wole than Deme shall I ;
Make amends, then, ere thou die.	And there-for, whylë þat þou may,
	Make Amend*is* or þou dye." 296

(38)

(*Man's Fourth Answer.*)

Lord, I have grieved Thee,	" I wote wele, lorde, frome yere to yere
	full gretely grevyd the, I have ;
	that I wete wele ; nor, þy m*er*cy were,
	My modyrs wombe hade be my grave. 300
	for what profyttytħe my levyng here
	But þou wolt affter-warde me save ?
but leave not my soul in the cave of hell.	But Ihesu, as þou boughttest me dere,
	Leve nat my soulë in hellë Cave ! 304

(29)

¶ " If þou ȝeue for my love a ferþinge,
þou doist it w*ith* an heuy harte ;
In almesse þou darist ȝeue no þing
 For drede þou schuldist falle i*n* pou*e*rte.   272
In wordis and in veyn spekynge,
 what eu*ere* þou waastist, þou myrie art ;
Of such y wole haue rekenynge ;
 On doomysday þou schalt not starte.   276

(30)

¶ " þa*n*ne schalt þou ȝeue acou*n*tis ful streite,
 How þou come to þi good, eu*ery* deel,
Wheþir þou it wan w*ith* trouþe or w*ith* disceite,
 And how þou spendist it, yuel or weel.   280
Noon oþer grace þa*n*ne aftir waite ;   [Page 201]
 For, as þou hast wrouȝte, so schalt þou feele.
What sch*a*l þa*n*ne pr*o*fite þi gowne y-pleite,
 Pou*n*dis or markis þat ȝe of þe peple peele?   284

(31)

¶ " A clene conscience schal in þat day
 More pr*o*fite, & be more sett by,
þan al þe muk & þe money
 þat eu*ere* was or schal be, vndir þe sky.   288
þa*n*ne wole not helpe to plete ne pray ;
 þerfore, as riȝt wole, þa*n*ne deme schal y :
And þer-for*e*, man, whilis þou may,
 Man, make amendis or þou die."   292

(32)

(Man's Fourth Answer.)

" **I** Woot weel, lord, fro*m* ȝeer to ȝeer   Man.
 Ful greetli greeued þee y haue ;
þat y wolde neer þi mercy were,
 My mod*ir*s wombe had be my graue.   296
For wh*a*t pr*o*fitiþ my lyuynge heere,
 But y myȝte aftirward be saaf ?
But ih*es*u, as þou bouȝtist me deere,
 Lete not my soule come i*n* hell*e* caaf !   300

(39)

[leaf 149, back]

I will cut off my wastefulness and vainglorious expenditure,

" My waste expensis I wyll with-drawe,

  Nowe, sertayne, ' waste,' wele colyd' þei be,

for þou were spent my boste to blowe,

  My name to bere by londe and' ssee. 308

wele I wott me thought' nat trewe

  with many A man of my cuntre ;

yff they me mett, they me nat knewe,

  Ne neuer yett harden) speke of me. 312

(40)

" fondely haue I wrought' & wyrchyd on wyse ;

which would have earned me reward if spent in almsdeeds :

  I myght' haue goton) mychë meede

had I spent hit in) goddis seruyce,

  On men) diseisyd and almys deede. 316

but now all my surplus

But thorowe thy grace I wyll A-Ryse,

  for, haue I and myne, oure bare mede,

I will spend on the needy ;

with the Remnaunt, lorde, at þy devyse,

  the poore, the nakyd, to cloþe & ffeede. 320

(41)

I will visit the sick

" Syk men) that lyen) in) goddis bondis,

  they haue no syluer for to spende,

and those in bonds,

And prisonners bounden with fete and hondis,

  Offt for to vesyte I wyll hem) Amende : 324

what I see howe hit with hem) stondis,

and give them all I can.

  Suche as I haue, I shall hem) fynde ;

Have mercy ! I will amend.

But, lorde, lett þy worke be þy bondis ;

  A, mercy, Ihesu, I wyll Amende ! " 328

(42)

(Christ's Fifth Complaint.)

Make amends by doing alms,

" **M**an, yff thowe wylt Amendis make,

  Do thyn Almes with thyne owne goode,

and taking no vengeance.

And wayte þou wyrkë no man) wrake,

  to venge Anodyr manys goode. 332

yff thowe ontrewly frome one take,

  And there-with fynde xl. her goode ;

Suche sacrefysis I for-saake,

  they been to me as sowre as soote. 336

(33)

¶ " My waast expensis y wole wi*th*-drawe ;   [Page 202]
  Now, certis, ' waast' weel callid þei be,
for þei were spent, my boost to blowe,
  My name to bere boþe on londe & see.   304
Weel y woot me dare not trowe,
  þou3 many a man of my cou*n*tree,
If þei me mette, þei me not knowe,
  Ne neu*ere* 3it herde speke of me.   308

(34)

¶ " Fo*n*nedli haue y wrou3t, as a wretche vnwijs,
  Where y my3te haue gete me myche meede
Had y it spend in god-is seruyce,
  On men diseesid, and almesdeede.   312
But þoru3 þi grace, lord, y wole rise ;
  For, haue y or myne, oure barë neede,
wi*th* the remenau*n*t, lord, at þi dyuyse,
  þe poore & nakid y wole cloþe & fede.   316

(35)

¶ " Sijke me*n* þat liggen in god-is boondis,
  þat han noo siluer for to spende,
And p*r*isoners bounde*n* feet and hondis,
  Ofte for to visite y wole to hem tende :   320
Whanne y se how it wi*th* hem stoondis,   [Page 203]
  Such as y haue, y schal hem sende ;
B*u*t, lord, lete þese werkis be þi sond*is* ;
  For, merciful lord, I wole amende ! "   324

(36)
(*Christ's Fifth Complaint.*)

" MAn, if þou wolt amendis make,   God.
  þan do þin almes of þi*n* owne good,
And waite þou worchë no man wrake,
  to venge anothir man-is mood.   328
And þou vntruli from oon take,
  And þerwi*th* fynde fourty her foode,
Al suche sacrificis y forsake,
  For þei ben to me as sour as sood.   332

(43)

Now thou oppressest the Poor;

" the poore peopułł þou doest opresse
　　wɩth flyghttɩs & wylys many also :

[leaf 150] but thou buildest churches and mendest roads.

thowe makyst chyrches, and syng messes,
　　thowe Amendystʼ wayes, men) on) to go ;　　340
and some men) ban) the, & some men) blesse :
　　Whedur shałł I here of theese twoo ?

Banish falseness from thee.

yff þou wolt haue grace as þou thenkɩs,
　　lett falsnes be Flemydł the froo.　　344

(44)

Moths eat thy clothes, and the poor go bare:

" the mothes that thy clothys etys,
　　andł þou lettestʼ poore men) go bare,
thy drynkɩs soweren), þou mouledestʼ metɩs
　　where-wɩth the febułł myghtʼ wele fare.　　348
thy Rustes þat thy syluer ffreete,

thy ill-gotten goods cry for vengeance on thee.

　　thy goodɩs that evyłł goton are,
they cryen) vppon) the vengeaunce grete,
　　there for to spyłł, yeet I þe spare.　　352

(45)

Thou withholdest thy servants' dues;

" wɩth-holdyn) hem) A-yenst the Ryghtʼ,
　　thoowȝe thy servaunttɩs vppon) þe crye ;
Andł, man), offtymes þou hast me hyghtʼ
　　thowe woulde Amende, & leve folye.　　356
thowe spekyst soore by day andł nyghtʼ,
　　thowe brekystʼ couinaunt contenually ;

yet I am loth to punish. Make amends.

yett is me lothe wɩth the to fyghtʼ ;　　359
　　yett make Amendɩs, man), or þou dye." [See note on p. 214]

(46)

(Man's Fifth Answer.)

" Swete lorde, I may nat Ayenst þe saye, [on leaf 152]
　　I have nat holden) þat I the heete :
I greve the gretely every daye,
　　I do nat as I am) in) dett,　　364

Lord, I have not kept my vow,

but I am beset with foes;

I woulde do wele, but wele-A-waye,
　　Wɩth Enemyes I am) euer by-sett ;

my flesh hinders me;

whan) my soule woulde faynest þe paye,
　　My flesche is the fyrstʼ þat wolc it lett.　　368

(37)

¶ " þe poore peple þou doist oppresse
  Wiþ sleitis and wilis ful manye also ;
þou makist chirchis, and doist singe messe,
  And mendist weies, men on to go ;   336
And sum men þee banne, & summë blesse :
  Which schal y heere of þeisë two ?
If þou wolt haue grace as þou doist gesse,
  Lete al falsnes be fleemyd þee fro.   340

(38)

¶ " þe moþþis þat þi cloþis ete,   [Page 204]
  And þou letist poore men go bare,
þi drinkis þat sowren, & þi mowlid mete
  Wherwith þe febil myȝte weel fare,   344
þe rust þat þi siluer doiþ freete,
  þi goodis þat yuel gote[n] are,
þei crien vpon þee veniaunce greete
  þee for to spille ; but ȝit y spare.   348

(39)

¶ " With-holden hire, aȝen þe riȝt
  Of þi seruanntis, vpon þee crye ;
And, man, ofte tyme þou hast me hiȝt
  þou woldist amende, & leue folie ;   352
þou spekist faire boþe day & nyght,
  þou brekist couenaunt contynuely ;
Me is ful looþ wiþe þee to fight ;
  þerfore make amendis, man, or þou die !"   356

(40)

(Man's Fifth Answer.)

" **S**weete lord, y may not aȝen say,   Man.
  Y haue not holden þat me hette :
Y greeued þee greetli euery day,
  Y do not as y am in dette ;   360
I wolde do weel ; but, welle-away !   [Page 205]
  Wiþ enemyes y am euere bisette !
Whanne y wolde þee faynest pay,
  My fleisch is þe first þat wole me lette.   364

(47)

" Eu*er* the fatt*er* that I [hit] Feede,

Eu*er* the Fressher hit is my foo,

and with it about me, yett must' wee bere hit Abowtë nede,

But febuĦ hit is, hit wole me sloo. 372

the worlde, the fende, my batayle byde

Some tyme w*ith* wele, some tyme w*ith* woo ;

how can I fight the world and the devil? whate may I do w*ith* a wykkyd weede,

to fy3te A-yeeɲ my enemyes soo ? 376

(48)

When I resolve to live a true life, " whan I iɲ-force me wother wyles,

And thynke I woulde lyve a trewe lyffe

and for-sooke aĦ batayll*is* & gylys,

the World challenges me. the worlde byddythe me bateĦ blyve, 380

And, but I wole vse wrenchis wylys,

to comyɲ wyse as I shaĦ nat stryve," 382

[MS. ends, and is incomplete.]

["The Stacyons of Rome" follows on leaf 152, back.]

[After line 360 the MS. runs on with line 383, p. 216, and transposes Man's Fifth Answer, ll. 361–382, to the end, p. 224. I fetch it back to its right place above.—F. J. F.]

(41)

¶ " Euere þe fattir þat y it feede,

Euere þe freischer it is my foo,

Ȝit y muste bere it a-boutë nede :

Ful febil it is, it wole me sloo.　　　　　　368

þe world, þe feend, me [bataile] beede,

Sumtyme wiþ weele, sumtyme wiþ woo ;

What may y do wiþ a wekkid[1] wede,　　[1 MS. welkid]

To fiȝte aȝen þree enemyes soo?　　　　　372

The fatter I feed my flesh, the more it fights against me.

The world and the devil tempt me too.

How can I fight these three foes ?

(42)

¶ " Whanne y enforsoþe me oþir whilis,

And þinke y wolde lyue a trewë lijf

And forsake all batailis & gilis,

þe world biddiþ me bataile blijf ;　　　　　376

And, but y wole vse wrenchis & wilis,

þe comoun uoice is, y schal not þrijf.

Summe at me mowis, summe at me smylis,

And counten me but a kynde caitif.　　　　380

When I strive to live a true life

the world bids me fight,

and the common voice mocks me.

(43)

¶ " But y þinke, not-wiþstonding þis,

To forsake falsnes wiþ-outen eende,

To restore aȝen þat y took mys,

And to paie my dettis fair and hende ;　　384

And whanne y haue ȝeuen eche man his,

As resoun is, þanne wole y spende,

And ȝeue myn almës þere nede is ;

Mercy, ihesu! y wole amende."　　　　388

[Page 206]
Nevertheless I purpose to for-sake sin, to restore all falsely gotten goods, pay my debts,

and give alms to all who need them.

(44)

(Christ's Sixth Complaint.)

" **M**An, y sente þee kindeli in-siȝte　　　God.

Of vndir-stondyng, skil, & witt,

To rewle þi silf bi resoun riȝt ;

More-ouer þou hast holi writt,　　　　　392

þat cleerli schewiþ þee goostli liȝt,

How þou schuldist deedli synne wiþ-sett,

And, how þou me pleasë myght :

What eiliþ þee, man, þin iȝe to schett?　　396

Man, I sent thee understanding

and Holy Writ

to show thee how to resist sin.

Why hast thou shut thine eye ?

(49)
(Man's Sixth Answer.)

" Swete Ihesu, answer I [ne] can),   383
    But oft I crye mercy with hart stable ;
    Alas for woo ! why is man)
wele woorse than beste onresonáble ?   386
All bestis, sithe this worllde by-gan),
    In kyndely wyrchyng be duráble,
Save onely I, off wyttys wanne,
    that wofull many dedis dampnáble.   390

(45)

¶ " Wordli richesse, & rial repaire,
    Iewels, and þingis, and myrþe of iolite,

If worldly riches and jewels,

Fischis, beestis, briddis of þe eir,
    þese þinkiþ þee semeli for to se.   400

and birds seem comely to thee,

If þo þingis þat schulen perische & paire,
    Vnto þi sighte þus semeli bee,

[Page 207]

Weel maist þou wite, y am weel faire,
    Of whom ech þing haþ his bewte.   404

thou mayst well know that I am fair, of Whom all have their beauty.

(46)

¶ " But, man, as þou wittlees were,
    þou lokist euere dounwarde as a beest ;

But thou ever lookest downward like a beast,

It heeuyeth þee of me to heere,
    Foule speche is to þee a feeste.   408

and delightest in foul talk.

I coumforte þee and make þe cheere,
    And þou aȝenward louest me leest ;

I am kind to thee

I calle þee to me ȝeer and ȝeer,
    Ȝit wolt þou not come at my request.   412

and call thee, and thou wilt not come.

(47)

¶ " A's from þi foo, þou from me flees,
    Y folewe feste, and on þee crye,

Thou fleest from Me,

þou wrappist þee wiþ vanytees,
    And þinkist my speche is but folie :   416

and wrappest thyself in vanities,

For þing þat nouȝt is, þou wolt leese[1]   [1 MS. lecsee]
    My ioie þat lastiþ euere eendeleesly.

losing for nought my endless joy.

Man, ȝit leue vice, and vertu chese,
    And amendis make, or þou die."   420

But, man, leave vice and amend ere thou diest.

(48)

(*Man's Sixth Answer.*)

" SWeete ihesu, answere noon y can,
    But ofte cry mercy wiþ herte stable :

Man.   [Page 208]

Alas for woo ! whi is a man
    weel worse þan a beeste vnresonáble ?   424

Alle bestis, siþen þis world bigan,
    In kindeli worchinge ben duráble,

Saaf oonly I, of wittis wan,
    þat haue doon manye dedis ful dampnáble.   428

(50)

I was made to
know my Maker,
" I, man, was made to knowe my maker,
  And to love hym ouer alle thyng ;
And I, A wreche, was neuer maker

[leaf 150, back]
  to cache kynde knowyng of my kynge ;   394
but have minded
only trifles;
to tryfyllis have I be tent-taker.
  A songe for sorowe wele may I synge,
for hade I of syn be for-saker,
  of cryst shoulde I have hade knowynge.   398

(51)

my spirit's eye
has been blinded
with covetous-
ness ;
" My gostely than blysefull off duste,
  Curssyd covetyse hathe so blyndedyd me,
they been shotyn with ffleschely luste,
  than hevenly thyngis may I noone see.   402
But, lorde, thowȝe I have been on[i]est,
but help me, Lord,
with penance to
cleanse my sight.
  thorowe helpe of thy Benyngnyte
I hope to Rube A-waye the Ruste,
  with penaunce, frome my gostely syhte.   406

(52)

" And where that I haue A-fore this
  My worledly synnys spente,
Henceforward
I will learn Thy
law,
frome hens forwarde my purpose is
  to lerne thy lawe to my lyvys ende.   410
and keep Thy Ten
Commands.
thy x comaundëmentis I-wys,
  hem for to kepe I wyll me bende,
And there as I haue doone A-mys,
Mercy! I will
amend.
  Mercy, Ihesu ! I wyll Amende."   414

(53)

(Christ's Seventh Complaint.)

Man, I have
showed thee
mercy oft,
" Man, my mercy, yf þou it mende,
  I have the hit shewed in many wyse
Sythen the tyme that þou fyrst synned
  Ayenst myne hest in paradyse.   418
In hell preson when þou were pynyd
  for doyng of the develys devyse,
have helped thee
from hell ;
owte of thy teene for to be tenyd,
  Mercy and love þe holpe or this.   422

(49)

¶ " I, man, was made to knowe my maker,
  And to loue him aboue al oþir þing ;
And y, a wrecche, was neu*e*re waker
  To catche kinde knowi*ng* of my kyng ;   432
To triflis y haue be a greet tent-taker ;
  A song of sorewe weel may I synge,
For hadde y of syn*n*e ben a v*e*rri forsaker,
  Of crist schulde y haue had knowyng.   436

(50)

¶ " Mi goostli iȝen ben ful of dust,
  Cursid coueitise haþ so blyndid me,
þei ben blood-schoten w*ith* fleischli lust,
  þat heue*n*ly þingis may y noon se.   440
But, lord, þouȝ y haue ben vniust,   [[Page 209]]
  ȝit þoruȝ þe help of þi benignite
I hope to rubbe aweye þe rust,
  W*ith* penaunce, from my goostli yȝe ;   444

(51)

¶ " *And* where þat y haue to-forë þis
  My witt in wordli þingis spende,
From hens forþward my purpos ys
  To leerne þi lawe to my lyuës eende.   448
þi ten comau*n*deme*n*tis, so haue y blis,
  Them for to kepe, y wole me bende ;
And þere as y haue a-fore doon mys,
  Now, merci, God ! y wole amende."   452

(52)

(*Christ's Seventh Complaint.*)

" **M**An, my m*e*rci, if þou it myn*n*ed,   God.
    Y haue schewid it þee on many wise
Siþen þat tyme was þat þou first synned
  Aȝens my precept in paradijs.   456
In helle prisou*n* whan*e* þou were pyn*n*ed
  For doinge of þe deuelis deuyce,
Out of þat pr*i*sou*n* for to be twyn*n*ed,
  Mercy and loue þee halp ; þinke on þese.   460

(54)

"Mercy was thyn advocate cheffe

    that I for the tooke Flesche & bloode ;

loue made the to me so leffe,

    that I for the was Rente on Roode ;   426

I suffyrde dethe to chaunge þy greffe,

    And In-to heƚƚ than doune I yeede ;

I brougħt' þe to preeffe to the blysse :

    Man ! I haue been thy frende fuƚƚ goode.   430

(55)

" I be-gan poore, thé Ryche to make ;

    to make thé whyte, I was made Rede ;

my sorowe, my syknes, made thé to slake,

    My hung*er* booke the blysfuƚƚ brede.   434

I bonde my selffe, þy bond*is* I braake ;

    to gett thy lyffe, I suffyrd' dede ;

what shoulde I do more for thy saake ?

    to hele thy foote, hurt was my hede.   438

(56)

" yff þou thynk I myght more do

    for thy saake, saye, I am Redy

to dye A-yeen, yff neede were there-too :

    Suche loue, man, to the haue I.   442

I hygħt' the myrthe & Ioyës moo,

    But þou Art thy moste Enemy,

for nougħt' that I do but þou wylt so ;

    Man ! make Amend*is* or thowe dye."   446

(57)

(Man's Seventh Answer.)

"Lorde, whan I thynke on þy pou*e*rte,

    and how wylfuƚƚ þou were and fayne ; [1]—

    to sle my syn, þou were slayne,[1]—

to suffyr for me wound*is* smarte ;   450

    And howe wylfuƚƚ þou were and fayne ;   450a

harder than Iren is my harte [1 Lines 449 and 448 are transposed,
                              and 450a repeated wrongly.]

    that hathe no pyte of thy payne !

Eu*er* the kynder to me þou arte,

    the more vnkynder I am A-gayne.   454

(53)

¶ " Mercy was þin aduoket cheef   [Page 210]
  þat y for þee took fleisch & blood ;
Loue madë þee to me so leef,
  þat y for þee was rent on roode ;   464
I suffride deeþ to chaunge þi greef,
  And vnto helle þan doun y ȝoode ;
Y brouȝte þee to blis from repreef :
  þus haue y be, man, þi freend ful good.   468

(54)

¶ " I bicame poore, þee riche to make ;
  To make þee whiȝt, y was made reed ;
Mi sorewe, my sijknesse, made þin to slake,
  Myn hungir book þi blisful breed.   472
I boond my silf, þi boondis y brake ;
  To gete þee lijf, y suffride þe deede ;
What schulde y more do for þi sake ?
  To hele þi foot, hurt was myn heed.   476

(55)

¶ " What woldist þou, man, þat y schuld do ?
  My mercy to þee is ful redy
Yf þou wolt dispose þee þerto ;
  Such loue tó þee, man, haue y,   480
I hiȝte þee myrþe and ioiës moo,   [Page 211]
  But þou art þin owne moost enemy ;
for ouȝt þat y þee bidde, þou wolt so ;
  Man ! make amendis or þou die."   484

(56)
(*Man's Seventh Answer.*)

" Lord, whanne y þinke on þi pouert,   Man.
  And how wilful þou were, & fayn,
To suffre for me woundis smert ;—
  To slee my synnës þou were slayn,—   488
Hardir than iren is myn hert,
  Which haþ no pitee of þi payn !
Euere þe kyndir to me þou art,
  þe more vnkyndir am y agayn.   492

(58)

Why shouldst
Thou be slain for
Thine enemy?

" Why wouledyst þou, lorde, be slayne for me ?

than) Am) I thyne Enemye moste vnhende,

Sithen) no man) hathe more charyte

than) deethe to suffyr for his Frende ?   458

what skyH is þou shouledyst slayne bee,

Sythen) I made þe thraH to þe Fende ?

Why didst Thou
not smite me?

I trespassyd, lorde, why smott*is* þou nat me ?

Nowe, blessyd be þou w*it*h-owttyn) eende !   462

(59)

[leaf 151, back]
I see Thou lovest
me.

" I see wele, lorde, that þ*o*u lovest us

for oure profyte, & nought for yeve ; [pyne]

for what were þ*o*u, ne were Ih*e*sus,

thougħe aH wee were in) eendeles payne.   466

But, alas, we are
so vicious that we
leave our gracious
and merciful God.

Alas, wee been) so vysyous,

And so onkyndely frome hyr declyne,

that is oure god so gracïus,

And is so lotħe, mannys soule to tyne.   470

(60)

Have mercy,
though, sweet
Lord,

" But, swete lorde, as þou haste bygoone,

so lett thy m*e*rcy fortħe extende ;

Put thy crosse and thy passyon)

By-twene my werk*is*, they ought to be brent,   474

And thy dome that I may nat shoone,

that bond*is* of heH can) me nat hend*e*.

help Thy son ;
I will amend !

Who but the fad*ur* shoulde helpe þe soone ?

Mercy, Ih*e*sus ! I wyH Amende."   478

(61)

(*Christ's Eighth Complaint.*)

If thou wantest
mercy,

" **M**an, yff þou wolte my m*e*rcy gete,

thorowe my passyon) of grete v*e*rtu,

why lovyst nat þou me for to bete ?   481

Eche day on) crosse þou doest me newe

why dost thou
crucify Me daily
with thy great
oaths,

w*i*th deedly syn), at morne, at mete,

thowe turment*is* me on-trewe,

And namely, w*it*h thyne othis grete,

to swere þou wolte nat me eschewe   486

(57)

¶ " Whi woldist þou, lord, be slayn for me,
  þat am þin enemy moost vnhende ?
Siþen no man haþ more charite,
  þan deeþ to suffre for his freende,   496
What skile is þou schuldist só slayn be,
  Siþen y made þee þral to þe feend ?
I trespaside, lord ; whi smoot þou not me ?
  Now, blessid be þou wiþ-outen eende !   500

(58)

¶ " I se weel, lord, þat þou louest us   [Page 212]
  For oure profite, & not for þine ;
For what were þou þee werse, ihesus,
  þouȝ alle we weren in eendelees peyne.   504
Alas, whi ben we so vi[ci]ouse,
  And so vnkyndeli from þee declynne
þat oure god art so gracïous,
  And so looþ art, mannis soule to tyne ?   508

(59)

¶ " But, sweete lord, as þou hast bigunne,
  So lete þi mercy forþ extende :
Putte þi crosse & þi passioun
  Bitweene my werkis worþi to be brende,   512
And þi doom þat y may not schounne,
  þat þe boondis of helle come me not hende.
Who but þe fadir schoulde helpe þe sonne ?
  Merciful ihesu, y wole amende."   516

(60)
(*Christ's Eighth Complaint.*)

" **M**An, if þou wolt my mercy gete   God.
  þoruȝ my passioun of myche vertu,
Whi leuest þou not of me to bete ?
  Eche day on crosse þou doist me newe   520
With deedli synne, at morn, at meete,   [Page 213]
  As a turmentour to me vntrewe,
And nameli, with þin oþis greete,
  To swerë þou wolt not eschewe.   524

(62)

rending my limbs, " No lymꝺ onꝺ me, man, þou for-beryste :

why doyst þou evyꝉ Ayenst goode ?

By my soule thowe offt-tyme swerystᵗ,

     by my body, and by my bloode ;   490

tearing Me to pieces with thy tongue ? *with* thy tunge me aꝉ to-terystᵗ,

     whanꝺ þou arte wroþe & wel ny woode ;

Manꝺ, *with* thy onkyndnes more me derestᵗ

     thanꝺ they that rent me onꝺ þe Roode.   494

(63)

Thou pitiest thy toe when it bleeds more than Me. " thowe haste more pyte vpponꝺ þy too

     yff hit be hurt, and lytyꝉ bleede,

thanꝺ eu*er* þou haddyst for aꝉ þe woo

     that eu*er* I Suffyrde for þy mysdeede.   498

[leaf 152]
But thou shalt soon be sorry for thy needless swearing. Whanꝺ þou arte toughᵗ, thanꝺ þou shalt woo

     of sweryng, but yff hit were neede :

thowe scorenest hemꝺ thanꝺ seyne þe soo,

     thowe takest to my heste no kepe.   [heede]   502

(64)

Thou liest loudly on me to get a halfpenny, " Lowde lesyng*is* on me þou makystᵗ,

     Some tyme to wynne An halpenye,

what tyme to wytnes þou me takyste,

     Andᵗ yeet the for-sweryst þe wyttyngly.   506

Byyng and syllyng, þou nat for-sakystᵗ ;

and often swearest wrongfully.   bothe veyne & wronge þou sweryst wronge ;

whanꝺ þou doestᵗ thus, there bale þou bakeste ;

Man, make amends.   Manꝺ ! make Amend*is* or thowe dye."   510

[*See note on p. 214.*]

(61)

¶ No lyme on me, man, þou forbeerist :
　　Whi doist þou yuel aȝens good ?
By my soule þou ofte tyme sweerist,
　　Bi my body, and bi my blood.　　　　　　528
Wiþ þi tunge þou me al to-teerist
　　Whanne þou art wrooþ, as wiȝt moost wood.
Man, with þin vnkindenes þou more me deerist
　　þan þei þat diden me on þe roode.　　　　532

(62)

¶ þou hast more pitee on þi too
　　If it be hurt, and a litil bleede,
þan euere þou haddist for al þe woo
　　þat euere y suffride for þi mys-deede.　　536
Whanne þou art tauȝt þat þou schuldist hoo
　　Of sweering, but whanne it were neede,
þou scornest hem þat sayn þee soo ;
　　To myn heestis takist þou noon hede.　　540

(63)

"Lowdë lesyngis on me þou makist,　　　　[Page 214]
　　Sum tyme to wynne an halpeny,
What tyme to witnes þou me takist,
　　And ȝit þou forsweerist þee wityngly.　　544
Biynge & sillynge þou not forsakist,
　　Boþe veyn & wrong to sweere me by ;
Whanne þou þus doist, þi bale þou bakist ;
　　Man ! make þou amendis or þou die."　　548

(64)

(*Man's Eighth Answer.*)

" **S**weete ihesu, how schulde y aȝen say,
　　But þat y caitife am, more curst
þan þo þat doon þee on þe crosse eche day
　　With greet ooþis & werkis wurst,　　552
And myche more þee greeueþ þan þei
　　þat on calueri slowen þee firste ;
For hadde þei knowe þee for god verray,
　　þee to deeþ þei hadde not durst.　　556

Man. Jesu! I can only
answer that I am
more curst a
caitiff

than those who
slew Thee on
Calvary.

They knew Thee
not for very God,

(65)

but I know Thee
as the Almighty,

¶ But y knowe, aftir my bileeue,

þat þou art god omnipotent,

and yet I cease
not grieving Thee.

And ȝit y ceesse not þee to greue !

Weel worþi am y to be schent ! 560

[Page 215]

How maist þou, lord, suffre me to meeue ?

Alle creaturis owen me to turment ;

I wonder that
I have not been
killed or burnt.

Merueile it is þat y not myscheeue,

þat y neere kild, drowned, or brent. 564

(66)

The earth
swallowed up
Dathan and
Abiram, who
were not so
wicked as I.

¶ The erþe opened and swelewid al quicke,

Daton & abiron for her synne ;

And y weene þei were neuere so wick

As y, moost caitife of mankynne ! 568

Though dire
disease prevails
now, I stick in
my sins.

In deedly synne men dien now þicke ;

Disese ful greet now dooþ bigynne,

And ȝit in my synne y stonde and sticke ;

Evil habits are
hard to give up.

Yuel custum ys ful hard to blynne. 572

(67)

I do evil,
and will let no one
reprove me.

¶ I wolde be wantowne, and do ille,

But y wolde noon me reprehende,

But lete me lyue aftir my wille :

þis was leefful, sumtyme y wende, 576

But now y se þat it is skille,

Send me light.

þat such light to me þou sende,

But if y leue synne, it wole me spille.

I will amend.

Merciful lord ihesu, y wole amende ! " 580

(68)

(*Christ's Ninth Complaint.*)

[Page 216]

" **M**an, of þi silf it schal be-long

If so be þi soule be spilt ;

Forgive those
who work thee
wrong, and I will
forgive thee.

Forȝeue þou hem þat worchen þee wrong,

And y schal forȝeue þee þi gilt ; 584

And if þou be of herte so strong,

And on no wise forȝeue þou wilt,

But venge þi silf with herte & tunge,

As a traitour þou schalt be ouer tilt. 588

(69)

¶ þou getist no merci, þi silf to saue,
   þat no mercy on oþir has :
How may þou me of merci craue,
   And þou wolt graunte no man grace?   592

   But thou shalt have no mercy if thou wilt show none.

Merciful men schulen mercy haue ;
   Fel folk, schal y fleeme fro my face ;
What ensaumple þat y þee 3aue,
   Whanne y deeþ suffride, no tent þou taas.   596

   Thou takest no bid of the example I set thee :

(70)

¶ I praied for hem þat me disesid,
   þou3 y my3te hem haue dampned for ay ;
For, and þou be a litil displeside,
   þou bannest & cursist nyght and day ;   600

   I prayed for those who injured Me,

For no preching wolt þou be pleside,
   But for to venge þee is þi wil alway ;
Ful foulë schulde þi foos be fesid
   If þou my3te ouer hem, as y ouer þee may.   604

   [Page 217] but thou cursest those who displease thee, and desirest revenge on them.

(71)

¶ Withoutë cause ofte art þou wrooþ
   Vnto þi freendis vnskilfully ;
Whanne þei þee techen & councelle boþe
   To leue þi wraþþe and þin enuye,   608

   Thou art wroth with thy friends without reason when they advise thee to give up sin.

With wordis greete and spiteful ooþ
   þou defendist þee of þi foule folie ;
But þee to leese, y am ful looþ ;
   Man, make amendis or þou die."   612

   Still I am loth to lose thee. Make amends.

(72)

(*Man's Ninth Answer.*)

" Sweete lord, þinke þou madist us alle,
   And how kinde and propir it is to þee,
On synful men þat to þee calle,
   On hem to haue mercy and pitee.   616

   Lord, it is Thine to have mercy on sinners.

þou3 y haue be as bettir as galle,
   For þi greet merci, haue mercy on me,
And fro þi loue þat y no more falle !
   But kindele þou me in charitee.   620

   Have mercy, then, on me, and kindle me in Charity.

(73)

[Page 218]

¶ For þouȝ y cowþe al kunnynge ken,
    And speke wíth aungils tungë cleer,

And þouȝ y delide among poore men
    My wordli goodis alle in feer,   624

And ȝaf my bodi for to brenne
    For loue of þee þat bouȝtist me dere,

Ȝit al þis profitiþ me not þen,
    In loue and charite but if y weere.   628

(74)

¶ And y woot it is more plesyng
    To þee, ihesu, my souereyne lord,

þat y loue þee ouer al þing,
    And be in charite and acoorde   632

Wíth alle my neiȝboris, oolde & ȝyng,
    þan for to faste & goo wollewarde,

And heere alle þe massis þat preestis syng ;
    But if y loue, y gete no coumfort.   636

(75)

¶ Alas ! whi haue y so wraþful ben,
    þat loue myn herte myȝte not come hende ?

I hatide hem þat me neuere dide teen,
    Y loued not hem þat me good kende,   640

[Page 219]

I castide me no þing to be in þat meen ;
    To loue myn enemyes, y wolde not entende ;

But ȝit schal y hem neuere curse, y weene ;
    Merciful ihesu ! y wole amende."   644

(76)

(*Christ's Tenth Complaint.*)

"**M**An, if þou wolt of bataile blynne,
    And charite kepe in echë chaunce,

My merci soonë schalt þou wynne,
    So þat þou do fruytis of penaunce.   648

Loke þin herte be contrite wíth-ynne,
    And sory for þi mys-gouernaunce :

What profiȝtiþ þee to schryue þee of þi synne
    But þou in herte haue repentaunce ?   652

Marginal glosses (left column):

For though I gave all my goods among the poor,

and my body to be burned,

all would be nought if I were not in Charity.

And it is more pleasing to Thee that I should love Thee and be in charity with my neighbours,

than that I should go wool-clad and hearing masses.

Alas ! why will not Love come to my heart ?

I have been full of hate ;

but I will curse my enemies no more : I will amend.

Man, if thou wilt cease from strife, bide in charity, and be contrite for thy sins, thou shalt have mercy.

(77)

¶ þou scornest, and penaunce doist þou noon

For þi synne, but þin herte be soor;

For wordli losse þou makist moone,

þou siȝest and sorewist myche þerfore.

And if þi body were woo bigoon,

What bittir medecyn ȝeuen þee wore,

Ioiyngly þou woldist it take anoon,

Thi bodily helë þee to restore.

But thou doest no penaunce except thy heart aches.

656 Thou sighest for worldly loss; and for bodily pain takest bitter medicine;

660

(78)

¶ þi soule with synne is goostly slayn,

And þou withoute sorewe þi synnë telłis,

To do such penaunce, þou art not fayn,

As þi schrift-fadir þee councellis.

Thou wolt neuere restore agayn

Fals-goten good þat þou wiþ mellis:

Man, þou must þerfore suffre payn

For þi synnes, heere or sumwhere ellis.

[Page 220]

but thou sorrowest not for thy sins, thou doest not penaunce ordained,

664

restorest not false-gotten goods.

For this thou must suffer.

668

(79)

¶ It is impossible, and may not be,

To passe fro ioie to ioie: for thi,

Take þi crosse to þee, and folewe me,

If þou wolt to my blis up stiȝe.

Greet sijknesse and al aduersite,

What-so-euere comeþ, suffre paciently;

Hate alway synne, and euere it flee,

And, man, make amendis or þou die."

Take up thy cross and follow Me,

672

suffer sickness and adversity,

hate sin, and make amends before you die.

676

(80)

(Man's Tenth Answer.)

" Lord, ȝeue me grace amendis to make,

For of my silf me failiþ poweer:

Synne þat is deedli y wole forsake,

And to do deedis þat worþi merite weere.

In þis world sende me woo & wrake

For synnis þat y haue doon ful seere:

Who haþ no desese, heere he may quake;

Hem þat þou louest, þou chastisist heere.

Give me grace, Lord, to forsake my sin and do good works.

680

[Page 221]

Punish me here; for whom Thou lovest Thou chastisest.

684

(81)

For my sake, þritti ȝeeris & moo,

Thou, Thy Mother, and apostles
    greet traueile for me in erþe þou hadde ;

þi modir, wiþ þin apostolis also,

suffered great distress on earth ;
    In greet disese her lijf þei ledde :   688

In aduersite and mychë woo

martyrs and confessors too ; I'll gladly go with them.
    martris & confessouris weren clad :

in such a companye to goo

    in þi leuerey, y schulde be glad.   692

(82)

For if they suffered in this life,
Siþen þi derlingis þat with þee dwelle

    hadden such aduersitee in þis lijf,

what tongue can tell what damned men shall endure in hell ?
what herte may þinke, or tungë telle,

    þe payne, þe anguische, & þe strijf   696

þat dampned men schulen haue in helle,

    þere eendelees woo & sorewis ben riyf ?

I will forsake my sins and shrive me ;
Y wole forsake my synnes so felle,

    & to a discreet preeste y wole me schryue.   700

(83)

[Page 222] will do penance, and keep Thy commandments.
¶ In trewe penaunce is myn entent,

    Fro hens forward my tyme to spende,

And kepe y wole þi comaundëment,

    Ellis in helle fier y schal be brende.   704

Rial repeire, riche roobis, and rent,

    What mowe þei helpe me at myn eende ?

Unless I do, I shall be ruined. I will amend.
But y þee serue, y schal be schende ;

    Mercy, lord ihesu, y schal amende."   708

(84)

(Christ's Eleventh and last Complaint.)

Man, I wait for thy repentance day by day.
"**M**An, do penaunce whilis þou may,

    Lest sudeynli y take veniaunce :

Do y not abide þee day bi day

    Bicause y wolde þou dide penaunce ?   712

I am ready to forgive
Man, y am more redy alway

    To forȝeue þee þi mys-gouernaunce

þan þou art mercy for to pray,

and to exalt thee.
    For my wille were þee to enhaunce.   716

(85)

¶ Whanne þou alle þi freendis hast asaied,

    þou schalt fynde no freend lijk me ;

' þou wolt amende,' þus ofte þou seide,

    And aȝen amendis wole y not be ;   720

Do trewe penaunce, & y am payed,

    From eendelees peine y wole make þee free ;

For whi? for þi loue my lijf y laied :

    What freend wolde haue so doon for þee?   724

Thou shalt find
no friend like Me.

[Page 223]
Repent,
and I will save
thee.
I gave My life
for love of thee.

(86)

¶ With soruful herte þi synne þou schryfe,

    Make amendis with þi myȝt & mayn,

And if þou þus leeue þi wickid lijf,

    Myn aungils wolen be þerof fayn.   728

þinke þou ofte on lottis wijf,

    And turne not to þi synne agayn ;

Lete not dispeirë þee doun drijf ;

    þinke on petir & on mawdeleyn.   732

Make amends for
thy sins.

Think on Lot's
wife :
return not to evil,

and do not
despair.

(87)

¶ Man, þus wipe awey þi wickidnes,

    And kepe my biddynge bi and by,

And þou schalt haue in my blis,

    Worschip wiþoute ony velonye,   736

No pouert, but al richesse,

    Hele, strenþe, & wijsdom eendeleesly ;

þou schalt be ful of al swetnesse

    Where þou schalt lyue & neuere die."   740

Do My bidding,
and thou shalt
have honour,

riches, health, and
wisdom, for ever,
in heaven,

where thou shalt
never die.

(88)

(Man's Eleventh and last Answer.)

" Graunte mercy, ihesu, crop & roote

    Of al frenschip, for þou neuere failis ;

Aȝens þee nyle y not moote,

    But, as ofte as me yue[þ] aylis,   744

I wole fallë flat to thi foote,

    To helpë me in goostli batailis.

Aȝens al bale, lord, þou be my boote,

    Whanne synne & sorowe me sore asailis.   748

[Page 224]

Jesu,
I will pray to
Thee whenever
sin tempts me ;

be Thou my help
and cure.

(89)

I will hide me

¶ Now woot y where y schal me hide
 Whanne y am stirid to ony synne ;

in the wounds of
Thy right side,.

In þe greet wounde of þi right side ;
 And, be y veryli hid þer-ynne,   752

there secure
against all the
fiend can do.

As in a tour þere may y a-bide
 For auȝt þat þe feend can ymagyne,
For al þis world þat is so wiyde,
 þere is for man moost souereyn medicyn. 756

(90)

I will not despair

¶ þere may no wanhope make me care,

if Thy angels
and Mother keep
me.

 þat haþ oon of þin aungils so good
To kepe me þat y not mys fare,
 And þi modir, myldest of mood, 760

[Page 225]

þat schewiþ to þee hir pappis[1] bare
 (For me) of which þou soukedist foode ;
And to-fore þi fadir, [&] mere[2] maree,
 þou schewist þi woundis rent on roode. 764

(91)

I shall not miss
Thy mercy.

¶ How myȝte y of þi mercy mys,
 Siþen to helpe man þou art so hende?
Now, ihesu, lord, þou weel us wisse,

Lord, send us
grace that we
may be with
Thee in bliss.

 And, whilis we lyue, such grace us sende 768
þat we may bide wiþ þee in blis,
 And wiþ aungils, world withouten eende,
þat to be chosen, ordeyned ys
 To leeue al synne, & hem amende. 772

Amen.

  Amen : Amen **: Amen** Amen."

["In my ȝonge age" follows in the MS., p. 226.]

[1] Compare Hoccleve's *Mother of God*, p. 47, l. 112; p. 54, l. 72. Are these paps referd to in English poetry before the 15th century?
[2] MS. not clear. ?mere = mother.

The Virgin's Complaint.[1]

Filius Regis Mortuus est.

[*Lambeth MS.* 853, *ab.* 1430 A.D., *page* 74, *written without breaks.*]

[12 stanzas of 12 lines each, *abab abab bcbc.*]

(1)

A S resou*n* rewlid my richelees my*n*de,
   Bi wielde waies as y hadde we*n*t,   As I walked by wild ways, .
A solempne citee me fortuned to fynde;
  To turne *þ*er*t*o was myne entent.   4 I turned to Jerusalem,
¶ A maiden y mette, a modir hynde,
   Sobbinge & si*ʒ*ynge, sche was neer sche*n*t;   and met a maiden mother sobbing,
Sche wepte, sche wailid, so sore sche pined;
  Hir heer, hir face, sche tuggid & rent,   8
   ¶ Sche tuggid, sche taar w*ith* greet turment,   tearing her hair, her face,
    Sche racide hir skyn, bothe body & brest;   her breast,
Sche seide *þ*eise wordis eu*er*e as sche went,
    "Filius regis mortuus est."   12 and saying ever, " The Son of the King is dead.

(2)

"The kingis sone," sche seide, "is deed,
  *þ*e ioie, *þ*e substaunce of my lijfe: My joy is gone.
*þ*e modir to se hir sone so blede,
  It kitti*þ* myn herte as w*ith* a knyf.   16 It cut my mother's heart to see Him bleed,
¶ My sone *þ*at y was woont to fede,
   To lulle, to lappe, w*ith* songis rijf;   my Son whom I lulled with songs.
Out of his herte his blood to schede,
  Maki*þ* me, his modir, in myche strijfe. 20
   ¶ I am bo*þ*e maiden, modir, & wijf,   [Page 75]
    And sones haue y no mo to souke my brest;   No more sons have I to suck my breast.
I may make sorewe w*ith*out relijf,   The King's Son
    For 'filius regis mortuus est.'   24 is dead;

---

[1] In the first edition, this and the following poem from Harl. 3954, having the same first two stanzas, were printed opposite one another, for the contrast of their later stanzas. But as in this second edition the parallel arrangement would have left p. 233 blank, the Resurrection poem is now put after the Death one.

(3)

Thus filius regis, myn owne dere child,

I saw Him on the
cross,
defiled with spit-
ting, wounded
with spear.
  Hangiþ on þe croos : y stoonde and se
How he is woundid & defilid
  With spittinge & speeris so piteuousli.   28

I cried to my own
dear Son.
¶ I cried upon him as y were wielde,
  ' Mi swete dere sone, seest þou not me,
þine owne dere modir ? ' þo he me biheld,

He said, 'Mourn
not, I shall come
to thee,'
  And seide, ' moorne not, modir, þi sorowe lete be ; 32
  ¶ I schal be þin & come to þee.'

and I swooned.
   He spak ; y swowned, y neuere ceest ;
  A ! sone myn, sone myn, upon a tree !
  Filius regis mortuus est.   36

(4)

My bliss is dead.
He dieþ, he dieþ, þat is my blis ;
  He swelte, y swowned, y cried a-las !

No wonder I am
wo !
He was my
Spouse, my
Brother, my all.
No wondir is of my greet heuynes !
  Mi fadir, my broþir, my spouse, he was, 40
¶ My modir, my socour, & al þat ys !

[Page 76]
Now I am
fatherless ;
  Now fadirlees & modirlees y mai forþ passe,
Broþerlees, spouselees, ful wrecchid y-wis,

a thing forsaken,
  As a þing forsaken þat no þing has ! 44

not full of grace,
  ¶ A ! gabriel, þou clepidist me ful of grace.

but full of sorrow,
   Nay ! ful of sorowe þou now me seest ;

weeping tears.
The King's Son
is dead.
þe teeris trikilen dowun on my face,
  For ' filius regis mortuus est.' 48

(5)

I asked the Jews
I lokide up," sche seid, " vn-to my child,

to hang the
mother by the
Son.
  I cried on þe iewis, & bad hem hang
þe modir bi þe sone þat neuere was filid :

O Death, thou
killedst my babe ;
  O deeþ, deeþ, þou doost me wrong ! 52
  ¶ Mi babe þou sleest, þat neuere was wielde ;

kill me !
   Come, sle þe modir ! whi tariest þou so long ?

Murderer, why
þou morþer man, whi art þou now myelde

Vn-to þe modir þat wolde deeþ fong? 56   spar'st thou me?
¶ þou pynest my sone with peynës strong;
  Pyne þan þe modir at hir reqwest!   Torture me too.
Alas, y may synge a soruful song,
  þat [1] 'filius regis mortuus est.' 60   [[1] Page 77]

(6)

A! þou erþe! on þee y clayme apeel   Oh earth, thou
  þat þou receyuedist his giltlees blood.   drankest His guiltless blood!
þou stoon! whi woldist þou be so freel   Oh stone, thou
  To be þe morteis þere þe crosse stood? 64   barest His cross!
¶ He made þe erþe and stoonis feele,
  And ȝe ben instrumentis now to þe roode   Ye help to slay your Maker,
To sle ȝoure maker! ȝe wite ful weel
  He dide neuere yuel, but euermore good. 68
  ¶ He was euere meeke & mylde of mood;   ever meek,
    Now is he stikid as it were a beest!   now stuck like a beast.
  Alas my babe, my lyuës foode,
    Filius regis mortuus est! 72

(7)

Thou tree, þou crosse, how durst þou be   Oh tree, oh cross,
  A galow to hang thi maker so?   ye made the gallows for your Maker.
Vnto his fadir y may apeele þee
  þat woldist be cause of þe sonës woo; 76
¶ Not cause, but help þat he deed be!
  ȝe trees! crie mercy, ȝe be my foo;
Hadde ȝe be ordeyned [2] a roode for me,   [[2] Page 78]
  To hang me bi him, it hadde ben weel doo. 80   Why did ye not make a cross too for me?
  ¶ But what may y seie? whidir schal y do? [go]
    þe tree haþ hangid a king, a preest;
  Of allë kingis suche ben no mo
    As 'filius regis mortuus est.' 84

(8)

O ȝe creaturis vnkynde! þou iren, þou steel,   Oh steel and thorn,
  þou scharp þorn!
How durst ȝe slee ȝoure best frend,   ye slew your best friend,

þe holiest child þat eue*r*e was born?   88

¶ ȝe haue hi*m* wou*n*did, ye haue hi*m* pyned ;
    Spere & nail his bodi haþ schorn !

þou spere ! whi suffridist þou þe smyth þe grynde
    So scharpe, þat al his herte þou hast to-torn ?   92
    ¶ I may crie out on þee boþe euen & morn ;

A wemlees maydens sone þou sleest !
    I wri*n*ge & wepe as þi*n*g for-lorn !
    Filius regis mortuu*s* est.   96

(9)

Thou scourgë maad of ful touȝ skyn,
    Knottid & gnaggid, y crie on þee !

þou ¹beet my barn þat neue*r*e dide synne :
    Whi beet þou him, & fórbare me ?   100
    ¶ Made he þee nouȝt? myȝte þou not blynne ?

For oue*r*myche þou fraiedist þat free ;
þoruȝ-out his bodi no place was i*n*ne,

Boþe fleisch & blood þou pullidist *with* þee :   104
    ¶ þou madist ful blac þat was briȝt of blee,
    þou schalt oonis come to oure conquest.

O fadir of heuene ! now haue pitee
    þat 'filius regis mortuus est.'   108

(10)

Also þou beest must bere þe galle
    þat he schulde dri*n*ke ; þou pynest hi*m* more !
Vpon my knees here dowu*n* y falle,

And axe iuggeme*n*t of heue*n* þerfore ;   112
    ¶ And moost y crie on ȝou iewis alle,
    For ȝit myȝte noon of he*m* so hi*m* haue to-tore,
Of alle þese þe instrumentis þat y on calle,

But ȝe he*m* made to greue hi*m* so sore.   116
    ¶ He made ȝou iewis : ȝou to restore
    He come to ȝe erþe ; & now ȝe encreest

His pyne : ²alas, þat eue*r*e ȝe were bore !
    For ' filiu*s* regi*s* mo*r*tuus est.'   120

(11)

O ȝe fals iewis! whi dide ȝe þus,   *Ye false Jews,*
   Him þus to slee, ȝoure sauyour ?
Whanne he sittiþ for iuge, whidir wole ȝe trus ?   *where will ye go*
   ȝe moun not hide ȝou from his reddour.   124   *when He sits as Judge?*
¶ Alle oþere creaturis ben peteuose ;   *All other creatures were*
   þe sunne, þe cloudis, for his dolour,   *pitiful; the sun and clouds were dark,*
Schewith her moornynge ; but ȝe viciose,
   ȝoure lauȝinge dooþ him dishonour.   128
   ¶ þe erþe qwakid temple & tour   *the earth quaked; but you mocked.*
     To bere ȝou synnful, proud, & prest ;
   þe sunne ȝeue ȝou no liȝt þis hour,   *May the sun give you no light.*
     For 'filius regis mortuus est.'   132

(12)

Now 'mortuus est' my fair lord !   *My lord, my child, is dead.*
   Now deed is my dere child, alas !
Now y may walke in þis world   *I, wretched, walk the world.*
   As a wrecche þat wantiþ grace !   136
¶ Al þis y seie to bere recorde ;
   Noo lengir myȝte y loke in his face ;   *I could no longer look in His face,*
þus y come fro calueriward,   *and now am coming from Calvary.*
   Weping & wailing þat y born was.   140
   ¶ If ony man loue me, lene me a plase   *Give me a place to weep my fill,*
     Where y may [1] wepe my fille & reste,   *[1 Page 81] and rest.*
   And my sone wole graunte him sum þat he has :
     Filius regis mortuus est."   144   *The Son of the King is dead."*

The Virgin's Complaint and Comfort.

Filius Regis Mortuus est. Resurrexit: Non Mortuus est.

[*Harl. MS.* 3954, *ab.* 1420 A.D.; *leaf* 90 *a.*]

[12 stanzas of 12 lines each, *abab abab bcbc.*]

(1)

as reson hathe rulyd my recles mynde,

As I wandered I found a solemn city,

Be a wey wandryng as I went,

A solom cite me fortunyd to fynde.

To turne þer-to was myne entent ; 4

and met a lady who mourned,

A louely lady, a maydyn hende,

I met here mornyng ; but wath sche ment

sighed, and swooned.

I kowde noȝt knowyn ; but fast sche pynyd,

Sche swonnyde, sche seyd, & was nere schent. 8

þat blissid beerde fro grownd I hent,

I dashed water on her. She cried "The King's Son is dead.

Wyth water I wesche here face & brest ;

Her here, her skyn, sche raside & rent,

And seyd " **filius regis mortuus est.** 12

(2)

þe kynges sone," sche seyd, " is dede !

His Father is God,

Hyest in heuene his fader is ;

His mother I :

I am his moder þorowe his manhede,

I bare Him in Bethlehem ;

In bedlem I bare ȝour alderes blisse, 16

In circumsicion I saw hym blede,

þat prince present I-wys.

I offered turtle-doves for Him,

In a tempille, as lawe gan lede,

Tirtildovys I offerid a-bouyn al þis ; 20

I took Him into Egypt,

In-to egipt I fled, as m[o]der his,

And lost hym, & fond hym at a fest

and found Him in Cana of Galilee.

þer he tornyd water in-to wyn I-wis ;

And nowe : **filius regis mortuus est.** 24

(3)

" Whan he was ded & hang on a tre,　　　　When He was on
　　　　　　　　　　　　　　　　　　　　the Cross
　　iiij flod*es* of p*a*radice fro hym ran ;

I c*r*ied, ' dere sone, seist þu noȝt me,　　　I cried out, full of
　　　　　　　　　　　　　　　　　　　　care, to Him,
　　Thi karefulle mod*er* blo & wanne ? '[1]　　　28

A doleful loke þan lokede he,

　　That p*er*cyd myn hert, boþe blode & bon ;

I c*r*iede on deth, ' why wilt þu fle ?　　　　and prayed Death
　　　　　　　　　　　　　　　　　　　　to slay me,
　　Cu*m*, sle his mod*er*, þu morder mañ !　　32

　　Why slest þou my sone ? cu*m*, sle me þan !

　　　　Why comst þu noȝt at my request ?

　　þou takist fro me alle þat I wan,　　　　now that my Son
　　　　　　　　　　　　　　　　　　　　is dead.
　　　　Nowe **filius reg*is* mortuus est.** '　　36

(4)

" What wond*er* is it þowe I be wo,

　　For he is dede þat soke my pappe ?

His cors-is grau*e* I come nowe fro,　　　　I come from
　　　　　　　　　　　　　　　　　　　　His grave,
　　þ*at* su*m*tyme lay quyke on my lappe.　　40　He who lay on
　　　　　　　　　　　　　　　　　　　　my lap.
A-las ! for sorwe I hau*e* no mo ;　　　　　Alas !

　　I, ka[r]fuHe mod*er*, where is myn happe ?　　[leaf 90, back]

Nowe ligiȝt he ded, boþe blok & blo !　　　He is dead.

　　þe so*nn*e lost his lith, þe clowd*es* gan clappe,　44　The sun lost its
　　　　　　　　　　　　　　　　　　　　light,
　　The element*es* go*nn*e to rusche & rappe,

　　　　And smet downe chirches & templis w*ith* crak,

　　Dede men out of here gr*a*ue gan skappe,　　dead men arose,
　　　　　　　　　　　　　　　　　　　　and said, ' The
　　　　And seyd **filius regis mortuus est.** "　48　Son of the King
　　　　　　　　　　　　　　　　　　　　is dead.' "

(5)

Why deyed þi sone, þou maydyn cha[s]t ?　　Why did He die ?

　　þe secund p*er*sone, & þe godhede nowt,

Nore þe thirde p*er*sone, þe holigost,

　　þis m*er*ueliȝt me meche in my thowt.　　52　I marvel why,
　　　　　　　　　　　　　　　　　　　　for wisdom was
For wysdome to þo sone was be-tawte[2]　　given Him.

　　Whan Adam to synne was browt,

iij for iij þat we xulde trespace nowt ;[2]

---

[1] MS. wanme.
[2] These lines do not rhyme with 1 and 3 of this stanza, as the others in the poem do.

He was before we
were created.

But maker of redempc*i*on was or we were wrowt. 56

Adam to a tre his hand*ës* cawt;

Crist*is* handis to a tre were fest;

He fought to fell
our foes,
and is dead.

To fe##e o*ur* fon o*ur* frendis fawt,

And þer **filius regis mortuus est.** 60

(6)

St. Paul says He
died for all.

Seynt poule seythe he deyed for alle;

Why wer*e* not alle men sauyd þan ?

St. Augustine
says for all be-
lievers.

Sent austyn answerid in gen*e*ra##e,

He deyid for eu*e*ry leuyṅg man. 64

Unbelievers will
not credit this.

Hym selfë þ*at* wille not god ca##e,

He wy##e not leue þ*at* he hy*m* whan ; [1]

What wond*e*r is it, þowe he be thra##e

That byndi3t hym selfe, & not vn-lose can ? 68

But for His
blood that was
shed I cry,
'The Son of the
King is dead.'

þe blod þat fro his syd*ës* ran

Whan a##e þis werlde was derke, est & west,

Ther-for I syng as I be-gan,

Filius regis mortuus est. 72

(7)

"Go and see
Him."

"Go, loke," sche seyid, "whi##e þou mayst se,

I may no leng*e*r taryon out of towne."

So I went to the
Cross,

I toke my gate up to þe tre

þ*é*r þe blod was rennyng downe : 76

iij dayis I dithe me þer to be,

For pete of his passïon,

Sithen to his gr*a*ue he went a-lone fro me.

and met three
women,

iij women I met w*ith* precessïon, 80

I askyd hem whedir þ*at* þei were bone ;

Fulle sone þei toke sorowe w*ith*-outyn rest,

who said,
[leaf 91]
'The Son of the
King is dead.'

3et þei answerid w*ith* dollefu##e sone,

And seyd, **Filius regis mortuus est.** 84

(8)

Then I went to
His grave,

So to his gr*a*ue 1 went ful rythe,

And pursuyd aft*e*r to wetyn an ende ;

---

[1] *for* wan.

I sawe angelis w*ith* gret lithe
   Of seraphy*nn*ys ord*er* adowne gan sende.   88
þe women, þei sobbid, & mornyd sore i*n* sithe ;
   þei seyd, " we leyd hym here w*ith* oure hande."
þe angelis answeryd w*ith* word*is* rythe,
   And seyd, " is not here þat ȝe wende ;   92
   He is resyn, as he ȝowe kennyd,
      And in to galalye forthe is prest."
Her*e* chere & comfort gan a-mende,
     For **resurrexit! non mortu*us* est!**   96

I saw Angels,
Seraphim,
descend from
heaven,

who told the
women that
Christ was risen.

He is not dead.

(9)

To telle þis tale I hied me fast,
   That **filius regis**. was resyn a-geyn ;
Bé a tempiłłe as I forthe past,
   I herd wepyng w*ith* mechë peyn ;   100
A woman I sawe þere at þe last
   That I first met, w*ith*-outyn layn,
Ful doofułły on me here eyn sche cast ;
   But howe sche ferd, fast I gan frayn :   104
   " A-las," sche sayd, " I am vn-fayn
      To se my sone in þis dissesse."
þan to þat ladi I answerid a-gayn,
   And seyd, " **filius regis** no*n* **mortu*us* est.**"   108

I hastened to
spread the tid-
ings ;

and by a temple
met the Mother

I had seen before.

Sad she was,

but I told her,
' The Son of the
King is not dead.

(10)

Seynt thomes seythe, & od*er* doctours an heppe,
   þ*at* first he apperid to o*ur* ladi dere ;
His dethe to her*e* hert sanke most depe
   For sche was most of his chere ;   112
So bryth, so gloriouce, þe so*n*ne increppe,
   His schynyng merk*es* her*e* bodi bare,
He salutyd his mod*er* w*ith* gret worchepe,
   þat salutacio*n* I herd neu*er*e are,   116
   " **Salué, sa*nc*ta parens!**" I trowe it ware,—
      In latyne is wretyn fulle honest,—
   "My blissid mod*er* for eu*er*-mare !
     For **resurrexit! no*n* mortu*us* est!**"   120

To Her, His
Mother, did He
first appear,

saying
Hail, holy parent !

I am risen, not
dead.'

(11)

" þis was gret mervayle for to se,
  þe ertdly moder þat kyng to susteyne ;

No such joy was
ever before or
since!
Sweche ioy and solemp[ni]te,
  Be-forn ne after was neuer seyn ;   124

[leaf 91, back]
The earth was
glad, the sun,
The erde is glad, þe sunne is fre,
  þe sunne is glad þat it brythe xalle bene,
And neuer after so blac to sene.

the world,
and all Chris-
tian men.
þe werlde[1] is glad, & hath grace sene,   128
  Alle cristen pepill glad xal bene

Christ is King!
    þat crist is boþë k[i]ng and prest ;

This day He rose.
He is not dead!
Nowe is seyd **hec dies** for ioye, I wene,
  That **resurrexit! non mortuus est!**"   132

(12)

Why did the
King of all die
Syn he was lord & k[i]ng ouer alle,
  Had mythe & powere of good & ille,
Whi wolde he not at oo word calle
  þe soulis fro heuene at his owyn wille,   136

and be in
thraldom ?
But þus to be ded & thralle ?
  To þis oure gloce wylle answere tylle :
He leet his mythe at þat tyme falle,
  And wrowt wisdomys folle sotylle,   140

To redeem our
souls from the
Devil,
who was con-
quered when
the Son of the
King died.
To bie our soulis þat were hese with skille.
  þe fende of mankende had gret tryste ;
There lost he his cause ; þat lekid hym ille,
  Whan **filius regis mortuus est.**   144

    Explicit Filius Regis . · .

        [1] MS. welrde

Part of a Meditation of St. Augustine.

IN the 1866 issue of the stereotyped edition of Mr. Craik's *Compendious History of the English Language*, v. 1, p. 193, is the following passage quoted from Sir Frederic Madden's Preface to *Havelok:* "Between the years 1244 and 1258, we know, was written the versification of part of a meditation of St. Augustine, as proved by the age of the prior who gave the MS. to the Durham Library, MS. Eccl. Dun. A. iii. 12, and Bodl. 42." On my applying to the Librarian at Durham for further information about this piece of verse, the Rev. W. Greenwell answered, "It is upon a small piece of vellum, inserted, and forms no part of the original volume. I send you a correct copy." The Rev. H. O. Coxe, Bodleian Librarian, has also kindly sent me a copy of the Bodleian version, which I print side by side with the Durham one. Mr. Coxe dates the Oxford copy at from 1300 to 1320 A.D.

MS. Eccl. Dun. A. III. 12.	*MS. Bodl.* 42, *fol.* 250.
Wyth was his halude brest	Wit was his nakede brest
and red of blod his syde	and red of blod his side
Bleye was his fair handled	Blod was his faire neb
his wund dop ant wide	his wnden depe an uide
And his arms ystreith	Starke waren his armes
hey up-hon þe rode	Hi-spred opon þe rode
On fif studes on his body	In fif steden in his bodi
þe stremes ran o blode.	Stremes hurne of blode.

(P.S.—See Sir F. Madden's print of the Oxford copy, with the original Latin, in *Warton*, v. 1, p. 24, note, ed. 1840.)

The Seven Deadly Sins,

OR "GYF ME LYSENS TO LYVE IN EASE."

[MS. Univ. Lib. Camb. Ff. 1. 6. fol. 56 *b*. Handwriting of the 15th century. Every *ll* has a stroke through it, and most of the final *n*'s have a stroke over them as here indicated.]

(1)

As I walkyd apoñ a day
    To take the eyre of fylde & floure,
Apon a mylde mornyng of may,
    when floures ben full of swete savoure,   4
I harde on say, " o god ! for ay ?
    hough long shall I leve in my doloure ? "
Apoñ hys knëys he gañ pray,
    " Swete Ihesu, sende me sum socoure,   8
Maryes soñ, most of honoure,
      That ryche & pore may ponyche & please,
lys me now in my longoure,
    And gyf me lysens to lyve in ease.   12

(2)

To lyve in ease, thy lawes to kepe,
    Graunt me grace, lorde in blys soo bryght,
That I neuer in that cabañ crepe
    Ther lusifer ys lokyñ with-outyñ lyght.   16
My myddell woundys, they beñ derne & depe,
    Ther ys no plaster that persyth aryght,
her smertyng wyll nat suffre me to slepe,
    Tyll a leche with dewte have thēm dyght.   20
hit most be a cnect, a crouned wyght,
      That knowth that quaysy from ben & pese,
Or ellys theyre medsyns they haue no myght
    To geve a mañ lysens to lyve in ease.   24

As I walked out on a May morning,

I heard one say, "O God, how long?

Succour me, Jesu, and comfort me now in my languor.

Grant that I may never creep into the cabin wherein Lucifer is locked.

None can cure my wounds but a 'knight,'

who knows that sickness from beans and peas.

(3)

This wound norysshyth woundes sevyn;
  'Superbia' ys the most prinsipall,
'pryde pertly' in englysshe steven,
  For he ys more bytter then euer was gall.
I haue had ther-to lechys aleven,
  and they gave me medysins all.
The souereynyst medysyn that ys vnder heven,
  hyt growes nother in ground nother wall;
  'vmylitas' I hard a clerke it call;
    had I hit, I were at ease.
  larde! sende it vnto the syke thralle,[1]
  and gyff me lysens to lyve in ease.

Of the seven wounds,

Pride is the principal,
28 *and is bitterer than gall.*
[leaf 57]

The best remedy for it is called
32 *Humility.*

Lord, send it me!

36

(4)

A wycked wound hath me walled,
  And traveyld me from topp to too;
This wracched worlde hit may be called,
  hit hath many a blayne black and bloo.
hit hurtys my soule, it makes me to halt,
  In hed, in hond, in hart al-soo.
Nad I ben babtyzyd in water and salt,
  This ferdly fester wolde neuer me froo.
  This leche lyssyd me, lazars, & moo,
    Davith and danyell, of her dysease.
  Amend my wound that doth me woo,
  And gyff me lysens to lyve in ease.

Another wound, which is called this World, hath scored me,

40 *and left me black and blue.*

Had I not been baptized in water
44 *and salt, it had never left me.*

48

(5)

'Invidia' the therd wound ys,
  A wyckkyd gnawer, or venym, or gowt;
he ys a wyckyd wound, I gess,
  Ther he hath power to Reyne or Rought.
The condyssion of the wound ys this,
  To bren my brest with-in and with-oute.
I asked a lech what myght me lyss,
  he toke me 'carytas,' and put it in a clout,

The 3rd wound (or 2nd sin)

52

is Envy, which burns my breast.

The remedy for it is Charity,
56 *or Love.*

---

[1] MS. tharlle.

[leaf 57, back]

And bade me bame me well aboute,
　wheñ hit wolde other water or wese ;
And sone aft*er*, wit*h*-outyn doute,
　Than shold I have lysens to lyve in ease.　　60

(6)

'Ira' ys a wyckyd wound ;
　he ravesshith me, both raw and rede ;
And all my cors he woll confound,
　so sore he swellyth in hart and hede ;　　64

There ys noñ erbe that growyth on grounde,
　Nor no coresy may queth that qued,
Set 'amor cum paciencia,' in a littyll stound ;
　For he wyll drey ham and make hañ ded.　　68

Lord ! sende me sum 'amor' sede,
　In my gardyn to rote and ryse ;
Or ellys, as seker as meñ ete bred,
　I shall neu*er* have lysens to lyve in ease.　　72

(7)

'Auaryssia' ys a [balefull bane,][1]
　he bladdyrth and byldeth all in my boure ;
he makyth me to swell, both flesh and veyne,
　And kepith me low lyke a cochoure.　　76
I have herde of an erbe to lyss that peyne,
　Meñ seyth it bereth a doubyll floure ;

'vigilate, et orate :' vse well they tweyne,
　That shall help the of thy doloure,　　80
As sekere as bred ys made of floure,

　Smell theñ in sesyñ wit*h* thy nese ;
The swetness of that savoure
　Shall geve the lysens to lyve in ease.　　84

(8)

[leaf 58]

'Accidia' ys a souking sore,
　he traveylyth me froñ day to day,
And eu*er* he wyll have more and more
　Plast*er*s thañ he purvey may.　　88

---

[1] MS. "a souking sore," copied from l. 85.

I axst a mayst*er* of fysyke lore,
  what wold hȳm drye and dryve away?
'Elymosina' ys an erbe ther-fore,
  Oon of the best that eu*er* I say;   92
Noynt hem̄ ther-wyth ay wheñ thow may,
  Thingk that Requiem shall in the rent & sese,
And sone aft*er*, w*ith*-in a nyght & a day,
  Thou shalt haue lysens to lyve in ease.   96

The remedy is a herb called Almsgiving,

with which you should anoint the wounds.

(9)

'Gula' ys a grevous gall;
  he bereueth my rest all in my bed;
So sore I streyne my stomake w*ith*-all,
  wyth many festys when I am full fed;   100
I walow as worme doth in wall,
  I may nat trest tyll a schamely sched.
Mercy! lorde! to the I call,
  For vs thou lettest thy brest be bled.   104
A leche hath layd hys hed to wed
  To make a plast*er* that wolde me please,
Off abstinaunce; and I it had,
  Then sholde I haue lysens to lyve in ease.   108

The 6th is Gluttony, which makes me strain my stomach.

A leech hath pledged himself to find a remedy

it is called Abstinence.

(10)

'Luxiria' ys a lyther mormale;
  Mercy! lorde! full of pite;
Thou bringest my body in bitt*er* bale,
  And fraill my sowle w*ith* thy frailte.   112
Sumtyme a surioune tolde me a tale;
  This was the lessyñ that he lerned me;
The rote of an erbe I sholde vp hale,
  Men call it 'chastite';[1]   116
and pounde it w*ith* penytencie;
  Wheñ the ryb wode wyll on the rese,
Drayne it and dringke it w*ith* confescionè,
  Theñ shalt thow haue lysens to lyve in ease. 120

The 7th is Luxury (Lechery), that imperils body and soul.

[leaf 58, back]

The remedy is a root called Chastity.

---

[1] This line and the next are written as one; cf. l. 128.

(11)

Other good herbs
are these three:
     other Erbys ther beñ alsoo,
         That suffer the sores they may nat swell;

Confession-with-
the-mouth,
     'Orys confescio' ys on of thoo,
         he wyll nat suffre no ded flessche for to dwell;   124

Contrition-of-
heart, and
     'Cordys contrycio' ys the too,
         A wasshyth the woundes as doth a well;

Satisfaction-by
works."
     'Operys satisfaccio' the souereyne sauetyff,[1]
         For soth as I yow tell."   128

God give us all
licence to live in
ease!
     God, that made both hevyn and hell,
         geve vs grace to serue and please,
     In that worthy blys that we may dwell,
         And gyff vs all lysens to lyve in ease!   132

Explicit in veritate
Da michi quod merui   }   Quod lewestoñ.

---

[1] Or 'sanetyff,' sanative.

SHORT RELIGIOUS POEMS

FROM MS. HARL. 7322

(FIRST TREATISE, OF THE END OF THE 14TH CENTURY, WHICH
HAS ENGLISH VERSES MIXED IN THE LATIN PROSE).

[The full stops are mostly those of the MS.]

Christ on the Cross.

Ho þat siþ him one þe Rode.
    iesus his lemmon.
And his moder bi him stonde
Sorë wepinde, and seynt iohan.   **4**
And his syden istongë sore.
For þe loue of þe, man.
Wel shulde he his sunne forsake.
Wetë terës and eke leten.   **8**
Þat of loue can.

[leaf 7]
Whoever sees Christ on the Cross

should forsake his sins.

All is Lost on Death.

[See p. 253.]

Memento nouissima tua, quia hec sunt signa mortis,
    videlicet :—

Whanne þe ffet coldetȝ.
    and þe tunge ffoldetȝ.
And þe shyne sharpetȝ.
And þe þrote Roteletȝ.   **4**
And þe hew ffalewetȝ.
And þe Eyȝen dasewetȝ

[leaf 7, back]

When the throat rattles

and the eyes dazzle,

And him atroketʒ his bretʒ.

and the soul goes, And þe soule a-wey getʒ.   8

And on flore me him strecchetʒ.

little is thought
of him who was
so proud. And litel of him þanne me recchetʒ

And he þas er so proud.

Ne shal he haue bote a cloud.   12

And of þat erer was his

Then he has
nothing. Nou shal he hauen mys.

Et nichil de mundo portabit.

All too Late.

[See p. 253.]

[leaf 169, back] Wonne þin eren dinet : and þi nese scharpet.

And þin hew dunnet : and þi sennewess starket.

When thine eyes
sink And þin eyen synket : and þi tunge foldet.

And þin honde stinket : and þin fet coldetʒ.   4

and thy lips turn
black and thy
throat rattles, And þin lippes blaket : and þin teth ratilet.

And þin hond quaket : and þi þrote ruteletʒ.

then is it too late;
the wain is at the
gate. —Al to late . al to late . þen is te wayn atte yate.

For may þor no man þenne : penaunce make.   8

Three Certainties of the Day of Death.

[leaf 8] Hit beoþ þreo tymes on þo day
　　　þat soþe to witen me mai :

1. I shall hence, þat on ys, þat i shal henne ;

2. I know not
when, þat oþer, þat y not whenne ;   4

þat þridde is my moste care,

3. or whither. þat y not whider i shal fare.

Marriage.

¶ Nupcie moriar, quia nubere dulce est.

For hit is mury to beon a wife.

Anglice sic :

ich wolle leose my life.

Sins of our Time.

[Written as prose.]

¶ ȝissinge and glosinge and felsship beon riue.   [leaf 64]
luþer lustes ouer floten. with fals gile and strife   Our Covetousness,
hardnesse and bakbiting wiþ scornes out bersten;   Backbiting, and
Bote almus dede and trouþe, wiþ semli plei þei resten. 4
vnkundenesse, vnkunninge, vnclannesse, beon arerd   Uncleanness
so þat harmes þei boden, as ich am aferd.   bode harm.

Some go up, and some go down, in this World.

[Printed in Rel. Ant., v. 1, p. 64.]

"Kinge i sitte, and loke aboute,   [leaf 79]
    to morwen y mai beon wiþoute."
"Wo is me, a kinge ich was;   I was once a king.
þis world, ich louede bote þat, ilas!   4
Nouth longe gon i was ful riche;
Now is riche and poure iliche."   Now poor and
                         rich are one.
"Ich shal beo kinge, þat men shulle seo,
When þou, wrecchë, ded shalt beo."   8   [leaf 79, back]

Four Proverbs.

[See Wright's Political Songs (Camden Soc., 1839), p. 386-7.]

¶ *primus* dixit { Mithȝ / lithȝ / Fithȝ } is { Rithȝ; / nithȝ; / flithȝ. }   [leaf 91, back] Might is Right.

¶ *secundus* dixit { On / frend / wil } is { two; / foo; / wo. }   Friend is Foe.

¶ *tercius* dixit { lust hath leue; / ȝist' is Reue; / prude hath sleue. }   Lust is rife.

¶ q*u*artus dixit
$\left\{ \begin{array}{l} \text{wil} \\ \text{wit} \\ \text{God} \end{array} \right\}$
is
$\left\{ \begin{array}{l} \text{Red} \\ \text{qued} \\ \text{ded} \end{array} \right.$

---

no*t*a de mirabilib*us* m*un*di.

Narrat solinus de mirabilibus mundi de quad*a*m aue, que in nido suo facit duo foramin*a*, vnu*m* ve*r*sus orientem, et aliud ve*r*sus occidentem, vt pe*r* p*r*imu*m* cicius videat solem de mane, & pe*r* 2ᵐ diucius de sero. Et pe*r* p*r*imu*m* exit de mane, & pe*r* secu*n*d*u*m intrat sero. Sp*irit*ualiter auis iste est quilibet fidelis qui sibi facit duo foramin*a* in nido, 1. in corde suo, & in p*r*ima porta orientali, pe*r* quam ingreditur mundu*m*, inue*n*ie*n*t tres ' welcomeres ' horribiles, videlicet.

Welcomers
$\left\{ \begin{array}{l} \text{nuditas} \\ \text{Fletus} \\ \text{debilitas} \end{array} \right\}$
Anglice
$\left\{ \begin{array}{l} \text{nakednesse} \\ \text{Reminge} \\ \text{feblesse} \end{array} \right.$

Vel alite*r* sic quilibet intrat pe*r* portas, s*cilic*et,

$\left. \begin{array}{l} \text{nasty} \\ \text{sory} \\ \text{vnmiȝty} \end{array} \right\{$
Et certe clamat .A. quod est p*r*imu*m* n*omin*is Ade ; in qua

litera sunt Anguli ad designandum tria incomoda, que quilibet n*os*tr*um* incurrit quando nosci*tur* ; vnde quilibet

nostru*m* q*u*a*n*do flet & clamat, .A. quasi dolens, diceret in Anglico sic, videlicet,

     Wiþ wo & drede i am born ;
     Al for adam y am lorn ;
     To wo and sorwe brouȝt y am,
     þat haþ mad þi sinne, Adam.

     Teone and t*r*auail shal beo my lif.
     ȝeruþe, Adam, haue þe stiþ.

Vt pro isto dici potest istud psalmi : " In p*e*ccatis concepit me mat*er* mea." iob., etc.

Signs of Death.

[Printed in Rel. Ant., v. 1, p. 64-5.   See p. 249-50 of this Text.]

Alle his frendes he shal beo loþ, [leaf 121]
And helud shal ben wiþ a cloþ, All his friends shall loathe him.
Hyse eres shullen dewen,
& his eyen shullen dymmen, 4
& his nese shal sharpen,
& his skyn shal starken,
& his hew shal falewen, His colour shall fade,
& his tonge shal stameren, oþ*er* famelen, 8
& his lippes shulle bliken,
& his hondes shulle quaken,
& his teþ shulle Ratelen, his teeth shall rattle;
& his þrote shal Rotelen, 12
& his feet shullen streken,
& his herte shal breken ; his heart break,
& of al þis wordles b[l]isse,
ne woldy ȝeue a pese iwis. 16
þou þat art so proud, and the proud man have but a clout.
Ne shalt þou haue bote a clout.

The Covetous Man.

On hit is, and ne haueþ noþer [leaf 121, back]
sone, ne suster, ne nouþer broþer ; He has no kin.
Ne he n*er*e blynneþ of t*r*auaillin*ge*,
he nis no child of god halewin*ge*, 4 He is no child of God's blessing.
for one him self⸵ he ne þenkeþ,
for wham he wakeþ and harde swinkeþ,
he wakkeþ boþe dai and niȝt,
& leteþ his soule ben vuel diȝt. 8

Death.

Death is　　Est eni*m* mors　$\left\{\begin{array}{l} \text{mendacissima} \\ \text{Occultissima} \\ \text{repacissima} \\ \text{seuerissima} \end{array}\right.$　　　4

false, still,　　þo ded*tur* so is fals and falende,

Stille and eke stalkinge,

greedy,　　Gredy and Crepynge,

and stern.　　steorne and eke stellende　　　8

Christ announces his Coming.

Christ comes to lead us:

" Nou ȝe alle beo glad and bliþe,

For i come to leden ou swiþe."

In q*uibus* ve*r*bis quatuor p*r*oponam q*uesti*ones. . .

quatuor q*uesti*one*s* sunt :

" Ho art þou þat comest so litel a*n*d so mithful ?　　4

Ho art þou þat comest so dredful　And so Rithful ?

Ho art þou þat comest so ȝonge　And so connynge ?

Ho art þou þat comest so pore　And al weldynge ? "

¶ Ad p*r*imam re*p*onem, & ad om*ne*s alias :—　　8

a Knight to fight for us,　　"ich am a knyth for ou to fithten ;

ich am a pledo*ur* ou lede to Rithte ;

a Master to teach us.　　ich am a maister to teche þe lawe ;

ich am an emp*er*our, a god felawe."　　　12

Learn Love from Christ's Sufferings.

See the knotted Scourge that beat my back;

Biholt, þou man wiþ Routhful herte,

þe sharpë scourge wiþ knottës smerte !

Mi blodi bak wiþ hit his beten :

Leornë, mon, þi lust to leten ;　　　4

the Spear that stung my heart,　　For, wiþ þis sper þat is so gril,

Min herte was stoungen, so was my uel,

for love of thee.　　For loue of þe þat was so dere ;

Wel auȝtest þou of loue to lere.　　　8

Lobe Christ who Lobes Thee.

Leorne to loue, as ich loue þe ;　　　　　[leaf 135, back]
On alle my lymës þou mith seo　　　　　　Love me, man,
　　　　　　　　　　　　　　　　　　　　as I love thee,
　　Hou sore ich quake for colde ;　　　3
For þe ich soffre muche colde & wo ;　　for whom I suffer.
Loue me wel, and nomo ;
　　To þe i take and holde.　　　　　　6

Et Re*g*ina mate*r* sua nichil habuit vn*de* posset eum
induer*e* ; *ideo* dixit sibi :—

(The Virgin's Song to her Baby Christ.)

(1)

Iesu, swetë sonë dere !　　　　　　　[leaf 135, back]
　　On porful bed, list þou here,　　　Son, I weep that
　　　　　　　　　　　　　　　　　　Thy bed is poor,
　　And þat me greueþ sore ;　　　　3
For þi cradel is ase a bere,
Oxe and assë beþ þi fere ;　　　　　　Thy fellows, ox
　　　　　　　　　　　　　　　　　　and ass.
　　Weope ich mai þar-fore.　　　　6

(2)

Iesu, swete, beo noth wroþ
þou ich nabbë clout ne cloþ　　　　　　I have no cloths
　　þe on for to folde,　　　　　　9
þe on to foldë ne to wrappe ;　　　　to wrap Thee in.
For ich nabbë clout ne lappe ;
Bote ley þou þi fet to my pappe,　　　Put Thy feet on
　　　　　　　　　　　　　　　　　　my breast.
　　And wite þe from þe colde.　　13

The Vanity of this Life.

þe lif of þis world　　　　　　　　　[leaf 136, back]
Ys Reuled wiþ wynd.　　　　　　　　This world's life
　　　　　　　　　　　　　　　　　　is governd by the
Wepinge, derknesse,[1] a[n]d steriyng*e* ;　wind.
Wiþ wind we blowen,　　　　　　　4
Wiþ wind we lassun.

[1] 'derknesse' probably for 'drednesse.' The Latin has Flatum,
　　Fletum, Motum, Metum.

We are born
weeping:
we die so.

Wiþ weopinge we comen,
Wiþ weopinge we passun.
Wiþ steriinge we byginnen,   8
Wiþ steriinge we enden;

We live and die
in fear.

Wiþ drede we dwellen,
Wiþ drede we wenden.

Man made God's Brother.

[leaf 138, back]
Christ has robd
Hell.

þis timë man haþ ouercome
    þe fend, and Robbed helle;
Lokë þat, on his seruise,
    Lenge þat þou ne dwelle;   4

He has made man
ruler of all things,

þis time man is mad kniȝth
    And shuppare ouer alle þinge;
Loke, on non erliche þinge
    þou settë þyn endinge;   8
For now is erlich man bicome

God's own
brother.

    Godës owene broþer;
Loke, man, on nonë wyse
    þou chaunge for non oþer.   12

In Weal think of Woe.

[leaf 139, back]

In die bonorum non inmemor sis malorum.
yn time of wele þenke on þi wo.
for þe wele of þis world wole sone go.

Four Evils.

[leaf 140, back]

. . & facit quatuor mala vbi regnant secundum quod
componitur ex quatuor literis.   P. R. E. D. Vnde
Anglice :

Anglice {
    Hey Priuetȝ gritliche;
    Hey Robbetȝ holliche :
    Hey Endetȝ shameliche :
    Hey Draweþ dredfulliche.

Humility.

A tokne of godes louiing*e*,   [leaf 141, back]
A sheld of mithful wynning*e*,
A Celer of siker keping*e*,
A keye of Redi vndoing*e*.   4

Eve, Mary, and Paradise.

þe ʒates of Parais   [leaf 143]
þoruth eue weren iloken ;
and þoruth oure swete ladi,
Aʒein hui beoþ nouþe open.   4

Ideo ista humilitas dici potest ' clauis Dauid,' de quo
habet*ur* Apoc*alypsi* 3, que claudit, & nemo ape*r*it.

Envy.

De isto malo dicit Augustinus, q*uo*d est aliene   [leaf 143, back]
felicitatis t*r*isticia, et adue*r*sitatis leticia : ista est mala
condic*i*o, & sum*m*e cauenda p*r*op*ter* quatuor: videl*i*cet:

q*uia* hit { Roteþ and brenneþ,
               Hit freteþ and twynneþ. }

& i*d*eo est sicut anglice dicit*ur*, videlicet :

Ase { þe worm on þe treo,
       and þe hul on þe see,
       and roust on þe knif*e*,
       and ase deþ to þe lif*e*.

The Evils of this Time.

Set heu . . . raro inuenitur amor siue caritas ! ideo   [leaf 145]
dolorose potest dici modo istud Anglice :

Loue is out of lond iwent ;
Defaute of loue þis lond haþ shent.   4   [leaf 145, back]
Reuthþe and treuthþe and charite
Beþ out of lond, alle þreo :

Prude, enuye, and lecherie,
Couetise, and tricherie,   8
Habbeþ þis lond one here baillye.

Cupidity.

hit falseþ
hit reymeþ   } Cupiditas.
hit falleþ
hit shendeþ

A Triad.

Frendsship ⎫   ⎧ worsshipful
serte   ⎬ þat is   ⎨ blisful
wonyinge   ⎭   ⎩ ioyeful

Inscriptions. (*See page* 260–1.)

þi wyckede dedis þe broutte to care. bot is þe
for3oin,[1] þou sinne no mare.

þe wickede dedis þe made syke sore. bot al i
for-3iue þe, & sinne no more.

Alius rex s[i] dedit coronam auream memoratiuam in
qua sic sculpebatur:

þeng wat þou art, & wat þou was, & þat al þi
worssepe of me has.

þou þeng wel on þese þinges þre; wat tou art,
& wat tou were, & al þe worsse[pe has of me.]

Propugnator dedit anulum in quo sic scribebatur
per girum.

Sicut te dilexi disce me diligere / nam in toto
corpore poteris illud cernere.

Lere to loue as Ic loue þe; on al my lemes þou
mait it se.   [*Repeated, p.* 262.]

For þe I suffrede mikel wo. þou loue [me] treuli
ant no mo

---

[1] for3ouin, p. 264, near the foot.

Anulum in quo sic insertum erat :

> Nóble þou art þat were a-file. be war be onis
> þat nout þe gile.   [*See p.* 261.]

Mediator dedit ei tercium anulum in quo sic scribebatur :

> Wou michel, ant wat, & werfore. wat I haue
> þoled for loue of þe.

Germanus proprius sibi dedit quartum anulum in
quo sic erat scriptum :

> I am þi broþer, be nout in wer ; be nout agast
> to come me ner ;
>
> I am þi broþer, be nout agast ; be hende, &
> trewe, & stedëfast.

A sponso proprio dabatur sibi sigillum vnum per
quod hereditas sibi assecurabatur in quo sic :

> Here I take þe to my liue ; tac þou non oþer to
> terme of liue.
>
> Here I take þe to my spouse ; & ȝiue þe boþë
> land & house.

The Signs of Faithful Love.

Nam quatuor sunt signa fidelis Amoris, que ostendit   [leaf 144, back]
Christus, in quibus nobis exemplum reliquit, videlicet,

> On word [and] ȝiuinge,
> On werke and soffringe.

Christ Comes.

> Wat is he þis þat comet so brith   [leaf 153, back]
> Wit blodi cloþes al be-dith ?
> respondentes superiores dixerunt :
> " He is boþe god and man :   4
> swilc ne sawe neuere nan.
> for adamis sinne he suffrede ded.
> & þerfore is his robe so red."

Love.

[leaf 145] Bene debent ista exempla nos mouere ad opera caritatis, & eciam valor ipsius amoris qui habet condiciones secundum quod ibi sunt quatuor litere, scilicet, L. O. V. E.

> Hit is Lawe þat sailleþ noth,
> Hit is Ouer al þat mai beo wrouȝth,
> Hit Werkeþ wonderliche,
> And Ernes ȝeueþ sikerliche.   4

Poverty.

[leaf 147, back] Nota. non habuit ubi capud potuit reclinare, Moriendo ubi capud potuit tegere. Inde, bene potuit dicere 'pauper sum ego.' Istud exemplum debemus sequi propter quatuor que faciunt in possessore :

> hit resteþ ⎫   ⎧ hit quemeþ
> hit richeþ ⎭ and ⎨ hit demeþ

Lechery.

[leaf 148]
> Luxuria   ⎧ hit wasteþ   ⎫
> facit hec   ⎨ hit Fileþ.   ⎬ primo
>   ⎪ hit wrappeþ ⎪
>   ⎩ hit bigileþ. ⎭

Chastity.

[leaf 149]
> Castitas est ⎧ A tresour of gret Richesse.
>   ⎪ A vertue of douthtynesse,
>   ⎨ And is a worsshipful Cloþinge
>   ⎩ And an help of gret wynn[i]nge.

Inscriptions, p. 258-9, repeated.

(y and þ are the same.)

[leaf 152] þi wyckede dedis þe broute to care ; bot is þe for-ȝoui ;
þou sinne no mare.

þe wickede dedis þe made syke sore; bot al i for-ȝiue
    þe; & sinne no more

þeng wat þou art & wat þou was; & þat al þi worssepe
    of me [þou] has.

þou þeng wel on þese þinges · yie, wat tou art, & wat
    tou were, & al þe woisse.   4

Lere to loue as Ic loue þe: on al my lemes þou mait
    it se;

For þe I suffrede mikel wo; þou loue [me] trueli, ant
    no mo.

Noble þou art, þat were afile; be war be onis þat none
    þe gile,

Wou michel, at wat, & werfore, wat I haue þoled for
    loue of þe.   8

I am þi broþer, be nout in wer; be nout agast to come
    me nere;

I am þi broþer, be nout agast; be hende & trewe, &
    stedefast.

Here I take þe to my line, tae þou non oþer to terme
    of liue;

Here I take þe to my spouse, & ȝiue þe boþe land
    & house.   12

_____

The Sinners' Lament.

al þe ioȝe of oure herte nou is went a-wey :   [leaf 153, back]
for into serwe & into wo, tornid is al oure pley.
þe croune of oure heued is felle to gronde :
þat euere we sennede, weylawey þe stonde!   4

_____

Christ's Woe.

ȝe þat be þis wey pace,   [leaf 154]
abidid & behaldit my face ;
& loket wer ani wo or pine
may be lienit nou to mine!   4

A Lover's Complaint.

Loue, þou art of mikel mit;
Mi day þou tornis into nit,
   & dos me sikë sore;   3
and al for on so swete a wit
þat onis þorw loue me troupë plit,
   to ben myn euere more.   6

Christ's Call to Love.

Lere to loue as .i. loue þe,
for on al mi lemes þou mait it se.   [*See* p. 258.]

True Love.

[leaf 155, back]
þey loue be stro[n]g & mikel of mith,
for wele, for wo, trewloue mat lith.

treuloue is largë, fre & hende,
& loue ȝif alleþing bleþeli to his frende.   4

in wele & wo, loue sto[n]dit faste,
for lif, for det, trewloue wil laste.

fer & frey loue hat on heu,
for trewloue is fress & euere neu.   8

Four Inscriptions.

(1) fir & watir, wind & lond.
   i desire bo haue vnder myn hond vel bond.

(2) bede faste, for i come sone.
   yif þou serwe onli for me,
   sikerly þou tit þi bone.   5

(3) wil ȝe biddin, redi i am;
   ȝif ȝe leuin, i go you fram.

[leaf 156]
(4) smertlike i helpe, & noman forsake;
   bleþeli i fitte, þe maistri forto take.   9

Trust not the World.

worldis blissë, strif hat wrout,   [leaf 157]
for it is wit serwe to endë brout.

worldes catel [1] passet sone.   [1 leaf 157, back]
þat wacset & wansit rit as te mone.   4

trist nout to þ[i]s wonder world þat lastit bot a
      wile;
for it is not bot wiles of wo a hasardour þat wil þe
      gile.

Purity.

He is wel siker þat hat clennesse;
for al þat oþer renenant [2] is not bot wrechedenesse.

Mortality.

allas! in gret sinne, alle beȝete we were: [leaf 158]
stronge pines þoleden þe moderis þat vs bere.
here we liue bisiliche wit strong serwe & care:
deȝe we ssulin sikerliche; bot god wot wanne &
      were.   4

Pride.

in alle maner þrifte,[3] y passe allë þingge;
ȝif oni þing be lic me, to det i ssal him bringe.

Mercy.

ȝif sinne nere, merci nere non;
wan Merci is cald, he comet anon.

þer merci is rediest wer sinne is mest.
þer merci is lattest were sinne is lest.   4

Merci abidet & loket aldai,
wan mon fro sinne wil torne away.

----

[2] remenant?   [3] or þristi

Christ, Man's Help.

god help hastou, man & prest;
þe moder here sone sewet here brest;
þe sone his fadir ssewet his side,
hise wondir wondis depe & wide;   4
þanne mai þer be no maner werning,
þer of so gret loue is so gret tocning.

The King's Letters to his Son.

Fulgencius in gestis romanorum : quidam rex duos
habuit filios, quorum senior cum patre in pallacio fuit;
Iunior vero in castro pernoctauit periculoso.   cui pater
litteras 5. transcripsit.   prima erat ista, sic :

sinne & folye[1] only for-sake;
to clennesse of lif, for mi loue tac.

   2ª fuit ista, sic :
loue god boþe wit herte & þout.
for to his licnesse þou art wrout.   4

   3ª erat ista, sic :
[leaf 158, back] wit-outin louë þou art lorn;
wose hat nout loue, were bettre on-born.

   4ᵗᵃ erat ista sic :
of al þi wele i bidde non oþer,
bot loue me wel, as dot þi broþer.
vel sic :
of al þi richesse i bidde no more,
bot loue me wel for euere more.

   5ᵗᵃ erat ista.
Come nou, my swete chilt, wan þou come wilt,
for redi is þin heritage, & forȝouin is þi gilt.

The Ills of our Time.

Charite, chaste, pite, arn waxin al colde;
[leaf 162] Couetise, Lust, & maistrie, arn be-comin al bolde;
Consel, god acord, & wedloc ben nou noþing of tolde. 3

---

¹ MS. may be ‘fulþe.’

Stro*n*ge, t*r*ewe, & corteis, kepte þe land ;
Bot now feynte, false, folis, it han vndir hand ;
þeues, liers & fowlwi*m*me*n* boldeli ferth stand.   6

Vnder dercnesse, darket lit of stedefastnesse.   [leaf 162, back]
vnder sleuþe, darkit þe loue of holinesse.
For faute of rit domusma*n*, þe lauwe slepit of
     ritwisnesse.   9

wif, wille, and richesse, han þe maist*r*ie ta[ke] ;
ve*r*tu, godede, & almisdede, arn al for-sake ;   11
Ok*er*, liey*n*g, & wa*n*tonesse, mickel se*r*we make.

Look to the End.

þis is a wondir m*er*ie pley, & longe ssal laste :
bot, for þi sete is p*er*ilous, war þe ate laste.

A Lover's Saying.

me þi*n*g Rit þou art so loueli, so fair, & so swete,
þat sik*er*li it were mi det, þi co*m*panie to lete.

Ware the Wheel!

þis wondir wel vndir þis t*r*one,
it changit ofte as dot þe mone ;
al þat eue*r*e come þe*r*-on,
it fondit forto gile :   4
& bot þey [1] be war be-forn,   [1 leaf 163]
it ȝelt he*m* euele her wile.

The Lion.

þe lion is wondirliche st*r*ong,
& ful of wiles of wo ;
& weþer he pleye
oþer take his p*r*eȝe,
he can not do bot slo.   5

Ware Bear's Play!

war þe from þe bere plei auantir / last he bite;
for selde he stintit of his pley, bot yif he bite or
　　smite.

The Dragon.

I wile ȝou alle swelewe wit-outin oni both:
dot[1] some wile y saue, & some wile y noth.

Fortune's Wheel.

þou most fort, wit wele or wo,
　　be þou lef, oþer be[2] þou lot,
forto gon vp on þis wel
　　þat eueremore aboutë got.　　　　　　　　　4

ȝif þou be cointë, þou ssalt liue:
& ellis dedis dint i ssal þe ȝiue.
vel sic
ȝif þou go cointeli on þis wel,　　　　　　　8
　　þou ssalt liue eueremore:
bot ȝif þou falle, & go amis,
　　wit dulful det i wonde þe sore.

Foolish Love.

I am a fol, i can no god:
ho þat me louit, hi halde him wod;

.I. brennë hote, I smitë sore,
ho þat me louit ssal þe no more.　　　　　　4

dredful det out of me sprong,
　　fo[r] i am welle of wo:
I slou a wis king, fair & strong;
　　& ȝit .i. ssal sle mo.　　　　　　　　　8

　　　　　[1] bot?　　　　　　　　[2] MS. bo

The Ten Stages of Man's Life.

Vita ho*min*is
dec*ur*rit in
⎰ 10. horis. ⎱
⎱ 10 dictis ⎰   In
⎰ 10 radiis ⎱
⎰ ten times of þe day
⎱ ten stappes of oure way
⎰ ten spokes þat tornen ay

1   waich & wreschede þou art i*n* sith ;
   of alle man*er* beste, lest is ti mith.

2   Al þis world þe tornit to play ;
   þe more þou playst, þe more þou may.

3   Richesse makes man beholden aboute ;
   for to þe riche, me*n* bowe & louthe.

4   Nou hastou fondin þat tou hast sout :
   be wel war ; it lastit nout.

5   stro*n*g þou was, nou failit þi mith ;
   þou waxist heui, þat was wel lit.

6   Al mi lif ic sorwe & care,
   for det comit sone, þat noman wil spar*e*.

7   Lore þou hast, boþe to*n*ge & mi*n*de :
   as tou hast liuid, þou ssalt sone finde.

8   al þis wo[r]ld þou ssal forsake,
   for det is comu*n*, þat wil þe take.

9   ma*n* & wimma*n* han on ende ;
   for, esye he comu*n* al ; esye ho[1] ssuln wende.

10 Of þi lif nou litel lete,   [1 *or* he]
   for þou art tornid to wormis mete.

Four Inducements to Repentance.   [leaf 166, back]

[Q]Vatuor mone*n*t ad p*en*ite*n*tiam. videl*icet* :

benignitas d*iu*ina,
*Christ*i doctr*i*na,
horrendu*m* dei iudi-
  ciu*m*. i*n* impeniten-
  tib*us* inferendum,
& premiu*m* eternum,
ve*r*e peni*t*entib*us* re-
  pr*o*missu*m*.   ⎬ ang*l*ice ⎨

Godes hore,   [leaf 167]
Cristes lore,
Godes gr*i*sliche dom,

And the blisse þat ner
  nis don.

God's Goodness.

expectat paciente*r*,   anglice   he abit þolemodliche,
p*ar*cit faciliter,   he fur-geft litliche,
susci*p*it li*b*eralit*er*,   he vnde*r*-fenget freliche,
& obliuiscit*ur* totali-   and he fur-þet holliche.
ter.

[leaf 168, back]   *Written at the foot of the page in pale ink.*

Hou þi fairnisse is bi-spit,
Hou þi swetnisse is i-betin and ipit,
Hou þi lotleschipe to scharp detȝ is of set.

Against Temptation.

[leaf 172]

of vr vife wittes, a wel witiynge ;
of þing þat vs egget, a vast vleynge ;
and of þe laste ende, a bisi biþenkynge.

Alas, that we ever Sinned!

[leaf 172, back]

Strong it hus to flitte   } 1
Fro worldes blisse to pitte ; /

Strengore is to misse   } 2
Heuene-richë blisse ; /   4

Strengest is to wende   } 3
To pine wit-outen ende. /

þe blisse of oure he*r*te, al it is ago ;
Al vre welë torned is to wo ;   8
þe croune of vre heued
Fallen is to grounde :
þat we euer syngeden,
Weylawey þe stounde !   12

Job said :

[leaf 181]

þat ylke day be out of Mui*n*de
þat y was bron to[1] Mo*n*nes kuy*n*de !

       [1] *do altered to to.*

The Saved says:

For foulë lustës .I. witstod,
In blisse .I. werë [1]ʒys garlond.

The Lost says:

Alas! worldes yissyng Me haueth scehent, [leaf 182]
[1]ʒat euere My soule in helle beth brent.

The Saved says:

In heuene blisse .I. am in hele,
For I forsok [1]ʒys worldes wele.

The Lost says:

Alas! helle me hath in[2] holt in ruyde; [leaf 183]
[1]ʒe deuel in pine for worldes pride. [2 *or* an. ? MS.]

The Reward of the Meek.

For þou were Meke, an laftuste pruyde, [leaf 183, back]
Wite blisse in heuene I schal þe scruyde.

Matthew's Feast.

Matheu hat mad a grete gesteny[n]g
te Ihesu at home in his whonyy[n]g.

The Virtues serve us.

Innitant *igitur* fides, pietas & beneuolencia;	vs preyen, bileue, god wille, & pite;	[leaf 184]
Recipiunt spes, humilitas & continencia;	vs kepen, god hope, Mekenes & kastite;	
Recumbunt pauperes caritate & paciencia;	vus sit by, pouert, wisdom, & god leuy[n]g;	
Ministrant sanctitas, zelus & modestia.	vus seruen clannesse, rych & feyr bery[n]g.	

---

[1] This scribe uses ʒ for þ; and þ for ʒ in 'fur-þet,' forgets, 268/4.

Lord, come to my Feast.

Lord .I. bidde boȝe day & nyth,
cum to my feste [1]ȝat .I. haue dyth.

ȝif hit queme Mi lord ȝe ky[n]g, ȝy[n]g[2] ȝat I
   him preye.
I bidde he come to My gesteni[n]g, wit vus to
   gomen & pleye.

ȝif in þi sith i grace haue fonde,
ȝif me Mi wille at [1]ȝis stonde.

Hindrances of the Debil.

promissio fallax.			A fals by-hety[n]g.
promocio mendax.	anglice		A lyeres auansyng.
prolacio Mordax.			A bitynde fondi[n]g.

---

[1] This scribe uses ȝ for þ.   [2] thing

An A B C Poem on the Passion of Christ.

[Harl. MS. 3954, leaf 87. The A B C, etc., are not rubricated in the MS., but are made black here to catch the eye. The initial þ and y are the same.]

(1)

IN place as man may se,
Quan a chyld to scole xal set be,
  A bok hym is browt,
Naylyd on a brede of tre,
þat men callyt an abece,
  Pratylych I-wrout.

When a child is put to school, a book calld an A B C is given him, naild on a slab of wood,

3

6

(2)

Wrout is on þe bok with-oute,
V. paraffys grete & stoute
  Bolyd in rose red ;
þat is set with-outyn doute,
[*No gap in the MS.*]
  In tokenyng of cristis ded.

and rubricated on the outside with five paraffes,

in token of Christ's death.

9

12

(3)

Red letter in parchemyn
Makyth a chyld good & fyn
  Lettrys to loke & se.
Be þis bok men may dyuyne
þat cristis body was ful of pyne
  þat deyid on rodë tre.

(Red letters tempt a child to look at them.)

By this book we may understand that Christ

15

18

(4)

On tre he was don ful blythe
With grete paraffys, þat be wondis .v.
  As ȝe mou vnder-stonde.
Loke in hys body, mayde & wyfe,
Qwon hee gun naylys dryue
  In fot & in honde.

was put on the Cross with Five Wounds,

when nails were driven through His feet and hands,

21

24

(5)

Hond & fout þer was ful woo,
And þer were lettrys many moo
　　Wiþ-in & wiþ-oute,　　　　　　　27

and He was
covered with
wounds and
stripes from
top to toe.
Wiþ rede wondis & strokis blo
He was dryue fro top to þe too,
　　Hys fayre body aboute.　　　　30

(6)

I will tell you
about this,
About þis, a pece I wyl spede,
þat I myth þis lettrys rede
　　Wiþ-outyn ony dystaunce ;　　　33

and may God
bring us to
heaven !
But god þat let hys body sprede
Vp-on þe rode for manys nede,
　　In heuene vs alle avaunce !　　36

(7)

Christ was sold
to death by Judas
to fill his purse.
God wiþ spere was wondyd for vs ;
Fals iudas, to mendyn hys purs,
　　To ded hath hym̄ sold :　　　　39

On Good Friday
clerks say,
'Jesus is dead.'
On goodfryday, clerkys seyn þus,
" Mortuus est, ded is Ihesus,
　　In ston is ded & cold."　　　　42

(8)

[leaf 87, col. 2]
A madful mone may men make
Quan þat suete Ihesu was take !
　　Lystyn a lytyl pas :　　　　　45

The Jews took
Him before
Bishop Caiaphas :
þe iewys wroutyn hym wo & wrake ;[1]　[1 MS. warke]
Hee ledyn hym forth a gret shake
　　Aforn busshop Cayfas.　　　　48

(9)

bound Him,
Bondyn he was for our bounte,
And suffryd strokis gret plente
　　Be-forn cayfas þat nyth.　　　51
On þe morn, I tel þe,
and beat Him
before Pilate.
Eft was he betyn at þe tre
　　Be-forn pylatis syth ;　　　　54

(10)

Cananis hym crodyn tó heroudis kyng,
þer had he gret scornyng,
   þei bodyn hym turne þe gate.   57
Hee leddyn þat maydynus sone ȝyng
For to takyn hys damnyng
   Be-forn iustice pylate.   60

Canaanites mocked Him before Herod,

and led Him for judgment to Justice Pilate.

(11)

Dempt he was on a stounde,
Sethen betyn with many wonde.
He tokyn a clout, as it is founde,
   And wondyn hus body þer-inne.   64
With dry blod quan was he bounde,
Tho iewys, egre as ony hounde,
Threwyn hus body to þe grounde,
   And rentyn of cloth & scynne :   68

Doomed He was, and beaten,

wrapped in a clout,

thrown on the ground, and His skin rent.

(12)

Euene in hus eyne greye
Hee spyttyd on hym, þe soþe to seye :
   He lokyd on hem ful mylde.   71
Mary hys moder went þe weye
To caluery þer he xuld deye,
   And waytyd þer here chylde.   74

Even in His grey eyes they spat,

and He looked tenderly on them.

Mary went to Calvary.

(13)

For feyntyce fel þat fayre fode,
Nakyd he bar þat hard rode
   To-ward caluery,   77
Al be-ronne with red blod ;
Among þe iewys wylde & wod,
   He suonnyd cekerly.   80

For faintness Christ fell, carrying His cross;

streaming with blood,

He swooned.

(14)

God ! with iewys gret was þi pyne,
Naylyd on rode, soth for to seyne.
   Hee leydyn þe on þe grounde   83

God, great was Thy suffering!

Laid on the ground,

[leaf 87, back]

nailed through
foot and hand.

And ryuyn þi body holy & dygne,—
On þe he madyn a gret sygne,—
  Hee naylyd þe fot & honnde ;   86

(15)

Hard they bound
the Cross, and
hung Him,bloody,
on it,

Harde þei bondyn þat heuy rode ;
þer-on hys body heng al on blode,
  As beryt wytnesse sen Ion.   89
þe wyckyd iewys, wyld & wode,

driven into a
mortice of stone.

Hard þei dryuyn þat heuy rode
  In-to a morteys of ston.   92

(16)

Jesus, great was
Thy suffering !
Hand and foot
torn,

Ihesu, with iewys gret was þi pyne !
Hand & fot, for soþe to seyne,
  Al to-toryn in þat tyde,   95

sinew and vein
burst !
Magdalene
saw the wounds.

Al to-broste synwe & veyne,
As beryt wytnesse Maudeleyne ;
  She sau þe wondis wyde.   98

(17)

King Christ
paid for our
sins full dear.

Kyng crist was klad in poure wede :
Al þe syn of manys dede
  He hath bout wol dere ;   101

To buy us heaven
He shed blood
and water.

To byȝyn vs heuene, þat mery mede,
Al hys blod he gan blede,
  And sythyn water clere.   104

(18)

Love made Him
dwell with man,

Loue made crist fro heuene to comyn,
Loue made hym with man to wonyn,—
  As clerkys in bokys rede,—   107

and made His
heart bleed
to feed our souls
and bring us to
bliss.

Loue made hus hert to bledyn,
With hus blod oure soulys to fedyn,
  To bryngyn vs to oure mede.   110

(19)

Man, to get thee
mercy, Maid
Mary's Son
died on Good
Friday

Man, for þi mekel mercy,
Maydynnus sone Mary,
  On godfryday þus deyide !   113

þus he heng on caluery
With wondis weyde cekerly,
   A thef on eyþer¹ syde.   [¹ MS. eyeryer]   116

(20)

Nout he hadde at hys nede
To restyn hus hed, as clerkys rede,
   But al was hym be-reuyd.   119
Fox & foul may reste & hede,
But crist, þat deyid for manus nede,
   Hat nout to reste in hus had.   122

(21)

Out ran hus blod þat was so bryth;
þan seyde our lord god almyth
   A word of gret pete,   [leaf 87, back, col. 2]   125
" Al þus with iewys I am dyth,
I seme a wyrm to manus syth."
   Man! for loue of þe,   128

(22)

Pryckis hym peynyd, ȝe may here;
Hys hed was broydyn on a brere,
   þis is þe soþe to seyne;   131
With red blod was wet hus lere;
þo pryckis, þoru hus panne so dere,
   Wentyn in-to þe brayn!   134

(23)

Qwen of heuene, wo was she
To sen hangyn on rode tre
   Ihesu, here sone so suete;   137
Here tendre hert myth breste on iij
Quan she sau here sonë fre
   On rode hys lyf lete.   140

(24)

Ragyd & rent, in red blod,
þus heng he vp-on þe rod
   Aȝen þe sonë glem.   143

Worse than mad
were the Jews
to slay Jesus so
good.

For soþe he weryn werse þan wod
To slon Ihesu so good,
þe iewys of ierusalem.[1]   [1 MS. ielrm]   146

(25)

Slit was His flesh,

Slyt was hus flech, & slawe;
þe iewys in here falcë lawe,
þei dedyn hym mekel peyne: 149
As seyt þe gospel in hus sawe,

limb torn from
limb.

Euery lyth fro oþer was drawe;
þat is nout to layne.   152

(26)

Tugged with
trouble was our
Lord,

and yet spake no
angry word,

Togyd with tene was god of prys;
To don hym sorwe was here delys:
He seydë no word loth.   155
Quan he was naylyd at here a-vys,

while the Jews
cast lots for His
clothes.

þo iewys kestyn at þe dys
Qweþer xuld han hys cloth.   158

(27)

Wide were His
wet wounds
from hand to foot.

Wyde weryn hus wondis wete,
Fro þe hond[es] to þe fete
With deth he was [i]slawe.   161

His blood will
conquer our foe.

Hys lomeber blod our bale may bete,
Of qwom spac Moyses þe prophete,
Ryth in þe held lawe.   164

(28)

Xt. (Christ) on
Cross was slain,
[leaf 88]

and cried to God,

'Father, why
hast Thou for-
saken Me?'

Xp̄c crist on croys was sleynt;
To hys fader he made a pleynt,
Hys cry was, "hely!   167
Fader god in trynite!
Qwy hast þou forsakë me?"
Cryst seyde on caluery.   170

(29)

(Y stands for I.)
Christ

Y for I, in wryt is set.
Cryst for vs on croys was knet,
Nalyd on þe rode: 173

Out of thraldam he vs fet,
þat we þoru syn hadde get,
   And bout vs *with* hys blode.   176

brought us out
of the thraldom
of sin,
and bought us
with His blood.

(30)

Ȝet he was *in* suffryng
Of trokys & nayl*is* clynkyng,
   Tyl it was pacyd non;   179
Ne blench*y*d he *neuer* for betyng;
To dede hee dedyn heuene kyng;
   þis was a ruful mon.   182

Ȝet, or still, did
He suffer

till past noon,

and heaven's
King was slain.

(31)

& is to seyn, god is ded,
Of hys blod hys body is red.
   He ros on estryn morwe;   185
To helle he ȝede *with*-outy*n* abod,
For to stroy*n* þe fendys wod,
   To sauy*n* vs fro sorwe.   188

& means God
is dead.

He rose on Easter
Morn,
to destroy the
fiends in hell,
and save us from
woe.

(32)

Loke þat we ben seker & kende,
And kepe þis apece[1] *in* oure mende,   [1 *for* abece]
þan sekere be we of blys *with*-outy*n* ende
   In tyme qu*a*n we xul dey;   192
Afte*r*ward me*n* xal vp-ryce,
And wende for, boþe fol & wyce,
   To Iosaphat sekerly;   195

Let us remember
this

when we die.

Hereafter all
shall rise,
and go to the
Valley of
Jehoshaphat,

(33)

And west, nort, & south,
Eue*r*y man, boþe fremyd & kouth,
   Xul comy*n with*-outyn ly.   198
þer xal be gret asyce
Be-forn ihe*s*u, þ*a*t hey Iustyce,
   W*ith* wou*n*d*is* al blody.   201

friend and
stranger too,

to the Great
Assize
before Jesus
with bleeding
wounds.

(34)

Qu*a*n ma*nn*us soule hat *in* mynde
þe blod þat cryst let for ma*n*kende
   W*ith* terys & wou*n*d*is* smerte,   204

Man, when thou
thinkest on the
blood Christ shed
for thee,

Ma*n* fynde þou no*n* vnkyndnesse

Qua*n* þe wey of suetnesse

[leaf 88, col. 2]   Wyl entry*n* i*n*-to þin herte ;   207

(35)

say, " Ah, Jesu,
why wert Thou
hurt for my sin ?   Sey, " a, ihe*s*u ! qu*a*t hast þou gylt ?

Qwy art þou for my syn spylt,

Flour of lowënesse ?   210

I am a thief,
and Thou payest   I am a thef, þou for me deyist,

I am gylty, & þou abeyst

For my wykydnesse ;   213

(36)

so great a ransom
for so vile a thing.
What benefit
hadst Thou by
this ?   So gret rau*n*som for so wyl thyng !

Qu*a*t hast þou wo*n*ne wi*th* þi peynyng,

þou hey i*n* blysce aboue ?   216

Thy great good-
ness alone made
Thee hang on the
cross for man's
soul.   Gret godnesse hat þe makyd

For to hangy*n* on rode nakyd

For ma*nnus* soulë loue !   219

(37)

Lord, I beseech
Thee,   But, lord ihe*s*u, I kan no more

But þe besekyn wi*th* al my myth,

make me weep
night and day
for Thy pains,   þat I motë wepyn sore   222

Thyn hardë peyn*us* day & nyth,

and that love for
Thee may be
stuck as fast in
my heart as the
spear was in
Thine when Thou
diedst for me."   And þat loue mote also faste

In-to my*n* hertë stykyd be,

As was þe spere i*n*-to þi*n* herte

Qu*a*n þou suffrydyst ded for me.   Amen.   226

The Fifty-First Psalm.

[*Additional MS.*, *No.* 10,036, *Brit. Mus.*, *leaf* 96, *bk.*[1]]

(Twenty 4-measure stanzas of 8, *abab abab*.)

(1)

MIserere mei deus, se*cundu*m magnam
  misericordiam tuam!

Mercy, god, of my mysdede!	Have mercy on me, O God!
For þi mercy þat mychel ys,	
Late þi pite sprynge & sprede,	
Off þi mercy þat I ne mys. 4	
Aftur gostliche g*r*ace I grede;	I cry for grace
Good god! þou g*r*aunt me þis,	
That I may lyue in loue & drede,	that I may sin no more.
And neu*er* eft*er* to do more amys. 8	

(2)

Et se*cundu*m multitudinem miseracionu*m*
tua*rum*, dele iniquitatem meam.

And aft*er* þi m*er*cies þat ben fele,	
Lord, fordo my wickydnesse.	Blot out my wickedness,
Ȝyue me g*r*ace to hyde & hele	
The blamë of my bruchelnesse. 12	
Ȝif any sterynge on me stele,	
Out of þe clos of þi clennesse	
Wysse me, lord, in wo & wele,	and guide me in wo and weal.
And kepë me fram vnkyndnesse. 16	

(3)

Amplius laua me ab iniquitate mea :
& a peccato meo munda me.

[1] There is another copy of this Poem in Harl. MS. 3810, Part I.

[leaf 97]
Wash me from
my sin.

More-ouer, wasche me of my synne,
     And of my gultës clanse þow me ;
And serche my soule with out & Inne,
     That I no more defowlid be.   20
And as þyn hert aclef atwynne
     With doleful deth on þe rodë tre,

Let me do no-
thing but what
pleases Thee.

Late me neuer no werke bigynne,
     Lord, but ȝif it lykë þee.   24

(4)

Qoniam iniquitatem meam ego cognosco :
& peccatum meum contra me est semper.

I acknowledge
my sin.

For al my wickidnesse I knowe,
     And my synne is euer me aȝeyn ;
Ther-fore late þi gracë growe,
     Ihesu, þat was with iewis sleyn.   28
Ryche & porë, hye & lowe,

Small and great
will be glad of
Thy mercy at
the day of judg-
ment.

     Smale & gret[ë], in certeyn,
Atte domesdaie, when þou schalt blowe,
     Of þi mercy schul be ful feyn.   32

(5)

Tibi soli peccaui, & malum coram te feci :
ut iustificeris in sermonibus tuis, &c.

Against Thee
only have I
sinned.

To þee only trespassed haue I,
     Wrouȝt wickidly aȝens þi glorie
With wordes & eke with trecherie.
     Thou demyst riȝt, & hast þe victórie ;   36

[leaf 97, back]

Ther-fore, þee biseche now I,—
     For tolde hit is in many story,—

Him that trusts
in Thy mercy,
Thou keepest ever
in mind.

That who so trusteþ to þi mercy,
     Is endëles in þi memórie.   40

(6)

Ecce enim in iniquitatibus conceptus sum :
& in peccatis concepit me mater mea.

I was conceived
in sin ;

Biholde, in synne I was conceyued
     Of my modre, as we ben alle :

Off my fadre I nouȝt conceyued
    But flesche ful frel, & fayn to falle.   44
And sithe þi flesche, lord, was furst perceyued,
    And for oure sake laide streiȝt in stalle,
Was neuer synful man deceyued,
    That to þi mercy woldë calle.   48

but since Thou wast laid in the stable,

no sinner ever cried in vain for mercy.

(7)

Ecce enim ueritatem dilexisti : incerta & occulta sapiencie tue manifestasti michi.

Lo! þou hast louyd ryȝt,
    And schewid me counceil of þi wyt,
How, þorw mercy & þorw myȝt,
    Two kyndës ben to-gidre knyt :   52
Thral ys fre, & knaue is knyȝt,
    And god is man, as gospel wryt ;
And ȝit my soule in perel be pyȝt,
    Mercyful god, help þou yt !   56

Thou hast showed me how two natures are knit together.

If my soul is in peril, God help it.

(8)

Asperges me ysopo, & mundabor : lauabis me, & super niuem dealbabor.

With holi water þou schalt me springe,
    And as þe snowe I schal bé whyt ;
And ȝif my soule in synnë stynke,
    With wepinge water I may it quyt.   60
Dedly drauȝtes al-þouȝ I drynke,
    Of répentaunce ȝyue me respit ;
For who-so on þi prowës þynke,
    In worldës welþe is no delit.   64

[leaf 98]

Sprinkle me, and I shall be white as snow.

He that thinks on Thy throes has no delight in worldly wealth.

(9)

Auditui meo gaudium & leticiam : et exultabunt ossa humiliata.

To myn heryng þou schalt ȝyue
    Gladnesse, to gladë bonës meke.
In lownesse lernë me to lyue,
    Leuë lord, I þee by-seke !   68

Cause me to hear gladness.

The thief was
forgiven on the
cross.

The þeuës gult, hit was forȝyue
On rodë wher his bonës breke.
A contryt hert, & clene yschryue,
Saueþ soule & body eke.   72

(10)

**Auerte faciem tuam a peccatis meis:
et omnes iniquitates meas dele.**

Turn Thy face
from my sins.

Fro my synnës turne þi face,
Do al my wickidnesse a-way!

[leaf 98, back]

Grete is my gult, gretter is þi[1] grace,
And ellis, faileþ al oure fay.   76

My faults face
me,

And fawtës fele þat me doþ face,
Makeþ þat I may noȝt say,

and make me cry
for mercy.

But crie mercy when I trespace;
I-wis I wote no better way.   80

(11)

**Cor mundum crea in me deus: & spiritum
rectum innoua in uisceribus meis.**

Make my heart
clean

God! make þou myn hert[ë] clene,
And a riȝtful spirit in me newe;
Fro seuene synnes þou make me schene,

that I may follow
Thee.

That where þou go, I may þee seewe.   84
Al þi turment and þi tene,
Thi bodi blacke, þi bonës blewe,—

May Thy grief
be seen in my
heart.

Now, graunt, cryst, þat it be sene
In myn hert, þat hidowes hewe.   88

(12)

**Ne proicias me a facie tua: & spiritum
sanctum tuum ne auferas a me.**

Cast me not away.

Cast me nouȝt fro þi visage,
Take noȝt fro me þine holigost!
To byholde þi faire ymage,
Of allë murþës hit is most.   92

A blessed bird
was born

A blisful bryd was born in cage,
Cowþe ykid in euery cost,

---

[1] my *alterd to* þi.

When he were drawe in tendre age,
To dryue adoun þe deueles bost.

96

[leaf 99]
to abate the
devil's boast.

(13)

REdde m*ich*i leticiam salutaris tui:
& sp*irit*u principali confirma me.

Of þine helþe ȝyue me þe blisse,
  And strengþe me w*ith* þi spirit cheef ;
And alle my fyuë wittes þou wisse,
  That I may lyue as þee is leef,

Give me the joy
of Thy salvation,

and guide my five
wits.

100

And þou maist my langor lysse,
  That brouȝtest man to gret boncheef ;
So late me neu*er* þi m*er*cy mysse,
  When I am gurt w*ith* gostly greef.

Let me never miss
Thy mercy when
I am smitten with
grief.

104

(14)

Docebo iniquos uias tuas:
& impij ad te co[n]uertent*ur*.

To þe wickid I schal þe[1] waies teche,
  The synneful schulle to þee co*n*uerte.
Synful man, be war of wreche,
  And þenke on crystës hede & herte !

I will teach the
wicked Thy ways.

Sinful man, think
in pity on Christ !

108

Brest & hert was bete to bleche,
  On barë bodi, w*ith*-outë sherte ;
To rewe on him I wol þee preche,
  But alas ! þ*er* wolde no teer oute sterte.

112

(15)

LIbera me de sang*uinib*us, deus meus salutis
mee : & exaltabit lingua mea iusticia*m* tua*m*.

Delyu*er*e me fram blameful[2] blode,
  My lord, god of myn[2] helþe ;
And my mouþe schal w*ith* myldë mode
  Apertely schewe þi sely selþe.

[leaf 99, back]
Deliver me from
blood, O Lord !

116

Thi riȝtful blode ran dou*n* on rode
  To waschen vs f*ram* oure fleschly felþe ;
Agayn many a storme þou stode
  To wyssen vs fro þe worldës welþe.

Thy blood ran
down to wash us
from our filth.

120

---

[1] *for* þi   [2] m, n, *altcrd.*

(16)

Domine, labia mea ape*r*ies:
& os meu*m* annunciabit laudem tuam.

Lord, my lippes þou schalt vndo,
     And my mouþe schal þi p*r*echinge[1] spelle ;
Thi m*er*cy & þi myȝt also,
     Soþfastly no tunge may telle ;   124
For when we dedly synnë do,
     Thi riȝt vs demeþ doun to helle ;

But when we ceesen & wol saie 'ho !'
     Thi m*er*cy is oure waschynge welle.   128

(17)

Quoniam si voluisses sac*r*ificiu*m* dissem
utiq*ue*: holocaustis non dilectaberis.

Ȝif sacrifice hadde ben offrynge,
     I hadde to þee ȝyuen w*ith* hert fre ;

But certeynly hit is none suche þinge,
     That, to þi, plesaunt may be.   132

Thi self was offrid a child ful ȝynge,
     And afterwarde on þe rodë tre
Oute of þin herte þat blode gan sprynge,

     And þ*er*-fore myn hert I offre to þee.   136

(18)

S*A*crificiu*m* deo sp*irit*us contribulat*us*:
cor cont*r*itu*m* & humiliatu*m*, d*eus*, no*n* despicies.

To god hit is a sacryfice,
     A synful spirit to sorwe sore ;
A meke hert [þou] schal noȝt despice,
     Whan répentaunce hit wol restore.   140

I haue for sleuþe [left] þi seruyce,
     And litel lyued aftur þi lore ;

But I repente, & wille now aryse ;
     Mercy, god ! I wolle no more.   144

[1] *for* preisinge

(19)

Benigne fac do*mi*ne in bona uolu*n*tate tua syon :
& edificent*ur* muri ier*u*s*a*lem.

> With benygne wil, do to syon,
>> That ier*u*s*a*lem walles were wrou3t.
> Ierusalem, as telleþ seynt Ion,
>> Is holy churche þat erreþ nou3t :
> Tho testamentis cordiþ in on.
>> The wallës were to-gidre brou3t,
> When cryst hym self was corne*r* ston,
>> That ma*n*nës synne haþ dere ybou3t.

Do good to Zion, and build Thou the walls of Jerusalem.

148   Jerusalem is holy Church ;

Christ, the corner-stone.

152

(20)

Tunc acceptabis sacrificiu*m* iusticie
oblaciones & holocausta : tunc im-
ponent sup*er* altare tuu*m* [vitulos][1] do*mi*ne.

[leaf 100, back]

> Than schalt þou sacrifice accepte
>> Of ri3twisnesse & treuþe entere ;
> And caluës, aftur þi precepte,
>> Schulle be leide on þine autere ;
> On caluarie a calf þer crepte.
>> Cryst on crosse, boþe clene & clere !
> For þo teeris þat þi modre wepte,
>> Thow schelde [us] fro þe fendes fere ! Amen !

Then shalt Thou accept sacrifice ;

calves shall be laid on Thine altar.

156

For Thy mother's tears, shield us from the fiend !

160

[*In a later hand :*]
now, lord, be thou our helpe & guide,
and pardon things that cause vs slide !

----

[1] vitulos *omitted.*

Verse Prolog and Epilog to a Book on Medicine.

Verses written as a Preface to an English Treatise on Medicine.
(From Dr. J. F. Payne's vellum MS. of the first half of the
15th century.)

The man þat wol of lechecraft lere,
Red ovyr this book, and he may here
Many medycinis both¹ good and trewe²
To helë³ sores both oolde and newe,   4
⁴And preciouse medycinis, þorw goddis *grace*,
To save men lyves in diverse place.
Cryst, þat made bothe Est and West,
Geve grace her sowlës have god rest,   8
Eve*re* more in hevene for to be,
In hevene wyt þᵉ Trinite.
    Her-inne be medycinis, wythout-yn fable,
To hele alle sores þat ben curáble,   12
Of swerd, of knyf, and of arwe,—
Be þe wounde wyde or narwe,—
Of sper, of quarel, of dagger, of⁵ dart,
To make him hool in ylkë⁶ part,   16
So⁷ þe seek wol do wysely,
And kepe him-self fro surfety.⁸
Be þe wounde neve*re* so deep,
þer-of dar⁹ him take no kep,   20

This book contains medicines to heal sores and save men's lives:

all kinds of sores made by knife,

spear or dart,

so that you keep rom surfeiting.

(S. is Sloane 1314; Sl. is Sloane 2584, of the same type as P.
¹ Many a medicyn S. Sl.   ² trewe S. Sl., newe P.
³ To alle S., To leche Sl.   ⁴ S. and Sl. leave out lines 5-10.
⁵ of dagger of PS., or . . . or Sl.   ⁶ in ilka S., on eche Sl.
⁷ ȝyf S., So þat Sl.   ⁸ from queysy S., fro serfetrie Sl.
⁹ thar S., þar hem (*om.* no kepe) Sl.

So þat he drynke save[1] or anteoche,   Drink sage,
Him dar not drede of þat outrage :[2]
Be þat on and twenti days be goon,[3]   and in 21 days
He schal be hol, both[4] flesch and bon, 24   you'll be well.
To ride and go in ylk[o]n[5] place,
Thorw þe verteu[6] of goddys grace ;
Thus seyth Ypocras, þe good surgien,   Hippocras and
And socrates and Galyen,   28   Galen say so,
þat weren[7] philisophres alle thre,
þat tyme þe best[8] in any countree :
In þis we[r]ld were non her pere,
As fer as any man coude[9] here.   32

[*Sloane* 1314 *adds :*]

þei[10] practised medicynus, wit[11] godus grace,   who practist me-
To saue men lyues[12] in many a[13] place.   dicine to save
Crist þat made bothe est and west,   men's lives.
Grant her soules in heuen,[14] good rest,   36
Euermore in ioy to be
In heuen with god in trinite.[15]
Amen ![16] Amen ! for charite.   39

(The verses in the Payne MS. are written in double
columns, and the order of the first eight verses is a
little confused; so I have corrected it.)

The above agrees very nearly with a poem printed
by the Rev. G. Henslow, in his *Medical Works of the
14th Century*, p. 125 (1899), from Sloane MS. 2584 ;
with variants from Sloane MS. 1314.

[1] ȝyf he drynk antioche or saue S., So þat þei drynke saue or
antioche Sl., So . . save or anteocke P.
[2] Hem . . of non outrage Sl., & Drede of hys wondes thar hym
non haue S.
[3] Be on & twenti dayes gone S., Be . . be comyn and goon P.,
Be þat .21. daies be come & gon Sl.
[4] both *om.* S., boþe Sl.   [5] ilka S., eche Sl.
[6] myht S., myȝht Sl.   [7] wore Sl.
[8] þe best þat were S., þe best Sl.
[9] Als wyde as men myht here S., As fer . . myght Sl.
[10] And Sl.   [11] be Sl.   [12] mannes lyf Sl.   [13] in dyuers Sl.
[14] Leue here soules haue Sl.   [15] In . . . trinite Sl., *om.* P.
[16] Amen P., *om.* Sl.

At the end are the following verses, which I have not seen elsewhere :—

This book hat Ypocras,
Oon of þe beest surgien þat evere was ;
And Galien his felaw, and Socrates,
To þis book þ[e]i beren witnesse,
Ffor alle þei were felawes & fere
Whil þei leveden in erde here ;
And þorw þe grace of hevene kyng,
þei practiseden medicines to helpe manky[n]d.
Prey we alle to ihesu, hevene kyng,
þat [he] gif her sowles god wonnyng.

These verses are at the end of the same treatise (fol. 20* or page 40), which appears to be quite complete. It refers to "the good Earl of Hereford, that was a noble surgeon"; and I think must have been composed in the 14th century.—J. F. Payne.

The Prentise unto woe,

By Henry Baradoun, ab. 1483.

Hodson MS. 39, leaf 4 ; 2nd flyleaf. (Mr. Hodson's 3rd MS. of Chaucer's Canterbury Tales.) [1]

(1)

Musyng' alone, voide of consolacion),	[leaf 4]
Drownèd in sorowe, sigħyng wondre sore,	Sad, my time
I may complayn), *with* deedly lamentacion),	
My tyme eviłł spent / sith first I was bore ; 4	ill-spent,
My yongë yeres, in Courte I haue forlore ;	my youth lost at Court,
3hit, not-*with*stondyng' howe I haue so do,	
Vnto more peyne then) I was into-fore,	I am a prentice
I haue me yoked, as prentice vnto woo. 8	unto woe.

(2)

¶ For[2] liber̄te is laide alone apart ;	I have lost liberty
My wiłł also, hath no dominacion) ;	
And as for easë, that most nedis depart ;	and ease.
A greuous payn), in myn) oppinïon) : 12	
labour & trouble hath predominacion)	
Of my spiritis, wher-eue*r* I ride or go :	
hertis ease & I be not at vnion) :	
Thus am I yoked / a prentise vnto wo. 16	

(3)

¶ In the courte, is many noble Roome ;	At Court,
But god knowith, I can) noon) sochë cacche :	
ffrom a maister, I am) be-come a grome,	I fell from master to groom,
And bonde mysiłff' to waytyng' & to wacche ; 20	
With euere gadrin), I stonde behynde the hacche,	
Gapyng & staryng' / wanderyng' to & fro ;	
3hit for ałł this, no good can) I cacche :	and could get no place.
Thus am I prentice & ser̄uaunt vnto woo. 24	

---

[1] Mr. Hodson's Librarian, Miss Constance Belliss, kindly copied the poem for me, and read the proof with the MS.

[2] MS. As for.

(4)

I can't eat,
¶ Whenɒ I wolde ete, nature for to sustaynɒ,
   Or I may haue it / myn appetite is past;
sleep,
When) I wolde slepë, to releve my paynɒ,
   I do but slumbre / for I most rise in hast;   28
speak,
When) I wolde speke / my lippes be closedᵗ fast;
or sport.
      When) I wolde sporte *with* company also,
   I dare not out / I am so sore agast:
      Thus am) I prentice to wrecchidnes & wo.   32

(5)

I can't pray,
¶ Whan I wolde pray, & se*r*ue my heuynly kyngᵗ,
   (As eu*er*y creature is bounde of verrey right,)
Anon) ther is some obstacle or thyngᵗ
      That pullyth me thens, magre of my migͪt;   36
   Soche is my liffᵗ, by day and eke by nygͪt;
or know friend
from foe.
[leaf 4, back]
      And be-side this, my frende weH fro my ffo
   I can) not knowe / this I, most wreccheᵈ wigͪt,
      haue bounde me prentice to misery and wo.   40

(6)

Happy is he who
lives on little at
home,
¶ WeH is he, that can) holde hym) content
      With a meane lifë, voide of gredynes,
Out of trouble leuyngᵗ, *with* litle rent,
      beyngᵗ at home in p*er*fite stedfastnes,   44
   Wher pompe nor envy is countedᵗ for mastres.
      Soche a life, not I, but othir moo
and does not
bind himself a
prentice unto
woe.
Mygͪt haue fuH wele; but ȝhit folissͪ wilfulnes
      Doth bynde ffolkys p*r*entise to wrecchidnes and wo.

      Baradoun) henricus t*r*aistulit istud opus þe*r*
            sem*et* ip*s*um.

Hymn to the Virgin.

By WILLIAM HUCHEN.

[MS. no. cccxx. in the Library of New College, Oxford.]

THE MS., written about 1460, contains the Psalter in the later Wyclif version (Purvey), and prose translations of various canticles. The hymn, which is on the last page, appears to be in the same handwriting as the rest. Each of the seven stanzas (in "rime royal") is an acrostic on the name *Stanlei*. The person meant may possibly be Sir Thomas Stanley, who was created Baron Stanley in 1456, and died in 1459.—HENRY BRADLEY.

(1)

Swete and benygne moder *and* may,   1 Sweet maiden,
   Turtill trew, flowre of women alle,
Aurora bryght, clere as the day,
   Noblest of hewe, þus we the calle ;
   Lyle fragrant eke of the walle ;   5 fragrant lily,
Ennewid wiþ bemys of blys,
In whom neuer was founden mys.   7

(2)

So fayre, so good, was neuer non ;   8
   Transcendyng is ther-for þi place   thy place is above angels,
Aungels alle and seyntis echone ;
   Next vnto god, such is þi grace.   next to God.
   Lo, þi mekenes þe did purchace   12
Euer in ioy so to endure
In þi grete lande [*sic*], o princes pure.

(3)

Surmountyng is þin excellence,   15 Thou excellest all,
   Thou rose of prys, thou flowre of may ;
And phebus lyke in his ascence,
   Natyff of blys where þou art ay,
   Lady saunzpere, þis is no nay.   19
Empres of helle also of righte,   and art Empress of Hell.
In þe is eke owre anker pight   21 We anchor on thee

(4)

against storms
of sin.

Stormys ageyne of cruell syn   22
    That puyssauntlye us do assayle;
And while we þis world be yn
    Now, lady fayre, þou us not fayle.
    Lat neuer vice on us prevayle.   26

Entreat thy Babe
for us!

Entrete þi babe, so, quene on hie,
In whom to þe is no denye.   28

(5)

Siþ here is nought but myserie;   29

Tho the Fiend,
Flesh and World
assault us,

    The fende, þe fleish, þe world also,
Assaute us ay wiþ-oute mercy.
    Not comfortles ȝit is owre wo;
    Lady, to þe resorte we do,   33
Euyr tristyng thi grace and ayde,

we trust thee.

In whom fully owre trist is layde.   35

(6)

Sewte and servise we owe, parde,   36
    To þi hiȝnesse of very due,
As royall most by pedigre,
    None lyke of grace ne of vertu,

Lovely lady,

    Louely lady, þi servauntes trew,   40
Entrikid wiþ passiouns wylde,

shield us in
our need!

In tyme of nede socour and shilde.   42

(7)

Saue hem fro syn *and* worldly shame   43
    That þe worship with humble herte,

Jesus, grant us

And to þi son, iesus by name,
    Not sete (*sic*) to pray that we not smert.
    Lord, þi iugement we may not sterte;   47

thy grace,
in honour of
thy Mother!

Euere þerfor thi grace us hight,
In worship of þi modere bright.   49

By William Huchen.

Peare of Provence and the fair Maguelone.

[*Lord Clifden of Lanhydrock, Cornwall, has two leaves, and two narrow strips of two other leaves, of a 15th-century paper MS. of the englisht Romance of 'Pierre de Provence.' He let Mr. W. H. Allnutt of the Bodleian copy them, and hand his copy to me to be printed. I have completed the story from the enlarged black-letter version as reproduced by A. V. in the Paris edition of 1845, but have left out several incidents for which there cannot have been room in the short English text, of which I hope a complete copy will turn up some day.*]

[This story was written in the year 1453, in honour of God, the Virgin Mary, and the Hospital of St. Peter of Maguelone, of which the knight Peare and the fair Maguelone were the first founders. Peare was the only child of the Count John of Cerise, of Provence, and his wife, the daughter of Count Alvaro of Albara. Peare was gentle and amiable, valiant, handsome and wise, and was loved by all the folk of his country.

[One day a tournament was held in Provence, at which Peare overcame all the other valiant knights, and won the prize. During talk in the court afterwards, much was said of the beauty of Maguelone, the daughter of the King of Naples, and how knights went there to tilt for the love of her. One of the knights present told Peare that he ought to go out into the world, and win this beauty's love. So he resolvd to do it, if his father and mother would give him leave to go. They, however, refused it when he askt them, as he was heir to their kingdom, and their only comfort. But at last they yielded to his entreaties, and he set off for Naples with a small and well-appointed train, plenty of money, and three valuable rings which his mother gave him. Reaching Naples safely, he hears that the king honours a late-come knight, Henry of Crapana, and has fixt Sunday next for a tournament. Wanting to see the fair Maguelone, Peare appears on the field, well armd and horst, bearing two silver Keys as his badge, in honour of St. Peter. Henry of Crapana tilts first, and unhorses his opponent, but the latter's lance falls between the legs of Crapana's horse, and brings him to the ground, so that the knight's friends claim that Crapana was upset, which angers him, and he refuses to tilt again. Peare then tilts with Crapana's opponent, and bears both rider and horse to the ground. The King, struck by Peare's prowess, sends to ask his name and country; but Peare will not tell them; says he is only a poor French knight, travelling to see fair ladies and girls, and win honour and praise. Maguelone thinks the unknown knight handsome, and gets her father to hold other jousts, that she may see the valiant deeds of this Knight of the Keys. The King then asks him (Peare) to dinner at [the Palace, and seats him before Maguelone, whose beauty, grace and sweetness inflame him with love for her; and she is as much in love with him. After dinner she speaks to him, accepts his offer to become her knight, and says she wants to talk with him in secret. She leaves the hall with her mother, and the King then asks Peare who he is, but can get nothing from him but that he is a poor French knight seeking adventures.

[Peare, when alone, can think of nothing but Maguelone, and she of nothing but him. She begs her nurse † to find out who and what he is; and on the nurse scolding her, she declares it'll be her death, and swoons. So the nurse finds out Peare in a chapel, and asks him of what parentage he is, that she may tell Maguelone. He will say no more than that he is of noble stock; and he gives the nurse one of his mother's valuable rings for Maguelone. With this, Maguelone is greatly delighted, and, when asleep, dreams that Peare will soon tell her who he is, and give her another ring. So the nurse meets him again, and tells him how her lady loves him. He promises to reveal to Maguelone, if she will meet him alone, his rank and country; and he then sends her a second ring.[1] Maguelone gladly agrees to meet Peare; and the nurse bids him to come to the girl's garden gate, and up to her room. This he does, and, after pledging her to secrecy, tells her that he is the son of the Count of Provence and nephew of the King of France, and that he has come to Naples solely for love of her. She confesses that she loves him and will marry him, and she puts her gold chain and locket round his neck, in token that she gives him possession of her body.]

keyis & [B iij?]	cioꝺ breke
armys	e knyght
iħu sen	oste ho
y shalle	were as
wᵗ you d	ht I woldᵉ
tented	thanke
norise † to	ne finally
did hir'	hathe
the norise	ke of
was bro	awe but
sat in R	court I
pleasa[nt]	that I
of the k	[S]ee y beseke
ryalle	a madame
verily th	t more þeꝺ
gladdist	s & in this
saw no	s symple
to breke p	me & gave
vpoꝺ h	modir did
preserve	he ioy in
cam to h	partid & cō
Sir ye b	[c]ontenvally
thime to a	nbir' theꝺ
in ffraun[ce]	said cartes
was born	thingᵗ &
as welle	ore to me
of youre	said the
tyme to v	þat ye shulde
nesse pl	in maꝺ he
en she [B iij, bk. ?] & god forbed	

when the knyhtt had thus muche his entent, he was fulle of ioy, that it was Inpossible forᵉ any man to deserue; & fulle gladly he thankid hir', & said: "in as gret confidence as ye haue put me in,

---

[1] This gift is in the MS. too   see below.

mabeale, certayne y put you in the same; & here is a nodir' Ryng'
whiche my modir' gave me; & th̄ꞇ y geve you, and alle my body,
w*ith* trew entent; & neue*r* tille I die, to ffaile you." & oꞃ this he
kissed hir', & toke his leve, & depa*r*tid as that tyme, for thei durst
no leng*er* talke. & when he was depa*r*tid, the lady loked vpon hir'
rynges, & she thought muche ioy ꞇn the knyhtt & of his demeanyng; & she thought longe that thei were a sundre; & he on his side
thoughtt as longe; & dyue*r*s tymes he cam vꞃ-to hir'; & in conclusion,[1] he toke hir' the iij^d Ryng, & axid 'in what man*er* thei shuld be
maryed.' & she answerde & said, she wist neu*er*; & said, "we can
neu*er* mary here, for' my fadir." then said the knyht: "dare ye putt
me in suche confid'ence, to depart w*ith* me in to my count*r*ay ?" &
she said, "if ye wille swere vnto me neu*er* to offir' me dishoneste,
but kepe me a virgyne, & youre true loue*r*', tille ye mary, I assent to
depa*r*t when ye wille." then said the knyht, & made a large othe,
that he wold so deale; & seid 'he wold ordayne that thei shuld depart in that man*er*, & that hir' fadir' shuld not know no thing of hit.
[" And on the third day hence, after your first night-sleep (*somme de
nuit*), I will be ready with my horses at the little gate of]
youre gardyne."

[c.?] at the owre appoyntid he cam thiddir', & she was there redy,
& brought hir' to horse: & oꞃ horse he had chargid w*ith* vetaile, &
anodir' horse that they bothe rood vpoꞃ.[2] & they depa*r*tid & rood
in ther iurnay; but he kept no[t] his way, but costid oue*r* the contray,
ffor persueing. & they rood the first nyght & the first day & alle
the secund nyght or thei did lihtt. & in a wood nere the see sid
thei arived, & did alihtt, & toke suche vetailes as thei had, &
refreshid them silf.

now we leve the knyht & the lady in the wood, & lett v*us* telle
how she was wantid in hir' fadirs courte.

at the owre that the norise was wont to c*um* vn-to hir' to make
hir' redy, she caꞃ & vnded the dore, & she found þe bed stille made,
& no body in hit. & when she saw that, she was a carefulle creature; & she went vꞃ-to Queenis loggyng', & axid if she [Maguelone]
came there; and the queene said "nay." "alas," said the norise,
"y cam to the chambir' to do my dute, & y founde the bedd makid,
& no body therin." then said the Queene, "alas! for woo my hert

---

[1] B iiij ?
[2] The print makes Peare bring three horses: an English hackney, a good
goer, for Maguelone, his charger for himself, and a sumpter horse laden with
bread, wine, and other food, so that the fugitives should be independent of inns.

brekithe." & she wrange hirʲ handes, & tered hirʲ herre; & anon) the kyng had word; & he callid the norise to examyn) hirʲ; & she excused hirʲ as welle as she kowd. the king sware she shuld be brent, but she cowd excuse hirʲ bettirʲ. the kyng a-none axid aftirʲ the knyhtt of the

[keys; & when he could not be found, the king bade his folk arm & search, & bring him the knight alive, to be so punisht that all the world would talk of it. The queen wept; the nurse vowd she knew nothing about the elopement; the king fasted the first day; every one sympathised. After a fortnight's search the knights found nothing. Let us turn to Peare and Maguelone.

nott there
& su) wᵗ xx
kyngᵗ was
& muche w
toke for the
& the que[ene]
how the k
woode whe
theʳ laboure
& she beg
gret serch
said no fo
shalle no
& she lay
soundly &
hiʳ necke
papps* &
he was
& betwix
of red ve[lvet]
& ther w
he gave
welle &
& she be [back]
lie into the see
fer she did a
the ther & flee
okid whiche
tt agayne þᵉ
epe & at the last

[After their meal, Peare and Maguelone talkt a long while, and then she, tired with riding all night, laid her head in Peare's lap and went to sleep. He feasted his heart with looking on her wondrous beauty, her pleasing face, her sweet little red mouth. Then he undid her dress, and gazed at her beautiful bosom, white as crystal, toucht her breasts,* and was quite ravisht with love, so that he seemd to be in paradise. On her bosom was a red sarcenet (*sendal*) packet; and on unfolding it, Peare found that it containd his mother's three rings which he had given to Maguelone. He folded them up again, laid the packet on a stone close to him, and turnd once more to contemplate the fair-breasted girl before him. While he was absorbd in this sight, a bird of prey pounst on the red sarcenet packet, which it thought a bit of flesh, and flew off with it.

[Peare at once put his cloak under Maguelone's head, and went after the bird. It settled on a little rock near the shore, but flew away when Peare threw a stone at it, and dropt its red packet into the sea. Peare couldn't swim; and thinking the packet might be on the rock, he got into a little old fishing boat, and tried to scull to the rock. But the wind rose and carried him out to sea. In despair about Maguelone and himself, he thought of suicide, but prayd to the Virgin instead; and about mid-day, some Moorish corsairs took him into their ship, saild off with him to Alexandria, and gave him to the Sultan. The Sultan was greatly pleasd with Peare, and treated him like a son. In a year he learnt Moorish and Greek, and was so amiable that all the folk lovd him as a brother; but he

syd & he toke
bote & wᵗ the
hen) he cam)
bote as wele
londe & there
et wynde foo
the scee
ethe see the
do thus his
ic that y was
at y shuld
virgyne
lle devoure hir'
eve so longe
pest was
scee the watʳ
ld & the knyht
tir' owt of the
owne alle
id the sonn)
rgine whiche
n the wid
arwele my
die & thouht
not see his
[fresh leaf]

[always sorrowd for Maguelone, and was a good catholic. We'll now leave Peare.

[When Maguelone had slept her fill, she woke, expecting her head to be still in Peare's lap. But no Peare could she see. She cald him ; no answer came. She wept, and ran about the wood crying for Peare till she swoond and fell. When she recoverd, she lamented her hard fate, and climbd a tree, but could see no Peare, only the sea. All day she ate nothing. At night she slept in a tree, for fear of wild beasts, and resolvd not to go home to her father. Next morning she found Peare's horses and loost them, and then hid on the road through the wood to Rome. Hiding herself, she saw folk going and coming, and among them a pilgrimess, whom she persuaded to change clothes with her. In pilgrim's garb she reacht Rome, went at once to St. Peter's, and prayd before the great altar for her lover's safety, and her ultimate marriage with him. On rising she saw her uncle, her mother's brother, with a large train, seeking her ; but no one recognised her. For a fortnight she prayd daily, and then thought she'd go to Peare's country, Provence.

[So she journeyd to Genoa, and there found a bark, which soon took her to Provence (*en aigues mortes*);

& the [lady (Maguelone), after that she came to land, went] vn)-to the duke*s* place,[1] & ther' [in the hospital, was put where a pilgrim] or a pore body shuld be, & logid ther that nyhtt. & on) the morowe she spake vn)-to the hospetlere, & prayd that she myht be hir' servaunt, " ffor y am wery of the world." & the hospetlere was glad of hir', & said "yf youre demeanyng be good, ye may conteuve here longe ; & ffulle welle ye shalle be cherisid ; for the duke & the ducheis, & alle the estates of this countery, han great deuocion) vnto this place." then) said the lady : " hathe the duke eny sonn alyve ? " & she answerd & said, " he hathe as noble a knyht vnto his sonn), as eny is in cristendame. & his ffadir' & modir' taken) great thouht for hime : he departid to seek aventure, but they neue*r* kowd here no tydyng*es* yett of hime ;" & more com*m*vnynge thei had ; & she contenvd

---

[1] The French text makes a pilgrimess kind to Maguelone, who then builds a small hospital at a Saracen port near there, and nurses the sick.

servaunt in this hospitale.   and in litle tyme the maistres hospetlere
died, & then the lady was made hospetlere ; & she contenvid ffulle
welle & vertuously in this hospitale, so muche that the people said
that she was su*m* seint ; & she was called " the holy hospetlere ; "
& alle countery came thiddir'.   & the duke dyu*er*s tymes examened
hir', of what place she had be*n* before, & wher she was borne.   &
she answerd & said, " y am) a napolitane borne, a pore mans child ;
& my ffadir' was nott able to fynde me ; & I went & wandred in the
world to aske my leuyng', ffor godd*es* loue ; & to this place y haue
deuocion ; & here y purpose to make my*n* end, in the seruyce of
god."   & then the duke said " hurd ye neu*er* of a knyhtt callid
' pearr' de pr*o*vence ' in any part þat ye haue travelid in ? "   & she
said, " y hurd of no*n* suche."   & the*n* hire hert was allmost to-brast
w*ith* that wurd.   & she thouht how that was his fadir' ; & thouht,
if eu*er* she shuld here of hime, it shuld be there.   then the duke
departid ; & she contenvid ther stille, & was very diligent vnto pore
traveling people, alway [nursing them and serving God].

[One day it happend that some fishermen of Provence caught a
bass or seawolf (*leu*) ; and as it was such a fine one, they gave it to
the Count and Countess.   On cutting it open in the kitchen, the
cook found a ball of red sarcenet in its belly.   This was taken to the
Countess, who undid it, and discoverd her three rings inside.   She
burst out weeping, as she thought her son had been drownd and
eaten by fishes.   The Count comforts her, and orders all the Court
to be hung in black.   Soon after the Countess visits Maguelone in
her hospital, shows her the rings, and they weep together.   Now let
us turn to Peare.

[In the Sultan's court, Peare grows in favour with him and his
lords, so that he treats Peare as a son.   After three years in the
Sultan's service, Peare longs for home, and asks the Sultan to grant
him a boon.   The Sultan at once promises to do so ; and Peare asks
leave to go and see his father and mother, relations and friends,
" for all these years that I have dwelt with you I have been] In ign-
[orance how they fare.   To you have I given all my care] and
my deligence, and now y wuld beseket you that y may goo see
my ffrendis in my cou*n*trey ; & y shalle cu*m* agayne in alle the
hast vnto you."   and in as muche as he [the Sowdan] had
grauntid hime his bene, he kowd nott say hime nay, butt gave
hime leve ; & for his .iij. yeris service he gave hime .iij. barelles
ffulle of gold, & said, " go & cu*m* agayne, & ye shalle haue a bettir'
reward," & gave hime wrytyng' w*ith* hime to the ports wher he
shuld take shipp, & comaundid the*m* to get hime a shippe, & to
passe w*ith* hime into his contray, & that they shuld bry*ng*' hime

agayne in the same shipp. & [when] the maistirs of the toune sawe
this wrytyng⸍, they obeyd hitt, & shortly they ordayned hime a shipp
& men). & when) they were redy, & the wynd was fayer, thei callid
eu*er* abord. & the knyhtt spake vn)to the maistir of the shipp, &
said, "y haue .iij. barellis w*it*ʜ saltt[1] of this cu*n*t*r*ay, & y purpose to
geve hit vn)to an) hospitale, & lett it be brouhtt aborde the shipp."
& incontenent itt[2] was brouhtt in-to the shipp, & they sailed forthe
Into the Sea toward his countery the space of xiiij daies. & then
the wynde contraryd ther curse, & vndir⸍ a vagant ylond they came
to an anker, & stoppd there a litle while tylle the wynd amendid.
& as they lay at an anker⸍, ther wer dyu*er*s w*it*ʜin bord that desirid
to go a-lond to take su*m* byrd*is*. & when) they cam to the lond ther
were many birdis ; & wythe ther handis thei toke them ; they were
in suche a vagaunt ylond, that ther⸍ birdis knew nott man, & thus
thei chasid the byrdis. butt the knyhtt wentt alone be hime sis-
silf⸍, & he souhtt a feyer⸍ plott to slepe on) ; & he founde a plott
ffulle of floures ; & in the middis of the floures ther was a floure that
exedid alle the odyr floures in swete sauoure & in beaute. & then)
he thouhtt vpon) the feyer lady & vpon) Arestotles p*r*overbe, & said
in this wise : " Sicut Rosa int*er* spinas, Sic amica int*er* filias."

["As this flower surpasses all others, so does Maguelone excel in
beauty all other ladies." Then he wept and slept. While he lay
asleep, a favourable wind sprang up ; and as the mariners couldn't
find him, they set sail, reacht the Saracen port, gave the barrels of
salt to Maguelone's hospital, and begd her to pray for the left-behind
Peare. One day she wanted some salt, but found gold when she
opend a barrel. With the three barrels of gold she built a fine new
hospital and church ; and when the Count and Countess of Provence
came to perform their devotions there, she comforted them, and said
they must not doubt that God would restore them their son. Now
let us turn to Peare who was left asleep on the Island.

[When Peare awoke, and found his ship gone, he wept, lamented
his hard fate, and prayd for death. But some fishermen who had
landed for fresh water found him, took him on board their ship, and
carried him to the town of Trepona, where they put him in the
hospital. There he stayd nine months, able to walk about the town,
but ill of grief. One day he found a ship and sailors from Provence,
and agreed to go with them to the Saracen port. The men talkt of
Maguelone's Church of St. Peter and her hospital, and advised Peare
to go there and be cured. He made a silent vow that he would, but
would keep himself unknown for a month. In due course he was
landed, and went to the hospital as a poor sick man. Maguelone,

---

[1] quatoze barilz de sel, D 6, 1516. quatorze petits barils de sel, p. 40, ed.
1714. [2] MS. itt hit

not knowing him, or he her, washt his feet and hands, and kist them, (as was her custom with all patients,) gave him clean sheets, and said she'd help him to get well. Under her care he quickly mends, but sighs for his Maguelone. She, hearing his sighs, asks him what troubles him, and he tells her his whole story, but says only that he was the son of a rich man. Maguelone then recognizes him, and weeps for joy, but tells him to pray to God and the Virgin, who, having savd him from so many dangers, will assuredly give him back the lady whom he has so loyally lovd. She kneels before St. Peter's altar, and thanks him for restoring her her lover. She has royal robes made for her, and put in her room. Thither she brings Peare; and having put on her robes in a private chamber, and coverd them and herself with her nun's garments, showing only her eyes and part of her nose, she tells Peare she is his love, throws off her nun's dress, and lets her fair hair fall to the ground.

Peare jumps up; and they hug and kiss one another, and weep for joy. Then they sit down, hear each other's mishaps, and chat and kiss till night comes, when they go to bed in separate rooms. Neither can sleep. Next morning Maguelone, in her nun's dress, visits Peare, and then goes to the Count and Countess of Provence, and tells them she has had a vision of St. Peter bringing her their son. She begs them to have all the black hangings removed from the Court, and to come to her church next Sunday. They come accordingly; and after mass, Maguelone takes them to her room, where Peare at once recognizes and kneels to them. They and all their train are fild with joy. Maguelone, having retired, reappears in her royal robes. They wonder who the beautiful lady is; but Peare kisses her and tells them. They embrace her and thank God.

The news of Peare's coming soon spreads, and all the folk of Provence flock to see him. The knights hold jousts and tournaments in his honour; the commons have dances and games. Peare weds Maguelone with a rich ring that his mother gives him; grand festivities go on for twenty-two days. After the marriage, the Count and Countess live in great content for ten years; then die, and are buried by Peare with full honours in St. Peter's church. Peare and Maguelone live eight years, and have a fine boy who is afterwards King of Naples and Count of Provence. They live a holy and honourable life, die holy folk, and are buried in St. Peter's. May the Trinity, St. Peter and St. Paul comfort us in our afflictions here, and may God make us possess Paradise hereafter!

SKETCH OF

THE UNIQUE INEDITED ROMANCE OF

Amoryus & Cleopes,

BY JOHN METHAM OF NORWICH, SCHOLAR OF CAMBRIDGE.

A.D. 1448-9.

[*Quaritch MS.*]

1 Thys ys *the* story off a knyght, howe he dyd
many wurthy dedys be *the* help off a lady,
the qwyche taught hym to ouercome a
meruulus dragon, *the* qwyche was a C
ffote longe. And *th*is knyght was clepyd
Amoryus, & *the* lady, Cleopes.

(1)

The chaunȝ of loue, and eke *the* peyn of Amoryus
the knyg[h]t   1

For Cleopes sake, and eke how bothe in ffere

Louyd, and aftyr deyd, my purpos ys to endyght;

And now, O Goddés, I *thee* beseche off kunnyng, *that*
Lauysyca hyght;   4

Help me to adorune *the*r chauns in sqwyche mane*r*e,

So *that*, qwere *th*is matere dotht yt reqwyre,

Bothe *the*r louys I may compleyne, to loue*r*ys dysyre.

I'm to tell you the sad story of Amoryus and Cleopes.

Minerva,

aid me!

(2)

In May, *tha*t modyr ys off monthys glade,   8

Qwan fflourys sprede, *the* qwyche, wi*th*-in *the* rote,

In wyntyr were clos, *that* *th*an wi*th* ffloure & blade

For Phebus exaltyng, wi*th* sundry hwys smellyd sote,

And byrdys, amonge *the* leuys grene, her myrthys made;

Qwan Nero, Asy gan to subdwe[2] to *the* empyre,

And besegyd *the* emperoure off Perse, kyng Camsyre.

In May, the glad month,

Nero besiegd Camsyr, the emperor of Persia.

(3)

For qwan *th*is Romaynys gan to subdw   15

The regyon off Persë and off Medys,

Camsyr, kyng off *that* cuntre, hys pepyl to rescwe,

[1] Sir Miles Stapleton, Knight, married Catherine, daughter of
Sir Thos. Poole, and died 1 Oct. 1466. Bloomfield gives his
coat-of-arms: Stapleton impaling Delapole, *azure*, on a fess
between 3 leopards faces, *or*, a mullet *sable*, *or*, a lion salient,
gules.   [2] MS. suldwe.

Camsyr fought
the Romans at
Pansophiris
and was kild.

A3ens *th*is emper*o*ur*e*, *in th*e pleyn off Pansophyr*ys*

Toke batel ; qwer*e* he was smit to deth at o*n*ys   19

W*ith th*e ston off an engyne, & hys pepyl put to
flyght :

[leaf 16, back]

Th*us th*ise Romayn*ys* became *ther* lordys w*ith* ffors
off fyght.   21

(4)

All Persia yielded
to them.

And, ffor ffere, *th*e lordys off *that* regyon   22

3eldyn *th*e keys to *th*e emp*er*our off *th*is fforsayd cyté,

Yeuyng hym omage and possessyon

Off alle *th*is forseyd regyon off P*e*rsé,

Besechyng hym, vndyr trybute for to be ;   26

And *ther*vppon, *ther* othe *th*ei toke,

Sweryng vpon *th*e tempyl-boke.   28

(5)

But, ffor *that th*is cu*n*tre was gret & popul*us*,   29

And ffeyth in thraldam ys selde seyn,

Nero and his
Council

Be sad auysement *th*e emp*er*our wrought ryght *thus* :

He co*m*mau*n*dyd to a counsel, in certeyn,

Alle erlys & barouns *that* to *ther* oste dyd p*er*teyn ;

In qwyche counsel, ffor surenes to reule *th*e cu*n*tre,

left 2 lords
(Palemedon
and Dydus) as
Governors, who,

They p*r*omotyd too lordys to be resyde*n*t i*n th*e
chef cyte.   35

(6)

THe qwyche lordys we*r*e Romaynys born,   36

That afftyr, for prudent port & goue*r*nauns,

Were crounyd kyngys off *th*e remys namyd be-fforn ;

And so *th*is emp*er*our, w*ith* vyctory*us* chauns

Returnyd to Rome w*ith* hys oste & pysauns,   40

after the Romans
left,
dwelt in Albanest,

Thyse p*r*incys dwellyng in pes & rest

In *th*e cheff cyte off Persys, namyd Albanest,   42

(7)

married,

Qwer*e th*ei despousyd wyuys off *th*e lynage   43

Of Dary*us*, su*m*tyme emp*er*our off *that* cu*n*tre,

as Fyrage says,

Multyplying *th*e world, as seyth my*n* auto*u*r Fyrag*e*,

Qwer*e* he tellyth *th*e ryalte off *ther* maryage,

and had children,
Amoryus and
Cleopes.
[leaf 17.]

Reme*m*bryng *th*e loue, & eke *th*e adu*er*syte,   47

Off Amory*us* & Cleopes, *that* we*r*e *th*e chyldyr der*e*

Off *th*ise lordys : how *th*ei louyd & dyid in ffere.

(8)

And *th*e sempyl wryt*er* besechyt̄h off supportaci*on*   50

For *th*e rude endytyng off *th*is story ;

But eu*er*y word ys wrytyn vndyr correcci*on*

Off *th*em *that* laboure in *th*is syens *con*tynwally,

For, ffulle herd yt ys, I knowe yt veryly,   54

To plese *th*e pepyl ; but *th*e qwete frute schewyth

*th*e ge*n*til tree,

And *th*e mowt̄h *th*e hert : yt wyl none odyr be. 56

I (John Metham), the writer, ask help in my bad work.

(9)

But cause̍ qwy *that* I *th*is boke endyght,   57

Is, *that* noqwer*e* in Latyne ner Englysch I coude

yt aspye ;

But in Grwe y had yt wrytyn, lymnyd bryght

W*ith* lettyrys off gold, *that* gay were wrowght to *th*e ye,

That causyd me to m*er*uel *that* *th*ei so gloryu*s*ly   61

Was adornyd : & offtyn I enqwyryd of lett*er*yd

clerk*ys*,

Qwat yt myght be, *that* poyntyd was w*ith* so m*er*-

wul*us* werk*ys*.   63

I undertook it, because the story

was in a hand-some Greek MS. only.

No men of letters knew

(10)

But alle *th*ei seyd *that* yt was, be supposyng,   64

Grwe ; but qwat yt ment, *th*ei nyst ryght noȝt at alle.

And as yt ffortunyd, *th*er come rydyng

To Norwyche, a Greke, to home I schewyd in specyal

Thys fforsayd boke ; & he, iche word, bothe gret &

smal,   68

In Latyne yt expugnyd ; & *thus*, be hys infforma-

ci*on*,

I had *th*e trwe grownd & very *con*clusyon.   70

what it meant ;

but a Greek who came to Norwich

turnd it into Latin for me.

I   Her*e* endyt̄h *th*e **prolog, And begynnyt̄h** *th*e **ffyrst boke /**
n Albynest, *th*e chef cyte off *th*e regyon of Parsé
Thyse lordys reulyd, *th*e wyche excellent wer*e* off fame . . . .

The properties of the lovers' fathers were separated only by a
stone wall. Amoryus's father was Palemedon of Thessaly ; Cleopes's
was Dydus, who founded a temple of Venus, in which the citizens
put up a pillar of brass in his honour, because this temple and the

city were destroyd by a storm, and he rebuilt them. They ask
Palemedon to come to the Dedication of the new temple. With the
Emperor's leave, Palemedon and his son Amoryus start. (A young
knight rides up and warns Amoryus of the troubles of love.) They
are welcomd by Dydus, and taken to their dwelling. Next day they
admire the Temple of Venus ; and the priest or necromancer says he'll
dedicate it that day week. What gold, &c., he requires, is given him.
He throws treasure and dead men's bones to the damned spirits, and
gets 700,000 of them to complete the magic Sphere, from the 1st circle
of which the planets' sweet harmony comes. The 2nd circle contains
the stars, and is the College of Gods. After much astrological talk,
and a vision of Venus and the ruin of her Temple, seen by her Priest
or Secretary, the Temple is dedicated. Amoryus sees Cleopes,
sends for his prayer-roll, and does his devotions to Apollo and
Venus. Then he and Cleopes fall in love with each other. She
has, in her Book of Devotions, a picture of a hind holding a heart,
which she shows him. The service ended, they separate, after con-
fessing their mutual love. They want to express their feelings ; and
as 'woman's wit is ready,' Cleopes holds up her Book of Devotions
in red and green, containing a picture of a hind lying down, holding
a heart, before which kneeld a knight holding in one hand another
heart, and in the other hand a ring. Amoryus sees this, speaks to
Cleopes, and wonders what her picture means. After service, his
fellows chaff him ; but he takes leave of his lady, and prepares for
the coming jousts. He gets a kerchief painted with a copy of
Cleopes's picture, and winds it round his right arm, and tells his
father that Venus bade him wear it as a token of victory. Cleopes
is delighted to see her champion wear her badge ; and in the eight
days' jousting, he proves to be the best man. He then gives a
general challenge to every knight, and unhorses many. A knight
adventurous then challenges him (sign. c 1, bk., c. 2), and Amoryus
runs him thru the brain at the first charge (c. 3), and salutes Cleopes.

The third book (c. 3, back) shows us the separated lovers grieving
bitterly. But Cleopes goes to her father's orchard, in whose wall is
a cranny (Pyramus-and-Thisbe wise) coverd with ivy (c. 4), and thru
it, she sees and hears Amoryus lamenting his hard fate. She throws
the bottom of a broken glass to him ; he comes to the rift in the
wall, and they have a love talk, agree to meet again, each putting a
gold ring in the cranny 'for true love's everlasting continuance'
(c. 5, back), and kissing the wall, instead of one another's person.

Then come tidings to King Palemedon of " a merulus dragon, *the* qwyche dystroyd *the* cuntre," the folk's goods, and eek 100 men of the city. This beast, Amoryus undertakes to fight, and, the same night, tells Cleopes of it. She warns him that he'll be kild. He'd better fight a lion than a serpent, whose venom 'll burn thru his armour. She then tells him about serpents—'*thi*se cokatrycys . . *the* serpent clepyd 'draconia' . . 'horne serpentys, . . a dragon . . namyd aspys, see . . dragounz and monstrys . . as *th*ise chyldrynyz, ydrys, & ypotamyȝ,' and the worst earth-dragon of all, 'serra cornuta' (c. 6), with the remedies for the venom of most of them.

Sarra cornuta is the name of the serpent that Amoryus is to fight; and for this he must have charms : 1. instead of his helm, a 'bugyl' gaping, with a bright carbuncle on its forehead; 2. the ring with a 'smaragd,' that Cleopes gave him the other day, and which is to be turnd towards the beast's eyes[1]; 3. a drink before the battle, made of herbs that she names, mixt with 5 powderd stones, 'orytes, lyguryus, demonius, agapys, acates,' for which he is to send to Walter jeweller in her name : a spoonful of this confection will cure any one. The 'bugyl' is to tempt the serpent to attack, and then the carbuncle will help.

Amoryus rides to the town, and next morning, having taken his drink and ring, proceeds to the dragon's den, and thrusts his spear into the brute's mouth (d 2, back). It kills his horse; but Amoryus puts out one of its eyes, and holds his ring to the other (d 3). Its stink is enough to kill a man. The carbuncle frightens the dragon; but it comes open-mouthed at Amoryus, who throws a phial of his potion between its jaws. This closes them at once, as if they were bound with iron chains, and is about to kill the dragon, whose bristled muzzle turns blue. It spreads its wings to fly, and Amoryus drives his sword up to the hilt into its heart (d 4). He then goes home triumphant, and arranges with Cleopes to meet him in the forest at a well. She gets there first, washes her hands and face, and, hearing a lion roar, rushes off to, and hides herself in, a den, dropping her headkerchief in her flight. This, the lion tousles with his bloody mouth; and having drunk some water, goes away. Amoryus comes, and on

---

[1] "insted off your helme, set a bugyl (an imitation young bull or buffalo) gapyng :

> A bryǵh carbunkyl, loke þer be set in *th*e fforhed;
> And in your hands halde *that* yche ryng
> With þe smaragd, þat I here delyue*re*d you þ*is* odyr day :
> Loke þ*a*t þe stone be toward hys eyn alwey."

seeing the kerchief, thinks a wild beast has kild and eaten Cleopes.
He laments her, and at last puts his sword-hilt on the ground, falls
on it, and drives its point into his left side. Cleopes, hearing his
last call on her, rushes up. He is just able to speak to her, and
then dies; whereupon she, after lamenting him, pulls his sword out
of him and kills herself. A pious hermit hears her last cry, and,
after prayer, comes up and sees the piteous sight. He then prays to
God to bring the two lovers to life again, which He does. The
hermit converts and baptizes them, takes them into the city, and
causes the image of Venus to tumble down, and the magical Sphere
to vanish. Then he marries Amoryus and Cleopes; they live long
and have children, die, and are buried together.

John Metham then praises highly his patron Sir Miles Stapleton,
and his lady, a Lloyd, of the family of De La Poole, Duke of Suffolk,
—whose arms, 3 horses' heads, were embroiderd on the velvet cover
of the MS. in the 17th century, while one is on the other side,—
and ends with the following Epilog:—

(a)

And yff I *th*e trwthe schuld her*e* wryght,   [top of page]

> As gret a style I schuld make in eu*er*y dregre,   [*so*]

As Chauncerys, off qwene Eleyne or Cresseyd, doht
    e*n*dyht,

> Or off Polyxchene, Grysyld, or Penelope.

As beuteu*us*, as womanly, as pacyent, as *th*ei wer*e*
    wu*n*t to be,

> Thys lady was, qwan I endytyd *th*is story,

.xxvii.

> Floryschyng, *th*e seuyn & twenty yer*e* off *th*e sext
    kyng He*n*ry.[1]

Marginal note: If I wrote the truth about Lady Stapleton, I should want Chaucer's style.

Marginal note: I write in 27 Henry VI, 1448-9.

(b)

Go now, lytyl boke, &, wi*th* alle obeychau*n*ʒ,

> Enterly me comende to my lord and mastyr eke,

And to hys ryght reu*er*e*n*d lady, wi*th* alle plesau*n*ʒ,

> Enfformyng *th*em, how ffeythful*l*y I hem beseke

Off supportaci*on* of *th*e rude endytyng owte of Greke;

> For alle *th*is wrytyng ys sayd vndyr correcci*on*,
> Bothe off *th*i rymyng, & eke off *th*i translaci*on*.

Marginal note: Little book, commend me to Sir Miles and his Lady!

[1] 27 Henry VI. is from 1 Sept. 1448 to 31 Aug. 1449.

(c)

For *th*ei *that* greyheryd be, afftyr ffolkys estymacion,
  Nedys must more cu*n*ne, be kendly nature,
In yche syens qwer*e*-in *th*ei haue *ther* op*er*acion,—
  Sythyn that craft comyth be co*n*tynwaun3 in-to
    eu*er*y creature,—
Than he *that* late begynnyth, as be demonstrac*i*on
  My mastyr Chau*n*cerys, I mene, *that* longe dyd endur*e*
  In practyk off rymyng ; qwerffore p*r*offoundëly
  W*ith* many p*r*oue*r*bys, hys bokys be rymyd
    naturelly.

(d)

Eke Ion Lydgate, su*m*tyme monke off Byry,
  His bokys endytyd w*ith* termys off retoryk
And halff chongyd Latyne, w*ith* co*n*seytys off poetry
And craffty Imagynac*i*onys off ym[a]gys ffantastyk,
[. . . . . *no gap in the MS.*]
  But eke hys qwyght her schewyd, & hys late werk,
  How *that* hys co*n*tynwaun3 made hym both a
    poyet & a clerk.

(e)

But nowe *th*ei bothe be pasyd ; & afft*er* schal I. [back]
  Qwer-ffor I make *th*is schort orysu*n* :
O welle off m*er*cy, Iesu,—*that* I, be ffreelnes & ffoly
  Haue *th*ee offendyd in dede or i*n* ony Imagynac*i*on,—
  Fully off fforyeffnes I *th*ee beseche, w*ith* my herty3
    hole em*m*oc*i*on,
  Purposyng to amende alle *that* I haue done amys ;
  To me, Iesu, now *th*i mercy, fful necessary ys.

(f)

And *th*ei *that* my sy*m*pyl wrytyng schal rede,
  Off storyis off elde tyme, yff *th*ei lyste, off *ther*
    godene3,
Qwer*e* *th*ei Ion Metham in boke3 ffynde, p*r*ay for
  hy*m* to spede
  In vertuys ; ffor he off rymyng toke *th*e besyne3
  To co*m*fforte *th*em *that* schuld[ë] falle in heuynes,

For tyme on-ocupyid, qwan ffolk haue lytyl to do,
On haly dayis to rede, me thynk yt [ys] best so.

**Here endyth *the* story off Amory*us* *the* knyght &
off Cleopes *the* lady.**

————

[? MS.] 1° fol., ad me . .   aȝus

The. translator signs his name several times in the
MS., once at the end of the Treatise on Physiognomy
which follows the Poem, as—

Quod Ion Metham, scoler*e* off Cambryg. . Am*en*.

At the end of the 1st treatise, of "Cyromancy"
[lf. 11, bk.] before the Poem, it is "q*uod* Ion Metham
. . . Metham."

Dr. J. W. Clark, the Registrary, writes that the
Cambridge University records do not mention John
Metham.

I am greatly obliged to Mr. Quaritch for letting
me see, and print this abstract of, his unique and
interesting little MS.

————

The contents of the Quaritch MS., all by Jn. Metham, to leaf
84, are :

1. The syens off pal[mistrye], lf. 2–12,
   . . . and owte off grew, doctor Aurelyan, *the* qwyche
   was born in Itayle, translatyd *th*is syens in-to Latyne;
   and owte of Latyne, Ion Metham, sympyl scoler of philosophie, tranlatyd yt in-to Englysch, *the* xxv. wyntyr
   off hys age, prayng alle *the* rederry*s*, of pacyens for *the*
   rwde endytyng; for, as myne autor pleynly endytyth
   in Latyne, so ys my purpose pleynly to endyte in
   englysch . . . .
   Her endyth þᵉ syens off cyromancy ⎱
   quod Jon Metham . . . . Metham ⎰
   A big hand is drawn on each side of the next leaf, 13.
   4 leaves, 14–17, blank.
2. Amoryus & Cleopes, lf. 18–57.
3. Treatise on Physionomy, lf. 58–76.
   2 leaves, 77–8, blank.
4. Treatise on Fortunate Days, lf. 79–84.
   3 leaves blank, 85–7.
5. 1 leaf, 88, on what happens (in another hand) if Christmas
   Day falls on a Sunday, Monday, Tuesday, Wednesday,
   Thursday; breaks off with "[I]ff crystemes day ffalle on
   yᵉ ffryday" . . . .
   signatures of names and 3 lines of prose.

AFTERWORDS.

OUR sins find us out. Owing to my not having cut up and dated the pages of the 1st edition of this book, and also owing to the want of knowledge and care of the reader of it for our Dictionary, and of Stratmann and Mätzner, Dr. Murray was led into saying of *drain*, vb.

"It is remarkable that, after the O.E. period, no example of this word is known to occur for 500 years, till the 16th c."

when our *Seven Deadly Sins*, p. 247, l. 119, had it in the 15th century, ab. 1440;[1] and Dr. Bradley was left with '1607, Topsell,' as his first user of *gnawer*, tho we had it in this same poem (p. 245, l. 50) about 167 years earlier :

> "*Invidia* the therd wound ys,
> A wyckkyd gnawer, or venym, or gowt . . ."

Our word *coignage*, 53/86, printed in 1866, is not in our Oxford Dictionary ; nor are these now-printed words either: *anteoche* (a potion), 287/21, sent me by Dr. J. F. Payne, and *ascence* (Phebus in his ascension) 291/17, sent me by Dr. Hy. Bradley.

I am greatly to blame for not having collated earlier the German edition of Lydgate's *Horse, Goose and Sheep*, which gives some improved, and many various, readings for our text, of which these are a few :

15/1 Of controversies, pleys, & of discordis ; 15/13, 17/44 geven *for* yove ; 16/18 depeynt ; 16/23 good kepe ; 16/54 callid Pegase ; 17/59 rider callid is ; 17/62 his *for* bi- ; 18/71 theyr horses ; 18/76 Chaucer ; 18/78 Betwene ; 18/87 hors *for* hew ; 20/117 bande *for* lond ; 20/126 horsis ; 20/129 from *for* 2nd to ; 21/140 of Roweyn (aftermath, see p. 311) ; 21/143 of *for* for ; 21/147 hors *for* we ; 21/159 hem *for* hir ; 21/160 seid the goos *for* trust me weel ; 22/172-3 lines transposed ; 22/184 *and* somme to noote ; 23/193 prudence *for* provident ; 23/197 goselyngis ; 23/202 all away ; 23/208 servid ; 24/222 fiers leoun ; 24/225 These mihty ; 24/226 Maken ; 25/22

---

[1] Dr. M. quoted our line as "c. 1500 *Spir. Remedies* in Halliw. *Nugæ Poet.* 67, Drayne it and dringke it with confescione."

temple so ; 26/248 rescoud ; 26/259 And riht . . they ; 26/263 as that som ; 27/286 ram here ; 27/290 his vocate ; 27/293 ut rectores gregum *for* O Egle & thou leoun ; 27/295 and roiall ; 28/301 named is ; 28/308 List take the *for* Took the meeke ; 28/318 this lamb ; 29/323 lyneally ; 29/339 briht *for* fresshe ; 29/344 cacle *for* gagle ; 30/355 fyndith ; 30/358 pelt ; 30/365 of the ; 30/368 and *for* in ; 31/374 right holsom ; 31/385 gely ; 31/388 jointys *for* bonys ; 31/389 Their dede ; 31/391 preve it ; 31/393 Unto *for* But to ; 32/413 prowde forsworn ; 32/415 that toun ; 32/418 *no* But ; 32/419 Hemself ; 33/424 forth *for* silf ; 34/447 All *transferd before* These ; 34/448 for *for* of ; 34/449 Theyr ; 34/459 look wel on eny ; 35/482 flees *for* wolle ; 35/489 bewite ; 36/515 grasen ; 36/516 of *for* bi ; 37/527 engendred is hattrede ; 37/531 who *for* who that ; 37/532 frendis ; 37/536 To *for* so ; 37/537 rother *for* tothir ; 38/544 comunaulte ; 38/549 beeris *for* Booris ; 38/557 theyr *for* the ; 38/560 hem dresse ; 38/563 to *for* nat ; 39/568 fieldis . . doth gret ; 39/569 not ; 39/572 A *for* As ; 39/573 Beth ; 39/574 or storme ; 39/583 witte was ; 39/586 example ; 39/592 grete fisshes ; 40/596 wroth ; 40/601 perilous ; 40/606 gabburdis ; 40/607 communaulte ; 41/635 Eche man beware his neihburgh to despise ; 41/640 have no *for* nat ; 41/648 her ; 42/654 horsis *for* stokkis ; 42/655 grase.[1]

The additions at the end of the present volumes—thanks to Mr. Laurence Hodson, Dr. Henry Bradley, and Mr. Bernard Quaritch—introduce us to three fresh writers of poor verse, Henry Baradoun, p. 289, William Huchen, p. 291, and John Metham of Norwich, scholar of Cambridge, who wrote his Pyramus-and-Thisbe-like romance *Amoryus and Cleopes*, p. 301–8, in 1458–9, and affected to english it from Greek, which is of course nonsense. The prose fragment of the romance of " Peare of Provence and the fair Maguelone" will, I trust, lead to the discovery of a complete copy of it. Its tale was told in 1883 by Mr. Ascot R. Hope in his *Stories of Old Renown*, p. 189–213. On *La belle Dame sans Merci*, the imitations of it, the answers to it, etc., see M. Piaget's article in the *Romania* 1901.

As the medicine *anteoche* is not otherwise known, Dr. J. F. Payne has kindly sent me this recipe for the mixture, from his MS, formerly Dr. Frazer's :

For to make drynke of anteoche.

Tak an handful of Bugyl, an oþer of strawebery wyse [juice?], an oþer of meny consoude, and oþer of petit consold, an oþer of confirie, an oþer of þe croppes of þe red coul, an oþer of þe croppes of the brere, an oþer of Osmound, an oþer of croppes of hemp, an oþer

---

[1] p. 258 : the line ' Lere to love, &c.' is also l. 5 on p. 261.

of Sanycle, an oþer of orpyn, an oþer of tansy, an oþer of þe croppes
of þe Red nettles, an oþer of Pympurnele, an oþer of mouscre, an oþer
of violet, fyue handful of auence croppes and rote, & fyue handful
of erbe Water, fyue handful of Betoyne croppes, þre handful of erbe
Robert croppes and rote, and mader þe thrid part wight, ageyn
alle (?) oþer. Wasch hem clene and stampe hem, and do hem in-to a
newe erden pot, and put þereto a galoun of white wyn; and ȝif þou
miȝt not fynde wyt, tak reed, and set ouer the fuir tyl hauendel be
wasted; and þan tak it doun, and let streyne him in-to a faire
vessel; and tak a potel of lyf hony,[1] and boyle it, and [*back of leaf*]
skyme it, and þenne do it in þi licour, so that þou haue of eyther
ilyche mech ; and let boyle them to-gedder be þe space of þis psalme
seyng " Miserere mei, deus " ; and þat þis be don to-fore myssomer ;
and than do thi licour in a vessel of peaudèr, or of leed, or of glas,
wel stopped ; and whenne þe syke schal drynke ther-of, gyf him a
sponful ther-of, and thre of lew water, an do it in a cuppe or in a
pece to-gydder, and gyf þe seek to drynke last and first; but loke
þat þi water be of a welle, that welle[2] of his owen kende, and þat it
be soden first ; and kepe it for þe nones.

p. 21, l. 140, *Roweyn*. This is the 2nd or autumn crop of grass,
whether mown or not, after the first or June crop is cut and carried.
In Lydgate's county, Suffolk, where I write, the outgoing tenant has
to leave his *rowen* for the cattle of the incoming tenant to feed on
during the winter; and he gets an allowance for it.[3] Mortimer, in
his *Art of Husbandry*, ed. 1721, i. 233, says :

For the Wintering of Cattle, about *September* you must turn
thém out that you design to keep up for a Winter or a Spring-
Market, and your Cows that give Milk, into your *Rowens*, till Snow
or a hard Frost comes, and they will need no Fodder.

And so, after a pleasant day of work and walk in this near-
harvest Suffolk land, of lying on the Green, and strolling down
pretty, sandy lanes, and over gorse-clad commons, of seeing cattle
and crops, chickens, ducks and geese, and greeting friendly country
folk, I take leave at last of this long-delayd Text, hoping to be
forgiven, by friends and readers far and near, for all its faults.

White House Farm, Benhall Green,
    Saxmundham, Sunday night, 9 Aug., 1903.

---

[1] '*live* honey' was the first that draind from the comb, of its own accord,
before it was squeezd.—See Mortimer's *Husbandry*, 1721. The passage, I've
sent to Oxford for our Dictionary Supplement.   [2] springs.
   [3] My landlord, Mr. George Boast, has kindly showd me his incoming
Valuation.

INDEX AND GLOSSARY.

elenge, *a.* 116/57, dreary, miserable.
Elymosina, almsgiving, 247/91.
empere, *n.* 174/12, empire.
emperor, 12/3, 11, 12, 13/5, 12.
emprise, *n.* 31/553, maxim.
emyred, *a.* 77/57, admired.
enchace, *v.t.* 95/416, drive.
endlessly, *adv.* 217/418.
endooryd, *pple.* 56/5, gilt, with spatterd yolks of eggs.
enfeofment, *n.* 193/38, gift of Paradise.
Englishmen's bows and arrows, 24/216.
ennewid, *pple.* 291/6, tinted, gilded.
entenderde, *vb.* 72/32, taken in tenderly ?
enterly, *a.* 69/11, entire, whole.
entircomon, *vb.* 37/536, share.
entremes, *n.* 86/156, entrée, dish of food.
entrikid, *pple.* 292/41, ensnared, beguiled.
envious, *n.* 53/92, envy, jealousy.
' Envy,' 257.
Envy, the 2nd Deadly Sin, 245/49.
eques, knight, from *equo*=horse, 17/57.
er, *adv.* 250/11 ; erer, *adv.* 250/13, before.
erde, *n.* 242/125, earth.
eritage, *n.* 128/177, inheritance, lands.
ernes, *n.* 260/4, earnest-money, reward.
ertdly, *a.* 242/122, earthly.
estat, *n.* 39/367, collective body, number.
examplir, *n.* 75/67, model.
executor, *n.* 7/33, performer, singer.
existence, *n.* 73/4.
Exodus, a Prologue to (by Wm. Tyndale, 1530), 62/17.
expenses, *n. pl.* 211/301.
expert, *a.* 22/170, tried, wise.
extortion grounded on falseness, 37/523.
extremities, *n.* 22/179, fingers, toes, etc. ; 34/471, extremes.

F. for the feterlock, the badge of the Earl of March (Edw. IV.), 2/41.
fable, *v.t.* 126/105, deceive.
face, *v.t.* 282/73, confront, accuse.
fail, *v.t.* 105/670, be wanting in.

failed, *n.* 99/513, weak, wanting.
faint, *a.* 191/5, cool, unloving.
faith dwells in the heart, and Christ in it, 65.
falewetȝ, *v.i.* 249/5 b, grows pallid.
famelen, *v.i.* 253/8, fumble, stammer.
fantastical, *a.* 72/25, existing only in the fancy.
Father and Son, the Disputation between (by Wm. Roy, 1530), 62/1.
Father of Heaven, 175/32.
fatherless, *a.* 234/42.
fat roast goose fit for a king, 23/206–8.
faute, *n.* 124/56, default of care.
fayne, *adv.* 192/56, fain, gladly.
fayne, *n.* 117/83, feigning.
Feasts, the 10 chief Church, 118/105.
feature, *n.* 203/199.
feeble, *v.t.* 207/253, weaken.
feeld, 18/70, field of battle.
feeling, *sensus*, 65.
feel strong wines, 60 (63).
feffith, *vb.* 97/472, burdens.
felþe, *n.* 283/118, filth, sin.
felsship, *n.* 251/1, falsity, falsness.
feminity, *n.* 71/21, 74/35, women's nature.
fenestrallys, *n.* 56/7, arm-holes in a pillory.
ferdly, *a.* 245/44, fearful, terrible.
ferret, *v.i.* 48, 49/26, hunt rabbits with ferrets.
fervently, *adv.* 138/158.
fesid, *pple.* 227/603, harast.
fester, *n.* 245/44.
fethirbeddis, 38/560.
feyntyce, *n.* 273/75, faintness.
Fight is Flight, 251/
figure, *n.* 28/297, 322, resemblance ; 171/858, image.
Filius Regis mortuus est, 233–237.
——*Resurrexit: Non mortuus est*, 238–242.
fill : had my fill, 124/31.
find, *v.t.* 298/8, provide for.
fine, *a.* 172/874, celebrated, famous.
fitte, *v.i.* 262/9 d, fight.
Five Wells of Christ's Mercy, 142/36.
five wits, 124/53.
Five Wounds, Christ's, 133/21, 142/37.

myscheeve, *v.i.* 226/563, come to grief.

myse, *n.* 140/36, wrong doing, sin.

myste, *n.* 39/574, mist.

nail, one that pierst Christ on the Cross: a relic in Rome, 160/498, 161, *n.* 11.

Nails, Christ's three, thru hands & feet, 141/11.

namis, *n.* 43/10, names.

namly, *adv.* 110/824, specially.

nar, 19/112 (if ships and horses) were not, didn't exist.

nasty, *a.* 252.

Nativity of the Virgin Mary, Feast of the, 118/116.

nature above craft, 73/3.

Nature, his giftis, 41/648.

Nature seen by Alanus, 73/20.

neb, *n.* 243/4, face.

necessity, *n.* 69/7, need to beg.

negligence, *n.* 24/232.

neme, *n.* 131/282, eme, uncle.

nemeled, *pple.* 43/10, named.

ner, *a.* 87/198, nigher.

ner, *adv.* 267 (at foot), never.

nere, *vb.* 263/1 e, were not, did not exist.

nese, *n.* 246/82, nose.

neven, *v.i.* 139/17, name.

newe, *adv.* 23/206, just, newly.

newe, *v.t.* 282/82, renew.

New Testament in English, 63/22.

New Year's Day, indulgences on, xliv.

New Year's Morning, a Greeting on, 66-7.

night & day, *adv.* 170/803.

nit, *n.* 262/2, night.

no, 18/69, nor.

no kyns wise, 88/224, no kind of way.

no-skynnes wyse, 94/384, in no kind of way.

nokkis, *n.* 31/380, nocks, notches.

nome, *n.* 146/107, name.

non, *n.* 277/179, noon.

noote, *v.i.* 22/184, make notes.

notable, *a.* 16/41, remarkable, advantageous.

noth, *adv.* 260/11, 266/2 b, not.

nother, *conj.* 20/129, 253/16, neither.

nought, nothing, a Tale of, 63.

November, 170/788.

nowne, *a.* 78/79, own.

noxiall, *a.* 71/15, nightly.

noynt, *v.t.* 247/93, anoint.

Numeri, the 4th book of Moses, Numbers, a Prologue to (by Wm. Tyndale, 1530), 63/19.

nutritive, *a.* 31/376.

nynne, *n.* 11/99, nine, extreme.

nyst, *vb.* 178/28, knowest not.

Obedience of a Christian Man, by Wm. Tyndale (1528), 63/24.

obedience (under thy), 174/19, rule, sway.

obstacle, *n.* 290/35.

obstinate, *a.* 138/154.

of, 40/593, by.

of, *prep.* 40/598, by ; 268/2 c, from.

oil & butter mixt with gooseturd as a salve, 23/197-201.

oil of olive, 31/390.

oil-wells, two miraculous, in Rome, xli, 171/828.

oker, *n.* 265/12, usury.

olifant, 29/333, elephant.

olive, *n.* 112/29, Virgin Mary.

on, *a.* 267/9, one.

one after another, 150/222.

One is two, now, 251.

one of the best that I ever saw, 247/92.

onethis, *adv.* 57 (13), hardly, with difficulty.

onhanged, *pple.* 194/67, hangd on the Cross.

oone, *n.* 177/5, self.

Operis satisfactio, 248/127, satisfaction for sin by good works, 248/127.

or, *conj.* 1/19, 61 (79), 290/26, before.

order of Chivalry binds men to do no wrong, 19/98.

order of troops in battle, 24/227.

Oris confessio, confession by the mouth, 248/123.

Ortulus Animae, in English, 62/11.

oþer, *conj.* 84/107. either.

otter, *n.* 49/25.

ou, *pron.* 254, you.

Our Lady, 170/794, 241/110 ; her portrait painted by Angels, 165/625-36.

outrage, *a.* 207/243, vicious.

over, *v.t.* 227/604, be over, have at will.

over floten, 251/2, float at the top, on the surface.

overmuch, *adv.* 236/102.

overschake, *v.i.* 107/726, pass over, go by.

overtilt, *pple.* 226/588, overthrown, upset.

owt, *n.* 9/61, anything.

ox & ass, the baby Christ's companions, 255/5 b.

'p. r. e. d.,' 4 evils, 256.

pace, an easy, 81/29.

pacyd, *pple.* 277/179, past.

paied, *pple.* 51/65, pleasd, satisfied.

paining, *n.* 181/15, punishment.

paint, *v.t.* 191/7, cover up, falsify.

paire, *v.i.* 217/401, impair, worsen.

palace, Diogenesis, a small barrel, 51/73.

palestre, 19/101, tournament-ground, athletic-field : ' pleyes palestral,' Chaucer, *Troilus,* v. 304.

palm, *n.* 151/252, a supposed print of Christ's foot.

palme, palmete, xxix, 151/252, foot-sole.

Palm Sunday, indulgence on, xxxix.

palysyd, *pple.* 152, *n.* 4, paled, palisaded, enclosed.

pan, *n.* 275/133, brain-pan, scull.

pap, *n.* 178/46, teat; 186/109, teat, 187/117, 239/38.

pap, *n.* 255/12 (this, bef. 1400, answers the query in note 1, p. 232) ; 296.

papes, *n.* 149/195, popes.

paps of the Virgin Mary, 232/761.

papynjaye, *n.* 131/251. ' Papegay : m. A Parrot or Popingay': Cotgrave.

Parable of the Wicked Mammon (by Wm. Tyndale, 1528), 63/23.

paraffys, *n.* 271/8, 20, 'paraf of a booke (or paragraf). *Paraphus,* paragraffus, Catholicon.'

parage, *n.* 115/29, parentage.

parais, *n.* 257/1 b, paradise.

paraunter, *adv.* 106/710, peradventure.

parchemyn, *n.* 30/367, 271/13, parchment.

pardon, French for ' forgiveness of sins,' 143/5, 6 ; is best had in Rome, 143–173.

pardon is the soul's cure, 143/3.

parker, *n.* 49/28, park-keeper.

'Parliament of Love,' the, 76–79.

parson, *n.* 97/463, person, self.

parted, *vb.* 109/798, departed.

partiality, *n.* 40/610.

party, *n.* 104/643, part, self.

party in a law-case, 15/8.

pas, *n.* 272/45, time.

pasaunt, *a.* 71/1, passing, exceeding.

Paschal lamb, 28/316, Christ.

pass, *v.i.* 6/7, die ; 113/35, pass, go from ; *v.i.* 146/87, sail.

passage, *n.* 53/78, journey.

passith, *v.t.* 29/348, passes, excels.

pasture, *n.* 22/162, feeding-place.

pasture, *v.i.* 33/441.

Pater noster, a, 8/44 ; 10/71, 11/95.

patrimony, *n.* 60 (56) (58), inherited estate.

pay, *n.* 74/46, pleasure.

paye, *v.t.* 197/92, please, satisfy; *n.* 196/96, pleasure, satisfaction.

payse, *v.t.* 74/45, weigh.

peace is better than war, 32/399 ; is the ground of all debate, 34/453 ; the benefits of, 51/68–70.

peacock-featherd arrows, 24/214.

' Peare of Provence and the fair Maguelone,' p. 293–300.

pece, *n.* 272/31, portion of time and talk.

peireth, *vb.* 88/228, impairs.

pele, *v.i.* 109/783, appeal.

pelican, *n.* 131/251.

Penitent Thief, xxxiv.

pens, *n.* 23/188, goose-quills.

Pentecost, Feast of, 118/113.

pere, *n.* 287/31, equal.

performyd, *a.* 60 (54), finisht.

perry, *n.* 73/9, precious stones.

pershyng, 16/21, piercing.

pese, *n.* 253/16, pea ?

pese, *v.t.* 136/115, appease, still.

peynyng, *n.* 278/215, suffering.

peyse, *v.t.* 57 (4), weigh, consider.

picture, *n.* 40/615, painting.

pieces, all to, *adv.* 88/207.

Pig-stye, xviii.

pilchis, *n.* (sheepskin), 30/366, cloaks.

pilet, *n.* 30/358, pelt, skin and fleece.

pillar of faith, *n.* 112/18.

pillory for false bakers and millers, p. 56.

pillows of goose-feathers, 23/192, 195.

mainder, or ' revenant' return, incoming.

renyth, *vb.* 71/10, 18, reigns.

repair, *n.* 22/163, 230/705, resort;
217/397, belongings.

repeale, *vb.* 104/649, call back, give
up.

repel, *v.t.* 59 (48), snub.

report, *v.t.* 195/79.

reprovable, *a.* 99/512, 142/38, blame-
worthy.

request, *n.* 84/122, 85/146, 142/40.

Requiem, *n.* 247/94.

rese, *v.i.* 247/118, shake?

reseyne, *vb.* 173/907, reveal, disclose.

reseyt, *n.* 100/553, receiving of the
thing sought.

residence, *n.* 47/5.

residue, *n.* 207/264, mispent money.

resort, *v.i.* 195/77, go.

respite, *v.t.* 106/724.

res publica, 16/34, 19/96, 29/331,
32/398, 36/502.

rest, *n.* 31/378, quiet, repose.

rest, *vb.* 275/118, 120.

restauracion, 31/372, restoring, set-
ting-up again.

Resurrection, Festival of Christ's,
118/111.

Resurrexit! Non mortuus est! 241-2,
241/96, 120, 242/132.

Revelation of Antichrist (by Richard
Brightwell, t. i. John Firth, 1529),
62/3.

reymeþ, *vb.* 258/2 b, guides, directs.

reynyed, 2/44, reignd.

reyste, *n.* 124/33, attack, combat?

rhetoricians indite epistles, 23/185.

rich & poor alike, 251/6.

richelees, *a.* 233/1, reckless.

riches the original of pride, 34/457.

richeþ, *v.i.* 260/2 b, enriches.

rings, the three, of Peare of Provence, 294-6, 298.

rithful, *a.* 254/5, rightful.

rolle vp, *v.t.* 38/562, meditate on.

roll up, *v.t.* 142/21, meditate on.

roo, *n.* 151/233, row.

Rood, the Holy, a piece of, at Rome,
167/715.

roof, *n.* 155/374.

room, *n.* 289/17, place, post (at
Court).

root, *v.i.* 246/70, take root.

roppis, *n.* 31/383, guts, entrails.

rose-red, *n.* 271/9, the colour so cald.

rotelen, 253/12, ruttle, gurgle.

roteletȝ, *v.i.* 249/46.

rought, *vb.* 128/162, reckt, cared.

roust, *n.* 257/5 c, rust.

roweyn, *n.* 21/140, rowen, aftermath,
the 2nd crop of grass, cut or
uncut, still used in Suffolk.

royal, *a.* 31/385, sovereign, excellent.

royal estate, 16/19.

royal judges, the lion and eagle,
16/22.

ruby, *n.* 73/10.

rudder, rider, in Dutch, a knight,
17/59.

rude, *a.* 111/842, unskilful.

rue, *v.i.* 177/15, 179/62, have pity.

ruinous, *a.* 57 (2).

rukkyng, *pple.* 39/569, lying down
and huddling together. rukkun,
or cowre down, *Incurvo* : 'to
ruck, to squat, or shrink down.'
Forby, Pr. Parv.

run to school, 142/26.

ruteletȝ, *v.i.* 250/6, gurgles.

ruyde, in = unruyde, 269/1 d, cruel.

ryb wode (rybaude: Bradley), *n.*
247/118, ribald. Lechery personi-
fied.

ryme, *v.i.* 81/38, write poetry.

rynnes, *vb.* 133/15, runs, charges.

ryuen, *pple.* 141/13, torn, split.

S. for Richard, Earl of Salisbury,
2/33.

sacring, *n.* 9, *n.* 2.

sad, *a.* 114/5.

sadil, *n.* 29/340, saddle.

sailleþ, *vb.* 260/1, assails.

sakkis, *n.* 32/415, sacks of wool.

salffe, *a.* safe; salffely, safely, xiv, *n.*

sall, *n.* 139/20, self.

salt & water for baptism, 245/43.

salvator, *n.* 155-6/375-6, a picture of
the Saviour, not painted by a man.

Salvator, an image of Christ, 171/
856-9, 172/869; sent by Christ to
our Lady, 159/464-9.

same : this same year, 119/134.

Santissimo Bambino, an image of
the infant Christ, xliii.

sapience, 49/41.

sark or shirt, that Mary made for
Jesus, a relic in Rome, 157/420.

sarplers, *n.* 32/415, large bales of

wool, of 160 stones apiece. 'Sarplar of Wool, a quantity of Wool, otherwise called a Pocket or a Half-Sack; a Sack containing 80 Tod, a Tod 2 Stones, & a Stone 14 Pounds.'—Phillips.

Satirical Proclamation, 12–14.

sauetyff, *n.* 248/127, healing, cure.

saunzpere, *a.* 291/19, without equal.

savacion, 17/42, salvation, saving of a life.

savage, *a.* 51/54, furious.

save, *n.* 287/21, sage.

savour, *n.* 131/256, scent.

sayne, *pple.* 93/361, seen.

scalding (of one's flesh), 23/199.

scarceness, *n.* 60 (61).

schanginge, 72/42, changing, *pple.*

sched, *n.* 247/102, shed, covering?

schoolmistress, *n.* 85/137, lady-love.

schools of coverd sneers, 92/327–9.

schortithe, *vb.* 72/28, grows short.

schrede, *n.* 137/134, shroud, garment.

scicio (sitio), I thirst, 160/497.

scleuȝe, *v.t.* 124/30, slew.

scons, 11/103, sconce, candle.

scorning, *n.* 273/56.

scourge that flogd Christ, 236/97.

screffe, *pple.* 159, *n.* 7, shriven.

scripture, *n.* 16/30, writings.

scruyde, *v.t.* 269/2 e, shroud, clothe.

seats of the Passions, 65.

seawolf, *n.* 298, bass, a fish.

Secrete, the, 122/224, a prayer.

secretness, *n.* 78/67.

secure & sure, *a.* 175/44.

seemliness, *n.* 77/52, beauty.

sees, *v.t.* 89/250, cease.

seis, *n.* 49/44, seas.

selle, *n.* 125/72, saddle, bonds.

sempiternel, *a.* 113/27.

sentence, 15/9, statement; 36/497, judgment, verdict.

seraphim, 241/88.

serte, *n.* 258/3 c, sort, lot?

servants, bad & good, 59 (47–50).

seste (of), *pple.* 137/123, ceast (from).

set-by, *pple.* 95/420, 209/286, thought of, valued.

sete (sese), *v.i.* 292/46, cease.

sette, *v.t.* 99/524, stake.

seven deadly sins, 139/23, 282/83.

sewet, *vb.* 264/2, 3, shows.

sewte, *n.* 292/36, suit.

shake, *n.* 272/47, hurry.

shameliche, *adv.* 256/3 d, shamefully.

sharpe, *v.t.* 49/22, sharpen.

sharpen, *v.i.* 253/5, grow sharp.

sharpetȝ, *v.i.* 249/3 b, 250/1, grows sharp, pointed.

shat, *vb.* 152/281, shalt.

shattered, *pp.* xiv, *n.*

sheep, the simple, 16/25; its usefulness to man, 35–6.

sheep's head, 31/384.

Shere-Thursday, 28/320, Maundy or Holy Thursday, the day before Good Friday, on which priests used to shear their hair; 156/382, *n.* 7; 157, *n.* 15.

shet, *pple.* 40/615, coffind, buried.

shevis (of grain), 20/136.

ship is a horse of wood, 20/113.

shirt, *n.* 182/28.

shooting at pricks on the frozen Thames, Jan. 1564, xiv, *n.*

shrewd wife to be chastisd with mirth, not smiting, 58 (32).

shrift-father, *n.* 229/664, confessor.

shun, *v.t.* 223/513.

shuppare, *n.* 256/6 b, shaper, governor.

shyne, *n.* 240/3 b, chin.

similitude, *n.* 16/17, picture; 32/402, parable, story; 39/580, allegory.

sinful, *n.* 131/271, 283/106, sinful person.

sink, *v.i.* 109/793.

sinning, *n.* 205/210.

'Sins of our Time,' 251.

Sins, the Seven Deadly, 126/102.

sit-by, *v.i.* 269/3 g, 'recumbunt.'

sith, *v.t.* 259/1, sees.

sitting in the Pillory, 56/12.

sity, *a.* 59 (35), shitten?

skafhes, *n.* 43/13, scathes, harms.

skappe, *v.i.* 239/47, escape, rise.

skill of song, *n.* 107/733.

skin & shoes, all that's used of a dead horse, 24/223–4.

slain with, 280/28, slain by.

slake, *a.* 81/41, stopt.

sleep better than talking, 60 (63).

sleeve, take him by the, 129/189.

sleke, *v.i.* 135/83, slack, quench.

sleynt, *pple.* 276/165, slain?

slide, *vi.* 285/162, sin.

sliper, *n.* 90/262, slippery.

slit, *pple.* 276/147.

stith, *a.* 252, brave (bear thyself bravely).

stodie, *v.i.* 99/508, study, ponder.

stoke, *n.* 4/6,11, stock, trunk, family.

stokkis (*v.r.* horses), 42/654, for 'stottis' horses or bullocks.

stone that St. Paul was beheaded on, 148/149.

stongke, *vb.* 116/52, stank.

store, in, *adv.* 87/199, to himself, without utterance.

stormy sea, *n.* 112/13, this world.

stoundis, *n.* 39/577, times.

stoungen, *pple.* 254/6 c, pierst.

strain my stomach, I, 247/99.

strange, *adv.* 133/4, strongly.

straw, litter for the stable, 23/196.

strecchetʒ, *v.t.* 250/9, stretchis.

streight, *a.* 31/392, pressing, great.

streite, *a.* 209/277, strict, accurate.

streken, *v.i.* 253/13, strike, kick? or stretch?

strengþe, *v.t.* 283/98, strengthen.

streyt, *a.* 80/18, strict, positive.

stroke, *n.* 272/28, 50, blow, stripe.

stroyn, *v.t.* 277/187, destroy.

strye, *v.t.* 91/304, destroy.

strynges, harpe, 81/383, harp-strings.

stryves, *n.* 32/410, strifes.

studes, *n.* 243/6, steads, places.

study, *v.i.* 205/205, seek, search.

stuff (*v.r.* turf), *n.* 20/121.

stuff, *v.t.* 40/616, fill.

styfe, *adv.* 133/4, stiffly.

stykyd, *pple.* 278/225, stuck, driven.

subdeue, *n.* 5/31, subduing.

submyt, *pple.* 89/234, submitted.

substance, *n.* 233/14.

sue, *v.t.* 88/227, follow, pursue.

suffering, *n.* 277/177.

suffisaunce, 51/65, a sufficiency.

Sum of Scripture (by Simon Fish, 1528, 1530?), 62/26.

summerstide, 1/1.

Sunday, 160/490.

sunne, 249/7, sins.

sunny, *a.* 174/9.

suonnyd, *v.i.* 273/80, swoond.

Superbia, pride, the 1st Deadly Sin, 245/26.

superfyne, *a.* 28/313, ? not 'excessive,' but put in to get a ryme to 'virgyne.'

supplanting, *n.* 40/604.

Supplication of Beggars (by Simon Fish, *c.* 1524), 62/2.

supportation, *n.* 111/841.

surcoat, *n.* 183/28.

sure, bread, as sure as men eat, 246/71.

surfeit, *n.* 53/104, excess (in speech).

surfeits, *n.* 142/38.

surfety, *n.* 286/18, excess in food & drink.

surfetys, *n.* 47/19, surfeits.

surioune, *n.* 247/113, surgeon.

surplice, a white, 129/188.

suspect, *a.* 58 (29), suspected, doubtful; 63/30, heretical.

swage, *v.i.* 175/44, lessen.

swan-featherd arrows, 24/214.

swearing, *n.* 94/378, oath-taking.

sweet smell of saints' corpses, 162/530.

swelte, *v.i.* 234/38, died.

symplesse, *n.* 80/17, simplicity, want of skill.

syne, *n.* 152/262, sign, mark.

syngeden, *v.i.* 268/11 d, sinned.

synket, *v.i.* 250/3, sink (in thy head).

synnewis, *n.* 31/389, sinews.

t for *d*: *ant*, and, 258 (at foot); *chilt*, child, 264/11 b.

t for *th*: *lovet*, loveth, 266/2, 4 d; *det*, death, 266/11 c; *stintit*, stinteth, 266/2; *dot*, doth, 264/8 b; *abidet & loket*, abideth & looketh, 263/5 e; *ti*, thy, 267/1.

tabernacle, *n.* 177/1, small chamber.

tabide, 22/165, to abide, live.

table of the Last Supper, 156/381.

table-cloth of the Last Supper, a relic in Rome, 157/418.

tables of stone, in Rome, on which Christ wrote the Law for Moses, 156/388-91.

tablets of the Law of Moses, xxxi.

tabreyden, 41/647, to draw out, exalt or puff up.

take away, *v.t.* 98/500, withdraw, subtract.

take the air, to, 244/2.

Tale of ryght Nought, 63.

talwe, *n.* 31/382, melted fat.

tascape, 17/46, to escape.

taster of wines, 60 (65).

taswage, *v.t.* 22/178, to aswage, soothe.

wytt, *v.t.* 128/185, know.

Xal, *v.i.* 242/129, 271/2; *pl.* 277/193, shall.
xul, *vb. pl.* 277/192.
xuld, *vb.* 273/73, 276/158, should.
xulde, *vb.* 239/55, should.

Y. for Richard, Duke of York, 2/25.
yatis, *n.* 130/244, 249, gates.
yave, *vb.* 170/799, gave.
yconomie, n. 57/3, of household-keeping.

year to year, from, 209/293.
yelt, *vb.* 265/6 c, yields, pays.
yeres, *n.* 92/332, ears.
yeuyth, *vb.* 36/497, give ye.
yie, *adv.* 261/3, yea.
Ynglysshmen, 24/216, Englishmen.
yong, *n.* 77/59, young girl.
yove, 15/13, 17/44, 24/230, given.
ypleite, *pple.* 209/283, pleated (gown).
yra, n. 178/37, anger.
ystreith, *pple.* 243/5, stretcht.

WORDS, &c., IN 'AMORYUS AND CLEOPES.'

acates, *n.* 305, agates.
adorune, *v.t.* 301/5, celebrate.
agapys, *n.* 305, a precious stone.
aspys, a dragon, 305.
avysement, *n.* 302/31, counsel.

besynez, *n.* 307 f, business, labour, trouble.
Book of Devotions, 304.
bugyl, *n.* 305, a young bull or buffalo.

chiromancy, *n.* 308.
Christmas Day: its influence on events, 308.
chyldryny3, *n.* 305, monstrous beasts.
cockatrices, *n.* 305.
College of Gods, 304.

demonius, *n.* a precious stone.
despousyd, *v.t.* 302/43, married.
draconia, the serpent, 305.
dragon: Amoryus's fight with one, 305.

emotion, *n.* 306 c.
exalting, *n.* 301/11.
expugnyd, *v.t.* 303/69, expounded, explained.

frailness, *n.* 307 e.

goddes, *n.* 301/4, goddess.
greyheryd, *a.* 307/1, grey-haird.

hermit who brings the dead to life, 306.
horn serpents, 305.

kissing a wall instead of a lover, 304, at foot.

letteryd, *a.* 303/62, learned.
lion tousles Cleopes's kerchief, 305.
lyguryus, *n.* 305, a precious stone.
lymnyd, *v.t.* 303/59, illuminated.

multiply, *v.t.* 302/45, increase, by having children.

noqwere, *adv.* 303/58, nowhere.

orytes, *n.* 305, a precious stone.

palmistry, *n.* 308.
pasyd, *pple.* 307 e, dead.
physionomy, *n.* 307.
planets' harmony, 304.
poyet, *n.* 307 d, poet.
poyntyd, *v.t.* 303/63, illuminated.
prayer-roll, 304.
profoundly, *adv.* 307 c.
promotyd, *v.t.* 302/35, appointed.
pysauns, *n.* 302/40, puissance, retinue.

qwan, *conj.* 301/15, when.
qwere, *conj.* 301/6, where.
qwerffore, *conj.* 307 c, wherfore.
qwete, *a.* 303/55, sweet.
qwy, *conj.* 303/57, why, for which.
qwyche, *n.* 301/9, which.
qwyght, *a.* 307 d, white.

remys, 302/38, realms.
resident, *a.* 302/35.
reverend, *a.* 306 b, worthy of reverence.
rift or chink in a wall, thru which Amoryus and Cleopes talk, 304.
ryalte, *n.* 302/46, grandeur.
ryming, *n.* 306 b, 307 c.

rymyd, *pple.* 307 c, rymed.

sad, *a.* 302/31, sound, trustworthy.

secretary, a priest of Venus, 304.

sempyl, *a.* 303/50, simple, unskild.

serra cornuta, an earth-dragon, 305.

smaragd, *n.* 305, a precious stone.

Sphere, the Magic, 304, 306.

sqwyche, *a.* 301/5, such.

subdue, *v.t.* 301/13, 15.

supportacion, *n.* 303/50 ; 306 b, support, help.

supposing, *n.* 303/64.

syens, *n.* 303/53, art of verse-writing.

temple-book, 302/28.

too, *a.* 302/35, two.

tribute, *n.* 302/26.

unoccupied, *a.* 308/1.

woman's wit is ready, 304.

wyntyr, *n.* year, 308.

ydrys, *n.* 305, monstrous beasts.

ypotamyz, *n.* 305, hippopotamuses.

NAMES OF PEOPLE AND PLACES.

AARON'S rod, a relic in Rome, 156/392.

Abacuk (Habbakuk), 40/38, brought potage to Daniel.

Abiram, 226/566.

Abraham, patriarch, 29/325.

Adam, 252 (at foot), 259 c ; 259 (at foot) ; & his apple, 131/268 ; we are lost thru him, 252.

Africa, 53/93.

Agapetus, St. Eustace's son, xliii, 171/853.

Agincourt, 25, *n.* 2.

Albanest, the chief city of Persia, 302/42, 303/71.

Albara, Count Alvaro of; his daughter, the Countess of Provence, 293, 296, 298, 300.

Albion, 24/211, England.

Alexander, 17/45 ; was 4 ft. 5 in. high, 61.

Alexander, 41/628, 51/72, 53/82, 85.

Alexandria, 296.

Aleyn, *n.* 73/17, Alanus.

Ambrose Castle, 57/5.

Amoryus, the knight, 301–8.

Ananias, who christend St. Paul, 146/111.

Anglond, 13/12, England.

Anjou, 25, *n.* 2; Louis & René, Duke of, 14/6, 8.

Apollo, 304.

Aristotle's proverb, 299.

Armagnac, Count of, 14.

Asy, 301/13, Asia.

Attila, repulse of, xxiv.

Aurora, 38/561, sunrise ; 291/3.

Aventine, Rome, church on the, xlii.

Aurelyan, doctor, 308.

Babylon, Emperor of, 12/3, 11.

Baradoun, Henry, his 'Prentice unto woe,' 289, 290.

Basilica Appiana, xxviii ; Constantiniana, or that of the Holy Apostles, xxxviii, 168/724; Eudoxiana, xxxviii ; the Prasinian, xliv.

Basilica of St. Paul, xxv–vi ; 146–7; of St. Peter, xxiii–xxv ; 144–6; of St. Peter's, Rome, xxiii, 144; of Santa Maria Maggiore, xxxv, 164/591 ; of San Pietro in Vincoli, xxxviii, 167/704–5.

Basterdfeld, Sir Wm. ; his Warning, 123 ; 123/7.

Bayard, blind, 25/235.

Baynard's Castle, xiv, *n.*

Beaufort-en-Vallée, 25, *n.* 2.

Beaugé, 25, *n.* 1.

Bedford, John, Duke of, xx.

Bedlem, 238/16, Bethlehem.

Belvoir, Leicestershire, 79.

Beme, 13/15, Bohemia.

Bermondsey, Abbot of, 10/73.

Bethlehem, 113/42 ; boards from